Risk Contracting and Capitation Answer Book
Strategies for Managed Care

Clifford C. Dacso, MD, MPH, MBA
Baylor College of Medicine
Houston, Texas

Sheryl Tatar Dacso, JD, DrPH
Jenkens & Gilchrist, P.C.
Houston, Texas

AN ASPEN PUBLICATION®
Aspen Publishers, Inc.
Gaithersburg, Maryland
1999

This publication is designed to provide accurate and authoritative information in regard to the Subject Matter covered. It is sold with the understanding that the publisher is not engaged in rendering legal, accounting, or other professional service. If legal advice or other expert assistance is required, the service of a competent professional person should be sought. (From a Declaration of Principles jointly adopted by a Committee of the American Bar Association and a Committee of Publishers and Associations.)

Library of Congress Cataloging-in-Publication Data

Risk contracting and capitation answer book : strategies for managed care /
[edited by] Clifford C. Dacso, Sheryl Tatar Dacso.
p. cm.
Includes bibliographical references and index.
ISBN 0-8342-0988-8 (alk. paper)
1. Health maintenance organizations—Economic aspects—United States. 2. Managed care plans (Medical care)—Economic aspects—United States. 3. Capitation fees (Medical care). 4. Risk assessment. I. Dacso, Clifford C. II. Dacso, Sheryl Tatar.
[DNLM: 1. Managed Care Programs—United States. 2. Risk Management.
W 130 AA1 R595 1999]
RA413.R53 1999
362.1'04258—dc 21
DNLM/DLC
for Library of Congress
99-11154
CIP

Orders: (800) 638-8437
Customer Service: (800) 234-1660

About Aspen Publishers • For more than 35 years, Aspen has been a leading professional publisher in a variety of disciplines. Aspen's vast information resources are available in both print and electronic formats. We are committed to providing the highest quality information available in the most appropriate format for our customers. Visit Aspen's Internet site for more information resources, directories, articles, and a searchable version of Aspen's full catalog, including the most recent publications: http://www.aspenpublishers.com
Aspen Publishers, Inc. • The hallmark of quality in publishing
Member of the worldwide Wolters Kluwer group.

Editorial Services: Stephanie Neuben
Library of Congress Catalog Card Number: 99-11154
ISBN: 0-8342-0988-8

Printed in the United States of America

1 2 3 4 5

*To Rebecca, Mara, and Matthew Dacso:
they are wonderful people and have made
immeasurable contributions to this work.*

TABLE OF CONTENTS

LIST OF QUESTIONS

Chapter 2 Delivery Systems

Chapter 3 Plan Design

Chapter 4 Health Services Management

Chapter 7 Legal Issues in HMO Contracts

Chapter 8 HMOs and Liability

Chapter 9 Medicare

Chapter 10 Managed Care and Medicaid

Chapter 11 Direct Contracting and Group Purchasing: An Employer and Regulatory Perspective

Chapter 12 Corporate Compliance Issues in Health Care Delivery

Chapter 13 Network and Integration Strategies

Chapter 14 Health Care Database and Information Management

ABOUT THE AUTHORS

CLIFFORD C. DACSO, MD, MPH, MBA, is the John S. Dunn, Sr., Research Chair in General Internal Medicine at Baylor College of Medicine in Houston, Texas. He is professor and vice chairman for clinical affairs in the college's Department of Medicine. He is senior medical advisor to Deloitte & Touche Consulting Group, and chair of the Medical Care Advisory Committee to the Texas Health and Human Services Commission. He has served as medical director for a number of institutions, most recently Community Health Choice, a not-for-profit HMO based in the Harris County Hospital District, and he has also served as the vice-chairman of its board. Dr. Dacso holds bachelor of arts and master of arts degrees from the University of Pennsylvania, a doctor of medicine degree from Baylor College of Medicine, a masters in public health from the University of Texas, and a master of business administration from Pepperdine University. He is certified in internal medicine, infectious diseases, and geriatric medicine and practices general internal medicine.

SHERYL TATAR DACSO, JD, DrPH, is a practicing health law attorney with the law firm of Jenkens and Gilchrist, PC, in its Houston office. She holds bachelor's, master's, and doctor of public health degrees from the University of Texas and a law degree from South Texas College of Law. Dr. Dacso has practiced widely in health law since the late 1970s, working originally as a litigator in an insurance defense firm, followed by several in-house positions, and culminating in her attainment of the position of Senior Vice President and General Counsel for the Providence Hospital in Mobile, Alabama. After moving to California, she became a shareholder with Jennings, Engstrand, and Henrikson, heading their health law section in San Diego. She joined Jenkens and Gilchrist shortly after returning to Houston. Dr. Dacso has held several academic positions, including San Diego State University Graduate School of Public Health, where she rose to the rank of Adjunct Associate Professor, and the University of Houston Institute for Law and Medicine, where she teaches at present. Dr. Dacso has a national health law practice and is widely sought as a visiting lecturer and consultant in complex health care system and managed care strategies. She is the author of several scholarly works in the area of managed care and is the co-editor of *The Managed Care Answer Book*, published by Panel, a division of Aspen Publishers, Inc., which is in its third edition.

JORGE A. FONT, MPH, is an international health care consultant based in Houston, Texas. His clients include major employers, national managed health care organizations, and international health care payers and providers. Mr. Font has approximately 20 years of experience in all phases of health plan evaluation, development, and implementation. Formerly, Mr. Font worked for more than five years as a consultant for The Wyatt Company, specializing in managed care program development and health data analysis. His clients included state governments, business coalitions, national hospital organizations, and Fortune 500 employers. He was a founder of the Houston Health Care Purchasing Organization, one of the largest employer purchasing coalitions in the United States, and pioneered risk-reward sharing programs between large regional employers and independent physician organizations and hospitals. Previously, Mr. Font managed a regional preferred provider organization (PPO) for a major commercial insurer and developed and managed HMO operations for two health plans in the mid-Atlantic region. He is published as a contributing author in *Managing Integration and Operations: A Guide to Quality Health Care Systems* (Thompson Publishing, September 1995), the Spring 1993 journal *Topics in Health Care Financing* (Aspen Publishers, Inc.), and in other journals. Mr. Font has participated on the faculty of the National Managed Health Care Congress in the 1993, 1994, and 1995 national conventions. In February 1994, he conducted a congressional briefing on the topic of marketplace reform. He is a frequent speaker and often is quoted in local and national media. Mr. Font received a bachelor of arts degree from Wake Forest University and a master of public health degree from The University of Tennessee. His administrative internship was served with The George Washington University Health Plan.

M. JAMES HENDERSON, MHA, has been with the Methodist Health Care System since 1974, where he now serves as an executive vice president for managed care and president and chief executive officer of MethodistCare, Inc., the system's health plan. He received his bachelor of science degree from Stanford University in 1967. He served in the U.S. Air Force from 1968 to 1973, reaching the rank of captain. After military discharge, he attended Washington University's graduate program in health care administration, receiving his master of health administration with honors. In 1979, he completed the executive program for health systems management at Harvard University. In the fall of 1992, he entered the Pew Doctoral Program in health policy, an on-job, on-campus program at the University of Michigan's School of Public Health. He is a member of the American Hospital Association; the Texas Hospital Association and other local, state, and national health care–related professional organizations; and is a Fellow with the American College of Health Care Executives. Mr. Henderson has been active in many community organizations. He served as chairman of the board of stewards at St. Luke's United Methodist Church, where he has been a member since 1977. He has held multiple positions in public education organizations and currently serves as chairman of the board of trustees of the Houston Community College System. He is also on the Covenant House Texas board of directors, is a board member and past chairman of the South Main Center Association, and holds memberships in several cultural and environmental organizations.

REGINA HOLLIMAN, RN, BSN, is a health care management consultant based in San Diego, California.

DONALD L. HOLMQUEST, MD, JD, is an attorney, physician and a principal in his own firm of Holmquest & Associates. Formerly a senior partner at Wood, Lucksinger & Epstein of Houston until its dissolution, Dr. Holmquest practices general health law with an emphasis on the complex regulatory and organizational interface between health care institutions and physicians. After receiving a degree in electrical engineering, summa cum laude, from Southern Methodist University, Dr. Holmquest attended Baylor College of Medicine in Houston where he received his doctor of medicine degree, cum laude, in 1967 and his doctor of philosophy degree in physiology in 1968. After completing his internship in internal medicine at The Methodist Hospital in Houston, he served as a scientist astronaut with the National Aeronautics and Space Administration. During that time, he earned Air Force wings and completed 2,000 hours in jet aircraft while training and working in the Apollo and Skylab programs. Following a period of training in nuclear medicine at Baylor, he served as chief of nuclear medicine at the Ben Taub General Hospital in Houston and then created the department of nuclear medicine at the Eisenhower Medical Center in Palm Desert, California. He returned to Texas as associate dean of medicine at Texas A&M University, working for three years to create the new College of Medicine there. In 1976, he left the academic environment and started private medical practice and his legal education. In 1980, he earned his doctor of laws degree, cum laude, from the University of Houston. In 1991, he established his own firm dedicated to the health care industry. Dr. Holmquest focuses his legal practice on the regulatory and organizational issues that confront hospitals, physicians, and other health care providers as they attempt to adapt to the competitive environment of modern medicine. His clients include community hospitals, HMOs, PPOs, IPAs, medical groups, and a number of physician/hospital joint ventures. He is active in integrating institutional and physician services through the creation of hospital-sponsored group practices and the implementation of joint ventures and managed care initiatives. Until recently, Dr. Holmquest served as general counsel for North American Medical Management, Inc., a subsidiary of PhyCor, specializing in the management of risk contracts for organizations of physicians. Dr. Holmquest is active in many organizations, including the American Medical Association, American College of Nuclear Physicians (member, board of regents for six years), Texas Medical Association, and American Fighter Pilots Association. Biographical listings may be found in *American Men and Women of Science* and *Who's Who in America*. In addition to his other professional interests, Dr. Holmquest has served on the board of directors of two national hospital systems and the executive committee of one of those.

CYNDI M. JEWELL, JD, MPH, is currently associate general counsel at Baylor College of Medicine, Houston, Texas. Previously, she worked at Fulbright & Jaworski's Houston office as an associate, where she concentrated her practice in litigation and transactional and regulatory matters related to health care and managed care. Ms. Jewell received a bachelor of science degree in microbiology from Allegheny College in 1985. In 1993, she received both a master of public health degree from The University of Texas School of Public Health and a doctor of laws, with honors, from the

University of Houston Law Center, where she was a member of the Order of the Barons and a research editor for the *Houston Journal of International Law*. Ms. Jewell was admitted to practice law in Texas in May 1994. She is a member of the Houston Bar Association, State Bar of Texas, the American Health Lawyers Association, Texas Association of Defense Counsel, Defense Research Institute, Greater Houston Society for Health Care Risk Management, and the Health Care Compliance Association. Ms. Jewell has experience in corporate, partnership and general business, and regulatory law advice with respect to physician/hospital arrangements, mergers and acquisitions, and other general contract issues, including managed care contracting. She also has experience in regulatory matters and government enforcement involving health care institutions and in developing and implementing corporate compliance for health care entities. Ms. Jewell also has defense litigation experience in medical malpractice, employment law, medical product liability, and personal injury matters.

KATHLEEN LOEB, MS, is a certified Project Management Professional (PMP), and is a partner with Deloitte & Touche Consulting Group's practice in Atlanta, Georgia. She specializes in the delivery of information technology professional consulting services to health care industry clientele. Ms. Loeb focused nearly 17 of her 20-year career in the field of information technology with the IBM Corporation, where she was recognized as a subject matter expert on enterprisewide data warehouse planning, design and implementation, and large-scale cross-industry project management. During her career, she has had the pleasure to serve multiple high-profile clients including Duke University Medical Center, Novant Health Care System, and several Blue Cross/Blue Shield plans in the Southeast.

MARIE OSER is director of development for THA, the Association of Texas Hospitals and Health Care Organizations in Austin, which includes the Texas Institute for Health Policy Research. She is a graduate of the University of Michigan in Ann Arbor with a bachelor of arts in history. Ms. Oser also received a secondary teacher's certificate. Most recently, she served as the health care risk manager for the central region of Prudential Health Care. She was the manager of government programs for the southwest region, which included managing Medicaid and Medicare risk applications, compliance coordination, and developing and implementing training programs. She also served as a member of the lobby team focusing on Medicaid and women's and children's issues. During her career, Ms. Oser has been involved in the planning and implementation of a number of health and human service projects. She served as executive director of the White House Conference for Children and Youth. Ms. Oser has received presidential appointments to national and international commissions, as well as gubernatorial appointments to state commissions involving health care. Among her publications is *Good Health Plan*, describing a model managed care program.

LES PAUL, MD, MS, FCCP, joined MethodistCare, Inc., in 1997 as the chief medical officer. He was formerly a physician consultant for Milliman & Robertson, Inc., Wakefield, Massachusetts. In that capacity, he served as a consultant to health systems and developed new physician hospital structures, medical quality management, implementation of health care practice guidelines, physician leadership development, and the actuarial and medical practice analysis of shared risk contracts. Prior to his work with Milliman & Robertson, Dr. Paul was the associate medical director and section leader of General Internal Medicine at Lahey-Hitchcock Clinic North, Peabody, Massachusetts. He was responsible for developing the primary care section, designing and implementing the quality program, and preparing the facility for Joint Commission on Accreditation of Healthcare Organizations site review. He served as the medical liaison for managed care issues, including the design of optimal case management systems for patients in capitated insurance contracts. Dr. Paul has conducted an active clinical practice for 14 years, first in pulmonary and critical care, and then as a general internist/pulmonary consultant. He is a graduate of the University of Illinois College of Medicine in Chicago, and he completed an internal medicine residency at the University of Minnesota. He completed his pulmonary fellowship at the University of Vermont and at the National Institutes of Health. In addition to his medical training, Dr. Paul has completed a master of science degree in medical management at the University of Wisconsin in Madison.

MARC B. SAMUELS, JD, MPH, is a senior partner of HPG Austin and chair of the company's state government consulting practice. He has acted as advocate, strategist, and consultant to several state health care trade associations, companies, and organizations, including primary care, multi-specialty, and specialty medical groups; surgery centers; 501(a) nonprofit health care corporations; physician practice management companies; investor-owned and nonprofit integrated health care systems; public rural hospitals; specialty hospital companies; managed care organizations; pharmaceutical and telemedicine companies; and health data and services companies. He is heavily experienced in strategic positioning of companies and organizations and specializes in identifying corporate and organizational issues and creating repositioning strategies and programs for dealing with them. Much of Mr. Samuels' work involves counseling clients about the competitive challenges facing companies and organizations as a result of new government regulation and health system change. His expertise is also applied to legislative and regulatory advocacy, with specific strength in the formal and "informal" rules of state legislatures and regulatory actors. Mr. Samuels holds a juris doctor degree from the University of Texas School of Law, a master's in public health in chronic disease epidemiology from Yale School of Medicine, and an undergraduate degree in neuropsychology from the University of Michigan. He is pursuing a doctorate program in health services management and expects to be finished in late 1998. Mr. Samuels also serves on the governing board of the University of Houston Health Law & Policy Institute. Mr. Samuels served former Commissioner of Health & Human Services Mike McKinney as chief advocate on agency matters to the legislature, the governor's office, industry, the media, and the public. He also served as a member of the policy office of President George H. W. Bush and was also a member of the policy office of his son, Governor George W. Bush (current Governor of Texas). Both roles focused on health policy and reform. Mr. Samuels also represented the President's Council on Competitiveness, chaired by Vice President Dan Quayle. His private sector experience includes serving as a legislative advocate for Jenkens & Gilchrist, P.C., and as an analyst with the law offices of Deborah L. Steelman and McManis Associates, management and research consultants. Mr. Samuels has been a featured speaker at meetings and symposia of many health care trade associations, such as the National Managed Health Care Congress, Health Care Financial Management Association, National Association of Managed Care Physicians, Southwest Conference of Rural & Community Hospitals, Pharmaceutical Research & Manufacturers Association, Texas Organization of Rural & Community Hospitals, Texas Rural Health Association, and the Texas Association of Surgical Centers. He has also facilitated meetings for health care vendors such as ICM, NYLCare Health Plans, Pfizer Inc., TAP Pharmaceuticals, Tenet Health Care Corporation, and Columbia Healthcare. He has authored several articles, most recently on "The managed care backlash" in *Health Systems Review* and "Future trends in the health care economy" in the *Journal of Health Care Finance*. He is a contributor to the second and third editions of *The Managed Care Answer Book*, published by Panel Publishers, New York.

FREDERICK W. SPONG, MD, MBA, FACP, is a health care management consultant with broad expertise in medical management, but with special expertise in physician education and communication, physician retraining, physician-patient communication, patient education and communication, and total quality management in health care. He has served managed care organizations, health care facilities, medical groups, independent practice associations, integrated groups, and employers. Additionally, he has been medical director of a 150,000-member HMO, associate medical director of an 800,000-member HMO, and principal of a leading health care management consulting company. Dr. Spong is board-certified in internal medicine and nephrology.

PREFACE

Health maintenance organizations (HMOs) have come a long way since they were vilified in the 1930s and 1940s as the vanguard of the communist incursion into American health care and a threat to our way of life. Now, HMOs have the capacity to bring a movie audience to its feet in universal approbation for a statement about how difficult it is to access clinical care through an HMO. Despite strong emotional sentiment, HMOs have been credited with holding down health care costs, increasing the awareness of quality issues in medical care, reviving the notion of a primary care physician, augmenting the status and role of nurse practitioners and physician assistants, and creating a host of new bureaucratic entities to manage what had once been the ultimate cottage industry—the practice of medicine.

This book examines managed care in the context of the HMO. The HMO envisioned by its early organizers has changed dramatically. From what was once a "lock-in" insurance product with care delivered within a self-contained and exclusive system, the HMO now has as broad a menu of options as that of its preferred provider organization (PPO) and indemnity predecessors. In fact, most HMOs today offer PPO and indemnity options at a point of service; consequently, although the letters "HMO" have the capacity to inflame passionate support or antagonism, we will show that the HMO has no normative value or moral worth by itself, but instead, is simply a way of paying for and, under some arrangements, delivering health care services.

Authoring a book on HMOs takes a certain amount of courage, like building a house in the Los Angeles canyons. There are constant tremors in the background, sometimes punctuated by major upheavals, and disaster is always on the horizon. We have attempted to present a spectrum of issues surrounding the modern HMO, including some of the legal and administrative challenges HMOs face. We have leveraged a number of experts in this work and they are cited in the About the Authors section. There are others who have made major contributions to our understanding of this medium of health care delivery. These include Merlin Olson and colleagues at Deloitte & Touche Consulting Group, and the Health Law Section of Jenkens & Gilchrist, P.C. Every piece that has been sent to us has been examined and we take full responsibility for errors, omissions, and failures of clarity. Our editors at Aspen Publishers, Inc. have also shown a remarkable amount of patience with us as we missed deadline after deadline, drop-dead date after drop-dead date. We hope that Kalen Conerly and Stephanie Neuben are happy with the final product and we thank them. LeeAnn Chastain at the Baylor College of Medicine in Houston has labored with us on this production and has lent a valuable editorial and administrative eye.

The production of a book is always a difficult task, but rarely more than with a house full of teenagers who have a different idea of the definition of fun. Once again we are grateful to Rebecca, Mara, and Matthew for their humor and intelligence. To them we dedicate this work.

CHAPTER 1

The Environment of Managed Care

Clifford C. Dacso and Sheryl Tatar Dacso

INTRODUCTION

That health care has come into its own as an industry is confirmed by the rise of a new brand of consultants dedicated to foretelling its future. There should be a Yogi Berra aphorism that says, "Those who foretell the future are condemned to live it." Yet, there are, and continue to be, a parade of pundits wishing to predict developments in health care. The Health Care Security Act of 1993 is now inextricably intertwined with President Clinton and emblematic of the failure of "big government" to repair what is fundamentally a business problem. Trends that have indeed contributed to the evolution of the delivery of health care in this country include:

- the rise of managed care, supplanting indemnity fee-for-service
- the condensation of physicians, hospitals, and payers into delivery systems
- the emergence of quality measurement and management
- the rise of credentialing and other signs of the institutionalization of medicine
- the backlash against health maintenance organizations (HMOs) by physicians and the public
- the rebound in the premium dollar rise after the early victories of capitation
- the opening of networks and point-of-service options
- the rise of the specialist in conjunction with disease-state management

1

There are, of course, trends that were missed by many observers. These include:

- the collapse of the equity market in managed care organizations
- the difficulties of the large hospital corporations
- the intense activity of the federal government in compliance
- the attacks on the Employee Retirement Income Security Act (ERISA)

Other major issues that have been more evolutionary than revolutionary include:

- maturation of physician practice management
- rise of the "consumer" and his or her influence
- emergence of provider-sponsored managed care in response to the Balanced Budget Act (BBA) and the opportunities provided by Medicare+Choice
- continued upward inflationary pressure of technology
- increased prominence of information technology
- development of novel insurance products

With the enactment of the BBA on August 7, 1997, Congress and the president have set the stage for changes in Medicare and Medicaid programs. Items to be considered by a 17-member commission charged with preserving Medicare into the next century include raising the age of eligibility from 65 to 67, raising premiums for wealthy beneficiaries, and implementing a $5.00 copayment per visit for home health visits. The net effect of the recently passed legislation was to cap Medicare Part A payments and not give hospitals an inflation increase. The BBA also delayed the implementation of previously proposed changes that were intended to allow practice expenses in Medicare's fee schedule that would have increased primary care reimbursement and decreased payment for specialty care.

Q 1:1   What is managed care?

Broadly speaking, managed care describes a health care delivery system in which a party other than the physician or the patient influences the type, nature, and extent of medical care delivered. Managed care is an affirmative process and does not include limiting access nonselectively. Similarly, many of the evils attributed to managed care are not implied or expressed in its definition. Restrictions on patient-physician contact time, for example, are a result of the business factors of performing managed care, not of managing the care itself. Some forms of indemnity insurance that limit benefits by various methods based on cost and utilization may fall under the rubric, but such a system is not truly a managed one. Benefit limitations are designed to limit access nonselectively. A managed care system may limit benefits to its customers, but will actively manage those limitations by assessing their outcomes. A managed care system actively manages both the medical and financial aspects of a patient's care.

Some early managed care systems contained cost by providing global care and putting the providers at risk. They emphasized preventive as well as crisis-oriented intervention. Others merely negotiated discounts with physicians and hospitals in return for volume considerations in pricing. These are systems that could be called managed cost, not managed care. Later generations of managed care organizations increasingly emphasize outcomes measures as indicators of success.

Defining managed care is difficult because it is an evolving concept that embraces disparate organizations. The sharp distinctions that once existed among different types of plans have blurred as plans have adopted various features. The characteristics most common to managed care include:

- arrangements with selected providers who furnish a package of services to enrollees
- explicit criteria for selection of providers
- quality assurance, utilization review, and outcome measures
- financial or program coverage incentives or penalties to enrollees who do not use selected providers
- provider risk-sharing arrangements
- management by providers to ensure that enrollees or members receive appropriate care from the most cost-efficient mix of providers

Q 1:2   How is managed care distinguished from other health care financing arrangements?

Managed care organizations should have at least the characteristics outlined in Q 1:1. Managed care systems should be distinguished from fiscal intermediaries, which channel a payer's funds to the health care provider. These intermediaries may perform utilization review and quality control functions but not manage or assume risk for an enrollee. A managed care provider takes at least some of the risk for the patient's health care. Rather than simply approving or denying coverage based on a benefit plan, the health care manager will intervene to provide what it considers appropriate medical care for the minimum cost.

This distinction becomes critical as the labels for care delivery proliferate. Even traditional insurance companies may vend to a self-insured employer a product called a third-party intermediary, whereby they perform no insurance function; but merely process claims and do precertification and other clerical tasks. The self-insured employer holds the risk.

In analyzing the structure-function relationships of a managed care organization, it is useful to heed Deep Throat's admonition: "Follow the money." It is also useful to follow the risk, because the party that holds the risk has the most monetary stake in successfully managing the patient's care.

Q 1:3   What is driving the growth of managed care?

Medical costs have always been irritants for patients and payers. Physicians, however, historically were at the top of the nation's most respected list despite the expense of their services. Hospitals, by virtue of their voluntary, nonprofit nature, were considered public treasures, spoken of with pride. It is difficult to remember that as recently as 50 years ago, community fund-raisers were undertaken to build hospital wings and that a goal of broad-ranging federal legislation was to place a hospital in every community.

The public perception of the medical profession may have changed when the ethical prohibition against physician advertising was lifted. The notion of a physician advertising was so contrary to patients' perception of a physician's priestly role that the medical profession immediately lost credibility and respect. The increase in medical malpractice litigation was symptomatic of the widely held feeling that if medicine cost so much, it should be perfect. Similarly, there grew a widespread notion that hospitals and physicians made too much money, and malpractice litigation was viewed as a way to spread the wealth. The medical profession was increasingly seen as avaricious and unresponsive to the needs of the public.

The feeling was, "If health care providers want to act like a business, they'll simply have to be treated like a business." This included increased regulation and price competition.

Managed care is viewed as an answer to the problems of increasing price, decreasing access, and uncertain quality. Cost-conscious employers or payers can better estimate at the beginning of the fiscal year what their medical costs will be at the end. Patients, on the other hand, feel insulated from medical price increases and catastrophic expenses that could completely deplete their assets.

Providing medical care to the population is expensive. Figure 1–1 shows health care expenditures and trends. Although medical care expenditures have continued to grow, the rate of growth is decelerating. The initial explosive growth in the number of HMOs eventually moderated, only to pick up again as government programs increasingly mandated care management. Analysis of the current number of HMOs is murky—primarily because of the large numbers of mergers and acquisitions. More significant than the absolute number of HMOs is the number of enrollees, which continues to increase (Figure 1–2).

Q 1:4   What are the barriers to continued growth in managed care?

The growth and potential cost-effectiveness of managed care arrangements may be inhibited by the statutory and regulatory systems, liability issues, demographic factors, environmental issues, and market forces.

Employer/Employee Issues. As the major purchasers of health care benefits, employers have influenced benefit coverage and plan structure (i.e., copayments, premiums, and network products). Many employers pay either the full cost or a fixed percentage of the premium of any health plan offered. This allows fee-for-service plans to have the greatest level of employer subsidy. Unless employees are given responsibility for paying more of their health insurance premium, they have little incentive to select the lower cost plans.[1] As employers become more active consumers of health care plans, their use of incentives to encourage employees' use of low-cost plans has been effective. In times of full employment, such as during 1997–1998, competition for the work force increases and there is concomitant upward pressure on benefits. This situation is somewhat analogous to the rise of health insurance itself after World War II.

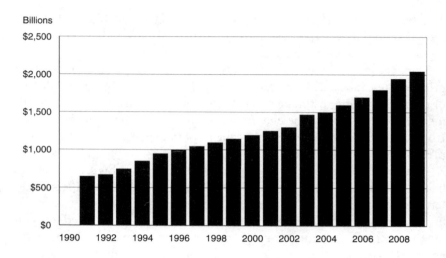

Figure 1–1 National Health Expenditures, 1990–2008 (est.). *Source:* Reprinted from Congressional Budget Office, 1997.

Demographic Issues. Most managed care arrangements require a specific mix of providers. For example, HMOs that serve Medicaid clients are required to have 25 percent of their enrollees from commercial payers (although these requirements are commonly waived by the states). Strictures also exist governing the population of Medicare HMOs. In view of the American preference for choice, significant incentives are needed to influence consumer behavior. This is much more pronounced among the elderly, whose level of attachment often is directly related to location of hospitals, drugstores, and clinics. Although many managed care arrangements have used economic incentives (i.e., copayments and deductibles) to influence choice, features such as point-of-service and other "opt-outs" are included in many managed care plans to allow more freedom of choice, but with higher out-of-pocket charges for using nonnetwork providers. Other issues relate to the special needs of the rural and inner city populations in which many managed care organizations are unable to provide adequate coverage because of the sparseness of providers.

Physician Issues. Managed care depends on an adequate supply of primary care physicians who can manage a patient's care and ensure that the patient receives only medically necessary services. These primary care

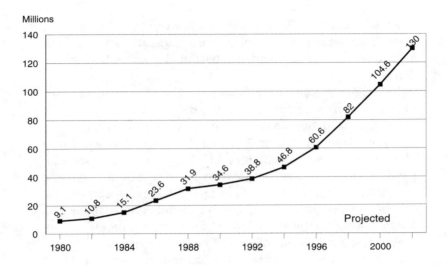

Figure 1–2 HMO Enrollment: Actual and Projected. *Source:* Reprinted from *Medical Benefits*, Vol. 13, p. 8, © 1996, Aspen Publishers, Inc.

physicians (i.e., family practice, general internal medicine, and general pediatrics) are in short supply because of emphasis on subspecialization. On the other hand, there is an oversupply of many types of specialists who are finding it increasingly difficult to survive without being associated with a managed care plan. These physician factors are in constant evolution and include the following:

> Some obstetrician-gynecologists are demanding to be considered primary care physicians for women. Heretofore, they had been universally considered specialists. Some, however, find that although managed care plans highly encourage their serving as "primes," they feel uncomfortable in that role. Data also suggest that specialists serving as primary care physicians may, in fact, utilize at a higher rate outside their specialty. The converse is also true in that specialists may utilize resources more appropriately within their specialties and, indeed, have superior outcomes to the generalist.
>
> Publicly held management corporations are consolidating physicians' practices and contracting as units. They are also consolidating themselves into large corporations capable of executing

nationwide contracts for care. Hospital based primary care groups, constructed originally as defensive measures, are suffering from a lack of profitability and demonstrated contribution to the margin.

Physicians' incomes are declining. The median income for physicians fell 3.8 percent in 1993, even among primary care physicians, and has stayed relatively steady since that time. Medicare payments to primary care physicians similarly fell in 1995 on a relative value unit (RVU) basis, however, Medicare payments to the specialist now show some sign of increasing.

Medical schools are considering decreases in class sizes. Funding for postgraduate training is generally limited to the first specialty board. Similarly, there is strong support for effectively eliminating funding for training of international medical graduates, who now form the core of house staff in many inner-city institutions. A bold experiment by the Health Care Finance Administration pays some New York hospitals *not* to train graduate physicians (*The Wall Street Journal* Interactive Edition, www.wsj.com).

Financial Issues. Many managed care arrangements are capital-intensive. In developing an integrated delivery system, the physical plant (offices and facilities), network development, and provider contracting costs may be prohibitive. This has stimulated significant activity in mergers and acquisitions of physician practice management organizations. Information technology (see Chapter 14) has emerged as perhaps the single most avid consumer of capital in the health care business as payers and providers alike seek to control the information flow and garner knowledge about enrollees.

Tax Incentives. The current tax structure does little to motivate employers to control health insurance costs because these expenses are tax deductible to the employer and not taxed to the employee. The net result is a federal subsidy of the purchase of health insurance, with the most expensive plans (e.g., fee-for-service plans) receiving the greatest subsidies. With the passage of the Health Insurance Portability and Accountability Act of 1996 (HIPAA), medical savings accounts (MSAs) will allow individuals to deduct amounts paid into an MSA during the taxable year, up to specific limits.

Legal Issues. Many legal issues at the state and federal level pose barriers to achieving health care reform through managed care. In addition to ERISA and state insurance regulations, the specter of medical malpractice liability becomes more acute in a managed care environment given the competing interests of the patient and physician and the physician and managed care organization. Recent efforts by the states and an abortive effort by the U.S. Congress in 1998 have been directed toward securing "patients rights." A sentinel event was the passage of Senate Bill 386 in Texas that allows causes of action against managed care organizations for their practice of medicine.

Legislative Issues. Managed care organizations are critical of the numerous anti–managed care laws and regulations in existence that pose barriers to the growth of managed care in the health care industry. Although wide variation exists among the constituencies as to the most significant "anti–managed care" legislation, the following are commonly raised as barriers: (1) networking legislation (e.g., "any willing provider" laws); (2) utilization review regulation; and (3) state benefit mandates.

Of late, however, under the pressure of Medicaid federal funding changes, there has been a change in the attitude of many legislators toward managed care. In fact, the regulatory barriers may be easing.

Q 1:5   Is the growth rate of medical care costs slowing down?

Several studies have suggested a leveling off or slight lessening in medical care costs' rate of increase—this is presumed to be in response to the increase in health care competition over the past 10 years. Based on a report prepared by Deloitte & Touche in conjunction with VHA, Inc.,[2] in the second quarter of 1996, the medical care price index dropped below the U.S. consumer price index for the first time in almost 20 years. An uptick in 1997 presages the return of inflation of health care costs, however. The financial performance of health care equities was still a respectable 6.2 percent in the first two quarters of 1998; however, many expect that increasing government regulation, public revulsion with HMOs, and mergers and consolidations will take their toll. Health care equities have certainly not been immune to the recent Wall Street implosion.

Although health insurance premium costs also decreased in their rate of growth, that trend is almost certain to reverse as managed care organizations become responsible for a more uniform segment of the population and technology costs continue to climb. Premiums for 1998–1999 are expected to increase at a significantly higher growth rate than in previous years.

Q 1:6   What happened to managed competition?

Managed competition is the macroeconomic principle propounded by Alain Enthoven and later adopted by the Jackson Hole Group as a way to allow economies of scale to be applied to the health care industry. This principle was incorporated into President Clinton's unsuccessful health reform package of 1994; however, the concept of managed competition—that purchasers of health care can come together into purchasing alliances to exert price pressure on health care delivery systems—exists in various forms today.

There has been a rise of purchasing organizations—such as the Houston Healthcare Purchasing Organization—and various business groups on health that have allowed medium-sized businesses to access discounts in physician fees, hospitalization, pharmacy, durable medical equipment, and other aspects of health care.

The Clinton plan envisaged a string of regulated health care insurance purchasing cooperatives throughout the country, with some of the larger purchasers forming their own cooperatives. Although these cooperatives never formed, the business alliances exert some group buying pressure. This technique, however, works best in a discounted fee-for-service environment and may be less successful if the alliances try to function as health care delivery services or to perform underwriting functions. As interim entities, they are performing many of the functions the cooperatives would have done. This is not true managed competition, though, which would have involved more stringent government regulation. The business groups do exemplify one important trend: stripping out costs at the expense of insurance companies.

The year 1998 saw the backlash against those very entities that helped kill the Healthcare Security Act. The insurers mounted the highly effective "Harry and Louise" television campaign featuring the "they win, we lose" slogan. Now the National Association of Health Plans, which represents more than 1,000 managed care organizations and HMOs, has been airing a series of ads in the Washington, D.C., area warning of decreasing benefits and increasing costs[3] as politicians grapple with reconciling cost containment with the public's desire for more access, more choice, and more quality at lower cost.

Q 1:7   What are the national economic drivers of managed care?

Industry, government, and even the medical profession want to slow the growth of health care's contribution to the gross domestic product. Managed care holds out that promise. If the recipients of health care benefits can be convinced that the change from fee-for-service medicine to managed care is in their best interest, so much the better.

Although both the actual dollar amount and the proportion of the gross domestic product are the largest in the world, the perceived value returned is not thought to be large enough to justify the expense. Nonetheless, the expense continues to grow. The drive to lower the cost, or at least the rate of increase, has several bases:

- Despite enormous affluence, Americans have a subjective sense of financial inadequacy.
- Medical care and medical care providers are perceived as too well-fed.
- Despite enormous successes, the medical care establishment is thought to give too little value for the money expended.
- Medical care is felt to be a fungible commodity.
- Entitlements are consuming what is seen as a disproportionate share of the federal budget.

The contribution of health care to the nation's economic environment has far-reaching implications. The question of value received is even more important for health care policy. Conventional wisdom says that the payers' perceived value of health care is not commensurate with the cost. But who is being asked? For the millions of eligible veterans who receive first-dollar health care from the Department of Veterans Affairs, the value received is infinite, because they pay nothing. Veterans argue that they paid for their health care in advance with their military service, and it is incontrovertible that some were promised health care for life should they develop a service-connected disability. Nonetheless, in terms of dollar outlay, the eligible veteran's return is highly satisfactory. An even more obvious example of value received is indigent health care (where it is available). In this setting, the patient makes no contribution to his or her health care and yet is afforded high-quality care by practitioners who are held to the same standard as those delivering compensated care.

The segment of the population least satisfied with its health care has yet to be identified. The call for reform emanates from the magnates and the politicians—and from workers whose health benefits are tied to their employment and who feel they have significant out-of-pocket expenses despite health insurance. The call also emanates from the representatives (self-appointed and otherwise) of the uninsured and those who must rely on indigent health care systems. From a social point of view, these representatives' claims of poor value are understandable. From a purely national economic perspective, it is inexplicable.

The focus of the national economic debate on the health care crisis has been centered on physicians and hospitals. Other major players in the health care scene are the manufacturers of durable medical equipment and pharmaceuticals. Although major public policy has not focused on them, these equipment manufacturers consume a substantial proportion of the health care dollar. Recognition of this has prompted the major pharmaceutical manufacturers to move to control the distribution of their products by acquiring managed care pharmacy distributors.

Q 1:8   What has happened to health care costs overall?

There is no question that the declining growth of health care costs promised by the Health Care Security Act and delivered by macroeconomic forces and resolve of purchasers has occurred. Figure 1–3 shows the relative changes in the consumer price indexes of medical care compared with all other items. A comparison of health care costs over time, however, shows a steady decline in the secular trend.

Although the general economy is in a noninflationary period, health care historically has been able to defy any trend of reduction. This is obviously no longer the case. Of interest, though, is the projection of expenditure increases over time (see Figure 1–1, Q 1:3).

Q 1:9   What is the basis for this change in health care cost inflation?

Several reasons have been adduced:

- Managed care, by judicious contracting, population selection, and risk management has reduced health care premiums paid by employers.

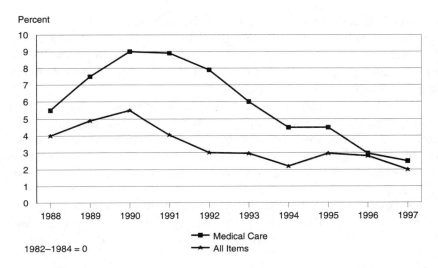

Percent

1982–1984 = 0

Medical Care
All Items

Figure 1–3 Consumer Price Indices. *Source:* Reprinted from *Setting Foundations for the Millennium*, Deloitte & Touche LLP, 1997, U.S. Bureau of Labor Statistics.

- Employers have drawn a line in the sand following the lead of large purchasers such as the California Public Employees' Retirement System (CalPERS) and have kept down the amount of money they are willing to pay for health care.
- Competition among providers for large blocks of lives has driven down price.
- Uniformity has been imposed on a previously anarchic and highly individualistic market.
- Objective measures of value and customer satisfaction and purchasing on that basis is beginning to be imposed.

Q 1:10   Can this trend be sustained or is it an isolated phenomenon that will be reduced as soon as competitive pressures change?

It can be argued that the price of health care has been artificially inflated only of late and that it is returning to previous levels. The impetus to return seems robust and powerful; however, there are some indications that the slowing in health care costs may be subsiding and that sectors of the economy may experience increases over the next several years. The National Coalition on Health Care projects that small employers will have a proportionately greater increase in expenditures on health care than will larger employers.

On the contrarian side, the respected health economist Eli Ginzberg observes that the decline in health care cost inflation is possibly only a one-time event resulting from the shift of populations from higher cost fee-for-service plans to managed care.[4] Ginzberg also identifies the immutable increase in expense accruing as a result of the wider availability of newer technology.

An important issue identified by Ginzberg and others is the rise of direct payer contracting. This technique allows risk sharers, employers, and providers to manage the lives without the intercession (and cost) of a third party.

Kassirer,[5] in an accompanying editorial, makes the strong argument for the current "lock-in" HMO as being a transitional model, a "failed experiment." He identifies several features of the emerging model:

- MCOs must assign the most appropriate medical personnel to the patient as dictated by the needs of the patient.
- MCOs must become better citizens by showing more interest in the community, the underserved, medical education, and research.
- Regulations will emerge to govern the activities of HMOs to a greater degree.

There is some evidence that these changes are already beginning. The March 25, 1997, interactive edition of *The Wall Street Journal* carried the headline "Oxford Health Plans To Let Specialists Oversee More Care." The article continued, "Oxford estimates that 75 percent, or $1.7 billion, of the company's $2.2 billion in medical spending last year went for services provided by specialists. We're asking primary care to control all of this. It's getting complicated, and it's something primary care doctors weren't trained to do." Mr. [Stephen F.] Wiggins [Chairman and CEO] says, "Payment will be made in stages that are keyed to, among other things, reports from patients themselves on how well they are doing weeks after a medical procedure. The physician will be paid out as long as he [*sic*] delivers good quality care." Oxford has seen some dramatic reverses in its economic fortunes, however.

Texas has been a leader in legislation regulating the HMO-physician and HMO-patient relationship. It is anticipated that such regulations will become more widespread.

Q 1:11   Are there federal policy drivers for managed care?

Since the failure of the Health Care Security Act, health care reform has been, at best, incremental, but the exigencies for reform have not changed. Congressional Budget Office data from 1996 confirm that the Medicare trust is plunging headlong toward bankruptcy. Recent political activities toward a balanced budget and a surging economy in 1997 allowed the Medicare Trust's demise to be postponed; however, it is conceivable that this demise will occur unless dramatic changes in the program occur (see Figure 1–4). The widespread disparity in Medicaid benefits around the country is putting a strain on wealthy and poor states alike. Long-term care is a national imperative that has not yet begun to be addressed by the federal government, the lead having been taken by the great private foundations.

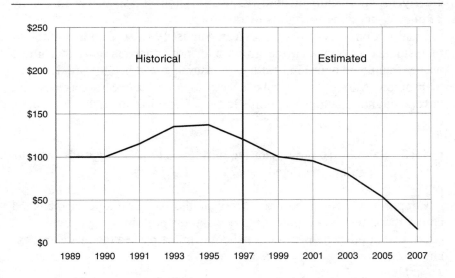

Figure 1–4 Medicare Health Insurance Trust Balance. *Source:* Reprinted from *Medicare Trustees Report*, 1998, Health Care Financing Administration.

MSAs have not had a sufficient assessment on a national scale; recently enacted federal legislation will provide for a pilot before the inauguration of a national mandate for that form of payment.

The question of the uninsured and uncovered continues to loom in the foreground of the health care debate with no obvious solution—short of universal coverage. Some suggestions include extensions of Medicaid eligibility to the medically indigent through a Section 1115 waiver. The impact of indigent care's growth cannot be overestimated. Not only is the absolute number increasing to more than 40 million in 1998, but the percentage of uninsured and underinsured older Americans continues to increase. As forced retirements, downsizing, and other labor cost–control measures pervade the marketplace, this demographic imperative can be expected to increase in influence.

A major national economic force is the attempt to make practicing medicine a commodity. As Blumenthal[6] points out, comodification may have an adverse effect on indigent health care because physicians feel less altruism and social responsibility. "After all," Blumenthal writes, "since when do banks, car dealers, stockbrokers, and supermarkets feel that they are obligated to give away services to persons who are unable to pay their bills?" The fundamental problem of vulnerable populations—the frail elderly, the chronically mentally ill, and children with special needs—may be poorly served by merciless market forces.

Finally, Congress passed HIPAA in August 1996 to provide portability of insurance coverage in the group and individual markets; to combat waste, fraud, and abuse in health care insurance and health care delivery; to promote MSAs; to improve access to long-term care services and coverage; and to simplify administration of health insurance.

Q 1:12   What are the legislative initiatives in place or underway to regulate managed care?

Congress is feeling the pressure of public backlash against managed care's more restrictive practices. Legislation prohibiting gag rules that restrict what physicians can tell patients almost passed the last Congress and is expected to be introduced once more.

The Health Care Financing Administration (HCFA) has already required disclosure of financial inducements paid to physicians. This type of regulation is also expected to be expanded and continued. Congress can be expected to influence managed care delivery in the programs over which it has the most influence, Medicare and Medicaid.[7]

Q 1:13   What is anticipated to be the impact of this rise in cost on the availability of employee and dependent health insurance coverage?

The majority of health coverage for the insured population continues to be employer based. The American Hospital Association and the Lewin Group, Inc., reported[8] that dependent coverage is projected to continue declining, causing the number of uninsured patients to rise to 45.6 million (16.2 percent of the population) by 2002. This report asserts that the majority of this increase will be a result of changes in employment status and the subsequent loss of health coverage. Another trend identified by the report is increased employee responsibility for health care expenses in the form of copays, deductibles, and other out-of-pocket expenses.

Although HIPAA could have been reasonably expected to change this trend, the existence of similar laws in the majority of states will likely decrease its overall impact.

NEW REGULATION AND LEGISLATION

Q 1:14   What is HIPAA and why is it important?

The Health Insurance Portability and Accountability Act of 1996 was the first insurance reform legislation enacted since ERISA. HIPAA imposes limits on group health insurer's ability to deny coverage for preexisting conditions and to discriminate against prospective or current enrollees based on health status. The law also requires guaranteed issue and guaranteed acceptance or renewal of policies in the group market and the group-to-individual market.

The important provisions of HIPAA include:

- Provides tax deductibility of MSA contributions under a pilot project and standards for catastrophic health insurance policies sold in conjunction with MSAs. Federally qualified HMOs are permitted to offer catastrophic health insurance policies.
- Amends the Consolidated Omnibus Budget Reconciliation Act continuation coverage rules.
- Makes health plan–related changes to Medicare-Medicaid antikickback law.
- Instructs the Department of Health and Human Services (HHS) to adopt uniform standards for health plan payer and provider transmission of electronic health care data.
- Revises Medicare supplemental insurance coverage.
- Gives tax-favored status to long-term care insurance policies that meet certain standards.

Other provisions of the law impose minimum maternity stay requirements and require mental health coverage parity for plans covering medical and mental services.

Q 1:15   How is HIPAA enforced?

The HHS has jurisdiction over health insurance requirements not adopted or enforced by the states, and the Department of Labor oversees enforcement of provisions related to ERISA plans. The Internal Revenue Service will tax health plans and insurers that do not comply with the provisions and will oversee employer compliance with the tax benefits available under the law.

Q 1:16   What are the BBA's important features as related to Title IV of the Social Security Act (Medicare and Medicaid)?

The BBA's Medicare provisions expand choices for seniors, create antifraud initiatives, provide a package of preventive care benefits, modernize Medicare's payment system, establish MSAs and a private fee-for-service option under the Medicare+Choice program, and are anticipated to extend the Medicare trust fund an additional 10 years while saving taxpayers $115 billion. The BBA creates a bipartisan commission to address Medicare's long-term solvency crisis expected with the retirement of baby boomers. The commission will look at the financial impact of the increased numbers of eligible people on the Medicare programs as the baby boom generation ages and make specific recommendations to Congress with respect to a comprehensive approach to preserving the Medicare program.

The BBA maintains Part B premiums at 25 percent of program costs and phases into the premium—over the next seven years—the cost of a home health reallocation. This plan achieves the following goals:

1. Extends the life of the Medicare Part A trust fund for 10 years.
2. Contains structural reform and expands choice through provider sponsored organizations (PSOs), preferred provider organizations (PPOs), private fee-for-service plans, and a demonstration project for MSAs. Private contracting for health care services is also allowed.
3. Includes expanded preventive health care benefits for mammography, Pap smears, diabetes, prostate and colorectal cancer screening, bone density measurement, and vaccines.
4. Increases accountability through fraud and abuse penalties and strengthens program integrity through increased disclosure of information to beneficiaries and encouragement of prudent purchasing decisions.

Choice for Medicare beneficiaries is ensured through the Medicare+Choice program, which will allow seniors to continue receiving traditional fee-for-service Medicare and to return to fee-for-service Medicare after trying another plan. The plan options available to the beneficiary will include PSOs, MSAs, private fee-for-service, private plans/HMOs, and PPOs. These Medicare+Choice plans will be reformed to encourage expansion into rural and low-cost urban areas by:

• setting minimum monthly payments to $367 beginning in 1998 (most current rural payments are $221)
• gradually moving the calculation of payment from its existing formula to a 50/50 blend of national average costs and local costs

- guaranteeing plans a minimum percentage increase
- replacing the 50/50 Medicare/non-Medicare enrollment rule with enhanced quality and outcome measures
- authorizing new competitive pricing demonstration projects
- carving graduate medical education costs (direct and indirect) from payments over 5 years and making these payments directly to the teaching hospitals

Q 1:17   What are the significant consumer protection features of the BBA?

There are significant consumer protections proposed, such as monthly disenrollment through year 2001, with annual enrollment with a 6-month disenrollment period in 2002, and annual with 3-month disenrollment in 2003 and after. Other protections include:

- requiring all plans to make medically necessary care available 7 days a week, 24 hours a day
- prohibiting plans from restricting providers' advice to beneficiaries about medical care and treatment (gag rules)
- requiring plans to have grievance and appeal mechanisms in place to protect beneficiary rights
- requiring plans to provide coverage for care that a "prudent lay person" would consider an emergency
- protecting patient confidentiality by requiring plans to safeguard the confidentiality of health information while allowing patient access to their medical records

Q 1:18   What are the Medicare payment reforms in BBA?

Among other payment reforms, the BBA includes a new prospective payment system for skilled nursing facilities, home health agencies, hospital outpatient departments, rehabilitation facilities and hospitals, and ambulance services. Medicaid disproportionate share hospital payments are reduced 5 percent over the 5-year period. Indirect medical education adjustment is reduced from 7.7 percent to 7 percent in 1998, 6.5 percent in 1999, 6.0 percent in 2000, and 5.57 percent from 2001 forward. The home health reallocation proposes a reallocation from Part A to Part B of the home health spending that does not follow a hospitalization or skilled nursing facility stay.

The legislation goes beyond HIPAA in addressing antifraud and abuse as a means of controlling cost of care. Measures include:

- a "three-strikes, you're out" hard line on frequent offenders
- the Secretary's discretion to call, "One strike, you're out"
- mandatory surety bonds and owner interest disclosures
- binding advisory options for physician self-referrals
- a new, toll-free number for beneficiaries to report suspected fraud and billing irregularities directly to the Inspector General of HHS

Q 1:19   Which provisions of the BBA affect Medicaid?

The BBA's goal is to achieve approximately $13 billion in net Medicaid savings over 5 years with increased state flexibility and program oversight. States will have the option of providing Medicaid services through managed care without a waiver. The requirement that states pay federally qualified health centers on a cost basis will be eliminated over a multiyear period. States can use Medicaid payment rates to determine whether cost sharing is owed for qualified Medicare beneficiaries and dual eligibles.

The legislation increases health coverage for children who are uninsured. It provides for $24 billion to be spent on children's health care, with more than 7 million of the country's uninsured children becoming eligible for coverage. The Child Health Insurance Assistance Program entitles states to grants to expand health insurance access for eligible children. Many states, such as Texas, adopted appropriate legislation to enable such funding and match federal funds through a specified formula.

States will also have considerable flexibility on how to spend the money, including the ability to define eligibility (with an income ceiling of 200 percent of poverty for states where current Medicaid eligibility is below 200 percent of poverty, and a ceiling of 50 percent above the current ceiling for states with Medicaid eligibility ceilings in excess of 200 percent when the measure is enacted). Options for states include:

- expanded Medicaid coverage
- enrollment of uninsured children in health plans by private health insurers
- direct provision of health services to children, including immunizations; well-child care; and services provided by disproportionate share [DSH] hospitals), although no more than 10 percent of the grant money can be used for noncoverage purposes (e.g., administration, outreach, or services)
- benefits must include either benefits equal to those provided in a benchmark benefits package, those provided by a state-administered program, or those of same actuarial value as one of the benchmark benefit packages and including at least inpatient and outpatient hospital services; physicians' surgical and medical services; lab and radiology services; and well-baby and well-child care, including age-appropriate immunizations

A benchmark benefit package would be one of the following:

- the standard Blue Cross/Blue Shield preferred provider option service benefit plan offered under the Federal Employees' Health Benefits Plan
- the health coverage that is offered and generally available to employees of the state in the relevant state
- the health coverage offered by an HMO with the largest commercial enrollment of the coverage offered by such an organization in the relevant state

IMPACT OF HEALTH CARE REFORM

Q 1:20   Is managed care an appropriate health care reform strategy?

It is clear that uncontrolled fee-for-service medicine or reimbursement is no longer a feasible economic strategy. No one realistically proposes a return to the "good old days." Fee-for-service reimbursement has been replaced by a number of arrangements that use some degree of managed care. The macroeconomic underpinnings seem to be based less on value than on certainty. Managed care, despite its flaws, does offer increasing predictability and capacity for budgeting as control increases and flexibility decreases. It is possible to know in the first-quarter budget what the costs will be in the fourth quarter.

It is interesting to speculate on why current indemnity-paying health care systems could not achieve that same degree of predictability. The large payers responsible for tens of thousands of lives should have been able to achieve a degree of actuarial certainty that would have allowed this predictability. The reason they could not probably had less to do with actuarial uncertainty than with shifting costs to payers from indigent care and government health programs. In recognition of this, virtually all the legislation before Congress had universal access as a principle, although it clearly was not compelling enough to secure passage.

When considering managed care and health care reform from the national economic perspective, the overall impact on the U.S. economy has to be ascertained. For example, pharmaceuticals and durable medical equipment manufacturers together employ hundreds of thousands of people and account for billions of dollars in sales. Contractions in these industries wrought by managed care would certainly have an impact on the gross domestic product.

As medicine becomes transformed into integrated delivery systems spanning communities and the nation, some risks become apparent. Market share can be garnered disproportionately by a small number of oligopolies with consequent impact on pricing, availability, and competition. Research, viewed as expensive overhead, may be dispensed with even by academic medical centers trying to stay afloat in a competitive sea while dragging the anchor of indigent care and community service. In fact, recent data suggest that in areas of high penetration of managed care, research programs are less robust. Large corporations become imbued with inertia and lose the culture that made them successful in the first place; they feel less connected to the community and may not view medical care as a community resource.

Nonetheless, some form of managed care offers the best hope for curtailing the growth of health care costs. The transition, however, will be spotty throughout the country, creating arbitrage opportunities that clever business people are likely not to pass up. Federal legislation will probably have to address this in the interests of public safety.

Q 1:21   What are the prospects for managed care in future health care reform?

It is likely that future health care proposals will contain many managed care features. Humphrey Taylor and J. Ian Morrison identify 10 key paradoxes:[9]

1. Consumers are very satisfied with the health care services they receive but are largely dissatisfied with the performance of the system as a whole.
2. HMO members have lower expectations but are more satisfied with their health care plans than consumers in indemnity systems.
3. Health care consumers seem to accept higher deductibles and copayments (when these plan changes are properly communicated), but they value low out-of-pocket costs in HMOs and PPOs.
4. Employers say they want to contain costs but have been unwilling to promote alternative options aggressively, such as severely limiting the choice of providers.
5. Traditional HMO models are the most financially viable, yet their growth has been slowest.
6. American doctors, especially older ones, publicly resist managed care, yet they are signing up at a rapid rate, and older doctors are just as likely as young physicians to be enrolled in a PPO.
7. Managed care was supposed to be a threat to physicians' incomes and yet, according to American Medical Association data, the mid-1980s proved to be a golden age of doctors' incomes.
8. HMO and indemnity plan enrollees under age 65 are fairly similar demographically, yet a significant number of employers claim to have experienced adverse selection.
9. The plans with the fastest growth in the mid-1980s are not the bellwether of managed care in the long run. For-profit independent practice associations with fee-for-service reimbursement methods proliferated from 1984 to 1986, and in the late 1980s began to encounter financial problems resulting in consolidation.
10. Americans want cost containment but will not pay for it in terms of rationing and rationalization of services.

Q 1:22   Do health care costs influence reform?

It is tempting to take a simplistic view when analyzing the question of the cost of health care in the United States. Any industry that occupies at least 14 percent of the gross domestic product must be complex. California has been one of the bellwether states for following the influence of managed care, and proponents now tout the decline in cost growth in California as proof that the system works. In reality, cost growth rate in California has declined, but that has only brought it to the level of the rest of the country. Health care can sometimes follow the law of unintended consequences, as demonstrated by the study showing increasing overall costs when drug formularies are restricted in an HMO.[10]

Q 1:23   How has managed care reform affected health care costs?

Although managed care has affected provider reimbursement and the growth of medical expenditures, it is not clear that this has occurred by virtue of management. Whether there has been a Hawthorne-like effect (i.e., improvement in performance because of the enormous scrutiny of health care costs) is yet to be determined. One of the major problems in making this assessment is the influence of the addition of administrative costs and profits to the mix. These were not a factor many years ago when the baseline data were being accumulated and health care was voluntary, not for profit. As an example, a recent analysis shows that 15 percent of the premium dollars in a prepaid, capitated system go to administrative costs, and this does not include corporate profits.

Despite possible alternative explanations, it appears that, at least in some markets, managed care has reduced costs. This has occurred, however, at the expense of traditional characteristics of the health care system:

- Hospitals will continue to close as the market for beds consolidates, leaving certain communities vulnerable. As a reaction to this, however, rural networks have begun to form and exert power.
- The poor and uninsured require safety-net institutions, which are required to compete on unfamiliar terrain. Public providers, though, are increasingly taking their lead from managed care in the private

sector and forming HMOs and other vehicles to compete for government-sponsored programs.

- "Value competition" is difficult for the general public to understand. The emergence of "direct to consumer" advertising by pharmaceutical houses seems to have galvanized a return to finding ways of publicizing successes. The impact of the *U.S.s News & World Report* ratings in the market has even caused analyses of that methodology to be published in respected medical journals.
- Vigilance regarding antitrust is required as large health care conglomerates emerge. Antitrust considerations seem to be assiduously observed by regulators.
- Continued analysis is required to see that initial cost reductions squeezed out by reengineering are maintained.

Q 1:24   What are some forces driving changes in health care?

In the private sector, purchasers and consumers are behind the changes in health care delivery and funding. Rising health costs—including increasing expenditures for retirees—have caused many employers to shift from passive purchasers to active consumers. Other major influences include government purchases of health care, private-sector initiatives including carve-out products, and intense local competition in a previously noncompetitive industry.

Q 1:25   How does society influence health care reform?

The influence of the electorate on health care reform is enormous. Recent events—such as the defeat of catastrophic Medicare by the American Association of Retired Persons and the death of the Health Care Security Act—demonstrate the voter's enormous power. In the face of a potentially bankrupt Medicare Trust Fund, the issue of health care reform should remain on the political front burner. The major source of influence at this time seems to be the purchasing power of those determining health care benefits for large institutions. As an example, CalPERS, the California state employees' retirement system, was able to effect price reductions in negotiations with managed care organizations simply as a result of its purchasing power. Other similar coalitions, such as the Houston Healthcare Purchasing Organization and similar business alliances, attempt to bring the power of large numbers to the health care debate. The poor and uninsured, however, have no such advocate but require the power of the state through Medicare and Medicaid to advocate for access on their behalf.

Q 1:26   How have policy makers responded to managed care?

Many of the changes being forced on the health care delivery system as a means to control cost and improve quality are encountering barriers in the form of existing federal and state laws. Some argue that federal antitrust laws, traditional state insurance laws and regulations, and newer rules such as any willing provider laws may pose barriers to the evolving relationships in the industry. Others are concerned that these new systems are developing outside of existing laws and regulations, thereby posing a threat to consumers and providers. Common issues that arise in the public policy debates related to managed care include:

- ERISA preemption of state laws
- medical liability reform
- role of local, state, and federal governments in health care reform
- accountability
- quality assurance
- access to care
- antitrust and competition
- provision of "safety nets" for vulnerable populations
- graduate medical education

THE ACADEMIC MEDICAL CENTER (AMC)

**Q 1:27   How has managed care affected graduate medical
            education?**

Academic health centers (AHCs) are unique institutions that combine the missions of education, research, and clinical care. They traditionally provide public access to the most sophisticated, and often the most expensive health care. Because of their structure and functions, they often have access to a variety of funds, both public and private, and are able to shift costs adroitly to cover shortfalls in areas of low funding. As funding for research constricts along with the payment for health care, AHCs are finding themselves under enormous pressure. In markets where there is intense competition and a variety of skills, this pressure is especially intense. Blumenthal and Meyer identify several clinical strategies:

- increasing sales of clinical services to private purchasers (this includes not only patient care services but management services (MSO) as well)
- reducing costs of clinical services
- increasing sale of clinical services to government payers
- increasing sales of nonclinical services in private markets: research and teaching

Other strategies for AMCs include developing international markets, becoming the provider of last resort for complex cases, and assuming a leadership role in quality and outcome measures and research.

AMCs play a major role in the nation's health care delivery system, and special accommodations may be needed to allow them to survive in a market where the majority of their services are no longer unique.

Q 1:28   What will be the fate of the teaching institutions?

AMCs are under tremendous pressure as the market consolidates. Traditional rivals such as Brigham and Women's Hospital and Massachusetts General Hospital, Presbyterian Hospital and New York Hospital, and New York University and Mt. Sinai have either announced mergers or taken serious steps toward consolidation to compete with the investor-owned, for-profit medical centers. Other AMCs, such as Tulane University, have entered into agreements with for-profits that devolve a varying amount of control to the investor-owned corporation. Even Catholic health care has been involved with the management agreement between the hospital of St. Louis University and Tenet.

The rapid expansion and increase in medical schools in the 1960s and 1970s placed pressure on the health care market, especially as it has constricted. The funding priorities of the 1970s generally promoted the establishment of a high-overhead research establishment that required the training of large numbers of medical scientists and narrow subspecialists. These physicians are now in their peak productive years in a shrinking market. Simultaneously, many of the new medical schools failed to develop intensive primary care programs or practices and are now left without a strong base.

AMCs find that the market is, in some cases, willing to pay a small premium, but this is not enough to offset the costs inherent in teaching and the indigent care burden they traditionally assume. The question is not, "Can the academic medical centers compete?" but rather, "Who will pay for their services?" The health care industry will ultimately bear the cost, either through cross-subsidization or direct support via a special tax or contribution. But, in return, the AMCs can expect to be held to a standard of market responsiveness blended with innovation and originality. Demanding complete market responsiveness to the exclusion of pure research is unreasonable. Pure research is critical to society and must be supported.

AMCs have adopted a number of strategies in response to the market challenge. These include:

- partnering with for-profit institutions
- expanding into the international market
- developing primary care networks
- acquiring or developing HMOs
- differentiating the product by measurable quality or excellence
- capitalizing on a well-known brand name
- marketing consumer education and health care information

Q 1:29   What changes are expected in medical education?

Some have argued that the subsidy for graduate medical education paid by government programs, especially Medicare, is an unwarranted contribution to the education of professionals who will later garner healthy incomes. Some analysts have suggested that the trainees themselves contribute to graduate medical education by taking starvation-level stipends. In fact, graduate physicians' stipends have changed little in constant dollars over the past 30 years, although their work week has declined to a mere 80 hours in response to the outrage over the death of Libby Zion in New York Hospital. Other important trends in education have created more barriers to entering the profession, which physicians in training have continued to be able to surmount. For example, many subspecialty training programs have increased the time required for certification from two to three or even four years; thus, it is possible for a student to remain in training for 11 to 14 years. If the reward for such delay of gratification is not sufficient, either financially or emotionally, fewer will do it—this is the argument some make for a cyclic supply of physicians and an eventual physician shortage as was touted in the 1960s. The evidence belies this; applications to medical schools continue apace and the scores required for admission continue to increase.

Q 1:30   How are academic medical centers and medical schools structured?

Generally, an AMC is a group of related institutions, including a teaching hospital or hospitals, a medical school and its affiliated faculty practice plan, and other health professional schools. This is not intended to be a homogenous definition because there are many differences in composition, number, and structure across the spectrum of academic medical centers.

The medical school fulfills several roles in an AMC. These include hiring faculty, setting faculty base salary and bonuses, granting tenure, operating a medical library, providing facilities for research and performing numerous administrative functions.[11]

Medical schools are financed by many sources, the most important being clinical income. Most schools recover these dollars through a "dean's tax," which can range from 5 to 20 percent of service income, and may be based on a fixed percentage of gross revenues, or a percentage of revenue net of expenses. Medical schools' sources of income depend on the following factors: whether the school is private or state supported, whether it has a health care system or a single hospital, its geographic location, the competitive nature of its environment, and the type and amount of research funding.

Industry-sponsored research is an important source of medical school financing, with some AMCs actually forming medical research organizations to compete for privately sponsored research dollars.

Q 1:31   **What is being done nationally to decrease the oversupply of physicians?**

Steven Schroeder identifies three responses to the impending physician oversupply:[12]

1. Reduce the number of residency slots, which would decrease the number of international medical graduates studying in this country. International medical graduates make up almost half the physicians in residency in New York State. Proposals exist to decrease the number of residency slots available from approximately 150 percent to 110 percent of graduates of allopathic schools in the United States, which would have the effect of virtually eliminating slots for international medical graduates. At present, there is a virtually unlimited supply of international graduates willing to take spots for accredited training in the United States. As the benchmarking analysis shows, there is not a corresponding demand in the medical marketplace. Residents are sometimes the sole source of in-hospital physicians in many hospitals. Many, particularly inner city hospitals, could not operate without them. A bold experiment is underway in New York City where HCFA is paying teaching hospitals not to train residents, hoping that they will hire midlevel professionals or physicians to function in the capacity of house physicians.
2. Decrease the number of medical students. Since the peak number, there has been only one medical school that has closed in the United States: the Oral Roberts University School of Medicine in Tulsa, Oklahoma. Another two, Hahnemann and Medical College of Pennsylvania have merged to become Allegheny, which, at the time of this writing, is emerging from financial disaster. Another proposed merger, that of New York University and Mount Sinai School of Medicine of the City University of New York unraveled initially, but now appears to be going forward. The demand for openings in medical schools continues to increase despite the manpower reality. Reducing the number of medical school positions, without a substantive decrease in postgraduate training slots only increases the percentage of international medical graduates.
3. Let market forces work. This is the "do nothing" strategy and is altogether too random to be a rational alternative for so significant a public policy issue.

Q 1:32   How can medical education be accomplished in a managed care setting?

There has been much discussion about integrating medical education into the managed care setting. Remembering that the fundamental principles of medical care are not different regardless of where the care is delivered, the primary function of medical education remains imparting medical knowledge to students. This is, and must remain, a time-consuming enterprise. There is a general perception that young physicians are not "prepared" for managed care when they finish training. In reality, young physicians finishing training are not "prepared" for any type of practice, which is why they commonly work with another physician or group to round out their training. Accepting for the moment that there is a necessary curricular component in managed care, what should that component look like?

1. It should be clear to the trainee that there is no difference in disease process that is determined by the way in which the physician is compensated for the care.
2. Managed care settings provide good opportunities for emphasizing the importance of primary care. Data are accumulating that the academic medical center does not impart to the student a sufficient appreciation for primary care.[13]
3. Cost-effective analysis, a necessary component of any health care intervention, can be well taught in an environment that is focused on it.
4. Managed care organizations tend to emphasize the role of teams in health care delivery. The trainee is more likely to work closely with a physician assistant, nurse practitioner, or nurse midwife in a managed care setting than in an academic medical center.[14]
5. One of the principles of HMOs is that it is population based. Thus, this type of analysis can be well taught in the HMO setting.
6. HMOs and managed care organizations have formal committee processes that are separate and distinct from the hospital. Students and trainees tend not to be versed in this aspect of practice.

As a result, exposure and experience in a managed care setting will provide the trainee with an amplified education experience separate and distinct from the traditional process.

Encouraging data show that physician compensation appears to be unrelated to the methodology by which the physician is paid. Costs are more determined by patient and plan benefit factors than by physician payment factors.[15]

Q 1:33   Is there a difference in the quality of educational experience garnered by a student in a for-profit or not-for-profit setting?

The literature on using HMOs for teaching is almost exclusively in the not-for-profit setting—it is also almost exclusively in the staff-model setting. As new models for the delivery of managed care become more prominent, attention will have to be paid to their role in medical education.

Q 1:34   Are there any examples of the impact of reduction in specialty training programs on physician supply?

There have been several studies of capacity and supply. A recent study demonstrates the effect of changing the population of a training program and its effect on the number of physicians available for practice.[16] Some specialties are so oversupplied that, were medical schools to cease further training in those specialties immediately, there would still be an adequate number of qualified specialist physicians nationwide 20 years hence. Interpretation of these data require knowledge of:

1. physician distribution by geographic unit
2. intensity and distribution of illness
3. prevalence of managed care
4. levels of care available within the community

Newer trends suggest that, with the advent of disease state management, the superabundance of specialists may be misleading. Major specialty societies have indicated a goal of increasing the number of primary care trainees. The result of this physician social engineering is not yet clear.

PHYSICIAN FACTORS

Q 1:35   How do physicians perceive managed care?

Physicians' attitudes toward managed care range from rage and resistance to enthusiastic acceptance. As could be expected, the majority fall in the middle. Some physicians are strongly opposed to any form of managed care. The reasons for this are complex and partially rooted in the ethos of professionals trained to be conservative and skeptical. For example, physicians in general were strongly opposed to Medicare for 20 years.

To understand physicians' attitudes on managed care, it is instructive to examine the way they are trained. From the very first, physicians are taught that they are to be the "captains of the ship" and accountable for anything happening to their patients. As any manager knows, accountability has to be married to authority and control to be effective. Managed care inserted a nonphysician into the sacred physician-patient relationship—a person who had no firsthand clinical knowledge of the management of the patient and whose only function was to restrict access to care the physician deemed necessary. Thus, an antagonistic relationship was created. Of late, physicians have moved into senior leadership positions in managed care organizations, and opportunities exist for them to control the full gamut of care; therefore, they are being reenfranchised with a resulting decrease in tension. Nonetheless, the restrictions of managed care are real, particularly on specialist physicians.

Under managed care, most major procedures and many minor ones must be precertified. Precertification is commonly done by algorithm and is not under the direct control of the ordering physician. Capitation can put a perverse incentive on the physician-patient relationship, whereby the physician can be rewarded for doing less.

Specialist and primary care physicians can have their natural alliance altered as traditional referral patterns and practice patterns are distorted by managed care.

Q 1:36   What impact has managed care had on the labor market for physicians?

The change in the financing and delivery of health care services has raised two issues affecting the physician labor market—the first is supply and the second is specialty mix. There are two market-related concerns, as well. The first is the effect of the changing market for physicians' services, and the second is the physician training pipeline. Unfortunately, these market factors are not entirely related, since market pressure to reduce physician supply may increase academic medical center and teaching hospital dependence on residents to meet service needs.

It is also expected that, because of the length of time of the training pipeline, short-term increases and incentives to increase numbers of primary care physicians will not begin to be realized for several years. In the short term, it is unlikely that changes in physician training will have an effect on the market.

Several initiatives have had a major effect on physician supply. These include:

- mandated reductions in specialty training
- reliance on board passage as a *sine qua non* for credentialing
- HCFA demonstration projects to reduce the number of residency slots
- increasing restriction on international medical graduates seeking post graduate training
- changes in compensation structures for physicians

Nonetheless, applications for medical school places are at historically high levels, and physicians continue to be seen as advocates for patients against restrictions imposed by managed care. Robert Blendon, professor of health policy at Harvard University says, "The backlash against insurance makes doctors by comparison look like the people's representatives."[17]

Q 1:37   How has managed care affected the way physicians practice?

Practice styles in the United States have always been varied. Physicians have practiced under the strict salaried arrangement of government medicine in the military, Department of Veterans Affairs, public health service, prison health service, and elsewhere. The group practice of medicine, with responsibilities, assets, and liabilities shared among members, dates back to the end of the nineteenth century with the founding of the Mayo Clinic. Some physicians practice wholly within an academic institution and see patients only in a teaching setting. Of course, the age-old model of American practice is the solo practitioner.

Managed care has added a new practice style to the repertoire, but the physician's role varies. In truth, however, the contemporary physician's professional life remains highly scrutinized, reviewed, and regulated. With managed care, the physician's cherished autonomy has eroded substantially under the influence of utilization review and sharp constraints on benefits paid. Virtually all payers have discovered that the physician is responsible for setting the cost of illness and have thus closely managed this aspect of medical practice.

Cost management has changed the relationship between physicians and patients because it has introduced the payer into the process of disease prevention and treatment. At one time, diagnosis and treatment decisions were made by the patient and physician and the bill was submitted to the payer, however, now the payer is placed in a decision-making role. Physicians are, therefore, in an awkward position. The physician's responsibility, legally and ethically, is only to the patient. The payer in a managed care system, however, will exercise discretion as to the dollars it will commit to an individual therapeutic decision, thus the physician is required to defend his or her therapeutic plan to any number of intermediaries who do not have the same fiduciary responsibility. The *Wickline* decision in California has rendered this relationship even more complex. The expansion of this situation to everyday practice is that, regardless of the payer's decision, the physician has the obligation to render full and complete medical care, even if the physician or hospital will not be paid for it.

Physicians are, therefore, feeling under siege. They are being publicly pilloried for avarice and at the same time being beggared by Medicare and some managed care providers. The outcome of this conflict is not easy to see, yet it is clear that the advent of managed care will radically alter the physician-patient relationship. One of the consequences that is already being felt is the loosening of the bonds between the primary care physician and the patient. Many managed care systems that tightly control physician time have already begun restricting the physician-patient encounter by setting performance standards and providing service on a first-come, first-served basis (rationing by queue). How that restrictive style of management will influence a new generation of physicians regarding their obligations to their patients is unknown.

Q 1:38   What effect has managed care had on physician income?

The Physician Payment Review Commission (PPRC) reports that physician median incomes for 1997 are at 1993 levels.[18] Median incomes for specialists continue to outdistance median incomes for primary care physicians.[19]

Q 1:39   Is the demand for physician services changing?

In previous reports, the PPRC noted that market indicators suggested an oversupply of physicians, overall. In its 1997 report, the PPRC indicates the data are less clear. Physician incomes have continued to grow, but at lower rates than in the past. The number of residents has grown, with decreases in areas such as anesthesiology, orthopedic surgery, and obstetrics-gynecology.[20] Some academic programs purposely decreased the size of their residency and fellowship classes in response to state and federal incentives.

Probably a more dramatic change has occurred in employment of physicians. In 1995, the share of physicians who were employees increased to 39 percent, up from 36 percent in 1994. At the same time, the share of self-employed physicians dropped to 55 percent from 58 percent.[21]

Based on the foregoing, national data indicate that positions in generalist fields are becoming more attractive, but that changes in relative incomes have been modest. Overall, job opportunities for physicians do not appear to be shrinking. The changing health care market does appear to be affecting whether physicians become employees rather than being self-employed.

Q 1:40   How does the turmoil in health care affect physicians?

For the physician, as opposed to the hospital, the incentives provided by capitation are clear. Whereas physicians were previously rewarded for maximum utilization, now they recover more by decreasing utilization. The perverse incentives are dramatically changed under managed care, but they become no less perverse. Remember that although the utilization of medical care in a hospital is largely controlled by the physician, the cost of services is not. Therefore, it is likely that as the transition to managed care is accomplished in communities where several systems now coexist, the average cost to the individual may still increase, although the rate of that increase should diminish. The potential for abuse by denying care looms large and demands the commensurate institution of quality metrics and standards.

For the primary care physician, managed care promised a golden age. Besides being courted by managed care operators, primary care physicians are able to do what they do best—care for individual patients. It is likely that plans allowing that relationship to exist will be the most successful. Overreliance on the primary care physician, or even the physician assistant or the nurse practitioner, has been destructive to the quality pronouncements of managed care organizations. Although having a personal physician is a laudable goal, data are accumulating that specialty issues are better managed by specialists. Managed care is struggling to define that border now; however, it is clear that specialty physicians are not as endangered a species as was once thought.

Choice will also be a significant determinant of success. As managed care matures in the United States, the promise of choice will probably be extended to the physician and the patient. As consumers of health care continue to be more demanding, the successful and popular groups will be able to negotiate more stringent terms with payers, and reject some plans in which they do not wish to participate. Even some physician management companies have recognized that the practice of medicine is best determined by medical practitioners in alignment with capable administrators. Of course, this places hospitals in the position of vendors instead of partners, with all the risk of misalignment attendant to that status.

Of interest, the dynamic tension between primary care and specialty practices is inducing some managed care organizations to pursue an aggressive carve-out strategy. This will have the consequence of fragmenting referral lines and natural alliances and cannot benefit the patient.

INDIGENT CARE

Q 1:41   How do indigent, uninsured, and underinsured people affect managed care organizations?

Managed care, for all its faults, has increased attention on primary care physicians and primary care delivery. Although there are many arguments about the extent of the abilities of the primary care physician in the care of the complex and hospitalized patient, there is no disagreement with the notion that primary care physicians are needed and are now lacking in the inner city. Data exist showing less use of preventive services in low-income areas, as well as lower rates of interventions for atherosclerotic disease and higher limb amputation rates for peripheral vascular disease and complications of diabetes. Figure 1–5 shows the cost of uncompensated care to total care costs.

Managed care is a technique capable of managing the health of a population and is ideally suited to address these issues; however, that intervention must be funded. The American College of Physicians, in a seminal report,[22] identified major interventions that affect inner city and urban health and must be strongly considered by the managed care community. These are:

1. Leverage all appropriate government and institutional resources to produce an adequate number of primary care physicians and other providers who are willing to practice in underserved inner city areas.
2. Create incentives to change medical school recruitment and education and residency training. Medical school recruitment policies, curricula, and clerkship programs must be retooled to address the health needs of inner city residents.
3. Provide substantial fiscal incentives to attract individual providers to inner city locations.
4. Deploy financial incentives and technical assistance to safety net providers who are being squeezed by reductions in public funding and competition for insured patients that have been brought on by the changing health care marketplace.
5. Require managed care organizations to contract with essential community providers (for example, those who serve low-income populations, such as community health centers) if the managed care organizations are serving persons in underserved, inner city locations and are financed in whole, or in part with federal funds.
6. Carefully scrutinize in advance all mergers, acquisitions, and conversions involving nonprofit hospitals and insurance plans by an objective representative of the public (for example, the state attorney general or an insurance commissioner) to evaluate potential effect on

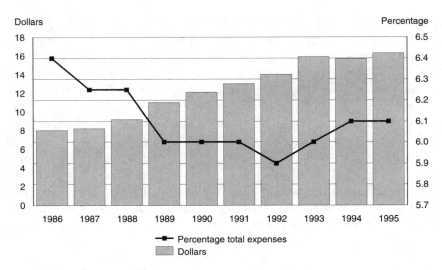

Figure 1–5 Uncompensated Care Costs. *Source:* Reprinted from *Medical Benefits*, Vol. 14, p. 9, © 1997, Aspen Publishers, Inc.

the community served by these nonprofit organizations. Community participation and vigilance are necessary to ensure that charitable resources remain dedicated to maintaining the well-being of the community.

It is incontrovertible that inner city hospitals rely on Medicaid payments wholly or in part. Many communities see managed care as a means to cut the overall cost of Medicaid; however, for the inner city public hospital, the safety net, the siphoning off of Medicaid normal deliveries and well-child examinations leaves it with the responsibility of providing care for the severely ill and those with complex health care problems. Further, since disproportionate share payments are paid on the basis of discharges, an efficient public sector HMO would have the effect of saving money on the MCO side while losing revenue on the DSH side.

The American College of Physicians has the following recommendations for regulation regarding federal waivers for Medicaid:

1. Require managed care organizations to provide special services that are essential in inner city environments such as primary care services

that are geographically accessible (providing transportation when necessary), after hours availability of primary and urgent care, outreach services, and self-care education. Managed care organizations must have linguistic and cultural competence and must be able to coordinate interaction with other social services, such as nutrition programs. Capitation rates would reflect the additional cost of providing specialized services and the savings from reduced emergency department and other hospital costs.

2. Restrict direct marketing and encourage enrollment and education through independent brokers to eliminate cherry picking and to provide objective information, thereby enabling enrollees to choose the health plans that meet their health care needs.

3. Provide case management for persons with human immunodeficiency virus (HIV) infections, acquired immune deficiency syndrome (AIDS), and other serious illnesses.

4. Include risk-adjustment mechanisms to protect plans with a higher than expected number of patients who have HIV, AIDS, and other costly diseases and conditions.

Further, the medical model is insufficient to answer the questions of health care for the poor and underinsured inner city resident.

Q 1:42   What can be expected to happen to indigent care?

1996 legislation provided an incremental improvement in the health care of the population by allowing portability of health insurance from job to job and by limiting the ability of insurance companies to refuse to insure a person because of a "preexisting condition." This will affect the uninsured population, because some of the people who would have been dropped from coverage would have joined their ranks. Nonetheless, in 1997, more than 40 million people had no health coverage for some time during the year. Changes in the welfare laws limiting the duration of Aid to Families with Dependent Children benefits will likely increase this number. Limitation of welfare benefits presages changes in Medicaid laws, and limitations in that coverage can be expected as well. Indigent care responsibility falls on government institutions and disproportionately on the academic medical centers that are often the providers of last resort.

As the indigent and underinsured question continues to burn, closer analysis of the problem shows that it is not only the uninsured who are having problems. Both the poor and the "near poor" elderly can devote nearly one third of their disposal income to health care despite Medicare. This is because the deductible in Medicare never caps out and the program does not cover prescription drugs.[23] Further, the so-called Medigap insurance plans that pay the deductible are becoming increasingly unaffordable for the elderly as managed care absorbs the well elders, and those requiring medical services remain with the indemnity product.[24]

The cost of indigent care is calculated not only in direct expenditures for care, but also in terms of lost productivity due to illness, increased costs from lack of preventive medicine, and costs of care of undocumented aliens. Several novel solutions include combining Medicaid with indigent care to provide one system for the low-income and the no-income population. Managed care solutions are being widely studied.

Q 1:43   What is behind the concept of cost shifting?

Although the cost savings in managed care can be substantial, there is still evidence of intense cost shifting. The data are difficult to assess, but evidence exists that medical care organizations are entered into at a loss. That is, organizations are paying for the privilege of doing managed care business. There is still a significant difference in payment realized by hospitals that use a discounted fee-for-service system and by hospitals that use a tightly controlled managed care system, such as Kaiser. Thus, there is an opportunity for cost shifting. As managed care and HMOs increase their penetration into markets and crowd out fee-for-service and discounted plans, this cost shifting will no longer be possible. Similarly, with changes in the payments for Medicare and the projected increase in the number of underinsured and uninsured, the opportunities for cost shifting can be expected to disappear. Paradoxically, then, it is possible that the average health care cost to the individual using institutional or hospital services will increase as hospitals are no longer able to sacrifice margin for market share.

What may seem like a trivial macroeconomic point becomes significant when the importance of cost shifting is considered. As long as there are deep pockets, costs can be shifted. As those opportunities disappear, providers can cut their costs, but, after that, quality would be the next area to receive cuts. The growing problem of the uninsured fuels the need to address this problem directly.

Q 1:44   How can managed care minimize cost shifting?

The potential for cost shifting by providers can be reduced in a number of ways. For one, a single-payer system would allow a uniform approach to the problem. Other countries, notably Canada, have a single-payer system in place, but attempts at this type of health care reform in the United States have not been successful. Another option is to extend Medicare to provide base coverage.

Medical savings accounts or medical individual retirement accounts (IRAs) allow a certain amount of money to be set aside to buy a high-deductible insurance policy and then to pay medical expenses. What is left at the end of the year goes to the consumer, tax free. There are obvious problems with this approach; notably, it does not address the issue of medical care for the poor. Particularly in the face of welfare reform that cuts eligibility for food stamps, the low-income and no-income segment of the population cannot be expected to set aside resources for medical expenses. The medical savings account approach also assumes that all consumers of health care are knowledgeable and will expend their discretionary resources on timely medical care and prevention.

Finally, a two-tiered system would provide minimum coverage for all with the ability to augment coverage according to personal resources available.

Q 1:45   How will health benefits be affected by payment reform?

Basic benefits are a core of services covered under any health plan. Strategies focused on reform of basic benefits can take two main paths. In one, a broad menu of benefits can be provided, but with a very high-deductible provision. This makes basic services essentially fee-for-service, while insurance is for catastrophic coverage. Although this has historic appeal (remember major medical) it is unlikely, after the battering Congress received on catastrophic coverage for Medicare, that this will form the cornerstone of health care reform. Medical savings accounts, or medical IRAs, have been incorporated into recently enacted federal legislation as a pilot project and have a great deal of support from conservative legislators and indemnity payers. In fact, some states such as Texas have passed legislation to require a pilot study of medical savings accounts for the state's Medicaid program. The evidence for the success of medical savings accounts is not yet in.

Another strategy is to broaden the availability of high-volume, low-cost procedures of proven benefits. These include immunization for children, breast cancer screening and Pap smears for women, prostate cancer evaluation for men, and colon cancer screening for all at risk. The major problems for basic benefits packages are likely to be mental health, prescription drugs, and long-term care.

TECHNOLOGY

Q 1:46   What new technologies can be expected to influence the cost of health care in the near future?

Major breakthroughs in medicine occur all the time. Sometimes, the most obscure discovery can translate into momentous changes. The discovery of the laws of natural selection in the 1860s by Gregor Mendel was unappreciated until discoveries in the early 1900s made them relevant. Similarly, penicillin was discovered to kill bacteria in 1929 by Alexander Fleming, yet the clinical uses of the drug were not evident until the 1940s, following the increasingly widespread uses of sulfa compounds as antibacterial agents. Thus, it is a bit risky to be oracular about trends in medicine and medical care delivery. Some emerging technologies, though, are almost sure winners.

Gene Therapy

This technology relies on insetting genes into the human chromosome to replace or repair defective genetic material that is causing disease. Examples of illnesses amenable to gene therapy include rare inborn errors of metabolism, such as Tay-Sachs disease in children, and common conditions such as diabetes and certain malignancies. Clinical trials of some of these technologies are under way, and there is intense interest on the part of both the scholarly and business community in this research. The completion of the human genome project will contribute to the knowledge necessary to advance gene therapy.

Immunotherapy

Elucidation of the mechanisms of inflammation will have a major impact on the treatment of a wide variety of illnesses including asthma, arthritis, and malignancies.

Joint Replacement Therapy

Advances in materials and surgical techniques will allow the replacement of joints with greater facility and fewer complications.

Organ Transplants

Advances in immunomodulation, surgical techniques, and organ preservation will allow the transplantation of more organs to replace diseased and worn out organs. Even metabolic illnesses such as diabetes and Parkinson's disease can be expected to result in successful therapy with organ and tissue transplantation.

Imaging

Radiologic imaging and other techniques continue to advance in sophistication. As they do, "exploratory" surgery can be expected to continue to decline, as there will be noninvasive techniques available that allow physicians to examine specific organs and metabolic processes.

Minimally Invasive Surgery

Advances in surgical and anesthesia technique will allow the continued advancement of laparoscopic (called "band-aid") surgery. This technique can be expected to advance beyond the abdomen, pelvis, sinuses, and joints into the chest and even the brain with resulting decrease in complications, length of hospital stay, and even costs.

Prenatal Diagnosis

Advances in diagnosis of newborn conditions before birth allow the detection of genetic and metabolic abnormalities in the fetus. Further advances in the field are beginning to allow detection of the same abnormalities from maternal blood without invading the uterus or the fetus. Early detection of abnormalities can be expected to allow in utero therapy.

Novel Cancer Therapies

Combinations of the modalities above can be expected to influence cancer treatment, particularly in cancer centers of excellence.

Q 1:47   What are the managed care issues specific to organ transplantation?

1. The age of the recipients of certain solid organ transplants, such as the heart and liver, is increasing. Although most heart transplant recipients are in the 50- to 64-year age group, this percentage is increasing. Those receiving a heart transplant at age greater than 64 is now more than 4 percent. Patients this age were previously excluded from consideration for heart transplantation. Similarly, liver transplantation is increasing in the over-64 age group. This age increase can be expected to have an impact on Medicare costs since transplants tend to be low-volume, high-cost procedures.
2. Solid organ retransplantation is increasingly common in the treatment of transplant failure or rejection. Particularly in children with liver transplantation, reoperation is more often indicated than in the past.
3. As end-stage renal disease is commonly caused by diabetes mellitus, combined kidney-pancreas transplants are more commonly being performed to address the underlying cause of the kidney failure.
4. Bone marrow transplantation is being used for an increasingly wide variety of indications, including the treatment of hematologic malignancies, solid tumors, and genetic illnesses such as severe combined immune deficiency. Advances in tissue typing and immunosuppres-

sion can be expected to increase the indications and survival of all forms of bone marrow transplantation. These include:

- Allogeneic transplantation occurs from a related donor and includes a syngeneic match, a genetically identical sibling.
- Autologous transplantation occurs when a patient's own cells are harvested and then returned to him or her, usually after chemotherapy or irradiation has destroyed the abnormal native marrow. Autologous bone marrow transplantation is used to repopulate the patient's marrow in illnesses such as breast cancer and lymphoma.

5. As opposed to liver, heart, and lung transplantation failure, kidney graft failure does not necessarily cause death because dialysis is a viable alternative and can keep end-stage renal disease patients alive for many years. Similarly, injectable erythropoietin can ameliorate the debilitating anemia to which dialysis patients were at one time subject. HCFA estimates a 10 percent per year increase in the approximately one-quarter million dialysis patients.

6. Advances in immunosuppression can be expected to increase the number of living solid organ recipients surviving their immediate postoperative period. This is particularly true in highly immunogenic organs such as the pancreas and the lung. The managed care implication is obvious. Patients are living longer and requiring chronic use of very costly drugs. The exchange, however, in quality of life for successful transplant recipients (and in many cases life itself) is compelling for transplantation as an acceptable mode of therapy for chronic conditions in both adults and children.

Q 1:48   What are the cost issues in organ transplantation and how can they be managed?

Organ transplantation is one set of procedures ideally suited for a center of excellence and for case management. Data on patient survival seem to indicate that survival rate increases and complications decrease in centers specializing in transplantation. Similarly, the concentration of transplantation in centers may allow price negotiations for volume.

When costs of transplantation are reckoned, it is important to look at the full episode of care including the pretransplantation evaluation and the expected posttransplant episode of care. With the possible exception of the cornea, transplant patients require chronic and expensive care, which needs to be added to the cost of the procedure itself.

NOTES

1. P. Taulbee and C.E. Cordero, "Employers are experimenting with managed competition," *Business and Health* 10, no. 3 (1992): 26–38.

2. VHA, Inc. and Deloitte & Touche, LLP, *1998 Environmental Assessment, Setting Foundations for the Millennium: An Assessment of the Health Care Environment in the United States* (Irving, TX: 1998).

3. J. Calmes, "Images of industry players shape debates nationwide," *The Wall Street Journal,* Interactive Edition, 25 June, 1998.

4. E. Ginzberg and M. Ostow, "Managed care—a look back and a look ahead," *New England Journal of Medicine* 336 (1997): 1018–1020.

5. J.P. Kassirer, "Is managed care here to stay?" *New England Journal of Medicine* 336 (1997): 1013–1014.

6. D. Blumenthal, "Effects of market reforms on doctors and their patients," *Health Affairs* 15 (1996): 179.

7. J.K. Iglehart, "Health Issues, the President, and the 105th Congress," *New England Journal of Medicine* 336 (1997): 671–675.

8. Medical Benefits 1996;13:19.

9. H. Taylor and J.I. Morrison, "Attitudes toward managed healthcare," in *Making Managed Healthcare Work: A Practical Guide to Strategies and Solutions*, ed. P. Boland (Gaithersburg, MD: Aspen Publishers, Inc., 1993).

10. S. Horn, "Intended and unintended consequences of HMO cost containment strategies," *American Journal of Managed Care* (1996):

11. J. Reuter et al., "HMOs' use of academic medical centers," IWP #96–103 (Washington, DC: Institute for Health Care Research and Policy, Georgetown University, 1996), as referenced in the "Physician Payment Review Commission Annual Report to Congress: Medicare and Medicaid Guide," *CCH* 955 (11 April, 1997): 358.

12. S. Schroeder, "How can we tell whether there are too many or too few physicians?" *Journal of the American Medical Association* 276 (1996): 841–843.

13. S.D. Block et al., "Academia's chilly climate for primary care," *Journal of the American Medical Association* 276 (1996): 677–682.

14. J. Veloski et al., "Medical student education in managed care settings," *Journal of the American Medical Association* 276 (1996): 667–671.

15. D. Conrad et al., "Primary care physician compensation method in medical groups: Does it influence the use and cost of health services for enrollees in managed care organizations?" *Journal of the American Medical Association* 279 (1998): 853–858.

16. G.S. Meyer, et al., "Gastroenterology workforce modeling," *Journal of the American Medical Association* 276 (1996): 689–694.

17. Calmes, "Images of industry players shape debates nationwide," 25 June, 1998.

18. Reuter et al., "HMOs' use of academic medical centers," 347.

19. Reuter et al., "HMOs' use of academic medical centers," 348.

20. Reuter et al., "HMOs' use of academic medical centers," 350–351.

21. M. Mitka, "Physician pay back up, but two-year trend still shows loss," *American Medical News* 1 (6 January, 1997) as referenced in the "Physician Payment Review Commission Annual Report to Congress: Medicare and Medicaid Guide," *CCH* 955 (11 April, 1997): 355.

22. American College of Physicians, "Inner city health care," *Annals of Internal Medicine* 127 (1997): 485–490.

23. M. Moon, *Restructuring Medicare's cost sharing* (New York: Commonwealth Fund, December 1996).

24. J.D. Cochrane, "Death of medigap coverage," *Integrated Healthcare Report* (December 1997–January 1998).

CHAPTER 2

Delivery Systems

Clifford C. Dacso and Sheryl Tatar Dacso

INTRODUCTION

Patients have looked to their physicians, small group, or local hospital for medical care. The advent of the health maintenance organization (HMO) has introduced health plans, insurers, employers, regulators, investors, health systems, and a host of other participants into the mix. This has had a far-reaching effect on medical care, as was described in Chapter 1. To manage the care of a population of patients, delivery system methodologies have evolved, along with the creation of a bewildering array of acronyms. Further, the definitions of the systems of care and their allied systems of payment are fluid. Rather than list each, this chapter looks at some of the salient underpinning questions of delivery systems.

PATIENT FACTORS IN DELIVERY SYSTEMS

Q 2:1   How are patients affected by managed care?

In traditional, fee-for-service plans, the payer compensates for an encounter between a covered individual and the health care system. If the encounter represents a covered benefit of the patient's plan, the indemnity payer pays the bill, subject to deductibles or other contractual reductions. If the patient does not have insurance coverage, or the encounter is not a covered benefit, he or she is liable for the bill. The patient chooses the physician or hospital to provide the service based on his or her own criteria, which may include reputation, proximity, perception of quality, amenities, religious or ethnic considerations, or even facility decor. Fee-for-service medicine is not highly price sensitive.

Managed care, on the other hand, generally presents the patient with a list of physicians. Often, after a physician has been chosen, it is difficult to change physicians, even if the patient is dissatisfied. Many managed care plans stipulate specific times during which patients may change physicians. Recently, and perhaps under the influence of Medicare managed care, this principle of locking in provider choice has started to break. Now, the ability to change providers is viewed as a competitive advantage, further weakening the bond between patient and physician.

Depending on the plan, patients may be required to see a primary care physician who will be responsible for making all assessments and determinations as to their medical needs. Patients generally are restricted in their ability to see specialists: The primary care physician must initiate referrals. Newer plans are entering the market with expanded choice and decreased restrictions, however. These are point-of-service plans that pay different schedules according to the patient's choice of provider and the point at which they enter the system.

Choice is often mentioned as a strong drive for patients to resist managed care. In this context, choice generally is taken to mean that patients can choose their physician for whatever reason they want. Thus, if a patient chooses to see an orthopedist for back pain (regardless of whether the back pain is caused by an orthopedic problem), that is considered exercising choice. If a patient is required to see a primary care physician who treats the back pain without referral to a specialist (successfully or unsuccessfully), that is restriction of choice. Responding to this perceived need for choice, managed care plans try to have the largest geographic, ethnic, and professional choices available. Choice is used as a marketing tool.

After choice, the patient is likely to be most favorably impressed by how managed care pays for medical services. The patient is likely to have a fixed copayment or fee for every visit, regardless of its complexity, and will probably not need to file insurance papers or be responsible for any other payment. Hospitalizations are likely to be covered entirely, with the exception of amenities such as a television or a private room. Prevention visits such as immunizations, Pap smears, and mammograms are likely to be covered benefits, with a required copayment.

When switching from an indemnity, fee-for-service system to managed care, patients are often required to change physicians to one who is on the list of the managed care company. In the past, this would have been viewed as unacceptable but then patients developed long-term relationships with physicians who may have delivered their babies, treated their parents, and then delivered their children's babies. Medical complexity, modern mores, physician specialization, advertising, litigation, and other factors have conspired to render the multigeneration patient-physician relationship anachronistic. The avuncular Dr. Marcus Welby is a rarity, particularly in the urban environment; thus, patients are not likely to miss someone with whom they never had meaningful contact. Interesting studies performed during the rise of managed care showed that a patient's loyalty to his or her physician is not strong and can be subverted by a relatively small amount of financial disincentive. As plans proliferate and more physicians participate in more plans, the patients may change payers without changing physicians.

Of interest, an unintended consequence of managed care has been the reemergence of primary care as a respected discipline among physicians and health educators. Pediatrics and family medicine have been joined at the primary care trough by general internal medicine, which is garnering a respectable percentage of the best graduates of medical schools.

Q 2:2   How are society and the public affected by managed care?

Society has decided that health care's current growth as a proportion of the gross domestic product is more than it is willing to pay. Organized medicine was told 20 years ago to police itself with regard to pricing. It did not; therefore, the promised external controls have been initiated in the form of diagnosis-related groups (DRGs), relative value-based payments, and strict utilization review and control. Managed care promises to place price controls in the market. That is to say, rather than vote for statutory price control, managed care promises to reduce cost (or at least slow its growth) by the application of market forces. But market forces reward efficiency and profitability. The "invisible hand" of the market does not particularly care about the infirm or poor. Market forces need to be allowed to act judiciously.

The competition among managed care strategies emphasizes generic relationships and benefits, not maintaining an individual patient-physician affiliation. Society appears to be deciding that the patient-physician relationship is dispensable in the face of the need for monetary savings.

Q 2:3   How is the health care workplace affected by managed care?

During the past five years, health care organizations have reorganized, reengineered, and restructured. Cost-cutting solutions have resulted in downsizing, layoffs, and reductions in non-nursing personnel. High technology has forced many employers to decide between the investment cost of acquiring "personnel-replacing" equipment and keeping the personnel.

The reengineering movement has changed how employers manage and deliver health care services. Downsizing has slowed from an annual rate of 8 to 10 percent over the past 10 years, to below 5 percent in the recent 3-year period from 1993 to 1995. Russ Coile, a futurist, reports on the following trends in the health care workplace:[1]

- "Virtual organizations" will evolve with the assistance of highly technological, mobile equipment with data and information to electronically communicate necessary patient information.
- The organization's focus will be patient centered rather than organization centered. Processes such as utilization and patient care management can come from any part of the organization, with the physical location of the care manager not as important as the information being communicated.
- There will be an increase in casual or part-time workers, with the use of temporary workers increasing significantly over the next 10 years.
- With health care becoming more efficient, staffing also will become more efficient. Limited-license personnel such as nurse assistants and physician assistants will become more predominant in the work force.
- There will be a dramatic increase in the use of electronic monitoring to allow improved employee decisions and evaluate performance. Clinical pathways and benchmarking will play an important role in setting standards and providing a means to flag potential problems.
- Computer capability will increase as means of storing and using electronic medical information evolves. Some health care organizations are developing the electronic medical record as a means of eliminating paper and improving the quality of the information, while increasing efficiency.
- The work force will become more diverse. According to U.S. Labor Department projections, by the year 2000, approximately 85 percent

of people entering the work force will be women or minorities. Multicultural work teams will become more common.

- The work force is aging. By the turn of the century, the median age of U.S. workers will be 45 years. In another 5 years, approximately 15 percent of employees will be over age 55. By the year 2015, more than one half of the American population will be over age 55.[2]

- A physician surplus will continue to exist, but not to the extent previously predicted.

- More physicians will accept salaried positions. Today, more than 30 percent of all physicians in the United States are salaried. This exceeds the number in solo practice.[3]

- There is a growing use of health care teams in patient care in view of the perception of reengineering experts that patients need multidisciplinary care. This is a response to previous concerns with fragmentation in the delivery of services, sometimes leading to serious errors in patient care.

- Information technology will be the foundation for these high-performance health care teams with the use of bedside computers and telemedicine capabilities to save time and improve the quality of information communicated. Even surgery can be performed using telesurgical robotic technology where the actual surgeon is nowhere near the incision site.

THE DELIVERY ENVIRONMENT

Q 2:4   What is reengineering as used in the health care environment?

Reengineering involves the fundamental rethinking and radical redesign of business processes intended to bring about dramatic changes in performance. According to Stephen Shortell et al., author of *Remaking Health Care in America*, the concept at the root of a reengineered system is to get to the point of thinking holographically, so that each component of the system can not only see where it sits in the system, but knows how it relates to each other component.[4]

Q 2:5   How reliable is enrollment reporting in HMOs?

Caution should be exercised in accepting any actual numbers of HMO enrollment statistics, because the definition of HMO can vary from lock-in plans to independent practice association (IPA) models with generous out-of-network benefits. Nonetheless, growth in managed care is reproducible regardless of definition. Much growth is estimated for HMOs and Medicare+Choice plans with the implementation of the Medicare+Choice program under the Balanced Budget Act (see Chapter 1, Figure 1–2).

Q 2:6   What type of managed care organization is experiencing the largest growth?

HMOs are clearly in the ascendancy but consumer choice is rebelling against the lock-in, closed-network model. Enrollment in staff model HMOs is declining rapidly, but growing in the group models and network models. Although the numbers are less accurate, preferred provider organization (PPO) eligibility has remained relatively constant. PPO enrollment is expected to decline because of its demonstrated incapacity to effect dramatic cost reductions; however, PPOs have piggybacked on the growth of managed care, which is now at the same rate as HMOs. In 1997, 31 percent of patients enrolled in plans were in PPOs, up from 25 percent the year before. This contrasts with HMO enrollment that has been steady at 33 percent for the past two years.

Q 2:7   How can benchmarking be used to assess needs for physicians?

There has been enormous discussion of the national manpower need for physicians since pioneering work in the early 1990s suggested a dramatic oversupply of physicians. Most planning for physician distribution is based on estimates of needs or projections of current demand. Goodman et al. has reviewed these methodologies and made a compelling argument for the use of benchmarking to assess physician manpower needs.[5]

A needs-based model looks at the prevalence of illnesses and conditions in a population and estimates the needs for physicians based on these conditions. A demand-based model looks at the requirements for physician services in certain environments and makes projections based on these. Goodman's approach to benchmarking identifies health plans and compares them with operating regions or systems. The goal is to examine the density of physicians relative to clinical outcome. Benchmarking is useful as a standardization tool using real-world, working examples. By this measure, there is an oversupply of both generalists and specialists nationwide.

Q 2:8   What are the problems likely to be encountered in the transition to managed care?

At one time, the transition steps to managed care seemed clear. First would come the PPOs and discounted fees in exchange for volume, then some tentative steps toward capitation and HMOs. With capitation comes consolidation in the physician market with large groups being necessary to take contracts. Hospitals similarly consolidate and close as the commercial health care systems enter the market and threaten the hegemony of the community hospitals. Consolidation likewise occurs at the level of the insurance companies, as only the large ones have networks of physicians and hospitals sufficient to manage contracts for lives. In the final stages, there are a few insurance companies and a few networks that manage the commodity of medical care with some form of prospective payment. Physicians, meanwhile, go through the stages of denial, rage, bargaining, and, finally, acceptance.

The problem is that it has not been quite as tidy as the pundits predicted. The spread of managed care throughout the country may not be too bad from the patient's point of view, depending on the degree to which the employer contributes to his or her medical coverage. This type of use adds to the aggregate of medical costs because it duplicates payment without efficiency in utilization. The industry has faced this problem in two ways. First, it has promoted the point-of-service product with limited out-of-network benefits. More important, though, there appears to be a move to increase the size of primary care networks while controlling access to specialists and expensive procedures. Thus, diversity and choice are seen by the managed care organizations as value added in the competitive environment. Some glimpse of how the network membership issue might come down is provided by the Medicaid experience. In some states that have moved to an HMO strategy, physicians are on multiple plans and patients choose both their plan and their physicians. Although data concerning the significance of physician choice are mixed, it cannot help but be a factor.

Because employers seek the best value for their employees, there may be several shifts of primary care and specialty providers for the patient, which is confusing, expensive, and bad for patients. Although there is no argument that continuity is beneficial, the markets are seeing this phenomenon. It is the responsibility of the purchaser of managed care to be certain to minimize the sort of activity that is destructive to the physician-patient relationship.

Q 2:9   How has the transition to managed care affected physicians?

For physicians, the transition to managed care will continue to be difficult. Not only are the incentives realigned in capitated managed care, but the transitional period is characterized by a hybrid practice. Unless the entire group practice "goes managed care," the physicians' offices are likely to have both prospective and some form of fee-for-service patients. This situation requires a substantial effort from both the physician and the payer. It also serves as a major impetus for physicians to leave their practices and sell them to a large system or to become part of the monolithic practices being developed as part of integrated health care delivery systems.

Holm and Zuba posit that large groups will be successful in managed care contracting.[6] They identify the following characteristics as promoting success:

- ability to document and report quality indicators, including patient satisfaction
- primary care orientation
- flexibility in accommodating a variety of payment systems, including capitation
- ability to manage a variety of risk situations, including global capitation
- wide geographic distribution of physicians within the contracted service area

Q 2:10   How will providers respond to the transition to managed care?

Providers are making a number of changes in response to managed care, such as:

- pricing services in relation to actual costs rather than prevailing market rates
- monitoring and disciplining peers aggressively for marginal practices or unacceptable cost, utilization, or quality of care
- designing balanced risk-sharing and gain-sharing reimbursement formulas that are equitable for all parties
- using resources more appropriately and being accountable for performance
- defining quality in operational terms and measuring it by its outcome
- forming closer relationships among different types of providers—hospitals, physicians, allied health, alternative health systems
- developing and sharing more meaningful data with purchasers and payers

Managed care seems to be evolving differently in different communities. Major influences on this transition seem to be the impact of government programs, the capacity of systems within the community to do managed care, the influence of employers, and the culture of the medical community and its entrepreneurial spirit.

Q 2:11   How has the transition to managed care affected physician-patient relationships?

For the patient, the transition to managed care poses a number of problems, most significant, the reasonable possibility that his or her physician will no longer be accessible. In that situation, the patient can either change physicians to one on the panel or pay cash for the personal physician's services. The number of people doing the latter has not been quantified, but it seems significant. From the point of view of the coverage provider, this is an ideal circumstance: The patient (or his or her employer) pays for medical care that is never used. This is also beneficial for HMOs, because they are paid prospectively for medical care they never deliver. The physician expectation of a long-term relationship that mirrors that of the patient has suffered with the notion of a "panel" replacing a "patient" or "family."

Q 2:12   How will payers and third-party administrators respond to managed care?

The definition of the payer is undergoing dramatic change—heretofore, "payer" was synonymous with "insurance company." The insurance company was a large company that accepted risk and spread it over a population. Increasingly, however, the "insurance company" may be a third-party administrator (TPA) for an Employee Retirement Income Security Act (ERISA) corporation or even a private-label HMO. In some cases, it provides no insurance function at all except maybe to reinsure a stop-loss. This shift has been accomplished with continuing strong financial performance by these firms. This function, however, is likely to be a target in the near term for recapturing profit margins given up by the providers.

An important trend has been the emerging alliances among health care payers and providers, specifically HMOs. This is analogous to a manufacturer controlling its distribution network. It has met with varying degrees of success.

Q 2:13   How have the markets responded to managed care?

Rather than proceeding in lockstep, markets are moving toward managed care in their own way. Regions where managed care and capitation have long been established consolidated early. Some of these consolidations are likely to break up, and some will re-form. Regions where there are a few dominant industries are likely to be pioneers in direct payer contracting. Areas where there is a large concentration of academic medical centers are likely to see consolidation of those services. Low-income areas are likely to experience a large number of enrollees from competition for Medicaid managed care–driven contracts. This strategy is vulnerable to constriction in government funding and changes in the nature of entitlement.

Payers (insurers and third-party administrators) are responding to changes in managed care by:

- passing more savings back to the purchaser
- affiliating with health plans that have rigorous credentialing and utilization review programs
- developing more effective techniques to manage psychiatric and chemical dependency cases appropriately, as well as other allied health services and long-term care
- improving health information systems to produce more data and focused reports
- improving on financial incentives and disincentives associated with plan design and high network compliance
- integrating medical benefits with workers' compensation programs (and disability management) into a managed care strategy
- developing private-sector mechanisms to deal with uninsured and underinsured groups

For TPAs, opportunities are burgeoning. Private-label HMOs will require their services, as will a host of HMO lookalikes and provider sponsored networks (PSNs). An interesting side effect of this proliferation is that, under the surface, all health plans will be more alike than different. The primary care networks will be more or less identical, as will the repertoire of services. The present TPAs will operate the back offices of these plans as vendors, taking no risk of their own but being rewarded according to performance criteria.

The key to understanding the relationships among PSNs is to follow the dollar. Whereas now a broad variety of mechanisms exist for taking health care risk, the trend is for the payers—that is, the employers—to assume some risk, but for the providers to assume the bulk of it. Those parties that now take money but not much risk will be eliminated from the stream as the health care dollar constricts. Similarly, the fundamental risk-reward relationship can be expected to come into play. Physician-led medical groups are likely to be major beneficiaries of this trend.

Q 2:14   How are purchasers of health care benefits and services dealing with managed care?

Purchasers have different responses to managed care depending on whether they are considered the enrollee or the employer. Enrollees are sharing more financial responsibility for the cost of medical care through copayments, deductibles, and coinsurance. They are accepting controlled access to providers and limitations on freedom of choice and assuming increasing responsibility for compliance and wellness programs. This transition is difficult for the enrollee. Because much of managed care still restricts provider number and access, the enrollee must learn to navigate physician and provider choice from a list of available options, not from personal or professional recommendations.

Financial schemes—such as medical savings accounts (MSAs)—also will affect consumers in that, for the first time in 50 years, they will be spending their own money on health care. Whether they will do this wisely, keeping in mind the long-term benefits of prevention and screening, remains to be seen. One can foresee full-scale marketing by health care providers promoting their high-margin screening and prevention programs with the same techniques used so successfully to create demand for other commercial products.

Employers have accepted greater financial responsibility for and management of employee health care costs through improved contract specifications, required compliance with performance standards, use of requests for proposals, and reduction in the number of health care plans available to employees for enrollment. Overall, employers are taking a much more active role in managed care activities as they move from being passive purchasers to active managers.

HOSPITAL FACTORS

Q 2:15   How will hospital mergers and takeovers affect managed care?

Health care provider mergers, particularly involving hospitals, occur for various reasons. Some mergers merely unite a number of weak institutions and bring no increase in access or quality or decrease in cost. Others occur as hospitals attempt to corner the market and regain a strong bargaining position in pricing. Recent Department of Justice guidelines on hospital mergers acknowledge the impact of managed care and health care reform.

Another motivation is domination of an integrated health system. If a successful health system must be driven by physicians, then a hospital-run health system is likely to be powerful, short-lived, and ultimately expensive. A well-constructed hospital merger, however, is likely to leave each institution stronger and more competitive. To evaluate a hospital merger as a candidate for managed care provision, several questions need to be asked:

- Is the resulting institution sufficiently capitalized to participate in risk?
- Is its administration able to manage risk?
- Is there a resulting match between available beds and the population served? If not, how does the institution propose to manage its excess capacity?
- Is the institution geographically positioned to participate in managed care? If not, are there sufficient contractual obligations to ensure broad geographic access to the fixed facilities?
- Is it prepared to integrate with physicians and other health care providers to provide a vertical system with substantial physician participation?
- Does the merger bring diversity to the system?
- Can the new entity provide not merely hospital beds, but also the full continuum of care?

Q 2:16   Can a hospital system readjust its business purpose and its place in health care to survive under managed care?

Traditionally, the hospital has managed beds and physician relationships. It has wooed physicians by providing amenities, recognizing that they alone were responsible for admitting patients. Hospital administrators managed profit centers and shifted costs. Of late, however, stimulated by the use of DRGs, hospital administrators have changed to manage costs under Medicare, but still without control of physician activity. The simple merger of a number of losing institutions in an attempt to realize economies of scale is not sufficient. Incentive integration and alignment are required for mergers to be long-term successes. Such mergers may be successful in the short term as cost is squeezed out of the system, case mix is adjusted, and competitors challenged, but it is likely that the aligned system will perform better.

Even the ill-fated Health Security Act recognized that the environment in which a hospital works might affect the spectrum of its services. A full-service hospital is not needed on every urban corner, but one is probably appropriate for a rural county with no health care facility for many miles. Thus, appropriate sizing of health care facilities, either within or without a merger, should be judged in the context of the population served.

THE MEDICAL DIRECTOR

Q 2:17   What is the role of the medical director in a managed care organization?

Most HMOs are required to have a full-time medical director. This person must be a physician and is responsible for a variety of functions, depending on the HMO. Some of these responsibilities include:

Quality of care. This may take the form of directing the quality improvement activities and credentialing.

Medical staff. This may include network design, peer review, and appeals process.

Medical care. This includes designing and implementation of pathways and protocols and overseeing and functioning as patient advocate in the review process.

Education. This includes educating fellow physicians and health care professionals about health care delivery in the managed care organization and educating patients regarding preventive care, access, and responsibilities.

Relationships with governance. The medical director is the physician to whom the board or owners of the managed care organization should look for guidance regarding the impact of financial decisions on the quality of care.

Q 2:18   To whom should the medical director report?

The answer to this question is more a function of opinion and local preference. Some of the medical director's reporting relationships are:

- The medical director has primary responsibility as a physician to ensure the care of the patients under management by the managed care organization. Any reporting arrangement that interferes with that duty is unsatisfactory.

- The medical director cannot be placed in a situation where he or she is pressured to violate the obligation to the patients cared for by the managed care organization.

Q 2:19 How has managed care affected physician-patient relationships?

Although managed care insulates patients from the act of paying their physicians, it also reduces the direct accountability of the physician. When patients pay fees for service, they contract directly for those services, know their costs, and feel connected to the outcome. This is communicated to the physician in a direct way by the continuation or discontinuation of the patient as a customer. In a managed care setting, regardless of the management paradigm, the physician and the patient do not have a direct financial bond. The financial relationship exists between the physician and the payer, because the patient is no longer the customer. This is not to say that the patient has no influence over the distribution of his or her dollars, but the accountability of the physician has been diluted for issues such as "customer service." The more restrictive the managed care setting, the more strongly this influence is realized. In a highly managed staff model HMO where physicians are essentially employees, patients are less able to vote with their feet. All such managed care systems try to build in safeguards for patient satisfaction, but these are externally imposed management tools, not the mutual accountability of a physician-patient relationship in which the latter has actively chosen the former.

Information concerning physician satisfaction is anecdotal, yet it seems that the change in practice style from an individual fee-for-service practice to an HMO is substantial. Younger physicians have grown up with the idea of managed care, and it seems, subjectively, that they would be more likely to adapt to being managed.

Q 2:20 What is the physician's role under managed care?

Many managed care plans require a physician to serve as a gatekeeper, interposed between the patient and specialty medical care. This is a role for which the physician formerly was rewarded with a return referral from the specialist. This is no longer the case. In some managed care programs, referral may actually cost the primary physician real money. Much of this confusion is alleviated in an integrated delivery system. Integration aligns the incentives of all providers to create the most favorable outcome for the patient.

MANAGED CARE AND MEDICAL ETHICS

Q 2:21   How does managed care intrude on traditional medical ethics?

The fundamental principle of the ethical practice of medicine relies on the relationship between the individual patient and the individual physician. On that mutual accountability rests the canon of ethics of the profession. When medicine consisted of that relationship only, all ethical questions of life and death, confidentiality and disclosure, and consent and autonomy were resolved according to the values and ethics of the two participants. Physicians assumed that their patients would be responsive and comply with instructions; patients assumed their physicians would be educated, compassionate—and not venal. Managed care increases the interests of a third party in the physician-patient relationship, because that third party is not bound by the same canon of ethics as the physician. As a result, ethical conflicts inevitably occur.

Q 2:22   How has the change in payment methodology affected the ethical relationships between physician and patient?

Before the end of the nineteenth century, payment for medical services was largely an issue between patient and physician. Hospitals were rarely used except in large cities and by the poor; medical care was generally rendered in the home. The physician rendered a bill and the patient paid it (or it was not paid). The introduction of third parties into medical care, which began with union- and organization-sponsored medical care, was a profound change for medicine. Nonetheless, third parties were, for the most part, benevolent. They viewed their role as financing medical care and were reluctant to enter into decisions concerning the delivery of that care. The view of the community supported the autonomy of the physician-patient axis. Because most hospitals were community supported, they were viewed as benevolent servants, as were physicians. A third party, bound by different ethics and with different motivations, is often at odds with the binary physician-patient relationship.

Q 2:23 How can managed care be reconciled with an ethical medical practice?

Managed care has the potential to reverse some of the excesses of the medical care system. With alignment of incentives, the physician has no reason to perform unnecessary or questionable procedures and has no stake in a bad outcome either. With proper alignment, the physician is most successful when the patient has the best result. Unfortunately, such accountability is rare in current managed care organizations. Accountability was one of the principles of the proposed Health Security Act, which foundered on the reef of political ineptitude. The amount of the health care dollar now going to monitoring physicians' activities under free-market managed care is really quite astounding.

The physician has a legal and ethical obligation to his or her patient to provide the most expert care regardless of payment capability. The medical profession and the courts have affirmed this many times over. The medical care system, however, has no interest in beggaring its providers. Moreover, physicians must never be placed in a position that is adversarial to their patients' interests. The challenge in analyzing extant payment mechanisms is to order the intellectual, moral, ethical, and financial incentives in a way that ensures the finest use of the appropriate medical care and preventive services for each individual in a compassionate and caring physician-patient relationship.

SYSTEMS AND INDIGENT CARE

Q 2:24 What would be the impact of extending HMO-type coverage to the medically uninsured population?

Bogard and colleagues[7] examined this question by comparing a population newly enrolled in an HMO with previously uninsured low-income persons newly enrolled in a similar plan. There were no differences in the utilization of services that are of major concern to organizations bearing financial risk: hospital days, hospital admissions, laboratory or pharmacy utilization, and radiology services. Previously uninsured people did have a higher frequency of outpatient visits than the control population, perhaps related to their poorer overall health. Both the control and the study populations exhibited what is commonly known as the start-up effect, in which a population with previously low rates of utilization exhibits a higher rate on entry into an HMO. This is generally felt to be a result of pent-up demand and not a characteristic of the population. Both the study group and the control group exhibited a start-up effect.

Thus, HMOs, with their defined services and the ability to predict costs based on population dynamics, may well serve to care for the indigent, uninsured and underinsured. Bogard et al.[8] affirm this and note several other salient points:

> As many physicians move into managed care practices where they may no longer control patient access and billing, the charity care that many physicians have traditionally provided to the uninsured by reducing or waiving fees may become more difficult to accomplish. In addition, the movement of many states toward contracting with managed care systems for Medicaid service delivery, driven by the desire to control Medicaid costs, has the potential for additional untoward effects on the uninsured. Public health delivery systems currently use Medicaid dollars to fund not only care for Medicaid recipients, but also to fund care for the medically indigent. If the expanding number of HMOs engaging in Medicaid contracts do not provide care for the medically indigent, access to services for the uninsured individuals may decline.

DELIVERY STRUCTURES

Q 2:25   What is happening to existing managed care products?

The lines between indemnity, HMO, and PPO plans are blurring. Insurers are developing HMO look-alike products such as exclusive provider organizations (EPOs) and HMOs with high-option benefits and low-option benefits. HMOs are also developing point-of-service products and indemnity opt-outs to compete with insurers and PPOs. PPOs are developing EPOs to compete with HMOs. HMOs and PPOs are being offered as local in-network providers, while insurers or third-party administrators are administering out-of-network benefits. This is creating a dilemma for purchasers of plans and services as they struggle to decide what to buy, whom to buy it from, and what is actually contained in the program called managed care.

Q 2:26   Can a competitive premium contribution model help the Medicare program?

Congress and the current Administration have developed a number of proposals that focus on the two goals of Medicare policy reform: broader choice of health plans and reduced growth in Medicare spending. These are reflected in the Balanced Budget Act of 1997.

Q 2:27   How does a premium contribution system work?

Instead of paying physicians and hospitals, or contracting with a limited number of health plans, this system would provide a contribution that beneficiaries would use toward the purchase of health insurance from a variety of approved plans. Plans would continue to charge different premiums for different levels of coverage; however, there would likely be a premium differential that would have to be addressed.

Q 2:28   What is the prototype model of a competitive premium contribution system?

Such a premium contribution system model contains five basic features:

1. The sponsor (typically an employer) solicits bids from health plans to provide a specific package of benefits.
2. Any health plan desiring to participate would compete for enrollees during an open enrollment period, at least annually.
3. The sponsor makes a contribution toward the cost of plan premiums, which is the same regardless of the plan chosen by the consumer.

4. The contribution typically is designed to be large enough to ensure that at least one plan in the system will be available at no additional cost to the consumer, but small enough to encourage consumers to select more expensive plans if they value the plan enough to pay the full difference between the contribution and the premium.
5. A core set of benefits is standardized to enhance plan comparison.

The intent of the model is to maximize consumer choice and minimize cost. It is based on an assumption that consumers will be more careful with their own money than that of their employer or the government. The model tracks employer-based models that often have the employer paying 80 percent of the premium cost, with the employee contributing the difference with choice of plan. With Medicare, the government would pay about 90 percent of the cost of benefits (excluding deductibles and coinsurance).

Q 2:29   Are there contribution systems in use at this time?

Yes. The Federal Employees Health Benefits Program (FEHBP) and California Public Employees' Retirement System offer excellent examples of successful models of the contribution system.

In these programs, the premium contributions are neither the same across all plans nor are they set at the level of the least costly plan. These programs had to compromise between competing goals of fostering premium competition, minimizing risk selection and controlling program costs. These programs do not allow all plans to compete and they do not rely solely on consumer choice to determine plan premiums. They do, however, engage in effective negotiations to control levels of plan profits.

Q 2:30   What issues must be resolved for Medicare to be able to move toward a premium contribution model similar to FEHBP and California Public Employees' Retirement System?

If Medicare premium contributions were considered, questions raised by the Physician Payment Review Commission would have to be answered:[9]

1. How should current and new beneficiaries be integrated into the system? Should the new system be voluntary for all current and future beneficiaries, or mandatory after a certain point in time?
2. How should the government's contribution be designed? Is it possible to stimulate price competition while maintaining the current level of federal support for the program? Is it possible to create incentives for beneficiaries and health plans to control costs without exacerbating the problem of adverse selection?
3. How should competition among plans be structured? How would the premium bidding process work? Should competitive behavior be promoted only through policies affecting consumers or also by allowing the program's administrators to negotiate aggressively for lower premium prices? Should the system restrict plan participation or be open to all plans? Should program administrators have the authority to remove plans with unacceptable bids from the competition?
4. How should the benefit package be structured? Should there be one core set of benefits with multiple supplements or a wide variety of benefit packages? Is it possible to maximize beneficiary choice without blurring the price and quality distinctions between plans or fueling adverse selection?

In addition to the foregoing questions, there would have to be some consideration of the integration of Medicare with Medicaid, which has separate benefits and eligibility considerations.

PROVIDER SPONSORED ORGANIZATIONS

Q 2:31   Should the federal government intervene in the regulation of provider sponsored organizations (PSOs)?

Assuming the continuation of the trend in most states to address PSOs by regulation, and the efforts of the National Association of Insurance Commissioners to develop uniform standards and guidelines for entities that assume risk, it is unlikely that the federal government will need to develop separate standards or rules related to PSOs except where specifically indicated or required under federal programs. PSOs that hold HMO licenses are already participating in Medicare risk programs. With the passage of the Balanced Budget Act of 1997, the PSO is identified as one of the Medicare+Choice organizations subject to specific solvency and related conditions of eligibility.

In a survey conducted by the American Association of Health Plans (AAHP),[10] many PSOs were found to be entering the health care market and seeking compliance with state HMO licensure requirements. The survey showed that 41 states reported licensing a total of 228 HMOs from 1995 to 1997, with 38 percent being provider owned. This fact, in the opinion of AAHP, contradicts the PSO proponents' claims that PSOs need exemptions from state health licensing laws to participate in the Medicare program and commercial market.

CENTERS OF EXCELLENCE

Q 2:32   What can be expected from centers of excellence?

A center of excellence is created when a health care system, sponsored by either a provider or a payer, centralizes high-tech or complex medical care for its providers. Alternatively, a tertiary care or academic medical center can create a center of excellence by bringing together a team of physicians, services, and hospital facilities to provide highly specialized care for a disease, procedure, or set of conditions. All patients with the problem cared for by the center of excellence generally are moved to that facility. The concept is that procedures that are rare or costly can be performed best by an experienced team. It is interesting that the types of procedures requiring a center of excellence are evolving as well. Only 25 years ago, coronary surgery was a highly specialized procedure, with only a few centers performing it competently. Now, of course, open-heart surgery is performed in most major institutions.

Centers of excellence answer a number of strategic questions for large and tertiary care institutions:

- What do we do with all the subspecialists? Most large and tertiary institutions have an excess of subspecialists for their catchment area, particularly in urban areas with teaching medical centers.
- How can we undertake disease-specific research? A center of excellence creates a concentration of patients with a particular disease or

condition, allowing clinical research and pharmaceutical development.

- How can we compete with community hospitals, particularly those that are part of chains? For the chain hospitals where the motto is faster, cheaper, and, if possible, better, diseases that are treated at centers of excellence (leukemia, organ transplantation, and others) are a major problem. Particularly if they participate in risk, the hospitals have to ensure that the specialized coverage is available. It is clearly impossible for the community hospitals to provide them. The tertiary care institutions thus turn the chains' problem into an improved strategic positioning. With telemedicine, electronic communication, and the Internet, competition among centers can become stiff.

- How can we exploit the international market? The services performed at centers of excellence are attractive to countries that are unable to provide needed services in an economical way for their citizens. Electronic communications media can be the key to success as well as differentiation within the market.

Q 2:33   How can a center of excellence be evaluated?

To evaluate a center of excellence, several questions must be asked.

Is it really excellent? There is no registration or specific qualification required for a health care institution to be called a center of excellence. The proliferation of such centers is akin to the widespread use of "cancer center" by institutions seeking to capitalize on the National Cancer Institute–designated cancer centers. A center of excellence should have a team of physicians and ancillary personnel specifically for the specialized task. They should be able to demonstrate that they perform the service better and more cheaply than a routine hospital or institute and should have a repertoire of quality metrics that allow comparison among centers— including established tools and data management techniques. The designation of such centers is often a marketing tool and represents neither a center nor excellence.

Does the center of excellence really improve the care of patients with the cited disease? During the time that rehabilitation hospitals were profitable because of DRG exemption, wound care centers of excellence sprang up all over the country. These centers purported to be able to take care of difficult and nonhealing wounds better than routine hospital or medical care. Often they included technology such as hyperbaric oxygen treatment, for which there is conflicting scientific evidence for improvement of outcome. Hyperbaric oxygen is, however, expensive and produces a high cash flow. A good retrospective method of analyzing the necessity of a center of excellence is whether it remains open after reimbursement profiles change.

Does the center of excellence work to refine the specific technique or procedure? One of the salient characteristics of a center of excellence should be the advancement of knowledge in that technique or procedure. Otherwise, there is no advantage other than economies of scale to lead a payer to contract with such a center.

Is it practical? Several payers have established centers of excellence throughout the country and the world. They propose to ship patients and their families many miles, perform the procedures, and then return them to their communities. Sometimes this is practical; sometimes it is only to the advantage of the payer.

Q 2:34   How does the concept of disease-state management affect what will be expected from centers of excellence?

Disease-state management is a technique care managers use to ensure that protocols are followed in the care of patients with certain high-cost complex conditions. Disease-state management usually involves assigning a case manager to a patient. The next step for the acute illness is the center of excellence, where all aspects of the patient's care are assumed for the episode of care. Of course, centers of excellence do not supplant disease-state management in the case of chronic illnesses that require continuity of care.

Q 2:35   Is integration the wave of the future?

The short answer is yes. There is no doubt that the greatest drains on the health care dollar have been the duplication of services, management, and administration in inpatient and outpatient settings. For example, a three-physician office must have a receptionist, nurses, and a business office. Integration allows centralization of certain functions. More important, integration aligns physicians and the health care organization. With joined boards, shared services, and mutual accountability, integrated health care systems allow the best use of the medical dollar. Integration is taking many forms to ensure this alignment. PSNs integrate through creative structures and partnerships. At its best, integration is the strategic alliance among payers, providers, and suppliers with alignment of incentives.

During the past several years, however, the concept of integration has changed. Initially, vertical integration was the key to success in managed care—that is, the managed care organization would own the insurance product, the hospital, the medical group, and the entire spectrum of care delivery. Now, integration is more likely to encompass the *continuum of care,* a concept pioneered by the long-term acute care industry. A horizontally integrated care system controls the venue of the patient—wherever the patient is. Horizontal integration, thus, is quite patient focused.

Q 2:36   What can be expected to happen to administrative costs?

Administrative costs can account for up to 20 percent of total health care costs in managed care. Much of this is invisible to the consumers, who think they are getting health care without the paperwork of indemnity coverage. The analysis of cost is tricky, because payers allocate their costs differently. Nonetheless, administrative costs, executive salaries, and investor payoffs are an important part of the health care dollar and must be considered when a benefits manager selects a plan.

That management compensation is an important feature of health care cost is indisputable. The 1998 trends are showing, however, that management compensation is more frequently being put at risk for performance.[11]

Q 2:37   As different forms of managed care spread throughout the country, what are some of the next developments likely to be?

Integration of providers will continue to be the key in urban areas; there will also be mergers among insurance companies and HMOs. The mergers of health plans and payers that we analyzed in the first edition of this book have continued. Large pharmaceutical companies have acquired or merged with distributors to ensure sales channels for their products. Eventually, only a few large insurance companies will remain. The varieties of risk sharing are proliferating so that traditional lock-in capitation will not be the only vehicle. Lock-in capitation is too restrictive for both consumers and providers, and there is backlash. Lock-in capitation, however, may continue to be the vehicle for care of the Medicaid population and the indigent.

Of interest, as managed care strategies spread throughout the country, the Tip O'Neill adage that "all politics is local" plays out. There are few data to suggest that managed care progresses in defined stages, one leading to another. In fact, it appears that the evolution of managed care is almost anarchical with the product changing to fit local economic conditions and mores.

Any form of prepayment requires integration because management of the capitated dollar requires alignment of goals among physicians, hospitals, and payers. In large cities, the trend toward integration is likely to persist, with health care systems assuming an increasing proportion of risk and ultimately becoming the payers. In smaller communities, the fee-for-service system is likely to persist, since the actuarial resources required for risk assumption will not be operative. There is some possibility that the health purchasing cooperatives envisioned in the proposed Health Security Act will find a home in the less densely populated parts of the country. To be competitive, these cooperatives will have to be subsidized either by the government or by a consortium of payers, which is somewhat akin to the risk pools in states where automobile insurance is mandatory. Business alliances and small employer pools may allow rural areas to participate in managed care savings without crippling the delivery system. Small community hospitals, previously the bulwark of philanthropy in towns, are being swallowed by the conglomerates, with the same potential effect on the town as the coming of a discount chain.

HMOs are at risk because of their increasing visibility. Regulation of the industry is increasing, with many states proposing "patient protection" legislation, physician protections limiting HMOs' ability to deselect, and increased financial security provisions. In a similar vein, continued pressure on prices will drive the HMOs to their limit in squeezing concessions from the providers. Finally, PSNs and hospital-based HMOs will exert tremendous pressure on the commercial market.

Q 2:38   With all the merger activity involving providers, insurers, and HMOs, is it likely there will be only a few insurance companies and health care systems left?

In the near term, it seems there will be a smaller number of insurance product providers. The inevitable consolidations will leave large participants, which, in some markets, will edge dangerously close to antitrust laws. Those issues are beyond the scope of this discussion, but it is fair to say that competitors will regularly raise them as consolidation occurs. As the market becomes constricted, new opportunities will arise for smaller participants. Similarly, alliances will form and dissolve as opportunities and the financial climate change. It seems likely that large blocks of patients will shift with price, but niche markets and boutique providers will continue to emerge.

NOTES

1. R. Coile, "Health care's workplace revolution," *Health Trends* 9 (1997): 3.
2. J.T. Rich, "Future compensation shock," *Compensation & Benefits Review* 28 (1996): 28.
3. R.A. Cooper, "Perspectives on the physician workforce to the year 2020," *Journal of the American Medical Association* 274 (1995): 1534.
4. S.M. Shortell et al., *Remaking Health Care in America, Building Organized Delivery Systems* (San Francisco: Jossey-Bass Publishers, 1996).
5. D.C. Goodman et al, "Benchmarking the US physician workforce," *Journal of the American Medical Association* 276 (1996): 1811–1817.
6. C.E. Holm and D.J. Zuza, "Positioning primary care networks: understand what managed care organizations really want," *Health Care Services Strategic Management* 15, no 8 (1997).
7. H.Y. Bogard et al., "Extending health maintenance organization insurance to the uninsured," *Journal of the American Medical Association* 277 (1997): 1067–1072.
8. Bogard et al., "Extending health maintenance organization to the uninsured," 1067–1072.
9. Physician Payment Review Commission Annual Report to Congress, *Medicare and Medicaid Guide*, CCH 955, no. 951 (1997): 187.
10. American Association of Health Plans, "Provider-sponsored health plans don't need special regulatory breaks," *Health Benefits* 12, no. 14 (1997): 8.
11. Coopers & Lybrand, "Total compensation in the health care industry, 1997," *Managed Care Compensation Monitor* (1998).

CHAPTER 3

Plan Design

Jorge A. Font

INTRODUCTION

With the emergence of so many variations of managed care plans from which employers can choose, purchasing and installing health maintenance organizations (HMOs) and related point-of-service (POS) plans has become an interesting mix of art and science for the purchasers. For many employers, HMO and POS plans are the only medical plan offerings; for others they are merely a component of a broad array of benefit plans. These complexities have led many large employers, especially those geographically dispersed, to rely on health and welfare consultants and brokers to guide them through the selection, negotiation, implementation, or ongoing interface with these plans. By conducting various objective and subjective studies, purchasers or their consultants can determine what best suits the needs of their organization and employees and begin the processes of plan evaluation, negotiation, selection, employee premium (contribution) setting, and implementation.

Organizations have purchased HMO and POS services primarily to reduce costs in their medical benefit programs. History, however, has taught many purchasers that, if not negotiated and implemented properly within the context of all their medical plans, an employer can exacerbate the aggregate medical cost problem in addition to creating significant long-term employee relations problems. The good news is that in today's more competitive environment, employers can be more proactive in dealing with HMOs and insurers. This chapter seeks to describe the determinants in successfully selecting, negotiating and implementing an HMO or POS plan.

Q 3:1   What self-study is required of an employer before evaluating a managed care plan offering?

In determining if or how an HMO or POS plan offering would meet a purchaser's needs, there are several fundamental issues that a purchaser should understand and/or address:

- the overall compensation and benefits philosophy
- the number and types of medical plans currently offered (including retiree medical plans)
- the age and sex demographics of the work force (by medical plan, including retirees)
- historical medical costs and trends for all plans (including employee contributions to cost)
- relative comparisons of the plan costs versus regional costs and for those organizations in the same industry
- geographic distribution of current and future work force and the percentage of work force in markets with adequate managed care plan penetration

Q 3:2   What external information should an employer be capturing as part of the plan evaluation process?

A great deal of information is available from both the state HMO regulatory agencies and the HMOs themselves. The following categories are offered as starting points for each managed care plan under consideration.

Q 3:3   What characteristics of ownership are important in the HMO evaluation process?

1. National or regional track record
   - Virtually all national news and business magazines have ranked HMOs and managed care products recently. With the fury of mergers and acquisitions in the HMO market as well as the rapid turnover in management, these rankings are, regrettably, of little utility in making a purchase decision as the published data lag behind the current status of the health plan.

2. Financial stability (Ratings by A.M. Best and others)
   - The most up-to-date data are usually available from the state insurance commission.
3. Years of operation in markets under consideration
4. Profit status (for-profit/nonprofit)
   - Once again, it is critical to obtain current information on the status of managed care organizations, as the trend is to convert to for-profit status.
5. Management team and management systems
   - Stable versus "in transition"
   - The medical director
     —The medical director is an active member of the management team and should be committed to improving quality and outcomes. It is generally accepted that the medical director should be a critical part of the management team, however, this is often not the case. An assessment of the degree of participation of the medical director can be difficult, however, certain clues can be gleaned from the organizational structure:

       (a) Is the medical director part of the executive committee of the HMO?

       (b) Does clinical decision making regarding care delivery and clinical guidelines emanate from the medical director's line of authority?

       (c) Is the medical director involved in credentialing, care management, and case review?
   - Management information system (MIS) used, number of months in place, and tenure of MIS director
     —MIS is a moving target in all health services. The HMO should have an MIS strategy that is responsive to changes in the environment and amenable to innovation as the technology shifts.
     —Is there a professionally-managed call center with 24-hour coverage for members?
     —Is the MIS Year 2000 compliant?
   - Customer/member services team structure and tenure of key staff
     —As all managed care becomes similar in pricing, the value-added services loom large as product differentiates.
     —It is worthwhile to inquire as to the system for handling physician and medical staff issues. This is often called "provider

relations" and is critical in ensuring continuity among the payer, the plan, and the medical care system.
6. Financial and utilization data (two years minimum)

Q 3:4   What type of financial data should be reviewed?

1. Premium trend (preferably three years)
   - Data regarding premium trend are complex and have to be analyzed in the context of the national premium trends, as well as change in premiums in the local market.
   - When comparing premiums, it is critical to compare plans that are alike. That is, value-added services differ among health plans.
   - After a five-year decline, HMO premiums are now increasing nationwide in recognition of the underpricing of HMO products, increased pharmaceutical costs, and poor market performance of HMOs in general.
2. Underwriting restrictions (i.e., thresholds of employer size to "experience-rate" versus "community rate")
   - Some size restrictions are established by payers (as in a cap for Medicaid patients in certain markets), whereas others are terms of the HMO's certificate of authority issued by the state.
   - It should not be assumed that the geographic area covered by an HMO is congruent with the service area desired by the purchaser. Service area characteristics of the certificate of authority should be determined carefully in the contracting process.
3. Net after-tax profit/loss
4. Equity per member
5. Ratio of assets to liabilities
6. Medical loss ratio (MLR) (total claims divided by total revenues)
   - The medical loss ratio is a proxy for how much the HMO projects spending on the actual care of the patient. This ratio has become the moral touchstone for HMO performance in that a low MLR can indicate overly aggressive profits or a restrictive access policy.
7. Claims coverage (total current assets divided by average monthly claim costs)
   - All HMOs are required to have the financial security necessary to pay claims for their patients in the event of a default or serious financial reversal. The claims coverage trend can be used as an element of assessing the HMO's exposure.

8. Membership levels and composition (commercial, Medicare, Medicaid)
9. Net worth as a percentage of annual revenues
10. Prior year incurred but not reported (IBNR) liabilities estimate per member versus actual claim costs
    - IBNR is the bane of the HMO industry. It is particularly critical in a young HMO that has not yet achieved a steady state in claims. When valuing an HMO, IBNR is an important measure.

Note that financial data above, which is produced by an HMO or state agency, may not directly relate to the dollar amount of premiums proposed to an employer. An employer must, nonetheless, evaluate the market as to competitive rates and the employer's historical cost data. Depending on the situation, an HMO may be willing to prepare a more competitive bid if it understands that the plan is under a competitive bid or, conversely, that it could get the business (exclusively) if it meets both price and performance conditions set out by the purchaser.

Q 3:5   What type of utilization data are collected by HMOs?

1. Hospital days and discharges per 1,000 members (all cases, maternity, psychiatric/substance abuse, medical/surgical). In assessing hospital days per 1,000 members, several features must be kept in mind:
   - The case mix. This represents the type and severity of illness cared for in the HMO population. Variations in the case mix can dramatically affect cost of care.
   - Demographic adjustment. Hospitalization rates are different for different ages and genders. This is particularly true with Medicare.
   - Standard of the community.
2. Hospital cost per day (all cases, maternity, psychiatric/substance abuse, medical/surgical)
   - Hospital costs are a complex variable depending on the costs of the community, as well as labor and professional costs. On the other hand, all other things being equal (including outcomes) this metric can be useful in comparing the cost/efficacy of several plans. When comparing plans, it is critical to be assured that all things are indeed equal, including value-added services.
3. Physician visits per 1,000 (primary care and all physicians)
4. Pharmacy (outpatient) utilization and cost per member per month, plus generic substitution rate

5. Delivery system
   - Ascertain the number and types of providers within the target market. The distribution and quality of providers may be the critical feature of an HMO network structure.
   - Current directory of providers (subjectively review general desirability and name recognition of the major hospitals and medical groups)
   - Primary care physician (PCP) to member ratio (both target and actual rates)
   - Percentage of PCPs and all physicians board-certified
   - Percentage of PCPs accepting new patients
   - Payment mechanisms for physicians (percentage under capitation, fee-for-service), including bonus pool arrangements for hospitalization, specialty referral, and pharmacy benefits
   - Pharmacy network providers
   - Pharmacy benefit program (description, formulary, and incentive arrangements with physicians)
   - Process for members accessing specialist care
   - Utilization and case management program documentation and clinical practice guidelines used
   - Centers of excellence contracted nationwide for high-cost procedures
   - Out-of-area network coverage and description (e.g., subcontracted national networks)
6. Member services
   - Appointment waiting time (routine and urgent care)
   - Member satisfaction survey results (grievance rate per 1,000, overall satisfaction rate, and percentage that would recommend the plan to others)
   - Claims turnaround times
   - Process for handling transitional members (those in process of receiving medical treatment that are changing plans)
   - Disenrollment rates
   - Client (employer) services
   - Extent of on-site support during enrollment periods
   - Provision of inventory control and distribution (i.e., yearlong enrollment materials, directories). This is a major consideration for purchasers with numerous employee locations.

- Process and timing of handling magnetic enrollment data, invoicing, and reconciliation
- Limits on retroactive membership count and related premium adjustments

Q 3:6   What are the particular areas where a purchaser can have some level of control in negotiating with HMO or POS plans?

The areas in which an employer can exercise varying degrees of control over attaining the most value for its health care dollar are negotiating HMO premiums, funding approaches (fully insured, self-insured, etc.), and benefit packages (HMO-specific); analyzing and determining appropriate employee premium contributions; establishing streamlined administrative services and performance requirements (including refunds if complaints exceed prenegotiated per 1,000-member levels) and telephone response times from customer service; and limiting the amount, nature, and timing of any marketing efforts to employees.

When an employer has significant leverage with an HMO (i.e., more than 10 percent of the lives in a market), the employer can typically influence other things, including which providers to add or delete (for its specific program), negotiating shared savings arrangements, and placing limitations on annual rate increases. Rate negotiation usually is the primary focus of the purchasing process. Being armed with information such as that suggested in questions 3:1, 3:2, 3:3, 3:4, and 3:5 can be key for the purchaser who would like to obtain the most favorable rate for its medical benefit program.

Q 3:7   When offering multiple plans, why is it important to carefully establish a strategy for consistent plan design across all plans and corresponding employee contribution levels?

Establishing a level playing field of all the benefit packages offered by different plans, or at least understanding the dollar value of those differences, is an important step in successfully offering multiple plans. An employee's selection of a medical plan will depend primarily on how much the plan costs him or her each pay period, the benefit coverage (deductibles, office visit costs), and the perceived quality and adequacy of participating providers. The employees' plan selection pattern is a major determinant in the financial health of the entire medical program. It will also determine, on another level, if the employer or the HMO wins in the game of risk. In an ideal world, a "win-win" situation results when the HMO profits, not by stealing healthier and lower cost members, but by efficiently managing the level of risk for which they are responsible (and for which they are commensurately paid).

To the extent an employer has in place an overall benefits strategy or clearly stated philosophy, the process of steering employees through employer/employee premium contribution rates can begin. Examples of a benefits philosophy might include: "It is the organization's position to offer employees a choice of plans" or "It is the organization's intent to move everyone into the lowest cost plan." With this fundamental under-standing, one can begin the evaluation process. In the 1980s, many employers learned firsthand the meaning of "adverse selection." Adverse selection, in this context, is a phenomenon whereby younger and suppos-edly healthier employees (who typically earn less than their older col-leagues) select an HMO (or other fully insured plan) based mostly on a lower (even if only marginally) premium cost to them, causing their employer's self-insured plan to lose the most desirable risks and therefore cause a disproportionate rise in the cost of that plan. Unfortunately, many employers that have intended to lower overall costs by offering a second, "less expensive" plan have actually exacerbated the cost spiral. The general principle of insurance involves the spreading of risk among the largest possible number of people. When an employer subdivides the risk pool by offering multiple plans in the name of "freedom of choice," they run an increased risk of creating adverse selection and raising the aggre-gate cost of their medical programs, especially if there is a self-insured plan in place. Unabated, this trend causes more and more people to flee the self-insured plan (which may be politically "untouchable"), and creates what is known in the actuarial business as the "death spiral." This fre-quently causes the employer to eventually terminate the self-insured plan, which brings with it painful employee relations consequences.

Whether negotiating the total premium with an HMO or establishing internal employee/employer contribution rates, the base benefit plan must be priced along with the actuarial cost differences of the benefits across different plans. Different benefits (e.g., vision, prescription drug) cost different amounts and often attract different categories of employees. For example, a 20-year-old male may be more interested in having coverage for prescription glasses and contact lenses (low actuarial cost) than a generous hospitalization benefit (high actuarial cost). The employers that require employees to pay the cost of the differences beyond the base benefit package have tended to be more successful in reducing adverse selection. Armed with an understanding of the benefit-cost differences among plans, for example, Base Plan A (1.00) and Plan B (1.05), an employer wanting to "level the playing field" may want to ensure that employees pay 5 percent more for plan B regardless of the total premium negotiated with the HMO (assuming there weren't other age/sex selection considerations). Next, consider the employee age/sex and other demographic selection differences.

Table 3–1 illustrates the relative cost weights by employee age and dependent coverage categories, based on a composite premium of 1.00. This clearly shows the extent of variation in costs among different age segments and coverage types.

When these factors are adjusted using actual employer data and geographic cost factors, one has a basis for adjusting the employee contribution levels internally (and negotiating or adjusting total premiums with an HMO rather than accepting their "off-the-shelf" community rates) to reflect either historic or actual enrollment patterns.

Table 3–1 Specimen Age Factors by Coverage Tier
Three Tier Rates

Employee Age Segment	Employee Only	Employee Plus Spouse or Child	Employee Plus Family
15–24	0.630	1.199	2.256
25–29	0.815	1.586	2.629
30–34	0.975	1.792	2.851
35–39	0.985	1.811	2.859
40–44	1.022	1.858	2.911
45–49	1.101	2.037	3.089
50–54	1.337	2.365	3.420
55–59	1.649	2.923	3.971
60–64	1.871	3.265	4.320
65+	2.030	3.611	4.667

Q 3:8   How does one evaluate a plan's ability to meet the geographic requirements for an employee/retiree population?

Employers can use any one of several commercial software products to map employees, doctors' offices, and hospitals by ZIP codes when conducting independent evaluations. There are several inexpensive, commercial software products such as Map Lynx and others that serve the purpose of graphing, for example, provider locations and employee residences on a printed map and giving the analyst a thumbnail sketch of geographic desirability.

For large or multisite employers, more sophisticated tools can be employed. For example, GeoNetworks, produced by GeoAccess, Inc., of Overland Park, Kansas, is a managed care–specific software package, typically leased by major consulting houses, large provider organizations, and managed care vendors. An employer may produce a simple ASCII file on diskette containing the addresses and ZIP codes of its employees (with other optional data elements, such as coverage type, sex, or active/retiree) for an HMO or other managed care plan, in order for them to match the covered population against their database of primary care physicians and hospitals. Some of the typical reports and specifications that can be requested include:

- percentage of employees within 8 miles (driving distance) of two primary care physicians (note: 10+ miles to one physician may be more appropriate for certain rural settings, and two PCPs within 5 miles for the larger metropolitan areas)
- percentage of employees within 10 miles of a full-service acute care hospital (30+ miles for rural areas)
- maps showing employees without desired access (with attached summaries listing county, city, and ZIP codes)

Employers should note that many plans, unless requested, will not differentiate types of PCPs in their reports, which may prove relevant given a particular population mix. Below are several suggested special reports to request. This, however, entails the employer providing the necessary demographic data (such as employee sex, family status, active/retiree):

- geographic distance of employees with family coverage to pediatricians
- geographic distance of single female employees and employees with two-party and family coverage to obstetricians/gynecologists
- geographic distance of all employees to adult medicine providers
- maps showing employees without desired access according to the above categories

In all cases, one must be certain that the physicians included in the analyses have practices that are open to new patients and that, if there are limitations on the types or ages of patients, then the necessary reference exists. In addition to the above mapping software reports, certain internal reports can be requested that may provide previews of potential problems, especially those dealing with hospital-based physicians. For example, a listing of all specialists sorted by participating hospital and medical specialty will indicate the holes in coverage of various specialties in the most commonly used hospitals, with particular emphasis on the hospital-based physician specialties (e.g., radiology, anesthesiology, pathology, and emergency medicine). Many employee complaints arise from a lack of "in-network" coverage within a hospital where an employee may have to pay higher out-of-pocket costs to these specialists (despite having complied with the plan by selecting in-network surgeons and facilities). Having this information can provide a basis for causing the HMO to fill its coverage holes before problems occur.

Q 3:9   What are the major administrative considerations for an employer in maintaining managed care plans?

The biggest administrative challenges for an employer in offering managed care plans are:

- conducting the enrollment process (with the added complexity of dependent enrollment and assignment to primary care physicians)
- reconciling membership counts (adds or deletes) and associated dollar disbursements
- dealing with questions and complaints

- acting as a medical ombudsman (i.e., dealing with employees' denials of payment for common outpatient services not preauthorized by a primary care physician, denied coverage for "experimental" treatments)
- rate renegotiations process (planning and execution)

Many of the larger, more geographically dispersed employers rely on consultants and specialty brokers to manage various or all aspects of their HMO relationships. Often, they are paid an hourly fee to perform these services, especially the services involving only premium rate analysis and negotiation. Others are paid on a percentage of premium basis, especially if it involves a full-service contract. The payment approach for these services must be considered carefully, much like an individual investor might hire a fee-only financial advisor versus a commissioned advisor, or vice versa.

In general, an employer's administrative workload should be somewhat less demanding with an HMO versus a self-funded indemnity plan; however, the HMO plan needs to be monitored throughout the year. Utilization and cost data should be provided regularly so that rate renegotiations can be undertaken with plenty of lead time before the employer's open enrollment period. Further, it is important to keep track of complaints, especially those relating to providers, so that corrective action (i.e., termination from employer's network) can be taken on contract renewal or sooner. Customer service and claims service complaints should be documented as well, and can be used in the renewal process, as well as in documenting performance requirements.

Q 3:10   What are the most useful means available today to evaluate the quality of care provided by a health plan?

Today, HMOs and other managed care plans compete more on the basis of total value: cost, service, and quality. Purchasers recognize that quality improvement in medical care delivery and plan administration usually results in lower costs and greater employee satisfaction. The following describes several emerging trends in plan quality assessment.

Published Report Cards

Several national report cards on health plans are being published. The most recognized is that from the National Committee for Quality Assurance (NCQA), an independent organization focusing on the assessment, measurement, and reporting on the quality of care provided by managed care organizations. The Quality Compass 1997[1] report released in October 1997 provides comparative data on 329 managed care plans that cover 37 million Americans. The report includes data from the Health Plan Employer Data and Information Set that addresses mostly preventive service performance plus the standard accreditation data maintained by NCQA. The NCQA accreditation process is conducted by physicians and other health professionals on-site for three or more days and assesses the following: (1) quality improvement, (2) provider credentialing, (3) member rights and responsibilities, (4) preventive health services, (5) utilization management, and (6) medical records.

To the extent a health plan subcontracts many of its services to large multispecialty provider groups, it is important to understand whether the NCQA or the Joint Commission on Accreditation of Healthcare Organizations has conducted a review of those entities.

Full accreditation from the NCQA is now recognized as a standard within the industry and should give the purchasing public some degree of comfort with the quality of processes for screening providers and overseeing the delivering of services. However, this and other quality reporting systems are still in their infancy. Although this type of accreditation and quality reporting offers useful pieces of information focusing mostly on preventive health services delivered (e.g., immunizations, mammography screening, smoking cessation), it still does not address the actual performance ("executional quality") of different providers in terms of outcomes for specific procedures (mortality and complication rates) for most services performed. Therefore, purchasers wanting to know the best place to have heart surgery may want to consider additional reference points on the outcomes data of contracted HMO providers as much as possible (versus the HMO itself). Other, more accessible reference points on plan quality improvement are offered in the following section.

Member Satisfaction Surveys

According to the American Association of Health Plans' 1995 HMO survey,[2] 95 percent of all HMOs use consumer satisfaction surveys, up from 97 percent in 1994. Member feedback is an important component in the quality improvement process. Surveys tell us how well employees are satisfied with the medical care and their perceptions of quality of clinical care, provider service, and functional status before and after medical intervention. In addition to the medical delivery aspects, surveys tell us how well a health plan is responding to the routine administrative demands of members. This tool gives purchasers the opportunity to influence the direction of quality improvement efforts for a given health plan, as well as an important component to performance standards used by many employers in the annual settlement and renegotiation processes.

NOTES

1. National Committee on Quality Assurance, *Quality Compass 1997* (Washington, DC: 1997).
2. American Association of Health Plans, "1995 Annual HMO industry survey," in *1995 Sourcebook on HMO Utilization Data* (95SRC) (Washington, DC: 1995).

CHAPTER 4

Health Services Management

Les Paul

INTRODUCTION

The medical director is responsible for ensuring that quality is provided by physicians in the health maintenance organization (HMO) provider network. Health services management utilizes tools to improve the health of a population. Health services management is performed by the physician in coordination with other health care professionals, such as nurses and social workers. Prior to the advent of managed care, health services management often took the form of coordinated discharge planning, the effort to provide continuity between the hospital and the outpatient setting, which was restricted to the care of patients with an individual illness episode. In a managed care setting, the goal of the HMO medical director is to improve the health of all health plan members, as well as to ensure that when an illness occurs, patients receive efficient and effective care.

Q 4:1 What is integrated health services management?

Integrated health services management emphasizes a number of features critical to success in a managed care environment:

- cost-effectiveness
- patient/member satisfaction
- health status outcomes for the individual and the population
- preventive care and disease management
- information management

Physicians in a managed care provider network assume responsibility for the continuum of care, including health promotion and disease prevention. Clinical pathways or "care maps," based on consensus and clinical evidence, have been developed by a variety of specialty societies, federal agencies, and commercial vendors. These guidelines can be important tools to assist physicians in ensuring that health plan members receive quality and cost-effective care.

Q 4:2   What are the goals of health services management?

Effective health services management is critical for the health plan's success. Physicians must agree to define and implement treatment plans with the goal of standardizing routine, uncomplicated care. Wide clinical practice variation is costly and has not been shown to improve the quality of care. Health services management does not seek to diminish the patient-physician relationship—on the contrary, this relationship is enhanced when outcomes are improved and costs are contained.

Q 4:3   What about concurrent review of hospitalizations?

Concurrent review is the preferred method of utilization review for hospitalized patients. It allows "real-time" communication between the health plan utilization management staff and the hospital clinical staff. Increasingly, physician groups financially at risk or capitated are aggressively participating in the concurrent review process. For the concurrent review process to be most effective, alternative venues of care (i.e., skilled nursing facilities, rehabilitation facilities, or home care services) must be available when clinically appropriate.

Q 4:4   What are continuum of care services?

Continuum of care services provide an appropriate level and location for medical care based on the intensity of a patient's illness and may include:

• acute care services

- long-term acute care
- subacute care
- skilled nursing
- rehabilitation
- custodial care
- home health
- adult day care
- hospice

Support services for the continuum of care include:

- durable medical equipment
- infusion services
- personal care and homemaker assistance
- nurse telephone triage
- transportation
- wellness programs

Q 4:5   What tools are available for the delivery of continuum of care services?

- clinical guidelines
- critical pathways
- delivery system infrastructure elements (i.e., rapid treatment sites)
- case management services
- disease management services

The Institute of Medicine has defined a clinical guideline as "a systematically developed statement to assist practitioners in patient decisions about appropriate health care for specific clinical circumstances."[1] Other names for guidelines are practice parameters, practice protocols, and practice algorithms. A critical pathway is "an optimal sequencing and timing of interventions by physicians, nurses and other disciplines for a particular diagnosis or procedure designed to minimize delays and resource utilization and to maximize the quality of care."[2]

When implemented, these two intervention systems are designed to produce the following five effects:

1. reduction in practice variation
2. improvement in the quality of outcomes
3. education of the providers
4. malpractice and litigation risk reduction
5. utilization review and cost control

Q 4:6   What sources are available to obtain clinical guidelines?

- Agency for Health Care Policy and Research—National Guideline Clearinghouse (Internet Web page available)
- American Medical Association Directory of Practice Parameters
- specialty societies
- integrated delivery systems (e.g., Intermountain Healthcare)
- consulting firms (e.g., Milliman & Robertson, Deloitte & Touche Consulting Group "Best Practices")

Q 4:7   How can physicians be encouraged to comply with guidelines?

Several factors aid physician acceptance and use of guidelines, including:

- education on the content and use of guidelines to decrease unnecessary admissions to the hospital
- information regarding costs associated with different modalities of care and unnecessary variation in practice patterns
- development of a physician-friendly information and reporting system
- use of "educational influentials" (clinical leaders) as change agents

For guidelines to be successful, there must be an efficient clinical support infrastructure. This may include some of the following elements:

- rapid treatment unit
- outpatient surgical center
- case manager/care manager
- 24/7 availability of services
- home health care
- outpatient intravenous therapy and pharmacy
- availability of facilities in the full continuum of care

Q 4:8   How does the medical director differentiate case management from disease management?

Case management provides a comprehensive plan of action to determine the level of clinical needs and to identify appropriate, quality alternative care when indicated. Disease management tracks the process of care delivery and the outcome of specific illnesses.

Q 4:9   What clinical conditions are amenable to disease management?

Common clinical conditions for which disease management guidelines may be helpful include:

- diabetes mellitus (type I and type II)
- hypertension
- asthma (adult and childhood asthma have different disease management challenges)
- emphysema
- congestive heart failure
- hyperlipidemia
- rheumatoid arthritis
- endometriosis

Q 4:10   How does a medical director define quality?

Quality is the critical goal of an effective care delivery model and it has many components. Important elements in the definition of quality include:

- cost-effectiveness
- appropriate use in the appropriate setting
- service
- patient/member satisfaction
- outcomes for the individual
- outcomes for a population of members under the care of the group
- safety
- limited variation

Q 4:11   What are the key components of a quality management program?

The fundamental principle of a good quality management program is accountability. This includes preparing and disseminating a written description of the program, reviewing it annually, and updating it as necessary. During this update, the quality work plan must include planning for future projects, tracking and accounting of past projects, and providing a global evaluation. This should be fully documented in the minutes of the plan's quality committee.

Another important feature of a quality management system is coordination. This requires documentation of support from the plan's leadership and board. Leadership must also review and comment on the periodic quality report and provide oversight of the quality management program. Quality activities must permeate the entire organization and be focused on the continuous improvement of health status for those served.

Q 4:12   What processes does a quality management program use to measure outcomes?

These processes include:

- measurable and objective data collection
- appropriate statistical methods for analysis
- normative data and benchmarks
- identifying appropriate and qualified people to analyze data
- devising methods to systematically track issues identified by the process

Q 4:13 How does the medical director analyze the risks and benefits of capitation?

By accepting risk, a medical group has the potential of improving practice efficiency. It gains control of the care process and diminishes the "step-check" of managed care to the extent to which it is willing to accept risk. Capitation has many potential disadvantages, as well. These include:

- adverse selection (nonrandom variation induced by such factors as location and reputation)
- small numbers (one "catastrophe" can affect a panel disproportionately when the overall numbers are small)
- a potential need for a new governance structure
- dissonance if the fee-for-service environment exists side by side
- physicians' increased concern about the interaction of cost savings and quality

To manage risk, the following strategies may be employed by a medical group:

- Take risk only for services that you control.
- Perform a thorough actuarial analysis of the population to be served.
- Investigate "carve-outs" for low frequency or resource-intensive services.
- Obtain adequate stop-loss coverage.
- Employ clinical guidelines.
- Share risk.
- Contract so that the payer and the provider have assigned incentives.
- Maximize the number of covered lives.

Q 4:14 How can the actuarial cost model be used to set goals of a care system?

Knowing the risk of utilization of services in the population that the group serves can lead to appropriate care and aggressive case management, thereby reducing inpatient length of stay, emergency department use, and promoting full use of outpatient facilities.

Q 4:15   What is the role of a physician compensation formula in aligning incentives?

In a group practice, the compensation formula must:

- Define productivity to reflect the best use of health care resources.
- Maximize incentives for increased workload.
- Use quality indicators *and* patient satisfaction as a basis for income distribution.
- Minimize "perverse incentives" such as rewards for denying care.

As a medical group makes the transition from fee-for-service environment to capitation, the compensation formula becomes very challenging. The transition can be accomplished in four stages:

1. Prepaid budget, which separates fee-for-service and capitated revenues and credits a fee-for-service equivalent for patient visits. This is useful when the number of capitated lives is small but is risky in that it does not reward the physician for conserving resources.
2. Transitional formula, which combines capitation and fee-for-service revenues.
3. Capitation, which is compensation based on number of covered lives per physician.
4. Salary/bonus, which provides a guaranteed base compensation plus incentive for individual and group quality-based productivity.

To be successful, however, a compensation formula must reflect the values and principles of the group and the physicians within the group. It requires leadership by physicians who are educated in management and compensation principles, and it requires an identifiable group culture. The information system employed by the group must be reliable and give adequate information regarding productivity and resource utilization by physicians. Finally, the group has to agree on specialty-specific work metrics.

NOTES

1. Institute of Medicine, *Guidelines for Clinical Practice: From Development to Use* (Washington, DC: 1992).
2. R.J. Coffey et al., "An introduction to critical paths," *Quality Management in Health Care* 1 (1992): 45.

CHAPTER 5

HMOs and Hospital Risk

M. James Henderson

INTRODUCTION

The growth of market share controlled by HMOs has been and continues to be dramatic. Hospitals must contract with HMOs or their share of the hospital services market will decline significantly. This chapter is designed to answer questions for "how" and "why" hospitals should contract with HMOs. The "why" is driven mainly by what level of risk a hospital is willing to assume and, in turn, can effectively manage.

Q 5:1 **What are the mechanisms used to reimburse hospitals for services rendered under a managed care contract with a health maintenance organization (HMO)?**

There are a variety of mechanisms available to pay for hospital services in an HMO contract. These range from arrangements wherein the hospital assumes no risk to arrangements where the hospital is sharing risk as a full partner with physicians and, in some instances, with the payer. The major categories of payment mechanism are:

- discounted charges
- per diems
- stratified per diems
- case rates
- capitation with a hospital risk pool and budgeted targets
- pure capitation

Q 5:2   Why are hospitals never paid full charge rates under an HMO contract?

The concept behind the managed care arrangement is that managed care patients will be directed or channeled to a participating hospital. Channeling is a process by which patients are referred to a network hospital, which includes only those institutions with which a contractual relationship exists; thus, justifying a discount in charges in exchange for patient volume. Networks are made up of health care providers that have entered into managed care arrangements with HMOs and other health plans. As networks open and the number of participating hospitals contracting with an HMO increases, this sacrifice of margin for volume becomes more illusory and may have an influence on negotiated price.

Q 5:3   How are discounted charge rates set?

Hospital charges in a fee-for-service environment evolved over decades from a complex interaction of market forces including third parties' willingness to pay and individual hospitals' efficiency in managing cost. HMOs pay at discounted rates when they pay on a charge basis—again, a discount in exchange for volume through channeling to a restricted network. These rates are set through negotiation based on market rates being paid to similar hospitals in similar circumstances.

Typically, the smaller (or more restricted) the network of participating hospitals in the HMO's network and the larger the volume of covered lives in the plan, the larger the discount sought and granted. On the other hand, specialty hospitals and niche market providers and "must have" institutions are commonly able to negotiate a more favorable reimbursement rate.

Q 5:4   What is a "must have" hospital?

In some markets, there are institutions that have either a broad repertoire of services combined with a reputation for highest quality or have a market cache that makes them more highly desirable than some others. This may be (and often is) location or it may be academic or other affiliation.

Q 5:5   What is a per diem rate and how does it work?

A per diem rate in its simplest form is a single set fee paid to a hospital for each day that a member of an HMO is hospitalized. This fee would be paid regardless of the diagnosis or condition of the patient and regardless of the level of services provided. However, there is usually not just one rate because, to be fair to both the payer and the hospital, it would need to be a "blended" rate based on a weighted-by-volume scale of the wide variety of types of hospital days—observation, obstetrical, medical, surgical, intensive care, step-down, telemetry-monitored, intermediate, or subacute. Rather than try to make a prediction (which would invariably be wrong) of the makeup of days to calculate a blended single rate, a series of rates are more commonly negotiated and used. The possible combinations of very specific per diems and blended per diems that might be negotiated into an HMO or hospital contract are limited only by the negotiators' creativity.

Failure to calculate a blended rate appropriately can be devastating to the integrity of the contract and will economically impact the parties. For example, a rate that incorrectly estimated the number of coronary intensive care days would have more utilization of expensive cardiac services than had been anticipated.

Q 5:6   What are the important factors in deciding what combination of per diem rates to use and how do the perspectives of the HMO and the hospital differ?

The range of services a hospital offers and its expected volume are the two most important factors affecting the variability of the types of patients and, in turn, the complexity of the per diem rate schedule needed. The wider the range of types of days the hospital offers (and is anticipated to be used by members of the HMO), the more types of per diem rates likely to be desired by the hospital. That is, in calculating hospital per diem rates, "one size does not fit all." Similarly, the greater the volume of activity anticipated by the hospital, the more interested its representatives become in having a wide range of per diem rates.

In both cases, the hospital is appropriately concerned about assuming financial risk created by potential variability when it has no way to control the same.

A hypothetical case illustrates the principle. Good-Hearted Hospital (GHH) signs a contract with Channelview HMO "Channelview". The agreed-on reimbursement rate is a single per diem rate based on the averaged experience of GHH over the last year for all of their inpatient activity. Included in this historical average are patients with a variety of admitting diagnoses and severity of illnesses. Once the contract is in place, Channelview instructs its physician panel to admit all of their severe cardiovascular cases to GHH, but all other admissions should continue to go to the other hospitals in the plan's network. GHH is financially disadvantaged by this chain of events and will immediately want to renegotiate a separate per diem rate for cardiovascular admissions or face tremendous losses as a result of the Channelview contract. The HMO, although perhaps winning in the short run, has seriously injured a network institution through intentional adverse selection. GHH, on the other hand, unable to control its case mix and contracting on the basis of historic experience, is woefully exposed financially as a result of the adverse case selection of Channelview.

The perspective of the HMO differs from that of the hospital. The HMO wants to be able to fix its anticipated provider costs as accurately and low as possible, which will allow it to price products and premiums competitively and gain market share while maintaining a good margin of profit. A single per diem rate is easier to administer and, therefore, less costly. The only cost variable for an HMO's hospital expense with a single per diem rate is the number of days that will be used. The HMO is at a financial advantage as long as the total number of days is at or below the projected level. The makeup of those days is of no consequence to the HMO, but as discussed above, it may be of grave consequence to the hospital. Naturally, as in the above example, it is not to the advantage of the HMO to cripple its network hospitals, as their capabilities and service reflect directly on the HMO.

Q 5:7   What is a stratified per diem rate and how is it used in HMO-hospital contracting?

In effect, any categorization of patient days into differing per diem reimbursement rates is "stratifying" per diems. This can be done by severity (e.g., subacute, routine, intensive), general diagnosis (e.g., medical, surgical, obstetrical), specialty (e.g., neurosurgical, cardiac, orthopedic), or any combination of these types (see Table 5–1). The use of stratifying per diems does not alter the potentially conflicting perspectives, but it represents mechanisms for compromise. Even when a mutually agreeable compromise between a single per diem (preferred by the HMO) and a highly complex stratified per diem (preferred by the hospital) is reached, another conflicting perspective remains and comes now to the forefront of a contractual relationship—this is, the total number of utilization days. After per diem rates are set, the HMO hopes to see the number of days used set as low as possible. The hospital, on the other hand, would like to see the utilization as high as possible because it is reimbursed on a "piecework" or "fee-for-service" basis—the larger the number of "units" the higher the payment.

Table 5–1 Per Diem Stratification Matrix

Severity	General Diagnostic Category	Specialty
Acute	Medical	Neurosurgical
Subacute	Surgical	Cardiac
Intensive	Obstetric	Orthopaedic
Step-down	Pediatric	Opthalmic

Q 5:8   What is a solution for conflicting perspectives and incentives?

Enter the concept of case rates. Any given hospital admission may involve a several-day stay by the patient. For some of the days, the level of services (and the commensurate costs of providing those services) may be very high, and some may be much lower in both the level and cost of services needed. Although there is variability in the types of days utilized for a given admitting diagnosis, over time and as repetitions of the same diagnosis increase, a normal pattern of days (and their commensurate costs) emerges. This normal pattern can be encapsulated in a case rate—a negotiated fixed rate per admission by admitting diagnosis category. The most well-known and widely used categorization of admitting diagnoses is the one used by the federal government for Medicare reimbursement to hospitals. It consists of more than 450 diagnosis-related groups or (DRGs).[1]

If an HMO contracts with a hospital using case rates rather than per diem rates, their financial incentives become more closely aligned.

Q 5:9   What are DRGs and how are they calculated?

DRGs are used for prospective payments for hospital services. They were constructed specifically for the Health Care Financing Administration's

(HCFA) use to pay hospitals prospectively, by diagnosis, for all services rendered to a Medicare beneficiary. As of 1995, 21 states were also using DRG methodology for Medicaid payments. The number of DRGs has changed over the years since the system's introduction in 1982, with some categories being dropped and new ones added.

DRGs are also widely used by commercial payers because of their standardization and the availability of software to manage payment under this system.

Q 5:10   Why are the financial incentives better aligned between HMOs and hospitals under case rate reimbursement than when per diem rates are used?

Both the HMO and the hospital are potentially rewarded for more efficient inpatient operations (i.e., fewer days and less costly days) in a case rate contractual arrangement; whereas, under per diem rate reimbursement contracts, the hospital may actually be financially disadvantaged by efficiency improvements that might result in fewer and/or less intense days. Using case rates, an HMO can fix its anticipated hospital costs by projecting the number of admissions by type and, simultaneously, the hospital has the opportunity to be financially rewarded for improving the efficiency of its operations.

Q 5:11   Are there any potential problems or risks for HMOs or hospitals when they use case rates?

Yes, but they are different for each. Although the HMO is able to transfer the variability risk of the number and type of inpatient days its members use, the HMO retains the risk of variability of the admission rates—both in total number and mix of admissions. For example, the total number of admissions for a covered population could prove to be higher than expected, or the mix of admissions might turn out to be skewed to the higher cost case rates, or both. Any combination of such occurrences could have adverse financial consequences for the HMO.

From the hospital's perspective, the risk is not the number and types of admissions, but rather an extreme case within a specific case rate category—the proverbial bad case or "train wreck." A single bad case could (and frequently does) cost a hospital hundreds of thousands of dollars under a case rate reimbursement contract.

Q 5:12 How can a hospital protect itself from a financial catastrophe caused by a bad case when being reimbursed under a case rate mechanism?

The hospital would need to obtain, prospectively, some type of stop-loss protection in its contractual arrangement with the HMO. Typically, this would be in the form of a negotiated amount of accumulated charges on a given admission that would trigger additional payment from the HMO to the hospital. The additional payment could be in the form of discounted fee-for-service or per diems. An example would be a contract provision that called for reimbursement to the hospital of $1,000 per day for all days a plan member remained hospitalized after that member's total accumulated charges exceeded $50,000.

Q 5:13 Because case rates allow HMOs to transfer some risk to the hospital, but stop-loss provisions transfer some of that risk back to the HMO, and the HMO still has risk for admission rates and mix, are there any other risk-sharing, HMO-hospital arrangements?

Yes, the next step on the HMO/hospital risk-transfer continuum is capitation. Actually, the next step is prospective capitation with a retrospective "true-up" of some type.

Q 5:14 How does capitation with a true-up work and how is the risk shared between the HMO and the hospital in such an arrangement?

As in the case of any capitation arrangement, the hospital would receive a negotiated per member per month rate multiplied by the total number of covered lives for which the hospital is responsible for rendering appropriate, needed services. However, because there is almost always more than one hospital in the HMO's network, the distribution of admissions among the various hospitals can (and typically will) have an unpredictable variability. To allow a prospective capitation payment rate for hospital services to be successfully negotiated and ensure equity of payment among the hospitals, assumptions regarding volume (number of admissions and number of inpatient days) and mix (by diagnosis and level of acuity) must be made by both the HMO and the hospital. If, as part of the negotiation process, these assumptions are agreed to by both parties, there then is the opportunity for both parties to reach agreement on what happens when actual variations from the assumed occur—which invariably will happen.

If the two parties agree that nothing happens, then the risk has been completely transferred from the HMO to the hospital and a pure capitation agreement exists. On the other hand, if some retrospective adjustment algorithm is agreed to, then the HMO is retaining some of the risk. How much risk the HMO retains is dependent on the specific algorithm. (The only exception to this would be if the HMO could negotiate a zero-sum game provision into all the network hospitals contracts—that is, the HMO only pays "x" amount of dollars to the hospitals, and the algorithm settles up the division of that set total amount among the individual hospitals.) Contracts including such retrospective algorithm adjustments would not be pure capitation (again, with the exception of the zero-sum game), but would represent capitation with a true-up.

Q 5:15   Can the risk transfer relation between HMOs and hospitals be summarized by a reimbursement mechanism?

Yes. See Table 5–2.

The total inpatient cost per enrollee is the cost per unit of service times the number of units of service per inpatient day times the number of

---

Table 5–2 Inpatient Risk Transferred from HMO to Hospital

Types of Inpatient Risk	Discounts	Per Diems	Case Rates	Capitation
Cost/unit of service	Yes	Yes	Yes	Yes
Number of units/inpatient day	No	Yes	Yes	Yes
Number of days/admission	No	No	Yes	Yes
Number of admissions/enrollee	No	No	No	Yes

inpatient days per admission times the number of admissions per enrollee. This result times the total number of enrollees yields the total inpatient cost for the HMO.

Q 5:16   If all of this applies only to inpatients, what about outpatients?

All the theoretical concepts discussed on the inpatient side apply to outpatient activity as well, but implementing the theory is much more complex because outpatient services can be offered by many more providers than just hospitals (e.g., home health agencies, ambulatory surgery centers, free-standing laboratories, and physician offices).

Q 5:17   Are there any other types of risk arrangements that can exist between HMOs and hospitals?

Yes. Specialty carve-outs and global capitation arrangements can be negotiated between an HMO and a hospital.

Q 5:18   What is a specialty carve-out and how does it work?

A hospital may have a highly specialized service capability that few, if any, other hospitals in the region have—for example, a burn unit, bone marrow transplant center, or a regional trauma facility. In such circumstances, an HMO may wish to contract with that hospital for that specialty service even if the hospital is not a part of the HMO's overall provider network. (It is assumed that if the hospital is part of the HMO's network, the HMO/hospital contract already includes the specialty service.) The same spectrum of reimbursement mechanisms previously discussed can be used for a specialty carve-out contract.

Q 5:19   How does global capitation affect the hospital?

Everything to this point has addressed only the facility component for HMO/hospital contracts. If a hospital owns or has a joint venture with a physician group or groups, the hospital or the joint venture entity can contract with an HMO for facility and professional components. Such a contract could, again, use the same spectrum of reimbursement mechanisms that has been previously discussed; however, such arrangements more commonly use global case rates or global capitation.

HCFA has recently awarded a demonstration project to examine the feasibility of a different payment mechanism. The Medicare provider partnership demonstration will pay one lump sum (i.e., a bundled payment) for both hospital and physician services when Medicare beneficiaries are admitted to acute care institutions participating in the project. The bundled payment will be paid to an organization representing both the physicians and hospital, such as a physician-hospital organization (PHO), for nearly all Medicare admissions to the hospital. The goal is to test how physicians and hospitals can organize in the management of clinical care, whether doing so can improve efficiency and quality of care, and whether it can save money.

Currently, hospital and physician payments are separate. The bundled payments for each patient case will cover all hospital, physician, and other health care professionals' services provided during a hospital stay. The payment formula will start with the DRG definitions that already are used to pay hospitals. The average historical total payment for hospital and physician services per DRG will be determined for each participating partnership.

All sites participating in the demonstration proposed a discount to Medicare from their historical reimbursement amounts.

The demonstration is limited to six sites in New Jersey, New York, and Pennsylvania. These states were chosen because they have relatively high medical costs but low Medicare managed care penetration, and therefore the greatest potential for better coordination of clinical care and program savings. The sites are:

- JFK Medical Center, Edison, New Jersey
- St. Peter's PHO, Albany, New York
- Crouse Irving Memorial PHO, Syracuse, New York
- The Chester County PHO, Inc., West Chester, Pennsylvania
- The PHO of Pennsylvania Hospital, Philadelphia, Pennsylvania
- St. Barnabas Health Care System Provider Partnership (including St. Barnabas Medical Center, Livingston, New Jersey; Newark Beth

Israel Medical Center, Newark, New Jersey; and Monmouth Medical Center, Monmouth, New Jersey)

Site selection was based on the site's ability to operate the demonstration, its geographic location, and ability to meet quality and financial criteria. The demonstration will begin in 1998 as each site becomes ready. It will run for three years, with a possible extension for up to six years.[2]

Q 5:20   If a hospital and its allied physicians agreed to global capitation with an HMO, haven't the providers then assumed all the risk?

Most, but not all. There will still be risk for out-of-area emergency services, ground transportation, ambulatory pharmacy, home health, etc. Typically, these risks are maintained by the HMO, but they could be assumed by a hospital and its allied physicians if they had the full range of services (either owned or contracted) and the necessary administrative infrastructure.

Q 5:21   Which payment strategy is the best for the hospital?

Hospital payment strategies are complex decisions and are based largely on the existing market forces. In a transition market where managed care

---

Exhibit 5–1 Formula for Calculating Health Services Costs/HMO Enrollees

Total cost =	
Total inpatient cost/enrollee	
Cost/unit of service	(1)
× number of units of service/inpatient day	(2)
× number of inpatient days/admission	(3)
× number of admissions/enrollee	(4)
Total outpatient cost/enrollee	
Cost/unit of service	(5)
× number of units of service/outpatient visit	(6)
× number of outpatient visits/enrollee	(7)
Total other cost/enrollee	
Cost/unit of service	(8)
× number of units of service/enrollee	(9)

is just entering and the predominant payment is discounted fee-for-service, case rates and per diems allow the hospital to manage some of the risk. It is essential, though, that the hospital find a mechanism by which the physicians also bear some of the risk. Physicians control the cost of a case. If they have no incentive to control this cost, the hospital cannot manage its exposure alone.

As an environment begins to move more toward provider risk, a hospital can be at an advantage if its information technology and cost structure can manage the risk early in the market. As the market matures and payment shifts to capitation, it is vital that the hospital seek a mechanism of contracting for lives along with its physicians.

Thus, an ideal payment strategy will likely be evolutionary. A hospital should decide what level of risk it can effectively manage and then match a reimbursement strategy to that level. Exhibit 5–1 displays the component parts that make up the total health services cost per enrollee in an HMO. If a hospital only is willing to assume and manage the risks for the cost/unit of service (ratios #1, 5, and 8 in Exhibit 5–1), then it should seek discounted charges contracts with HMOs. If also willing to assume and manage the risk for the number of units for inpatient days (ratio #2), a hospital can contract on a per diem reimbursement rate. If a hospital believes it can assume and manage the risk for ratios #3 and 6, it is ready for care rates. Finally, only when it can assume and manage the risk for all nine ratios in Exhibit 5–1, can a hospital consider capitation and its commensurate risk and reward.

NOTES

1. Health Care Financing Administration, *Medicare Provider Analysis and Review (MEDPAR) Issued Prospective Payment System* (Washington, DC: U.S. Government Printing Office, 1983).

2. Health Care Financing Administration, "Physician and hospital demonstration to increase health care efficiency," 10 September, 1997. Press release.

CHAPTER 6

Case Management

Frederick W. Spong and Regina Holliman

INTRODUCTION

The case management concept has changed considerably over the past two decades. What started out as discharge planning evolved into hospital based case management for specific patients admitted out of area, with injuries or with specific high cost illnesses. Hospital based case management further encompassed care of those patient populations with specific chronic and costly illnesses and included aspects of disease management. For those health care organizations that are financially at risk, case and disease management across the inpatient and outpatient spectrum now can provide improved quality of care as well as greater efficiency and lower cost.

Q 6:1   What is case management?

Case management is intended to improve the quality of medical care by improving the management of health care delivery outcomes. It encompasses a range of strategies that culminate in the design and implementation of comprehensive plans of action. Case management determines the level and extent of medical care needs and identifies appropriate treatment modalities and settings.

The Case Management Society of America (CMSA), founded in 1990, is an international, not-for-profit professional society with more than 7,000 members. CMSA describes case management as "a collaborative process which assesses, plans, implements, coordinates, monitors and evaluates options and services to meet an individual's health needs through communication and available resources to promote quality, cost-effective outcomes."[1] Ideally, case management acts to ensure continuity, timeliness, and appropriateness of care to produce planned clinical and resource management outcomes. The process involves a myriad of health care resources and professionals to achieve these outcomes. Physicians, nurses, social workers, discharge planners, hospitals, home health agencies, skilled nursing, and extended care facilities are among the providers mobilized to meet patient and family needs.

Comprehensive case management is more than coordinating health care providers and services; it is an ongoing process of patient, family, and provider education. The case manager assists all stakeholders (i.e., patients, families, providers, community agencies, and payers) to understand available care and treatment options, participate in health care decision making, effectively navigate the delivery system, and adhere to the plan of care.

In 1995, CMSA released the *Standards of Practice for Case Management,*[1] which delineated guidelines for case management that were drawn from a variety of disciplines. CMSA also issued the *Ethics Statement on Case Management Practice,*[1] a primer on the application of ethical principles to the practice of case management. Presently, the CMSA is developing the Center for Case Management Accountability, an outcomes study intended to create a replicable model of accountability; define and standardize reporting mechanisms; and compare performance measurement throughout the industry.

Q 6:2   What are the origins of case management?

During the late 1970s and early 1980s, case management emerged from its origins in nursing and social work as a distinct discipline. The earliest case managers were hospital discharge planners, responsible for evaluating the need for and arranging postdischarge care. Early discharge planners assessed patients during the latter part of a hospital stay. Although discharge planning was never a leisurely pursuit, discharge planners had considerably more time and latitude than they have today. If, for example, a patient required placement in an extended care facility and a bed was not immediately available, the patient spent an additional day or two in the hospital.

Sharply reduced average length of stay, coupled with prospective hospital payment and the need to ensure continued quality of care, intensified the importance of timely, effective discharge planning. Further, as the population of hospitalized patients shifted to include older and more acutely ill patients, referral to discharge planning occurred more frequently. Today, plans for posthospital care are developed before elective hospitalization or on the first day of unscheduled hospital admission.

Early case management activities concentrated on catastrophic illness and those patients requiring intensive, long-term, or unusually costly forms of care. Referral to case management was triggered by the costs associated with an acute episode of care or the anticipated costs of long-term care, such as institutional care of a ventilator-dependent patient.

Payers of workers' compensation, catastrophic automobile accident claims, and other commercial payers were among the first purchasers of case management services. Drawing on nursing and utilization management techniques, initial case management activities primarily focused on the identification of high-risk and high-cost cases and implementation of strategies to control costs.

Q 6:3   What are the key components of traditional case management?

Case management involves a number of interrelated processes derived from nursing practice. The processes are often performed simultaneously.

Assessment. Relying on information from the patient, family, and providers, the case manager develops a preliminary assessment and treatment plan. The plan includes measurable objectives such as projected length of stay (LOS), recovery in terms of ability to perform activities of daily living, and anticipated need for postdischarge care (e.g., transfer to a subacute facility, home health care, outpatient treatment).

Planning. The case manager must develop consensus about the treatment plan among all stakeholders. It is especially important that the patient and family participate in the planning process and concur with treatment goals since in the absence of such support, adherence to proscribed treatment and satisfaction with care are compromised.

Implementation. Before enacting the treatment plan, the case manager must conduct a benefits review and obtain the necessary authorizations. Often, extensive community resources are required to complete a treatment plan. The plan commences when all parties are informed and concur about the actions needed to produce the desired clinical and resource management outcomes.

Coordination. This process ensures timely access to needed services. Coordination also prevents duplication or provision of unnecessary services and enhances continuity of care.

Monitoring. The plan must be monitored to ensure adherence and may be altered or fine-tuned in response to the patient's needs.

Evaluation. Case managers determine the extent to which clinical and resource management objectives are achieved as well as patient, family, provider, and payer satisfaction with the course of treatment and planned follow-up.

Communication. Case management requires clear and frequent communication with patients and families, providers, and payers. Along with in-person and telephone meetings, case managers must maintain detailed written records and document authorization for treatment, changes to the care plan, follow-up, and evaluation.

Cost-benefit analysis. Because one desirable outcome of case management is optimal, cost-effective resource utilization, case managers must continually assess the costs and benefits of all planned treatment. Conversant with available community health care resources, they are often instrumental in guiding providers and directing patients to the most appropriate treatment setting.

Q 6:4   How is case management practiced?

Historically, case management has been performed episodically in response to catastrophic illness or in anticipation of prolonged hospitalization or highly intensive, costly service provision. This form of inpatient case management bears a strong resemblance to clinical crisis intervention. It is a patient-focused, payer-driven process; provider-organized by consultants firms. It is short-term, intense, and performed external to use management. In contrast, outpatient case management seeks to prevent the very episodes of care monitored by hospital-based case managers. Identifying individuals at risk (e.g., patients suffering from chronic diseases or frequent users of hospital-based urgent or emergency services), case managers educate patients about their illnesses to prevent exacerbation of illness that result in hospitalization. Case managers also focus on changing patterns of outpatient utilization by redirecting patients from the acute setting to lower levels of care. For example, patients diagnosed with chronic conditions such as asthma, hypertension, low back pain, or diabetes may be referred to patient education or peer support groups mediated by allied health professionals in place of frequent office or clinic visits. In the most sophisticated centers for care, chronic care for a given population is formalized as disease state management with maintenance of prevention goals.

Outpatient case management also has been applied to managing community-based health and social services for chronically impaired older adults. By bridging the chasm between the formal medical care delivery system and informal helping networks, several states have developed fully integrated models of managed care for older adults.

These model programs provide incentives for delivering appropriate acute and long-term care in the least restrictive setting. Case managers coordinate and facilitate service delivery for frail older adults requiring complex, multidisciplinary care in a continuum of settings ranging from acute, day hospital, and skilled nursing care to home care and respite for caregivers.

Q 6:5   Are case managers certified, licensed, or regulated?

One of the goals of the CMSA is to implement uniform standards for case management practice. Currently the practice of case management requires neither licensure nor mandatory certification. Voluntary certification is available from the Commission for Case Management Certification (CCMC), an independent credentialing body established in 1995.

The CCMC defines case management as a specialized area of practice, rather than a profession. CCMC credentialing establishes a national certification process attesting to an individual's mastery of fundamental case management principles and practice. The designation of certified case manager (CCM) was designed to serve as an adjunct to other professional credentials in the health and human services profession.

The renewable, five-year CCM credential is awarded to practitioners who satisfy specific educational and employment requirements and pass the CCM examination. Applicants for certification renewal must verify that they continue to maintain the license or certificate they held at the time the credential was issued and must demonstrate ongoing professional development by completing an approved program of continuing education or reexamination.

Efforts to license and stipulate training of case managers have been endorsed by a number of other professional organizations including the American Nurses Association, Association of Rehabilitation Nurses, and the National Association of Professionals in the Private Sector. Although the optimal education, training, and experience of case managers is debated within professional societies, all concur that to perform effectively, case managers must possess an expertise in traditional nursing process components, and superb interpersonal, communication, and teaching skills.

Utilization management organizations and firms that offer case management services are subject to regulation in at least 28 states. Most states require utilization review (UR) organizations to notify the provider or enrollee about UR decisions; use written, clinical review procedures that are periodically reviewed and updated; disseminate a written description of the appeal process to providers; allow ample time for providers to submit necessary clinical information for review; and prohibit reimbursement tied to the number or frequency of claims denials. Since 1991, utilization management companies conforming to national standards established by the Utilization Review Accreditation Commission (URAC) have been granted voluntary accreditation. The URAC standards are to:

- Encourage consistency in the procedures for interaction between utilization review organizations and providers, payers, and consumers of health care.
- Establish UR processes that cause minimal disruption to the health care delivery system.
- Establish standards for the procedures to certify health care services and to process appeals of the determinations.
- Provide the basis for an efficient process for accrediting utilization review organizations.
- Provide an accreditation mechanism that can be applied efficiently nationwide for those states that choose to regulate utilization review organization activities.

By late 1995, more than 150 utilization management and quality assurance systems providing service to more than 120 million managed care members had received URAC accreditation. Presently, some states waive the requirement for a utilization review organization to secure state certification if the company is accredited by the URAC.

Q 6:6   Who performs case management?

Case managers have emerged from medicine, nursing, social work, rehabilitation, physical therapy, health education, pharmacy, and behavioral health. Intuitively, clinical practice experience seems a desirable prerequisite for case managers, if only to ease communication and collaboration among the practitioners involved in patient care. In practice, however, case managers without clinical expertise can and do perform effectively, especially when trained to facilitate certain components of the entire case management process.

Q 6:7   What is hospital-based case management?

Hospital-based case management is intended to improve quality by providing planned outcomes, which include a goal of length of stay, and anticipated needs for postdischarge care or continuing care for chronic disease management.

Coordination and continuity of care. The case manager facilitates communication among caregivers, family, and payer to avoid unnecessary or duplicative service provision and to expedite timely referral, transfer, or discharge.

Early patient and family education. The case manager assists the patient and family to develop realistic expectations about the course of treatment and plan of care. When expectations are congruent, adherence to treatment and satisfaction with care are enhanced.

Demonstrated value. Case management produces measurable value by predicting, quantifying, and documenting the provision of health care services in the most appropriate setting. Employers and other purchasers of health care services can determine the degree of case management using standardized performance measures—such as the Health Plan Employer Data and Information Set.

Many payers and providers have instituted case management programs to control hospital-related costs. Case management has been demonstrated as an effective cost-saving measure when applied to selected cases—such as claims anticipated to exceed $25,000, patients with protracted hospital stays, and complex cases involving multiple severe, chronic, or progressive diseases.

Case management has been applied effectively to patients suffering from injuries (e.g., extensive burns, traumatic brain injury, spinal cord injuries); high-risk pregnancies; acquired immune deficiency syndrome (AIDS), and organ transplant patients; and patients suffering from degenerative neuromuscular diseases. It also has been used to manage aspects of mental health care and behavioral medicine—including care for people with acute and chronic psychiatric illnesses—as well as treatment for substance abuse.

Cost containment should not be designated as the primary goal of hospital-based case management. Rather, it should be considered a desirable outcome of optimal resource utilization (i.e., the result of effective case management).

Q 6:8   What are the basic mechanisms of hospital-based case management?

Hospital-based case management begins with preadmission screening to determine the medical necessity of the admission and the appropriate level of care.

Preadmission Screening

During preadmission screening, the patient and family are the focus of teaching to prepare for the planned activities of the admission (e.g., diagnostic testing, surgical or medical intervention); identify post-hospitalization needs for discharge planning; communicate discharge plan options to the patient and family; and initiate the community resource referral process and, when necessary, perform financial screening.

Admission Review

Generally conducted within 24 hours of admission, the admission review entails a comparison of clinical guidelines with the documented admission data to establish medically necessary treatment in an acute care setting. Admission review targets nonelective entry to the hospital (i.e., direct admissions from the physician's office and patients admitted through the hospital emergency department).

Continued Stay Review

At various points during the hospital stay, focused chart review is used to confirm or question the need for continuing care in the acute setting. It also may be used to modify or amend the discharge plan.

Discharge Planning

Discharge planning occurs during preadmission screening for all elective admissions. The discharge plan must retain considerable flexibility to respond to changing needs and circumstances of the patient and family. Along with continued stay review, ongoing communication with multiple caregivers is required to observe the need for changes in the goal length of stay or the discharge plan.

Q 6:9   What are the roles of physicians and nurses in hospital-based case management?

Essentially a collaborative process, case management involves the patient and family, case manager, physician, nurses, and allied health professionals. In many instances, case management also may be subject to institutional review from a provider or payer utilization management group.

The physician is responsible for diagnosis and treatment as well as development and direction of the care plan. Physicians engaged in the case management process must regularly confer with the nurses who implement and document the plan, the case manager tracking the plan, and the patient and family.

Effective case management requires considerable support from nursing personnel. They must be thoroughly conversant with the case management guidelines in their specialties (e.g., medicine, surgery, obstetrics, rehabilitation). Individual nursing departments often must be realigned to support overall utilization management goals. For example, preoperative testing and screening provide the opportunity for the nurse to preassess discharge planning needs and discuss the goal LOS with the patient and family. Case management guidelines and criteria must be incorporated in the nursing care plan. The nursing care plan should document the goal LOS and any potential obstacles (e.g., medical, family, social, or financial impediments to discharge) to achieving the goal LOS. Nurses facilitate timely communication between all stakeholders. They notify case managers when family members are available for conferences, participate in multidisciplinary rounds and alert attending physicians when the results of laboratory or other diagnostic tests arrive. Further, nurses promote timely changes in the care plan by apprising the physician of patient progress throughout the day, such as improving dietary tolerance. They also may intervene to clarify ambiguous orders, such as "D/C when OK with surgery."

Q 6:10   How does traditional, hospital-based case management differ from practice, health maintenance organization (HMO) case management?

Hospital-based case management addresses resource utilization during and after inpatient admission. It is characterized by short-term, intense case management relationships aimed at optimizing individual patient outcomes. Patient and family education centers on management of the illness or condition that precipitated hospitalization. The effectiveness of hospital-based case management is measured in terms of clinical outcomes, such as goal length of stay. Financial outcomes are assessed by determining the cost-savings per patient.

HMO case management not only incorporates hospital-based case management techniques, but also considers outpatient care. Its emphasis is on preventing hospitalization and illness. The case manager seeks to educate members about illness avoidance by promoting primary prevention and wellness programs.

Targeting members considered to be at risk for hospitalization or greater than average utilization (e.g., older adults, members with multiple medical problems or chronic illnesses), HMO case managers maintain long-term relationships with members. In general, they are less frequently called on to perform the crisis intervention services associated with management of catastrophic illness than their hospital-based counterparts. Applied to populations as opposed to individuals, the efficacy of HMO case management is measured using population-based outcomes such as hospital days per month, use of emergency or urgent care services, and overall cost savings per population.

Q 6:11   What are the goals of HMO case management?

Along with coordinating care and ensuring timely treatment in the most appropriate setting, HMO case management aims to enhance quality service delivery by preventing morbidity associated with chronic diseases. It has assumed an increasingly prominent role in HMO utilization management programs in response to the swelling numbers of older adults enrolling in Medicare-risk and other HMO programs.

Although most HMOs provide only limited skilled nursing or extended care facility benefits, many HMO case managers make use of a continuum of long-term care resources to shift frail elderly, chronically, or terminally ill members from higher cost hospital settings to nursing homes and home care programs. These innovative case managers follow members over time and across treatment settings.

The education goals of HMO case management differ significantly from the patient teaching conducted by hospital-based case managers. Proactive HMO case management encourages assessment and teaching of medical self-care skills and adherence to proscribed treatment regimens. Case managers also instruct HMO members about how best to negotiate the delivery system (e.g., how to seek urgent care, obtain a referral to a specialist, or resolve claims disputes).

Case managers play a pivotal role in monitoring and improving HMO member satisfaction. Many case managers assist members in selecting a personal physician, orient them to the HMO service delivery system, and provide referral to HMO and community-based health programs and support groups. Able to identify, document, and intervene to resolve recurring delivery system problems, case managers serve to increase reported levels of member and provider satisfaction.

As previously stated, optimal clinical outcomes and resource utilization, as opposed to cost containment, should be the overriding goals or stated purposes of case management activities, especially HMO case management. Designating cost containment as the HMO case manager's primary goal only serves to exacerbate tension resulting from the case manager's competing roles of advocacy and gatekeeping. Ultimately, the financial outcomes of HMO case management should be assessed as population savings, using lifetime expense profiling, as opposed to the individual cost savings attributable to catastrophic care or hospital-based case management.

Q 6:12   When should HMO case management begin?

When instituted as a primary prevention program, HMO case management must identify the need for active intervention at enrollment and before service utilization. Early identification, via new member surveys, health status questionnaires, and other member self-report mechanisms enables the case manager to triage members to office or clinic visits with physicians, midlevel practitioners, and nurses. The case manager also may refer members to HMO-sponsored and community-based health education, wellness, chronic, disease management, screening, and support group programs.

Many HMOs have reported successful implementation of disease management programs. Although disease management strategies vary, most include clinical practice guideline or critical pathway adherence and formularies and patient education programs to improve compliance. To date, these programs have targeted coronary artery disease, diabetes mellitus, chronic obstructive pulmonary disease, hypertension, chronic hepatitis, AIDS, asthma, high-risk obstetrics, depression, and chemical dependency.

Case management is a vital component of HMO disease management programs. To prevent disease-related morbidity, case managers identify members at risk, coordinate their care, and refer them to patient education programs to promote adherence to treatment and reduce health risks attributable to lifestyle or behavior.

Q 6:13   What are the key requirements for a successful case management program?

Effective case management programs share the following characteristics.

Management commitment. Without an earnest management commitment, the case manager will neither be accepted as a member of the provider team nor have the authority to intervene to effect change.

Physician commitment. Strong physician support for the case management process is essential. Physician involvement in the design of the case management program; inservice education delineating the goals, objectives, and mechanics of the program; and incentives for participation are among the strategies used by HMOs to generate physician enthusiasm for the case management process.

Designated case managers. Although case management is a collaborative process, conducted by a team of providers working in concert with patients and families, it requires a central locus of control. The designated case manager performs this function, serving simultaneously as a clearing-house for information, a source of referral, a patient advocate, an educator, and a coordinator of quality-driven care.

Accountability. Every individual involved in case management should have a clear understanding of his or her roles and responsibilities in the process. Despite considerable overlap of functions (e.g., multiple members of the case management team may communicate with the patient and family), written statements of accountability should, for example, identify each team member's responsibility in the case management process.

Ongoing team member education. All people involved in case management require regular updates about service utilization patterns and resource availability, as well as feedback about the overall effectiveness of the case management program. It is essential that continuing education regarding regulatory and industry standards be communicated to all team members.

Data collection and analysis. The case management process presents multiple opportunities to identify and address patient care and delivery system problems. To fulfill this promise, case managers must systematically document and communicate quality issues related to coordination, timeliness and appropriateness of care.

Q 6:14   To perform effectively, which resources must be available to the HMO case manager?

Case managers need the availability of physician management/advice on an ongoing basis.

Along with support from administrators and providers, the case manager must be equipped with a complete understanding of the HMO delivery system, benefits, and covered services. Similarly, case managers should have full knowledge of and referral relationships with local community health and social service agencies, organizations, and other providers.

From an organizational standpoint, the practice of case management requires operative management information and communication systems. Case managers and providers must have reliable, timely data to permit advances in the plan of care. Delayed laboratory or other diagnostic test findings may result in an unnecessary hospital admission or prolonged hospitalization. For example, an HMO member with chest pain admitted to a short stay or observation unit may linger unnecessarily if the laboratory data confirming noncardiac chest pain are not reported and conveyed quickly.

Lapses in communication not only have the potential to delay access to care but also may compromise adherence to treatment and satisfaction with care. If provider consent, payer authorization, or cooperation from agencies outside the HMO are not obtained or if the case manager fails to deliver even one element of the agreed on plan of care (e.g., referral to a physician specialist, reliable home health care, institutional placement), the case management process disappoints all the stakeholders.

Although not requisite to the effective practice of case management, the availability of immediate electronic information transfer streamlines the process. Handheld computer notepads enable the case manager to generate requests for referrals, coding, and billing at the patient's bedside. Future technological advances promise ever-increasing ease and speed of information transfer and the design of entirely paperless case management documentation systems.

Q 6:15   Which subpopulations of HMO enrollees benefit from case management?

Certain HMO members may qualify for comprehensive case management. The following criteria are some key indicators that would trigger the initiation of case management activities:

- active chronic disease
- multiple medications or certain categories of medications
- multiple hospitalizations
- age 75 years or greater
- multiple visits to the emergency department
- significant impairment in the activities of daily living

Q 6:16   Where should the responsibility for case management rest in HMOs?

There is a compelling argument favoring responsibility for case management by the component of the delivery system that bears substantial financial risk. Some HMOs place hospitals at risk and many require medical groups or independent practice associations to assume a share of the financial risk associated with providing care for the enrolled population. Others place an integrated delivery system at risk for financial performance. Proponents of assignment of responsibility to the entity or group at greatest financial risk contend that case management is best performed by those with the financial imperative and incentive to do it.

Other industry observers believe that the HMO's health plan or medical administration should assume responsibility for supervision of the case management function. Advocates of health plan or administrative oversight view case management as a key component of quality improvement, rather than simply a cost-containment program. They contend that the tangible results of case management (i.e., planned, predictable, clinical, and financial outcomes) constitute administrative accountability. Further, case management outcomes, when reported as performance measures of quality, significantly enhance HMO marketability among employer and consumer groups. The bottom line is that all delivery systems warrant some degree of case management.

Q 6:17   How are the outcomes of case management measured?

Traditionally, case management has been measured and its effectiveness assessed in dollars saved per patient. Case management consistently and unequivocally demonstrates the ability to control the costs associated with health care delivery. To date, the most dramatic savings have been realized as the result of hospital-based case management. These savings are immediate and easily documented. The cost savings resulting from proactive, preventive case management are still largely estimates of lifetime expense profiles (i.e., long-term, projected savings per population).

Case management can and should be appraised by its capacity to improve quality by reducing variance from established norms (i.e., critical paths or clinical practice guidelines). It should act to optimize resource management and utilization and measurably contribute to consumer and provider satisfaction with the delivery of health care services.

Case management programs must continue to demonstrate and communicate success in improving health care delivery quality using clinical, financial and patient satisfaction outcome measures. In the presence of quantifiable objectives and tangible results, case management programs will earn the support of all managed care stakeholders (i.e., employers, providers, payers, and consumers).

NOTE

1. Consolidated Metropolitan Statistical Area, *CMSA Standards of Practice for Case Management* and *Ethics Statement on Case Management Practice* (Little Rock, AR: 1995).

SUGGESTED READINGS

1. S.T. Dacso and C.C. Dacso, *Managed Care Answer Book: 1996 Supplement* (Gaithersburg, MD: Aspen Publishers, Inc., 1996), Q7:42–Q7:50.
2. M. Pinney, *Case Management: A New Generation* (Radnor, PA: Milliman & Robertson, 1996).
3. F.W. Spong, Case Management: Necessary for Disease Management (Presented to NMHCC Cardiovascular Disease Management Program, West Palm Beach, Florida, December 1995 and UCLA Healthcare Management Group, Los Angeles, California, March 1996).
4. E. Zablockki, "Keeping at-risk members healthy," *HMO Magazine* (September/October 1995): 73–76.
5. "Turbulent changes in CM provide for calmer waters after restructuring," *Hospital Case Management* (August 1995): 117–132.
6. J.O. Hillman, "Case management: creativity in the ambulatory environment," *Medical Interface* (November 1994): 71–76.
7. S.Z. Nelson et al., "An integrated continuum of care," *HMO Practice* 9, no. 1 (1995): 40–43.
8. T. Fama and P.D. Fox, "Beyond the benefits package," *HMO Practice* 9, no. 4 (1995): 179–181.
9. S.L. Aliotta, "Case management programs: investment in the future," *HMO Practice* 9, no. 4 (1995): 174–178.
10. L. Mahonen, "Challenges in the practice of case management within a managed care organization," *Medical Interface* (November 1993): 47–52.

11. Utilization Review Accreditation Committee, *URAC Standards* (Washington, DC: 1997).

12. F.W. Spong, "Demonstrating and communicating quality, models for measuring quality in managed care," in *Analysis and Impact* (New York: Faulkner & Gray, 1997), 279–296.

CHAPTER 7

Legal Issues in HMO Contracts

Donald L. Holmquest

INTRODUCTION

Physicians are frustrated that attempts to address the challenges posed by the shift of the marketplace to managed care seem to be barred by some technical legal restraint. Some of these challenges include:

- setting prices collectively
- having too many physicians in independent practice associations (IPAs)
- having too few physicians in IPAs
- contracting directly with employers
- accepting a share of hospital surplus funds
- removing or not removing a competing physician from a panel of physicians

Analysis leads to paralysis. This chapter identifies the barriers that actually exist, explains their basis and scope, and illuminates the options and pathways that allow, and even promote, positive action in the development and operation of health maintenance organization (HMO) products.

Q 7:1   How has the marketplace influenced regulation?

From the physician's perspective, managed care is not a new industry or even a new phenomenon. It is, instead, merely a new approach to the

133

buying and selling behavior made necessary by the relatively new emergence of competition for customers. For the most part, HMOs and managed care have not diminished the obligation of the individual physician to the individual patient. It is fair to say that these relationships have become more complex with the injection of an intermediary between patient and physician. Similarly, the HMO as a subset of managed care is not new either in terms of the law or the marketplace.

Q 7:2   How has the marketplace dynamic made HMO development unique?

Unfortunately, the emergence of competition for patients has not happened under the circumstances that permit traditional responses to competition. The health care industry has a significant oversupply of resources and manpower and archaic organizational structures on both the physician and institutional sides. Structures that normally develop in an industry have not developed in health care because of the:

- unique, private, and personal aspect of the physician-patient relationship
- inaccessibility of medical knowledge (the "art" of medicine)
- lack of standardization of procedures in health care delivery
- internal, self-policing of the profession
- self-certification of the medical profession
- previous view of the apparently inexhaustible supply of money available for health care
- social and political influence of physicians and organized medicine

Now, however, many of the influences are waning and the homogeneity of health care is beginning to dissolve and is beginning to show some of the same ruthless characteristics as the airline industry. That patients are not the purchasers of their own health care services makes developing a health care market that would parallel that of the airline industry impossible. The air travel market has developed rather logically since the federal government ceased its market distortion business by shutting down the Civil Aeronautics Board.

For the health care industry, concentrating purchasing power in the large insurance companies and the federal and state governments further complicates competitive responses, and the complex regulatory overlay of federal and state insurance and employee benefit rules creates additional limitations on how physicians can respond. The previous factors influencing the lack of regulation in health care can thus be refocused to represent the following trends:

1. Although the physician-patient relationship is still intensely private, there is a growing public aspect of the medical transaction. The injection of third (and fourth and fifth) parties has increased the volume of information flow and decreased the amount of privacy. Insurance companies that pay for health care routinely evaluate individual patient-physician episodes. Electronic media have made records available to anyone with a password, and the movement toward quality measures has made data available to regulators and outside quality assurance organizations.

2. Although most physicians still consider medicine an art, the arcane nature of the patient-physician transaction has been illuminated by the wide availability of medical knowledge packaged for the nonprofessional "consumer."

3. Managed care organizations—and HMOs in particular—cannot tolerate the enormous variation in procedures inherent in medical care delivery. Although each patient and each illness episode has its unique characteristics, there is increasing desire by health care delivery organizations and payers alike to standardize procedures, which allows them to institute protocols and estimate costs. Pejoratively, physicians call this "cookbook" medicine and fear the loss of autonomy that comes with "care pathways."

4. The process of "policing" a profession is traditionally assigned to those in that profession. This has been true for medicine, as well, where even the licensing authorities were responsive to medicine. Beginning with the appearance of members of the public on licensing boards and the growing awareness of physicians' reluctance to identify and correct poor performers among their ranks, there has been increasing public attention to medical quality and outcomes. Although medical licensing boards still possess the final say on granting medical licenses, participation in HMO contracts can be decided internally within the structure of the payer. Similarly, quality and outcome measures are becoming increasingly available to the public. With the publication of crude mortality data for hospitals, quality and

outcome measures increasingly have been sought and disseminated. The Health Employer Data Information Set, National Committee on Quality Assurance, and Joint Commission on the Accreditation of Healthcare Organizations disseminate quality and outcome information to payers and consumers of health care alike. Late 1997 saw the publication and dissemination, via the Internet, of outcome statistics for infertility clinics around the country by the Centers for Disease Control and Prevention. Quality and outcome data publication and dissemination pose intense legal and regulatory challenges to both the HMO and the physician. Typically, the quality assurance function of an HMO as applied to an individual physician is protected from discovery. These data, however, form the core of reports to regulatory agencies in the process of licensure monitoring for the HMO.

5. Medicine has long certified its own practitioners with training programs internally accredited and trainees certified by boards created by the profession. Only recently have specialty boards even required periodic recertification; previously, board certification was "evergreen." Certification by a specialty board is not required by any state for licensure; however, HMOs increasingly require this certification for credentialing. Nonetheless, boards are still internally regulated and, because board certification has become more important, there has been a proliferation of new boards, which are not recognized by the governing body, the American Board of Medical Specialties. With this growth in specialty "boards," additional regulatory procedures will be inevitable.

6. The constriction of resources available for medical care has shifted the burden of cost containment from the payer to the provider. An increasing amount of litigation has appeared against HMOs on the theory that they are skimping on quality to maintain profits.

Q 7:3   What are the major categories of legal principles that impact on the practice of medicine?

Legal principles that influence how physicians can adapt to competition can be lumped into several broad categories. Although every problem situation usually involves an overlap of several types of legal issues, we will deal with them individually.

Q 7:4   What effect has contracting had on physicians?

Perhaps the most fundamental change in the physician's life brought by managed care has been the blizzard of paper contracts that regularly blow across the physician's desk. Physicians are faced with questions about what traditional contract language really means. What is the significance of those "whereas" statements? What does termination for cause really mean? Must the physician read that confusing list of trivia in the concluding "miscellaneous" section?

Most physicians have developed some familiarity with contract principles through the other economic aspects of their lives, and professional associations of every sort have highlighted contract issues. There are, however, certain principles of contract law of which the physician should be aware, and certain patterns of managed care contracts worth noting. A checklist at the conclusion of this chapter describes the concerns that should be considered in each of the typical sections of a managed care contract.

Q 7:5   What is the "integrity of the promise?"

Contract law has one principal purpose: to protect the integrity of commercial promises. It is based on traditional notions of rational marketplace behavior that date back thousands of years. If all parties cannot be counted on to uphold their economic promises, any enterprise or society will fall apart; thus, a fundamental part of the law of contracts is to enforce binding promises. But the law will not just enforce any promise; a mere promise to do something is not a contract. A contract is an exchange between parties of promises or of something else of value for a promise, and the law will either make the defaulting party live up to the promise or else make the other party whole economically.

Q 7:6   Does a contract have to be in writing?

Although a verbal exchange of promises is technically as enforceable as a written one (with a few statutory exceptions, such as the sale of real estate or certain long-term contracts), the difficulty of proving verbal promises means that, for all practical purposes, contracts involving issues of substance need to be written down.

Even when a contract is in writing, it is not always clear what is the real transaction involved. Sometimes the difficulty comes from unskillful drafting, and sometimes from an intention to deceive. Occasionally, legalistic language is used that attempts to put the nonlawyer at a disadvantage. Fortunately, when interpreting a contract that has reached a court, what matters really is *the intent* of the parties in entering the contract.

A contract between a managed care organization and one or more physicians must not only be thoughtfully drafted and carefully reviewed by all parties, but also other evidence of what the party intended should be kept. Legally obtained letters, notes, witnesses, and recordings can be extremely valuable in ensuring that the promised benefit is delivered. Larger organizations such as group practices, larger IPAs, or physician-owned health plans will likely be using knowledgeable lawyers to protect their interests; individual physicians unfortunately are less willing to do so.

Q 7:7   How is a contract reviewed?

Ensure that all promises are obtained in writing. Then document, when possible, the specific intent of both sides and seek legal advice before signing any critical contract. The next step depends on the character of the transaction. When dealing with a typical agreement between an IPA and a physician (a contract with an HMO should be essentially identical and should be reviewed similarly), consider which parts of that agreement deserve scrutiny.

Q 7:8   What is the contract header?

The opening statement at the top of a contract is often called the "header" and contains information critical to the contract. Not paying attention to simple features of the header (e.g., using the wrong name or putting the contract in a personal name when it should be in the name of a professional corporation or group) is a common error. Other important points include:

- who the other side is
- in which state the other entity is incorporated

- an attempt in the miscellaneous section to impose the law of another state if the contract is litigated
- the effective date
- retroactive obligations and risks

Q 7:9   What are the duties and obligations of the physician?

Because most contracts contain an exchange of promises, one of the most important sections—no matter what it is called—is the duties (or covenants) of the physician. This needs to be read carefully, not only for what it includes, but also for what it might omit. An omission might be to the advantage of one party. Living with contracts that inaccurately describe obligations invites a later disagreement and possible litigation. The contract should not impose duties that a physician did not expect, does not want, or cannot fulfill. Pleas from the other side just to ignore unpleasant provisions, and assurances that they are pure formalities are to be ignored. If the provisions are not real or important, then they should be omitted. It is much easier to eliminate provisions in the negotiations than to later defend a failure to fulfill duties that the physician expected to be able to "ignore."

An interesting legal issue arises when the IPA wants the physician to agree not to provide services to any other IPAs (i.e., to be exclusive). Under some circumstances, exclusivity can serve to make life difficult for the payer's competitors by limiting the number of potential contracting physicians. The legal risk here is not for the physician, but for the IPA. Interestingly, some court cases have made the IPA's legal arguments sounder if the IPA pays the physician a higher compensation in return for the exclusivity.

Q 7:10   What are the duties and obligations of an IPA?

Just as important as listing the physician's duties is the catalog of services the IPA will provide. The list of duties to be performed by the IPA need not be exhaustive, but it is important that they and those of the physician are clearly delineated.

Q 7:11   What are some important aspects of the compensation section of the contract?

Usually the IPA's compensation duty is placed in a separate section of the contract because of its importance. Also, because of frequent changes in fee schedules and capitation rates, the real details are often placed in an attachment (exhibit, schedule, or appendix) to the contract that can be revised without amending the whole contract. A common mistake physicians make is accepting a contract in which the compensation appendix is missing completely or is obsolete or inaccurate. Obviously, a physician would never agree to work for the IPA without pay, so similarly a physician should not sign the contract without a clear provision stating what and how the physician is to be paid.

Although the amount and method (i.e., fee-for-service or capitation) of payment is important, the manner by which the physician is to receive payments is also important. For example, will the capitation payment be made on the 5th of the month or the 20th? The cash flow difference is substantial if many lives are involved. Because of the huge implications for the HMO, there is a real incentive for the payments to the IPA to be later rather than earlier. Then, of course, the IPA must turn those capitation payments around to the individual physicians. Thus, the time of payment is of critical concern to the HMO and may well be an item of contract. The implication for the IPA is less important because the number of lives is generally smaller, therefore, the IPA may be tempted not to specify timing. When the IPA's number of capitated lives increases, the issue may become proportionally more important for the physician group.

If payments are not received on time, there should be a fairly immediate remedy. For example, it is often attractive to be able to terminate the contract if payments are more than five days late more than two consecutive months. The payment of a late fee may also be appropriately agreed on. The presence and strength of such remedies will be determined by both the IPA's bargaining position and the importance that each party attaches to timely payment.

Those entering into capitation arrangements should be extremely careful. Although this style of payment may well be the wave of the future, it carries a number of risks—among which is adverse selection. Some physicians or groups attract patients with multiple serious problems. Good actuarial advice is needed on how to adjust capitation rates for this eventuality. Occasionally, contracts will provide for stop-loss insurance, in which the physician is paid additional sums when annual expenditures (based on what the patient would have cost under a fee-for-service payment system) exceed a fixed target amount.

"Term" and "termination" are two concepts frequently grouped together in contracts; however, they are different concepts entirely. The term of a contract is its stated duration. Termination refers to how the contract may be brought to a premature end before the completion of the term. Simply stating that a contract lasts indefinitely until it is terminated blends the two concepts. The interplay between term and termination is occasionally used to the disadvantage of the physician. For example, it is not uncommon to tell a physician that he or she is being given a one- or two-year contract, which is clearly stated in the contract. Buried in the termination section, however, may be a provision that the IPA or HMO can terminate the contract without reason with 60 days' written notice. Such a contract is, in reality, only a 60-day contract.

The contract's duration depends on the desires and relative bargaining position of the parties. Generally, the party getting the better long-term bargain desires a longer term. If one party is unsure of the deal's fairness or the reputation of the other party, it will want a shorter term contract. An important component of term provisions in contracts that automatically renew for additional terms is how much notice, if any, must be given if one party desires to exercise the option not to renew the contract. A one-year, automatically renewing contract with a required 6 months' notice not to renew creates the circumstance where the minimum remaining duration of the contract varies from 6 to 18 months. Fairly common terms in the industry today are one-year, automatically renewing contracts with 90-day, no-cause termination provisions. These contracts enable either party to end the contractual relationship fairly easily.

Termination provisions provide a means of stopping the contractual relationship because of the occurrence of some event or condition—or for no reason whatsoever. The HMO or IPA will insist it can terminate the contract rather quickly if the physician's character or competence is called into question. This would apply in the event of a sanction by the medical staff of a hospital, an accusation by the Office of the Inspector General, or a suspension or limitation of the physician's medical license. Typically, there is a fairly long list of events that can trigger a quick, for-cause termination of the agreement by the paying party. Because of the regulatory demands imposed directly or indirectly on HMOs and IPAs—as well as their vicarious liability exposure for actions by the physician—physicians typically are unsuccessful in reducing the timing or number of such triggers.

The physician should also consider what events should trigger his or her own right to terminate the agreement. For example, some contracts give the physician the right to terminate in the event that the paying party has not delivered more than a specified number of patients within a specified time period. Certainly the physician should have the right to terminate promptly if he or she is not paid as promised. However, the contract is likely to impose the duty on the physician to continue services to patients for some period of time even though he or she is not being paid. This is called the "hold harmless" provision and is imposed on HMOs by state insurance departments as a condition of lowering the HMO's cash reserve requirements. Most states do not technically require it; however, the HMO would be punished financially if it did not get that agreement from the physician.

Most contracts today provide the physician and the IPA the opportunity to terminate the contract prematurely with only 90 days' written notice (i.e., without cause). Absent special circumstances, such provisions make sense in that the relationship only continues over the long term if it is mutually beneficial.

The miscellaneous section of any contract is frequently ignored—to the peril of the reviewer. It often contains critical provisions. For example, contracts often state that the contract will be governed by the laws of, and even litigated in, a particular state. Failure to ensure that this is the state in which the practice or IPA resides can mean hiring lawyers in another state to fight a lawsuit at a distant site. The steps necessary to amend the contract are often given in the miscellaneous section, and occasionally provisions state that the IPA can amend the contract unilaterally, merely by giving the physician notice.

Q 7:12   What are the major features of antitrust applicable to medical practice?

Few legal concepts are more confusing to physicians than those comprising one of the most powerful concepts of commercial law: antitrust. Enacted in 1890 during the "trust busting" period of suspecting the abuse of large companies' economic power, the Sherman Act forbade certain types of behavior that were deemed to be harmful to the natural competitive forces of the American marketplace.

Three federal statutes provide the legal basis for most antitrust enforcement against health care providers—each one states a broad prohibition against a particular type of conduct that may, under certain circumstances, impermissibly restrain competition. The difficulty in predicting when these statutes apply stems from the unlimited scope of conduct they are used to measure. The same statutes govern competition in virtually every industry, from auto manufacturing to professional basketball, to banking, to health care. Every state has antitrust laws that, in most cases, closely mirror federal statutes.

Section 1 of the Sherman Act is the most commonly applied statute in the health care context. It prohibits contracts, agreements, and "conspiracies" between two or more people or entities found to "unreasonably" restrain competition. This prohibition has been applied to a wide variety of "joint conduct," including:

- exclusive contracts
- arrangements tying the purchase of one product or service to the purchase of a second
- organized resistance to managed care (i.e., boycotts)
- peer review process to exclude competitors
- IPA fee schedules and agreements between hospitals allocating the provision of specific services to each
- limiting advertising

Section 2 of the Sherman Act proscribes monopolization, attempted monopolization, and conspiracies to monopolize. Whether monopolization has occurred is generally determined by reference to the market share of an alleged monopolist, as well as the tactics used to obtain or maintain that market share. It is not a violation to obtain a monopoly through aggressive competition. The difficulty here is distinguishing aggressive competition from predatory, exclusionary, or otherwise unfair tactics. There is no simple test for distinguishing permitted from prohibited conduct, but aggressive conduct that goes beyond conventional "price, quality, and terms" competition is likely to come under scrutiny if it disadvantages rivals; for example, by "locking up" access to a large group of physicians.

Section 7 of the Clayton Act prohibits mergers, acquisitions, and joint ventures that may substantially lessen competition or tend to create a monopoly. This statute governs mergers and joint ventures. The significant feature of section 7 is that it does not require proof of an actual, immediate effect on competition. It requires only proof that the challenged transaction is likely to eventually lessen competition. Unlike the Sherman Act, which focuses on conduct, section 7 of the Clayton Act considers potential results (e.g., whether a change to the structure of the market such as the elimination of one competitor is likely to make the market less competitive).

For the practicing physician dealing with managed care, the most common antitrust issues arise in the context of choosing:

- how to avoid managed care
- how to pick partners to engage in managed care
- how to create IPAs or HMOs
- how to set fee schedules or capitation rates
- how to exclude or remove participating physicians
- how to contract with physicians on an exclusive basis

Q 7:13   What is price fixing?

Traditions of collegiality and fee-for-service physician payment have caused major price fixing problems for physicians. Because each physician or group of physicians is technically a competitor of other physicians, when physicians wish to band together for a preferred provider organization (PPO)-type of initiative, or even an IPA that contracts with HMOs on a fee-for-service basis, they are immediately at risk for the *per se* antitrust violation of price fixing if they create a fee schedule that is to be applied to all. *Per se* means that the conduct is condemned simply because it occurred, and that a challenger in court will be able to prevent the violator from offering any justifications whatsoever for the actions as evidence in a trial. Courts have been extremely strict on price fixing cases, and jail terms and huge fines are common in punitive judgments.

In 1992, after indictment sought by the Justice Department and a full trial, a jury convicted three dentists in Arizona of participating in a criminal conspiracy to fix prices in violation of the federal antitrust laws. Thus, price fixing challenges are to be avoided, even at the cost of extraordinary precautionary measures.

A recent expression of regulatory intent[1] by the two federal agencies enforcing the federal antitrust laws, the Antitrust Division of the Department of Justice and the Federal Trade Commission, states that unless groups of nonintegrated physicians such as IPAs, PPO panels, and physician-hospital organizations (PHOs) share some degree of risk and offer critical new services such as quality review and utilization management that promise the ultimate payers better prices, all price schedules must be prepared by the payers and agreed to individually by the physicians. The use of a "super messenger" that acts as a go-between for the payer and each physician, with little if any power to negotiate, is a means of avoiding the development of a single, unified fee schedule. However, it is quite cumbersome in all but the rural markets where it may be the only option in many cases.

Q 7:14   How may physicians achieve a status of "integrated economic entity" so that price fixing is not a risk when fee schedules are used?

In simplest terms, the integrated entity, such as a group practice, is a stand-alone business entity, separate from the physicians who participate in it. A PPO that merely markets a group of physicians to fee-for-service payers is not an entity receiving revenues for a sold product. The physicians provide the services and are paid individually for them. A capitated IPA, on the other hand, actually sells a bundle of services for a single price based on the number (and probably age and gender) of patients to be cared for. The IPA has revenues and it has a product. It can make money; it can lose money. It is even easier to understand why setting a fee schedule is acceptable for a capitated IPA that pays its physicians on a fee-for-service basis—it is the buyer, not the seller. Setting prices high artificially would harm the IPA, not help it. Further, if a capitated IPA were to raise the prices it pays artificially high, it would soon be out of business, to the detriment of its owners. Thus, integration involves the group of physicians being in a position such that the incentives to keep prices lower rather than higher are present.

Q 7:15   What is a boycott?

Another *per se* violation of antitrust laws is a boycott. Usually arising as organized efforts by medical societies or medical staff members to generate resistance to managed care, boycotts of managed care can take many forms. In the past, physicians have formed unions, thinking somehow that the narrow exemption from the antitrust laws granted to employees by the collective bargaining laws[2] would apply equally to collections of businesses that otherwise compete with one another. More subtle efforts sometimes take the shape of PPOs and IPAs that tie up a large segment of the community's physicians with exclusive contracts. They then negotiate with HMOs or PPOs, ostensibly on nonprice issues of quality or access, in a manner that makes penetration of the market by the managed care organization extremely difficult. Occasionally, federal agencies have challenged outright letter-writing campaigns to patients, newspaper advertisements, and medical staff harassment—all attacking physicians supportive of managed care. To avoid boycott risks, physicians should avoid sham organizations whose primary purpose is to restrain the advance of managed care in the community. Physicians should also avoid IPAs or other physician contracting organizations that contain a disproportionate share of the eligible physicians in the community.

Q 7:16   What are the contracting decisions compelled by antitrust considerations?

Many physicians are concerned about the potential for allegations of anticompetitive behavior arising from an IPA's refusal to grant a contract to a particular physician. A physician may complain, for example, that a group of physicians (the IPA board or credentials committee) is conspiring to restrict the physician from the market and that such activity will cause harm to the physician and to the community. Fortunately, laws relating to a physician's right to hospital medical staff membership is wholly different from those that apply to the IPA. There are few state laws dealing with a provider's right to participate in managed care organizations (e.g., the "any willing provider" laws), and these typically grant only limited appeal rights. There are few, if any, federal constitutional protections that apply. Provided that the HMO (and perhaps an IPA) has taken the extra steps to comply with the Health Care Quality Improvement Act,[3] an antitrust challenge is unlikely to be successful. Fortunately, physicians and their attorneys are beginning to understand this, and legal challenges are becoming less of an issue for physicians who participate in IPA governance.

Unless state laws provide otherwise, an IPA that is not dominant in its market (i.e., one that cannot dictate prices to payers or keep other IPAs from forming) can pick and choose among physicians with little regard for those sensitivities that apply so often in the medical staff context. Physicians can be rejected (i.e., be denied a contract or have their existing contract terminated or not renewed) for any of the following reasons:

- They are viewed as less skilled.
- They are inattentive to marketing needs.
- They deal with competitors of the IPA.
- They are not needed.
- They are merely unpopular.
- For no reason at all.

However, to minimize legal liability and to protect what remains of collegiality, physicians should take careful steps to see that other physicians are treated fairly and with a process that, while not due process, is at least polite.

Q 7:17   What is tortuous interference?

In many states, another legal theory of recovery, unrelated to antitrust but often arising in similar contexts, is tortuous interference (with existing or prospective contractual relationships). It also dictates careful treatment of physicians by an IPA. A tortuous interference scenario exists, for example, when a physician serves on the IPA committee making decisions about physician contracts, and his or her biggest competitor applies for a contract. The physician on the committee might want to take steps to ensure that this competitor does not later sue him or her alleging that the physician's position on the IPA committee was unfairly used to cause harm. It is permissible for the IPA to make harsh decisions based on its own needs; it is often not acceptable for an individual to use his or her position with an organization to further personal ends by excluding competitors or enemies.

Q 7:18   What is monopolization?

Section 2 of the Sherman Act does not prohibit an organization from being a monopoly; it only prohibits efforts to attain a monopoly. Enforcement of the Act focuses on certain types of behavior that are predatory, exclusionary, or otherwise unfair. Additionally, section 7 of the Clayton Act prohibits mergers, acquisitions, and joint ventures that could lessen competition substantially or might tend to create a monopoly. For most physicians, worries about a managed care organization getting so big that it has a monopolization problem are highly speculative in today's market. If they become principals in such a successful organization, they can afford excellent antitrust advice. Until then, concerns about too much size or success should be put aside and left to the lawyers.

Q 7:19   What, then, is the ideal size of a physician organization for HMO contracting?

The proper size for an IPA or PHO is an important issue for many nonlegal reasons. For example, for an IPA to attract physicians who are willing to accept reduced charges or capitation, the IPA must fulfill its promise to deliver new patients. It cannot do so if all of the physicians in the community are included. Because truly functional IPAs and PPOs tend to be small, antitrust authorities have stated that they were more concerned about IPAs and PPOs being overly inclusive rather than very restrictive on membership. An IPA or network that is too large often indicates an effort to block entry by other managed care organizations, especially if the IPA or network restricts its physicians from joining other similar organizations through exclusive contracts.

The *Statements of Antitrust Enforcement Policy in Health Care,*[4] issued by the Department of Justice and the Federal Trade Commission, provide insight on how the size of a physician organization will be viewed by the two agencies. For example, an IPA that only has nonexclusive contracts with its physicians will be in a safety zone for enforcement purposes as long as it includes less than 30 percent by specialty of the physicians in the market area. Should the contracts with the physicians be exclusive (i.e., restrict them from participating in any other IPA), then the limit on size is 20 percent by specialty. These size numbers are somewhat smaller than most antitrust experts have recommended in the past, and the agencies have recently approved larger groups who have formally requested guidance.

Q 7:20   What is the impact of the McCarran-Ferguson Act?

Physicians often wonder why insurance companies do not seem to follow the antitrust rules against price fixing and collusion that apply to everyone else in the industry. There is a good reason. Because insurance companies are highly regulated by the states, the Congress decided many years ago that it was appropriate to leave oversight of insurance company activities to the states. This act of Congress specifically exempts insurance companies from most applications of the federal antitrust laws. In the area of mergers and acquisitions, of course, the usual rules still apply. An insurance company also can set physician fee schedules because it is an integrated economic entity and is the buyer, not a collection of competitive sellers.

Q 7:21   What is the impact of state regulations on physician contracting?

Although there are some federal statutes and rules relating to HMOs—primarily those relating to federal qualification and special rules relating to coverage of Medicare and Medicaid patients—most of the rules that will affect how physicians can structure managed care contractual arrangements are determined at the state level by state insurance departments. These state agencies have been very aggressive in implementing their mandates to protect people with health insurance benefits. Although the federal Employee Retirement Income Security Act (ERISA)[5] exempts certain properly qualified employer health benefit plans from regulation by such state agencies, many state departments have limited the approaches available to providers who seek exclusive access to this pool of paying patients.

The regulation of HMOs is fairly straightforward; that of PPOs is more complex because there are two types: state-approved plans and ERISA plans. IPAs typically find rules governing their structure within the rules governing the character of organizations with which HMOs may contract.

Q 7:22   What are the two types of state-approved plans?

State-approved PPO plans. In virtually all states, the traditional freedom-of-choice provisions in state insurance codes have been amended to permit licensed insurance companies to offer health benefit plans that steer patients to certain physicians and hospitals with financial incentives. These PPOs are subject to prior approval by the state's insurance department and they must comply with all applicable state statutes and regulations. These PPOs also are subject to the "any willing provider" rules and any other organization, reimbursement, or coverage rules that might exist at the state level. For example, there may be special state rules mandating certain levels of coverage for patients with mental health impairments, with acquired immune deficiency syndrome (AIDS), or requiring coverage of chiropractic benefits.

ERISA PPO plans. Federal statute empowers employers to act as their own insurance companies for purposes of health benefits and to assume all of the actuarial risks of the employees' health plan. While employers often feel a great need to be attentive to the needs and desires of their employees, ERISA permits an employer to offer as many or as few benefits as it chooses, including none at all. Thus, should the employer wish to require all of its employees to seek care from only a single hospital and a small panel of physicians, it can do so. If it wants to steer its employees and their dependents to some providers with financial incentives tied to differential deductibles and coinsurance amounts, it can do so. State insurance rules do not apply, including any willing provider rules and mandated coverage rules.[6] (The Health Insurance Portability and Accountability Act of 1996, signed by President Clinton on August 21, 1996, mandating certain levels of parity for mental health benefits, somewhat modifies this freedom from mandates.) Thus, physicians and their hospital partners have a great deal of freedom in structuring arrangements targeted to patients covered by ERISA plans; however, one freedom that usually is not included is that of accepting capitation from the employer.

Q 7:23   How do PPOs capitate?

Capitation in the PPO context is usually both an operational impracticality and legal misdeed. Unless there is a captive population of patients, which is only possible in the context of HMOs, capitation is not feasible (with the exception, perhaps, of some type of per patient payment to the occasional PPO gatekeeper physician). When patients can choose to go outside of a restricted panel of providers, it is extremely difficult for actuaries to predict appropriate capitation levels.

Q 7:24   What is a point-of-service HMO?

A point-of-service HMO is one with an additional wraparound policy included that attempts, for all of the pool of patients, to guess the out-of-panel costs. Although it is an attractive marketing tool, HMOs are not sure it will be practical to implement. As to the legal issue, the problem is that capitation puts the receiver of the capitation into the business of insurance, an activity regulated by the state. Unless a physician, group of physicians, or physician-hospital organization meets a statutory or regulatory exemption, capitation is not permitted. An IPA is usually permitted to accept and pay capitation because of certain statements in the state's HMO act about how HMOs can pay physicians. In a few states, a medical group—in Texas, for example, even an IPA wholly owned by physicians—may be able to accept capitation from employers for physician services only.

Q 7:25   What defines an HMO?

HMOs are creatures of state law. Although the federal government grants privileges, such as federal qualification or the right to enroll Medicare and Medicaid patients to HMOs that comply with certain federal requirements, the technical rules about how physicians, hospitals, and provider joint ventures can engage in initiatives designed to attract HMO patients are almost entirely those of the local state government. In every case, a physician with specific questions will have to consult with an attorney or other consultant knowledgeable about their state's laws.

Frequently, HMOs contract directly with individual physicians and pay them directly. Payment can be made on a fee-for-service or capitation basis. Variations abound in whether the capitation goes only to the primary care physicians, to specialists, to both, or to neither. Formulas commonly establish mathematical risk accounts that pool the risk among varying groups of physicians. It is common to put primary care physicians at risk for specialty physician referrals, as well as hospital and even pharmacy use.

Some experts have expressed the opinion that physicians who contract directly with HMOs are at a negotiating disadvantage because the HMO can pit one physician against another. These experts believe that when physicians have set up the network or IPA and bargain with the HMO for a block of dollars (or percentage of premium) representing the entire physician services budget, they have increased the pressure on the HMO to bargain in good faith. For an IPA that is properly established and assumes enough risk as an entity, this structure creates in a legally permissible manner some of the collective bargaining power that physicians have often sought. It is usually possible under state law for a properly organized IPA to accept capitation payments from an HMO and to pay the physicians with whom it contracts on a fee-for-service or capitation basis. A controversy in a number of states is whether the IPA can assume the risk that a fixed capitation payment represents, because assuming actuarial risk is technically identical to being in the business of insurance. However, the weight of opinion in most states is that when the capitation payment to the IPA, or whatever the group of physicians is called, comes from a licensed HMO, all of whose contracts and relationships are subject to state regulatory scrutiny, the capitation payment is acceptable.

In a few states, there is even a controversy as to whether an IPA, as opposed to an HMO, can pay physicians on a capitation basis. Generally, payment by an IPA on this basis creates no regulatory risk for the physician and little for the IPA. If such payments are impermissible, state enforcement activities will generally be directed at the HMO. The usual argument against capitation for physicians and physician groups is that acceptance of a fixed payment in return for a variable amount of services—the volume of which is dependent on the occurrence of illness—puts the physician or group in the business of insurance. Fortunately, many HMO acts clearly make such payments permissible, thus avoiding the violation of the state's insurance code. Similar problems occasionally appear when an HMO wishes to pay hospitals based on capitation. For a single hospital or integrated hospital system, the counterargument is that a fixed payment for variable services constitutes not an actuarial risk, but merely a pricing risk, much like the open salad bar at the local steak house.

Payment of a global capitation amount that covers both physician and institutional services to any entity causes regulatory concerns in most states. Typical HMO statutes state with some specificity how hospitals and physicians may be paid, and few provide for a shifting of such huge actuarial risk downstream to a nonregulated entity. When individual physicians or individual hospitals are capitated, the argument can be made with some force that the payment represents merely a pricing risk—like the open salad bar. When a new entity is holding money that must be paid to others, however, it is usually characterized as an entity engaged in the business of insurance. Despite great fanfare about how global capitation to

PHOs and HMOs is the wave of the future, little progress toward this end has occurred. Part of the problem is overcoming the serious regulatory hurdles (including the possibility of fines on the magnitude of $10,000 per day); the other part is that many HMOs are not willing to pass on the potential profit margins that global capitation can represent. Despite the regulatory barriers, separate contractual agreements between an HMO and physicians or an IPA can usually provide for additional payments from the HMO if certain institutional budget targets are met—thus accomplishing much the same objective. And in some states (e.g., Tennessee), new statutes specifically authorize payment of global capitation by an HMO to a PHO.

Q 7:26   What are the tax consequences of an IPA?

It is common for IPAs to operate on an entrepreneurial basis, with the owners or investors who provide the sweat equity and capital sharing in the surplus remaining after the capitation payment has been used to pay all of the IPA's payment obligations. If the IPA is a nonprofit corporation, which is common, care will have to be exercised in shifting the money to owners and investors because dividends or payments resembling dividends cannot be paid by a nonprofit corporation. This often is achieved through a management company. Note that nonprofit corporate status has different names in different states and that nonprofit status is completely different in principle and concept from federal or state tax-exempt status. A nonprofit corporate IPA will almost certainly be taxable just as any other corporation. It is extremely rare for IPAs or even HMOs to achieve tax-exempt status, and the industry generally is moving away from tax exemption.

Q 7:27   What are the implications for capitation in the context of self-insured employer benefit plans?

When physicians become comfortable with capitation, they often assume that the next objective is to leave the HMO out of the loop and contract directly with employers for a fixed payment for covered employees and beneficiaries. This type of initiative is very challenging legally because the HMOs lobby hard with state regulators to prevent this loss of business. Further, state regulators do not favor self-funded employer plans because they shift premiums away from licensed insurance companies and HMOs, all of which pay state premium taxes.

Insurance departments typically argue that acceptance by a group of physicians (or a PHO) of a fixed monthly payment from an employer for a variable amount of services constitutes the business of insurance that requires the entity to be licensed as an insurance company by the state. Fortunately, a group practice can argue with considerable legal force that it is a single *person* that is merely accepting a pricing risk, like the open salad bar. This dispute has even been the subject of litigation in a number of states with varying results. In many states now, however, physician groups are feeling confident enough to accept capitation for physician services only. It is unlikely, however, that similar confidence can be afforded to PHOs and networks of providers that are not truly integrated businesses.

Q 7:28   What are the legal implications for managed care in Medicare and Medicaid?

During most of its history, Medicare paid for inpatient hospital services on a formula related to attributable costs. In 1983, it shifted to fixed, diagnosis-related, predetermined payments per admission. This step was the beginning of the effort to shift certain financial risks to hospitals where efforts to manage costs could be more effective. In 1982, however, the real beginning of risk shifting had already occurred with the authorization by the Tax Equity and Fiscal Responsibility Act[7] (TEFRA) of enrollment of Medicare patients by HMOs.

HMOs may enroll Medicare patients in their health plans provided they have taken the proper steps to obtain that privilege. Federally qualified HMOs may proceed directly to the regional offices of the Health Care Financing Administration (HCFA) to negotiate contracts covering Medicare plans. However, even for those HMOs that choose to skip federal qualification, there is a process by which they can obtain the same right to go to the regional office for contract negotiations. Once approved, the HMO can enroll Medicare patients according to a set of federal guidelines that makes it very difficult for the HMO to attempt to select only for healthy patients. On enrollment of Medicare patients in one of its plans, HCFA pays the HMO a monthly premium that is tied to the patient's age, sex, and whether the patient was institutionalized just before enrollment.

For physicians, the main difference in contracting with an HMO to provide medical services to Medicare patients compared to commercial patients is the compensation. Because Medicare patients consume many more medical and institutional services than do non-Medicare patients, the federal premium payment is often three or more times that of commercial patients. For fee-for-service contracts with HMOs or IPAs, payments are in no manner tied to the usual Medicare fee schedule and are often set at some discount rate. For capitation contracts, the capitation amount should be three to four times what the capitation amount is for commercial patients in the same market.

From the regulatory perspective, the Medicare HMO patient is treated primarily as a non-Medicare patient. Thus, for example, it appears that such a patient can be admitted to a skilled nursing facility without the prior hospitalization always required of a regular Medicare patient. Although the usual Medicare rules concerning fraud and abuse technically apply, it is now the HMO that is at risk for payment for unnecessary services; therefore, any enforcement efforts are more likely to come from that quarter. To a degree much greater than for commercial enrollees, Medicare HMO patients have the ability to shift easily into, out of, and between HMOs.

Perhaps the most intrusive requirement for health plans covering Medicare (and Medicaid) HMO enrollees is the recently finalized rule[8] concerning physician incentives. Through a statutory and regulatory journey that began in 1986, a new set of regulations strictly limits the degree of risk and reward that can be passed on to physicians treating such patients. The net effect is to set limits on the potential upside rewards (usually in the form of end-of-quarter or end-of-year bonus payments) or downside penalties (through withholds) to physicians by means of reduced use of specialty or institutional services. Fortunately, it will be the HMOs that will have the burden of disclosing the presence of applicable incentive arrangements and determining that appropriate limits (or stop-loss insurance) are in place. Unfortunately, the regulations may have the untoward effect of limiting the degree to which physicians can assume economic control over the majority of services that consume so much of the Medicare managed care dollar.

A growing number of states permit managed care plans to enroll Medicaid patients; however, each state administers its own Medicaid plan using both state and federal funds. Generally a state can shift some or all of its patients eligible for Medicaid into managed care plans according to a written plan approved by the federal government agency that monitors Medicaid. Such waivers can be unique to each state. Physicians interested in Medicaid managed care should contact their state medical association. Some physician groups have reported enthusiasm and success for Medicaid managed care; however, they also report an approach very different from that for the usual managed care patient. We can expect that the legal requirements associated with such plans will likewise be somewhat unique. Market forces in Medicaid are moving rapidly and can be expected to follow the stresses that Medicare is placing on HMOs.

Physicians must accept expert help as they move into new business arrangements for which medical school and residency did not train them. Like it or not, big is going to be better in most cases, and collective behavior, carefully crafted along legally permissible lines, is essential to survival. Information of every sort will be critical to success, and it will only be available to those who know how to create it, purchase it, or capture it. Lawyers, accountants, actuaries, and, occasionally, investment bankers, will become necessary partners with physicians as new ways of selling health care services emerge. With careful attention to detail, physicians can capitalize on their unique statutory franchise to regain control over their industry. Failure to do so will only further the dominance of monolithic insurance companies over both patients and physicians.

Managed care is a large and growing segment of the economic lives of physicians and requires full attention. Physicians should take great care that they do not, through inadvertence or haste, create organizations or arrangements that run afoul of technical legal requirements. Adverse results can vary from marketing delays while things are fixed, to huge fines, lost contracts, or jail time. Inattention to the technical rules that govern contracts can create huge losses or avoidable requirements that are burdensome. Above all, physicians should understand that this is an era where legal mistakes are no longer acceptable. Either the enforcement authorities will discover them or, more likely, former colleagues will take advantage of them.

Table 7–1 provides a checklist for managed care contracting.

Table 7–1 Managed Care Agreement Checklist

Provisions	*Recommendations*
DEFINITIONS	
Covered person/member	Need to know who will be eligible to receive services. Are dependents included?
Covered services	Should be those services for which payer is obligated to pay under member's health plan. Definition should not imply that the physician must provide services that he or she does not customarily provide.
Emergency or emergency service	Definition must be broad enough to cover Consolidated Omnibus Budget Reconciliation Act screening and stabilization of treatment required by law.
Medical necessity	Definition should be reasonably specific and be based on community standards rather than dictated solely by payer.
Noncovered services	If defined, should not imply that physician cannot bill for noncovered services.
Payer	If the independent practice association, preferred provider organization (PPO), or health maintenance organization (HMO) will extend the contractual discounts to other payers, the agreement needs to include an attachment listing all such payers, and all additional payers must be approved in advance (i.e., no "silent PPOs").
OBLIGATIONS OF THE PHYSICIAN	
Acceptance of new patients	Must the physician accept payer's members and for how long? Is there an upper or lower limit on the number of new patients that can or must be accepted?
Closing physician's practice	How much advance notice must be given before closing the practice to new patients? Can the physician eventually close practice to new managed care patients but continue taking other patients?
Credentialing standards	Review the standards and be sure that they are reasonable. Are they based on

continues

Table 7–1 continued

	National Committee for Quality Assurance standards?
Deselection process and rights	Review payer's policy to be sure it is fair. If possible, the physician should be able to appeal deselection if it is based on professional competence or quality of care, especially if a National Practitioner Data Bank report is involved.
Encounter reports	Most payers require encounter reports for statistical purposes. Be sure the requirements are not unduly burdensome.
Indemnification	Many physicians' insurers will not agree to cover liabilities assumed under indemnification provisions. If included, make sure indemnification is mutual and that each party is only indemnified for the acts or omissions of its own employees and agents.
INSURANCE	
Limits	The usual limits are a maximum of $1 million/$3 million and are much lower in many markets.
Tail insurance	Should be limited to a reasonable time period, such as three to five years following termination of contract. Check the applicable statutes of limitations.
Malpractice reports	Be sure the reporting requirements are reasonable. Physician should not have to report minor nuisance settlements.
Payer access to books and records	Permit access only to books and records related to the provision of services under the contract. Payer must give reasonable advance notice and must not disrupt the usual activities of the physician's practice.
Primary care physician duties	Duties should be clearly defined. What gatekeeper duties are required?
Referrals to nonparticipating physicians	Requirements and procedures should be clear. Under what circumstances can the physician obtain call coverage by a nonparticipating physician? Can emergency patients be referred without prior approval?
Scope of services	Restrict to those services customarily

continues

Table 7–1 continued

	provided by physicians.
Standards of care	Standards should be based on community standards if possible.
Termination of physician/ patient relationship	Should be able to terminate relationship with a disruptive or noncompliant patient.
Utilization review (UR)/quality assurance (QA) cooperation	Review the UR/QA plan. Is it reasonable?

OBLIGATIONS OF THE PAYER

Claims administration	Will claims be administered by the payer or a third-party administrator (TPA)? Payer should retain ultimate responsibility for making sure claims are administered properly.
Claims payment	Payment of complete and undisputed claims should be made within 30 to 45 days of receipt. Failure to pay in a timely manner should result in the loss of negotiated discounts.
Credentialing duties	Will credentialing be conducted by the payer or by some other entity? If conducted by a third party, or if required to use payer's credentialing standards, payer should retain ultimate liability.
Demographic reports on members	Payer should offer physician periodic reports showing demographic information on members and payers, including geographic concentration and utilization patterns.

ELIGIBILITY VERIFICATION

Prompt availability	24-hour, toll-free telephone service is optimal. If 24-hour service is not available, are the hours convenient? How long must the physician wait for a response?
Verification binding	The physician should be entitled to rely on verification that has been properly obtained. If the payer erroneously verifies eligibility, it should be obligated to pay for care given in reliance on the verification.
Indemnification	If included, make sure that each party only indemnifies for the acts or omissions of its own employees and agents.

continues

Table 7–1 continued

Liability insurance	Payer should have adequate general liability insurance and insolvency insurance or reinsurance.
Marketing	Payer should agree to include the physician's name and specialty in all directories. Physician's prior approval should be required for any marketing material that includes references to the physician.
Report payer insolvency	Payer should be required to notify the physician if it becomes insolvent, in which case the physician should not be required to continue providing services to the payer's members except during acute episodes of care.
State license or certification	If the payer is subject to certification by the state, copies of such approvals should be obtained.
Steerage incentives	Make sure that incentives offered by payers to their members are adequate and that members are not made aware of these incentives. Do NOT agree to any waiver or discount of copayments or deductibles that might violate state or federal laws.
UR/QA PLAN	
Administration	Who administers the UR/QA plan—the payer, a TPA, a physician hospital association, or a hospital?
Identity of reviewer	Is the reviewer a qualified nurse, physician, or specialist?
MEDICAL RECORDS	
Payment for copies	If possible, the payer should be required to pay for copies at a reasonable fee.
Patient consent	The payer should obtain the member's advance written consent to the release of medical records at the time the member applies for insurance coverage.
Maintain confidentiality	All patient records should be maintained in compliance with state and federal confidentiality laws.
Modification to UR requirements	Changes in UR requirements should be agreed to in writing by both parties before

continues

Table 7–1 continued

	they can become effective. Do not agree to unilateral modifications by the payer if possible. At least insist on prior notification.
On-site UR visits	On-site visits should be announced at least 24 hours in advance, and reviewers should agree to comply with physician's policies and requirements. Visits must not interfere with patient care or disrupt the physician's usual course of business.
PRECERTIFICATION	
Prompt availability	Toll-free telephone service is optimal. If 24-hour service is not available, are the hours convenient? How long must the physician wait for a response?
Exemption for emergencies	The physician must not be required to obtain precertification in an emergency, since delays could endanger the patient and violate state and federal laws.
Advance approval for elective admission	How many days prior to admission?
Concurrent review	Will on-site visits at the hospital be required?
Retrospective review	If retrospective denials are allowed, the contract should include a clause that prohibits such denials based on medical necessity as long as the physician obtained valid precertification prior to providing services.
TERM AND TERMINATION	
Automatic renewal	Never include an automatic renewal unless the contract can be terminated without cause after a reasonable period of notice.
Length of term	A long term is acceptable if this is an extremely desirable contract. If physician is unsure of the benefits, a shorter term is preferable.
TERMINATION WITH CAUSE	
Advance written notice	30 days is recommended.
Opportunity to cure	Should be allowed to cure breach to the reasonable satisfaction of the other party.

continues

Table 7–1 continued

Repeated breach	Immediate termination should be allowed, without opportunity to cure, upon repeated breach.
Insolvency	Immediate termination is vital, without opportunity to cure, if payer becomes insolvent.

TERMINATION WITHOUT CAUSE

Advance written notice	Anywhere from 45 to 90 days is recommended.
When effective	Will termination be effective at the end of the notice period or not until the end of the current term?

POSTTERMINATION
TREATMENT OF MEMBERS

Length of time	Try to limit to lesser of 30 days or completion of current course of treatment. Try to avoid any requirement that treatment be continued until the end of the term of the member's health plan.
Reimbursement	If long-term continued treatment is required, reimbursements should revert to a discount from charges rather than capitated or per case rates.
Posttermination contact with members	Some payers will not allow posttermination solicitation or contact with members or payers. However, physician should be allowed to conduct his or her usual marketing activities as long as derogatory or negative statements about payer are not made.
Termination if laws change	The parties should be required to re-negotiate in good faith in order to bring the agreement into compliance with the new laws, but if they are unable to agree, the contract should terminate automatically.

REIMBURSEMENT

AUDITS AND DISPUTED CLAIMS

Explanation	The payer should give the physician a written explanation of his or her claims that are being audited.

continues

Table 7–1 continued

Offsets or withholds before appeal	Before any funds are withheld, the physician should have the opportunity to appeal.
Claim forms	Should be similar to the standard forms used by Medicare and other payers. If electronic billing is required, physician must be sure he or she is equipped to comply.

COLLECTION FROM MEMBER

Deductible and copayments	Find out in advance the amounts set out in payer's health plans. Avoid waiving or discounting deductibles and copayments, as this could violate some insurance laws unless fully disclosed.
When collected	Are copayments collected prior to hospital admission, at time of service, or after payer has paid?
Hold harmless if payer defaults	This type of provision should be restricted, if possible, to HMO members. Try to reserve the right to collect payment from non-HMO members if payer becomes insolvent or otherwise fails to pay.
Member requests noncovered services	If member requests a noncovered service, physician should have the right to collect payment from the member.
Coordination of benefits	Should allow physician to collect 100% of his or her usual and customary charges as long as the payer's share of the bill does not exceed the negotiated rates.
"Most favored nations" clause	Avoid these clauses if at all possible. They require the physician to inform the payer of any lower rates given to other payers and to extend the same low rates to the payer. By releasing information about rates given to other payers, the physician will probably be in violation of the other payer's contractual confidentiality requirements. Additionally, it is often very difficult to compare different payment methodologies to determine who is getting the lowest overall rate.
Payment for new services	If new services are added after the original rates were set, the new services should either be subject to separate

continues

Table 7–1 continued

	reimbursement rather than included in a capitated or per case rate, or else the rates should be renegotiated to compensate physician for additional costs.
Rate changes	If the physician's charges are increased, does the discount automatically change so that the overall reimbursement stays the same? The physician should have the right to renegotiate rates periodically, and if the parties cannot agree on new rates, consider adding an automatic increase based on the consumer price index.
Stop-loss provision	Make sure stop-loss protection (such as outlier limits or reinsurance) is included in case of unexpectedly expensive or lengthy treatment.
Time frame for submitting clean fee-for-service claims	The physician should have at least 60 days in which to submit clean claims and longer if a delay is beyond the physician's reasonable control. Payer should notify physician promptly if additional information is needed in order to process a claim.
Time frame for paying claims	The payer should pay within 30 to 45 days of receiving a clean claim. If payer does not pay in time, the claim should revert to 100% of usual and customary charges rather than the negotiated rates.
TYPE OF PAYMENT	
Discount off charges	Make sure the discount is based on the physician's usual and customary charges, rather than on what the payer decides is a reasonable charge.
Per case or bundled services	Are there different rates for different levels of care?
CAPITATED	
Withholds or risk pools	What percentage is withheld? What other physicians are included in the risk pool, and are they appropriate utilizers? How often are the risk pools reconciled and paid out?
Clear financial responsibility matrix	Who is responsible for what payments? Who pays for out-of-plan services?

continues

Table 7–1 continued

MISCELLANEOUS
Amendments
        Should not agree to unilateral amendments by payer. All amendments must be in writing and signed by both parties.

Assignment
        Neither party should assign without the written consent of the other party.

CONFIDENTIALITY
Medical records
        Medical records must be kept confidential in accordance with applicable laws.

Financial records
        The payer must agree not to divulge financial information provided by the physician, including rates and charge master information.

Policies and procedures
        The payer must agree to return all confidential policies upon termination or expiration of the contract.

Subcontracting of services
        The physician should not agree to a prohibition on subcontracting of services. Such a prohibition would prevent the physician from subcontracting for ancillary services. The physician should be allowed to subcontract for various services as long as he or she retains licensure and overall responsibility for all such services.

Source: Reprinted with permission from *Making Sense of Managed Care*, pp. 167–176, © 1997, American College of Physician Executives.

NOTES

1. Department of Justice and the Federal Trade Commission, *Statements of Antitrust Enforcement Policy in Health Care* (Washington, DC: U.S. Government Printing Office, 28 August, 1996).
2. National Labor Relations Act, 29 U.S.C. §§ 151 *et seq.*
3. Health Care Quality Improvement Act, 42 U.S.C. §§ 11101 *et seq.*
4. National Labor Relations Act, 29 U.S.C. §§ 151 *et seq.*
5. Employee Retirement Income and Security Act of 1974, 29 U.S.C. §§ 1001 *et seq.*
6. The Health Insurance Portability and Accountability Act of 1996. U.S. Government Printing Office.
7. The Tax Equity and Fiscal Responsibility Act. U.S. Government Printing Office.
8. "Medicare and Medicaid Programs 42 C.R.F. part 1003, Final Regulations of Requirements for Physician Incentive Plans in Prepaid Health Care Organizations," *Federal Register* 61 (27 March, 1996), 60.

CHAPTER 8

HMOs and Liability

Cyndi M. Jewell and Sheryl Tatar Dacso

INTRODUCTION

On May 22, 1997, Texas Governor George W. Bush allowed Senate Bill (SB) 386[1] to pass into law without his signature, making Texas the first state to enact a statute authorizing suits against managed care entities.[2] The avowed purpose of SB 386 is to make managed care entities liable in the same manner that physicians and other health care providers are liable. Such accountability was not possible without legislation, according to the senate committee that considered the bill, because Texas law prohibits the corporate practice of medicine. The committee, in formulating the legislation, concluded that the corporate practice prohibition "prevents managed care organizations from being held legally accountable when making health care decisions which affect the quality of diagnosis, care and treatment of an enrollee in a health plan." SB 386 does more than merely overturn the bar to vicarious liability for provider decisions. It also makes managed care entities liable for any "determination which affects the quality of the diagnosis, care, or treatment provided to the plan's . . . enrollees," thus providing the basis for lawsuits related to denial of treatment and other usage issues. This chapter reviews the major areas of health maintenance organization (HMO) liability, discusses the reasons behind the enactment of SB 386, and addresses some of the positive and negative implications of this legislation as a model for other states.

LIABILITY ISSUES—BACKGROUND

Q 8:1   What are the major areas of liability exposure for an HMO under managed care?

Tort liability. Tort liability exposure for an HMO can arise through its relationships with providers, other insurers, plan administrators, utilization review agents, and even employers. An HMO's liability can also occur as a consequence of its own acts or omissions that result in injury or harm to people or property. Because managed care arrangements involve financial issues associated with care delivery, there are evolving issues associated with fundamental utilization management activities of health plans and managed care organizations.

An HMO may be liable for malpractice and professional liability under an independent corporate liability theory for failure to supervise and monitor its program and providers or it can be directly liable for the utilization review process itself. An HMO can also be vicariously liable for the activities of providers who are either employed or under contract with the HMO. Finally, an HMO may be liable for intentional or negligent infliction of emotional distress, unfair business practices, or wrongful interference in the doctor-patient relationship.

Liability exposure has been identified in the following areas:

- Intentional interference with the doctor-patient relationship. In *DeMeurers v. Health Net*, 1 BNA's Managed Care Reporter 415, November 1, 1995, an arbitration panel found that HMO officials had forced a physician to reverse his treatment decision.[3]
- Breach of fiduciary duty. In *Wickline v. State of California*, 192 Cal. App. 3d 1630 (1986), the court noted a physician's fiduciary duty to the patient to give priority to the patient's needs over the concerns of all others, including the physician. In the later case of *Ching v. Gaines et. al.*, Cal. Super. Ct., Ventura County No. 137878 (November 15, 1995), a judge overruled the HMO's pretrial attempts to eliminate a cause of action based on breach of fiduciary duty related to financial incentives not to refer patients to specialists.[4]
- Negligence *per se*. Another cause of action could be raised by violation of criminal statutes in a civil action to show negligence *per se*. For example, the California Penal Code 206 states, "Every person who, with the intent to cause cruel or extreme pain and suffering for the

purpose of revenge, extortion, persuasion or for any other sadistic purpose, inflicts great bodily injury . . . upon the person of another, is guilty of torture." This has not yet been presented as a cause of action under managed care.

- Negligence and vicarious liability related to treatment and negligent selection and credentialing of physician providers. In *Dukes v. U.S. Health Care Systems of Pennsylvania*, 57 F.3d 350 (3d Cir. 1995); *cert. denied*, U.S. 116 S. Ct. 564, 133 L. Ed. 2d 489 (1995), the widow of a plan subscriber was successful in maintaining a cause of action despite the defendant's efforts to seek Employee Retirement Income Security Act (ERISA) preemption on the basis of the fact that the HMO arranged for the actual medical treatment for plan participants. A plaintiff's efforts to hold an HMO liable under a theory of vicarious liability for its selected physicians' activities was also upheld in the case of *Chaghervand v. CareFirst*, 909 F. Supp. 304 (D. Md. 1995).

- Restrictions on access and choice of provider. In the case of *Rodriguez v. Pacificare of Texas, Inc.*, 980 F.2d 1014 (5th Cir. 1993), *cert. denied*, 113 S. Ct. 2456, 124 L. Ed. 2d 671 (1993), an employee went outside his HMO to consult an orthopaedic surgeon who placed him in therapy. When the HMO refused to cover the unapproved expenses, Rodriguez filed suit in Texas (state court) against the HMO and primary care physician for failing to provide prompt and adequate medical care and coverage.

- Negligent utilization review decisions. In *Corcoran v. United Healthcare, Inc.*, 956 F.2d 1321 (5th Cir. 1992), *cert. denied*, 506 U.S. 1033, 113 S. Ct. 812, 121 L. Ed. 2d 684 (1992), the court determined that despite the adverse outcome of the utilization review decision regarding benefits, the role of utilization review affects the benefits available under a benefit plan and, therefore, is subject to ERISA preemption.

- Negligent design of financial incentives or cost-containment programs. In *Shea v. Esensten*, 107 F.3d 625 (8th Cir. 1997), *cert. denied*, 118 S. Ct. 297 (October 14, 1997), the court ruled that an HMO has a fiduciary duty under ERISA to disclose physician financial incentives discouraging patient referrals to specialists.

Contract liability. ERISA imposes a fiduciary duty on plan administrators and even on employers. Liability arising out of a breach of this duty has been found when employers mislead employees regarding future employment benefits (*Varity Corp. v. Howe*, 516 U.S. 134 L. Ed. 2d 130, 116 S. Ct. 1065 [1996]), financial incentives to contracted physicians (see *Shea* above), and fraudulent inducement to forgo benefits and breach of contract (*Smith v. Texas Children's Hospital*, 84 F.3d 152 [5th Cir. 1996]). Insurance professionals may also become liable for professional negligence outside of ERISA (see *Coyne & Delany v. Selman*, 98 F.3d 1457 [4th Cir. 1996]).

Breach of contract claims are also part of the claim of bad faith. Many courts have held that insurance companies owe those they insure a duty of good faith and fair dealing in evaluating claims. This theory has a logical extension to direct contract arrangements. The elements of a bad-faith claim include the absence of a reasonable basis for denying benefits and the insurer's knowledge or reckless disregard of the lack of a reasonable basis for denying the claim. Factors viewed by the courts as having significance in determining bad faith include: (1) an insurer's failure to contact the member's attending physician to discuss the patient's condition before denying coverage; (2) failure to obtain the patient's progress notes and follow procedures for claims review before determining the services were not medically necessary; and (3) failure to inform a member of his or her right to appeal an adverse decision and settle disputes through arbitration.

Q 8:2   What are the more recent legal threats to physicians who practice under managed care arrangements?

Physicians operating under managed care arrangements are encountering novel theories of liability beyond claims for medical malpractice. These theories, such as breach of fiduciary duty, are often based on the results of economic credentialing directed patient care, gatekeeping, and using economic incentives to ration or withhold care (see *Wickline v. State of California*, 239 Cal. Rptr. 810 [Ct. App. 1986], *rev dismissed*, remanded 741 P. 2d 613 [Cal. 1987]). Causes of action brought against groups that participate in managed care arrangements include:

- medical malpractice
- intentional or negligent interference with a contractual relationship

- intentional or negligent infliction of emotional distress
- wrongful interference with the doctor-patient relationship
- intentional or negligent misrepresentation
- breach of fiduciary duty

Physicians have become more aggressive in challenging some of the actions and policies being undertaken by managed care organizations (MCOs), which may range from economic or punitive fiscal policies to deselection of physicians from the plan. Physicians are responding by bringing legal actions against MCOs under theories of slander, breach of contract, or failure to afford due process and retaliation.

Q 8:3   How does a managed care entity become legally liable?

The MCO has a duty of care. In the context of managed care, most lawsuits brought against an HMO for negligence relate to either the HMO's exercise of judgment in medical decisions or the selection and retention of participating providers. As discussed in Q 8:1, the effect of an HMO's making a coverage determination is subject to ERISA preemption. This relates most often to decisions affecting utilization and medical necessity.

Selection of providers. Because an MCO directs its enrollees or sub-scribers to use particular providers, it has a duty to exercise care in selecting and monitoring those who serve as its participating providers. This independent duty of care has been established over the years for hospitals and has direct applicability to MCOs. In *Harrell v. Total Health Care, Inc.* (1989 WL 153066 [Mo. App.], *aff'd*, 781 S.W.2d 58 [Mo. 1989]), the concept of corporate responsibility for provider selection was imposed on an HMO after a patient injury. In *McClellan v. Health Maintenance Organization of Pennsylvania* (604 A. 2d 1053 [Pa. Super. 1992]), the court held that an independent practice association (IPA)-model HMO had a nondelegable duty to select and retain only competent primary care physicians. The court noted that to establish liability against the HMO the plaintiff would have to show that: (1) the HMO had undertaken to render services to subscribers that it should recognize as necessary for the subscribers' protection; (2) the HMO failed to use reasonable care in selecting, retaining, or evaluating the primary care physician; and (3) the risk of harm to the subscriber was increased as a result of the HMO's failure to use reasonable care.

Selection of utilization review organizations. When a managed care organization contracts with a utilization review organization (URO), it exposes itself to liability for negligent selection of its URO. As with provider selection, an MCO should focus on the following criteria in selecting and monitoring UROs: (1) Determine whether the URO or personnel are properly licensed (if required by state law) and comply with the American Board of Quality Assurance and Utilization Review Physicians or other certification groups; (2) make sure the policies and procedures are clear and are followed consistently; and (3) review the qualifications of the URO personnel (e.g., nurse reviewers should be appropriately licensed and trained, with specified experience). Utilization review (UR) procedures should ensure that:

1. The proper personnel review the cases.
2. Physician reviewers practice in the area of medicine relevant to the cases they review.
3. There is discussion with the attending physician before issuing a denial.
4. The basis of denials and protocols followed are documented.
5. Patients and physicians have the right to appeal denials and a procedure exists for doing so.
6. Medical criteria are based on local practice standards (unless dealing with a specialty hospital).
7. Denials are communicated to the patient, who is informed about his or her rights.

Q 8:4   What is the potential liability of an MCO that performs utilization reviews?

An MCO that performs utilization reviews may have liability exposure for bad patient outcomes if the UR procedure is defective, if it is applied improperly, or if the UR decision is negligent. The leading case in this area, *Wickline v. State of California,* (239 Cal. Rptr. 810 [Ct. App. 1986], *rev dismissed,* remanded 741 P. 2d 613 [Cal. 1987]) recognized the potential liability of third-party payers. Liability in the UR process can result from failure to gather appropriate information before making a UR determination, failure to inform members of their right to appeal adverse UR decisions, or failure to issue a timely UR decision.

Based on the current state of the law under the *Corcoran* case (see Q 8:1), however, to the extent that the utilization review affects the determination of benefits and their availability under a health plan, the activities are subject to ERISA and state tort or contract claims will most likely be preempted.

Q 8:5   How can a managed care entity be at risk for medical malpractice claims?

Hospitals and other health care providers have been liable under conventional theories of liability such as vicarious liability, *respondeat superior*, and corporate negligence. Managed care organizations can incur similar liability exposure through the negligent acts of their employees or medical staff or through the negligence of those perceived by enrollees or members as having a relationship (agency or otherwise) on an ostensible basis. Managed care organizations also have liability for their own negligence in allowing an incompetent physician to practice with the plan.

Under several theories of liability, an MCO may be held liable for not only its own negligence, but also the negligence of others. These theories include:

Respondeat superior (employer) liability. In a bona fide employment relationship, an employer is liable for the negligent acts of the employee under the theory of *respondeat superior.* In *Shleier v. Kaiser Foundation Health Plan* (876 F. 2d 174 [D.C. Cir. 1989]), the court returned a $825,000 verdict against an HMO for wrongful death arising out of an employed physician's negligent failure to diagnosis and treat a patient's coronary disease. In states with a strong corporate practice prohibition, the courts have rejected liability under this theory on the basis that physicians had to be independent contractors since they could not be employees.

Ostensible or apparent agency liability. A managed care organization may have vicarious liability exposure for its nonemployed participating providers under a theory of ostensible or apparent agency if the patient reasonably views the entity, rather than the individual provider, as the source of care, and the entity engages in conduct that leads the patient to reasonably believe that the source of the care is the entity, or the provider is an employee of the entity. In the case of *Boyd v. Albert Einstein Medical*

Center (547 A. 2d 1229 [Pa. Super. Ct. 1988]), a plaintiff sued the HMO for negligent failure to diagnose breast cancer, alleging that the HMO should be liable under apparent agency for the negligence of its nonemployed participating physicians. The court considered the following factors as sufficient to justify the patient's perception of an agency relationship: (1) the payment of fees to the HMO and not the physician, (2) HMO control over the list of physicians from whom the patient could choose for care, (3) the requirement of referral by the primary care physician to a specialist, and (4) other representations that would cause the patient to perceive the HMO as the provider of care. However, in the case of *Raglin v. HMO Illinois, Inc.* (595 N.E. 2d 153 [Ill. App. Ct. 1992]), the court did not deem the HMO's quality assurance program as having sufficient control over the medical groups or physicians with which it contracted for medical services.

Direct corporate liability. An MCO may also incur direct liability for negligent provider selection and retention. In the case of *McClellan v. Health Maintenance Organization of Pennsylvania* (604 A. 2d 1053 [Pa. Super. Ct. 1992]), the HMO was sued on a theory of both apparent agency and negligent credentialing. In addition to finding support for a theory of apparent agency, the court also found sufficient allegations to state a cause of action for negligent credentialing on the basis that the HMO had a duty of care to "select and retain only competent physicians [and] formulate, adopt and enforce adequate rules and policies to ensure quality care for [its subscribers]."

Q 8:6   What can be done to reduce tort liability exposure of an MCO?

To minimize vicarious liability exposure, a formal mechanism is needed to reduce the providers' risk of malpractice. Adequate insurance, comprehensive risk management, and programs for quality management are essential components of such a system. To minimize liability for corporate negligence, there should be an ongoing mechanism for reviewing the clinical competence of physicians and other participating providers using techniques similar to those used by hospitals in credentialing and peer review. Under either theory, careful attention to the system's structure and contractual obligations are important elements of a risk management program. Express indemnification agreements should be avoided.

Q 8:7   What are some of the risk management approaches that can be taken to reduce liability exposure in managed care?

The following checklist is intended to assist MCOs, HMOs, plan sponsors, and other entities in minimizing risk in managed care.

Vicarious Liability Checklist

- Ensure provider contracts make the provider an independent contractor.
- Ensure marketing materials and written documents describe the role and relationship of the provider and plan.
- Avoid gag clauses.
- Ensure providers carry adequate insurance with reputable carriers.
- Include dispute resolution provisions.

Credentialing Checklist

- Conduct a thorough due diligence review of provider qualifications.
- Query the National Practitioner Data Base (NPDB) as part of the due diligence review.
- Verify references and other information.
- Contract for the right to audit and access records to monitor provider performance.
- Monitor provider performance.

Utilization Review Checklist

- Adopt utilization review standards and procedures that take into account the accrediting organization standards.
- Ensure utilization review standards and procedures are clearly communicated to enrollees, beneficiaries, and providers.
- Leave patient care to the physician.
- Ensure plan coverage conditions are clearly described.
- Delegate eligibility determination to plan administrator.
- Design provider compensation to avoid improper incentives.

- Obtain stop-loss insurance where appropriate.
- Disclose provider incentives to beneficiaries.
- Continuously improve claims review process.
- Obtain, if possible, contract indemnification.

Q 8:8   Is the current system of resolving medical liability claims appropriate for managed care?

Experts suggest that the current medical liability system does not adequately prevent medical injuries or compensate injured patients. As managed care expands, the medical liability system's performance will become increasingly important to maintain quality of care and not impede efforts to provide appropriate, cost-effective care. This has been reflected in the numerous proposals by state and federal governments to reform the medical liability system. These issues were discussed in depth in the Annual Report to Congress of the Prospective Payment Review Commission in 1991, which listed reduction of medical injury as the number one goal. A second goal was to compensate fairly those patients who experienced a medical injury. It was noted that the existing liability system promotes the practice of defensive medicine and may impede efforts to improve the cost-effectiveness of care.

Q 8:9   What are the major liability issues associated with denial of benefits and withholding of care in HMOs?

There has been significant attention given over the past few years to managed care and health insurance coverage litigation involving utilization decisions related to denial of care. These have come under scrutiny by state regulators and have been the subject of recent legislative reform. Advocates of patients who have been denied health care benefits describe the optimal outcome as one where the patient can obtain the desired treatment without personal financial responsibility. Where ERISA does not preempt the case, factors to consider are: (1) the specificity of the plan documents or insurance policy, (2) the grievance and dispute resolution system, and (3) the disclosures to and expectations of the patients.

Q 8:10   What effect does ERISA have on tort claims against HMOs?

As a general rule, ERISA provisions will govern employee benefits issues if the plaintiff receives these benefits from a private employer; therefore, any lawsuit will be heard in federal court. State law will govern if the plaintiff fits within certain exceptions such as for school district employees, church employees, or one who directly contracts for health care benefits with the HMO.

The purpose of the federal statute, as stated in section 2 of ERISA, 29 U.S.C. 1001(b), is to protect participants in employee benefits plans and their beneficiaries by requiring the disclosure and reporting to participants and beneficiaries of financial and other information with respect thereto; by establishing standards of conduct, responsibility, and obligation for fiduciaries of employee benefit plans; and by providing for appropriate remedies, sanctions, and ready access to the federal courts. Accordingly, ERISA preempts any state laws that may relate to an employee benefit plan. The courts have broadly interpreted the term related to an employee benefit plan, which means that a state tort claim filed against an HMO for negligence or breach of contract for wrongful denial of benefits is generally preempted by ERISA.

If, however, the claim's basis is related to the corporate or administrative aspects of the plan, including quality of care, then the ERISA preemption may not apply to bar the state law–based claim. The courts are not in agreement on whether the ERISA preemption applies to malpractice claims. Pure malpractice actions are more likely to escape the ERISA preemption under theories such as vicarious liability of the MCO or HMO for the acts of its agents or employees. It seems that the cases around ERISA preemption make a distinction between utilization review and benefit determination (which are preempted), and cases involving clinical decision making during treatment. For example, in *Dukes v. U.S. Healthcare, Inc.*, the plaintiff brought action in state court alleging medical malpractice against several defendants, including the physicians and the ERISA-covered HMO. When the HMO sought removal to federal court under ERISA, the plaintiffs sought to remand the case to state court on the ground that ERISA did not preempt their state claims. The case was ultimately remanded by the appellate court to have the case remain in state court with the court finding that the claim about the quality of a benefit received is not a claim under 502(a)(1)(B) to "recover benefits due . . . under the terms of [the] plan."

Until the case of *New York State Conference of Blue Cross & Blue Shield Plans v. Travelers*, U.S., 115 S. Ct. 1671, 131 L. Ed. 2d 695 (1995), ERISA preemption was given broad interpretation to encompass claims based on state laws which even remotely related to an ERISA plan. However, because of the rapidly changing role of the HMO in providing or arranging for medical care, the scope of the ERISA preemption has been narrowed dramatically. The trend today indicates claims for medical malpractice and negligent selection and retention of physicians will increasingly be found to fall outside of the ERISA preemption.

Q 8:11   What have been other legal barriers to HMO liability?

In states that strictly adhere to the prohibition against the corporate practice of medicine, there is a legal barrier to holding an HMO directly liable or accountable for patient care outcomes because the HMO does not engage in the practice of medicine. As a matter of law, then, the HMO cannot be liable for malpractice. Under this doctrine, a corporation may not practice medicine or employ or retain a physician as its agent to practice medicine. This doctrine, which exists in a number of states, prohibits a lay corporation or individuals from employing a licensed physician, receiving his or her fees, or in any way influencing the delivery of medical services unless the individual is a physician or the corporation or entity is owned or controlled entirely by physicians. This doctrine is based on the principle that businesses, organizations, and entities not licensed by the state to practice medicine cannot engage in medical practice and exploit the special relationship between a physician and his or her patient.

Q 8:12   Does managed care create additional liability exposure to providers?

The provider's liability for its own malpractice is well settled in law; however, where a managed care organization or other party becomes involved in the management of a patient's care, there is the potential for new liability issues. For example, physicians who perform the role of gatekeeper (i.e., controlling the patient's access to other providers as part of a managed care plan) may incur liability for a patient's care even where there has been no direct physician/patient contact. In the case of *Hand v. Tavera*, 864 S.W.2d 678 (Tex. App.—San Antonio 1993, no wit), the court found that the on-call physician (who had never seen the patient before) had a duty of care because he was the primary care gatekeeper for that patient under the terms of the managed care contract.

In the case of *DeGenova v. Ansel*, 555 A.2d 147 (Pa. Super. 1989), the insurer was held liable where its selected physician was asked to render a second surgical opinion as to whether the patient actually needed surgery recommended by another physician.

MODEL LEGISLATIVE INITIATIVES AFFECTING HMO LIABILITY

Q 8:13   What has been the impetus behind managed care reform?

A major impetus behind managed care reform has been the growing dissatisfaction with certain forms of managed care that limit access to care, choice of provider, and disclosure about the plan; restrict coverage; and establish incentives for health care providers to ration health care services. Many states have introduced legislation intended to address these concerns. The federal government is looking at enacting a patient's bill of rights as part of its efforts to address issues such as access and choice, disclosure, grievance procedures, and quality of care. Recently, one of the most dramatic legislative enactments came as part of a package of six managed care bills in Texas—this became SB 386, also known as the HMO Liability Bill. Since this law is precedent setting, it is instructive to examine its provisions.

SENATE BILL 386

Q 8:14   What types of entities are subject to SB 386?

SB 386 amends title 4 of the Texas Civil Practice and Remedies Code by adding chapter 88, which applies to any health insurance carrier, health maintenance organization, and managed care entity (i.e., MCOs). Chapter 88 defines a managed care entity as "any entity which delivers, administers, or assumes risk for health care services with systems or techniques to control or influence the quality, accessibility, utilization, or costs and prices of such services to a defined enrollee population." An MCO does not include an employer purchasing coverage or acting on behalf of one or more subsidiaries or affiliated corporations of the employer. It does not extend to a pharmacy licensed by the state board of pharmacy.[5]

Organizations subject to SB 386 can be individual entities or multiple entity networks such as preferred provider organizations, physician hospital organizations, IPAs, and other integrated delivery systems.

Q 8:15   How does SB 386 apply to MCOs?

Chapter 88 imposes two primary duties on MCOs. First, they have "the duty to exercise ordinary care when making health care treatment decisions and are liable for damages for harm to an insured or enrollee proximately caused by [their] failure to exercise such ordinary care." Ordinary care is "that degree of care that [an MCO] of ordinary prudence . . . would use under the same or similar circumstances." Health care treatment decisions are broadly defined to include both "determinations made when medical services are actually provided" and "decision[s] which affect the quality of the diagnosis, care, or treatment provided to the plan's insureds or enrollees." The latter forms the basis for denial of treatment and other utilization review–related claims. Second, chapter 88 makes MCOs liable for damages for harm to an insured or enrollee proximately caused by the health care treatment decisions made by its employees, agents, ostensible agents, or representatives who are acting on its behalf, and over whom it has the right to exercise influence or control, or has actually exercised influence or control that result in the failure to exercise ordinary care.[6]

Q 8:16   How does SB 386 get around ERISA preemption?

At this writing, there is a pending action in the U.S. District Court, Southern District of Texas, in that Aetna and its affiliates have sued the Texas Department of Insurance for a declaratory judgment on the basis that the liability cause of action contained in the bill is preempted by ERISA. (See *Corporate Health Insurance Inc. v. The Texas Department of Insur-*

ance, U.S. District Court, No. H-97-2072 [S.D. Tex. filed June 16, 1997]). The Texas Department of Insurance's position is that the focus of SB 386 is to permit a cause of action for HMO medical treatment decisions that do not implicate ERISA plan coverage determinations. The position of Aetna is that SB 386 relates to ERISA and Federal Employee Health Benefit Act (FEHBA) plans under the line of cases led by *Corcoran*.

Q 8:17   How does SB 386 get around the prohibition of the corporate practice of medicine?

Chapter 88 further provides that "[n]othing in any law of this state prohibiting [an MCO] from practicing medicine or being licensed to practice medicine may be asserted as a defense by such [MCO] in an action brought against it pursuant to this section or any other law."[7] Under this doctrine, a corporation may not practice medicine or employ or retain a physician as its agent to practice medicine. This doctrine, which exists in a number of states including Texas, prohibits a lay corporation or individual from employing a licensed physician, receiving his or her fees, or in any way influencing the delivery of medical services unless the individual is a physician or the corporation or entity is owned or controlled entirely by physicians. This doctrine is based on the principle that businesses, organizations, and entities not licensed by the state to practice medicine cannot engage in medical practice and exploit the special relationship between a physician and his or her patients.

Finally, an MCO cannot contract away the liability potentially imposed on it by requiring health care providers to indemnify it for the acts or conduct of the MCO. The strict prohibition on indemnification in chapter 88 arguably assists in leveling the playing field for physicians who frequently were not aware of the indemnification provisions in their managed care contracts.

Q 8:18   Are there any limits on an MCO's exposure under SB 386?

Chapter 88 contains provisions designed to protect MCOs from unlimited liability by giving them certain evidentiary protections. Chapter 88 expressly provides that a finding that a physician or other health care provider is an employee, agent, ostensible agent, or representative of the MCO *shall not be based solely* on proof that such person's name appears in a listing of approved physicians or health care providers made available to insureds or enrollees under a health care plan. This prohibits a *per se* allegation of agency merely because a health care provider is a member of the MCO's panel.

Second, chapter 88 affords MCOs certain procedural protections. Enrollees filing actions under chapter 88 must comply with the requirements of section 13.01 of the Medical Liability and Insurance Improvement Act of Texas (MLIIA). That section of MLIIA contains certain "gatekeeping" devices for medical malpractice and health care liability lawsuits. The Texas legislature enacted these procedural safeguards, which include cost bonds, monetary deposits, and expert reports in 1995 in an effort to stop the filing of frivolous medical malpractice lawsuits.

Third, chapter 88 also creates a quasi-administrative review process for adverse utilization review determinations and requires an enrollee to exhaust his or her health plan's appeals and reviews or submit the claim to independent review before filing suit. This process may encourage resolution of disputes without resorting to litigation.

Fourth, chapter 88 provides statutory defense to liability where an MCO did not, directly or indirectly, control, influence, or participate in the health care treatment decision or deny or delay payment for any treatment recommended or prescribed by a provider. Consequently, an MCO can still argue that because it is prohibited by law from practicing medicine, it is not liable for an adverse treatment outcome. The physician contracts entered into by many MCOs specifically disclaim any control by the MCO over treatment decisions. MCOs likely will rely on such language in defending claims brought under this statute. Chapter 88 also provides that MCOs are not required to provide an enrollee with "treatment which is not covered by the health care plan or entity." This provision may become critical when, in litigation, MCOs attempt to distinguish between treatment decisions and coverage decisions.

These provisions go a long way toward ensuring the equitable application of duties created by chapter 88. Nevertheless, a closer examination of the statute reveals that they are far from sufficient to ensure that MCOs are made liable in the same manner as physicians and other direct providers of care.

Q 8:19 **What have been some of the problems with interpreting and enforcing SB 386?**

Scope of liability undefined. SB 386 creates more questions than it answers. Chapter 88 makes an MCO accountable for health care treatment decisions made by its agents and representatives, but does not define such essential terms as "agent," "ostensible agent," and, with respect to representatives of the MCO, "influence" or "control." Without such clarification, it may be expected that determinations of agency and representation will be based on the facts and circumstances of each case, leading to considerable litigation. Until the scope of this duty is further defined by the courts, MCOs and health care providers will lack guidance as to precisely the sorts of relationships that fall within the ambit of chapter 88—and precisely how to avoid creating such relationships.

Potential for multiple recoveries. Equally important, chapter 88 is silent about the relationship between its newly created causes of action and the traditional malpractice claims against physicians and other health care providers. To the extent that causes of action created by chapter 88 are deemed to involve distinct "injuries," a patient may be able to recover both from the MCO that arranged for his or her care and from his or her physician for malpractice. This raises the possibility of patients receiving a double recovery or, at a minimum, an attractive choice of remedies.

Uneven playing field. Chapter 88 fails in its express purpose of making MCOs liable in the same manner as physicians and other health care providers. The statutory limitations on liability available to health care providers under the MLIIA are extended to MCOs in only a piecemeal fashion. Concededly, the requirement that plaintiffs post bond or place cash in escrow is carried over, as is the requirement that plaintiffs furnish defendants' counsel an expert report and curriculum vitae of each expert, or face dismissal of the claim and monetary sanctions. Also carried over are stringent standards for qualifications as an expert witness.

Chapter 88 does not extend the significant protections available to physicians and other health care providers to MCOs. First, the statutory limitations on actions under the MLIIA are not available to MCOs. MLIIA generally imposes a statute of limitations that covers a period two years from the date of the occurrence of the breach or tort or the date medical treatment is completed, while making special provision for suits filed by minors. In contrast, chapter 88 is silent on the applicable statute of limitations and when the statute will begin to run for minors. As a result, Texas courts likely will impose a longer statute of limitations on MCOs than on entities that qualify for the MLIIA protections. For example, in Texas, the statute of limitations in non–health care liability wrongful death actions runs from the date of death, *not* the date of treatment. The MLIIA also caps damages for wrongful death according to a consumer price index measure, which currently stands at approximately $1.27 million per defendant. This cap is not available to MCOs. Restrictions on prejudgment interests under the MLIIA also are not applicable to MCOs.

The MLIIA also creates a number of hurdles before recovery of damages. For example, a health care provider is entitled to 60 days' notice before the lawsuit is filed. If notice is not provided before filing a claim, the lawsuit may be abated or suspended for a period of 60 days. Buttressing these procedural hurdles, the MLIIA creates evidentiary hurdles to recovery by a plaintiff. For example, the use of *res ipsa loquitur* is limited to those situations in which it had been applied prior to MLIIA's effective date. Apparently, however, a plaintiff proceeding against an MCO need not clear any of these hurdles. Just as with the limitation on actions and damages, the procedural and evidentiary hurdles insulating physicians and other health care providers within the MLIIA are nowhere to be found in chapter 88 of SB 386.

Because fewer hurdles exist for filing lawsuits against MCOs, such entities may be more prone to suits than their physician and direct provider counterparts. This lack of hurdles creates an uneven playing field for MCOs in lawsuits in which health care providers also are defendants, because only the provider defendants have the full benefit of MLIIA tort reform measures.

Potential legal responsibility for what cannot be legally controlled. Although overturning the holding of *Williams v. Good Health Plus,* 743 S.W.2d 373 (Tex. Civ. App. 1987), which precluded a finding of vicarious liability on the basis that an HMO was prohibited from practicing medicine as a matter of law, chapter 88 leaves in place the statutory provisions that form the basis for Texas's prohibition of the corporate practice of medicine. This is most problematic for claims against an MCO for vicarious liability for health care decisions made by physicians over which the MCO may not exert control because of the corporate practice prohibition. That is, with the enactment of SB 386, an MCO now may be responsible for a physician's treatment decisions without the ability to seek indemnification from the physician for his or her negligent actions.[8] The net result of SB 386 is to place MCOs in the untenable position of being responsible for decisions of physicians and other health care providers that they are legally barred from controlling.

Q 8:20   What is the legal significance of this disconnection between an HMO's ability to control medical conduct and its liability under SB 386?

This disjunction of control and liability may have other consequences as well. Most managed care systems rely on utilization review to contain costs. Utilization review often takes the form of requiring precertification of medical necessity of a particular procedure, referral, or hospital admission, without which the MCO will not pay for treatment. Health care providers may now have greater incentive to conclude medical necessity exists for a particular treatment and let patients sue the MCO for any denial of treatment, rather than concluding otherwise and being sued for malpractice themselves. Similarly, MCOs will have an incentive to authorize unneeded treatment in cases in which an enrollee disputes the MCO's decision rather than risk exposure to liability, whereas previously an enrollee's remedies were limited in regard to an MCO's decision. Ironically, chapter 88 and similar statutes may hasten a return to the era of defensive medicine.

Q 8:21   How extensive is the potential scope of a health care treatment decision for purposes of imposing SB 386 liability on an MCO?

Chapter 88 imposes a duty of ordinary care on MCOs when making health care treatment decisions. This standard is similar to that placed on physicians and, as such, seems unremarkable at first. Nonetheless, a closer inspection of the definition of "health care treatment decisions" reveals the breadth of the duty created by this provision. Under chapter 88, a health care treatment decision includes not only "determination[s] made when medical services are actually provided by the health care plan," such as physician treatment decisions, but a far broader class of activities, namely, "decisions [which affect] the quality of the diagnosis, care, or treatment provided to the plan's insureds or enrollees." Although chapter 88 provides little guidance on the scope of such decisions, the latter clause arguably includes any manner of utilization review decision, including denials of certification for hospital admission, for particular procedures, or for referral to a specialist. In addition to utilization review decisions, an MCO's quality assurance decisions, development of practice guidelines, adoption of drug formularies, and network participation criteria may all constitute "health care treatment decisions" within the ambit of the statute. Consequently, MCOs operating in Texas should carefully examine their operating documents and protocols to determine areas of potential liability exposure, as these documents may become significant in defending future claims.

Q 8:22   Is there potential liability for out-of-network providers?

As noted earlier, chapter 88 makes MCOs accountable not only for the acts of employees, agents, and representatives, but for ostensible agents as well. A particularly troublesome aspect of this duty is its application to point-of-service plans and out-of-network providers. An MCO's "relationship" to such providers is nothing other than the traditional one of a fee-for-service insurer and independent physician. Unfortunately, in Texas, the ability to control or influence a purported agent is *not* required to establish a claim of ostensible agency. Although some act of "holding out" must be shown to succeed on a claim of ostensible agency, it is difficult for an MCO to protect itself from such liability, short of ferreting out and correcting any misunderstandings as to agency held by enrollees and insureds.

Although the question is not yet resolved, out-of-network physicians may constitute agents, ostensible agents, or representatives of an MCO, making the MCO liable for their acts. MCOs, however, lack mechanisms by which to ensure the quality of care provided by such physicians. Unlike its participating providers, for example, out-of-network physicians are not subject to an MCO's participation requirements or other "credentialing" mechanisms. Because MCOs have virtually no way to ensure the quality of out-of-network providers—but may be held liable nevertheless—it may be expected that MCOs will phase out or reduce access to providers outside their health plans. In that instance, consumers will have lost considerable flexibility.

Q 8:23   Is the independent review process described under SB 386 that uses an independent review organization likely to be effective in minimizing claims against MCOs?[9]

It is unlikely that the prefiling review process added to chapter 88 by the Texas House of Representatives would stem the tide of malpractice actions. A close reading of this portion of the bill confirms that it is more of a sieve than a shunt. In fact, enrollees have several opportunities to bypass the requirement of internal review or independent review.

First, the failure to exhaust internal review or submit a claim to independent review does not result in dismissal of the case. Rather, a court may, in its discretion, order the parties to submit to nonbinding alternative dispute resolution and may abate the action for up to 30 days.

Second, an enrollee can bypass the requirement altogether by alleging that "harm" to the enrollee has already occurred because of the MCO's conduct or that of its representative or agent and that the review would not be beneficial. Although a court, on motion and finding that the plaintiff's claim of harm was not made in good faith, may abate the case for up to 30 days, this is the "sole remedy" for the failure to comply with the internal or independent review requirement. Because exhaustion of an internal review or independent review is itself likely to consume 30 days, plaintiffs lose nothing by proceeding directly to court.

Third, the internal appeal or independent review requirement does not prohibit an enrollee from pursuing other remedies, such as declaratory judgment or injunctive relief, if the review requirement places the insured's "health in serious jeopardy." Therefore, yet another loophole is created when a plaintiff makes an allegation of serious jeopardy to health in his or her pleading. Moreover, in contrast to the harm pleading exception, if a plaintiff alleges serious jeopardy to health, no express requirement of a good faith showing exists, nor is the court given the power to abate the case if the allegations prove to be unfounded.

The net result is that enrollees may go directly to the courthouse with the new causes of action created by chapter 88, and the prefiling requirement emerges as a sham that will have minimal impact on the actual resolution of disputes.

Q 8:24   What is the potential impact of SB 386 on other managed care arrangements?

An unintended result of chapter 88 may be to expose a variety of entities used by physicians and hospitals as contracting vehicles—such as physician-hospital organizations, provider-sponsored organizations, physician group practices, and other networks of health care providers—to liability. This stems from the loose definition of MCOs, which appears to encompass not only the intended targets of health insurers and HMOs, but also multiple provider networks and their components. Thus, for example, preferred provider organizations, integrated delivery systems, and component entities that take administrative or financial responsibility for services provided to enrollees would appear to constitute entities "which deliver, administer, or assume risk for health care services . . . to a defined enrollee population."

The danger of this loose definition is profound and far-reaching. A 1997 American Medical Association survey of 4,100 physicians found that 32.5 percent of all physicians in the United States (and 75.2 percent of physicians practicing in large groups) participate in capitated contracts in which they "assume risk for health care services." Thus, many Texas physicians are likely to be surprised to find that their contracting vehicles may be subject to suit on the same basis as HMOs and other traditional managed care providers.

Q 8:25   What lessons can be drawn from the Texas initiative to hold HMOs legally accountable?

As other state legislatures, such as Georgia, look at Texas and propose similar legislation to hold HMOs accountable for their actions or inactions, there are some important lessons to be learned from the Texas experiment in legislating managed care liability. These include the following suggestions:

Define key terms affecting the scope of the legislation. Terms such as "managed care entity" and "medical treatment decisions" should be more precisely defined. Without more specificity, MCOs are unfairly exposed to litigation and are not given sufficient opportunity to comply with the legislation.

Apply any tort reform protections equitably to MCOs. Although some may disagree, MCOs are an integral part of our health care delivery system. The next generation of health care litigation now emerging will involve both MCOs and health care providers as defendants. If a state has enacted tort reform protections for health care providers in health care liability litigation, MCOs should be given equal benefit of those protections.

Put teeth into any independent review process. To be an effective method for resolving disputes without resorting to litigation, any internal or independent review process should be mandatory, with an exception only for instances in which the enrollee can show imminent, immediate harm to health or safety. Similarly, if an enrollee fails to exhaust his or her internal or independent review requirements, it should result in dismissal of the case. By strengthening the independent review process, legislatures will encourage MCOs and enrollees to resolve disputes earlier and without the expense and burden of litigation.

Consider repealing the corporate practice of medicine prohibition. The corporate practice of medicine prohibition, which is recognized in some form in a majority of states, can create an unlevel playing field for MCOs given the enactment of managed care liability laws. If MCOs now are to be held accountable for the actions of the health care providers with whom they contract to deliver care, MCOs should be given the legal authority and right to control the providers' actions through repeal of any corporate practice of medicine prohibition. If such control by MCOs is not desired or is deemed contrary to public policy, however, then the statutory causes of action should be drafted to hold an MCO accountable only for its actions, not for the actions of health care providers.

NOTES

1. Sibley et al., SB 386, chapter 88: Health Care Liability, amendment to section 1, title 4 of the Civil Practice and Remedies Code. 75th Legislature (R), Texas Senate 1997.

2. On 28 May, 1996, Governor Lawton Chiles vetoed similar legislation passed by the Florida Legislature authorizing civil actions against health maintenance organizations (H.R. 1853, 1996 regular session, Florida General Assembly, 1996). In 1997, legislation authorizing suits against managed care entities was proposed and defeated in at least six states. The Connecticut General Assembly proposed a bill that would hold

liable an MCO that proposes treatment alternatives contrary to those proposed by the attending physician and that subsequently cause complications (H. IL. 6136, 1997 regular session). Proposed House and Senate bills that would authorize a cause of action if an HMO fails to provide a covered service when it should have done so in good faith and when the treating physician thought it was necessary were proposed (H.R. 1547, 1997 regular session, Florida General Assembly and 1997 5.1168, 1997 regular session, Florida Senate). The Maryland General Assembly proposed a bill that would create liability for damages if an HMO failed to approve a covered service when such a service was recommended by a provider with a contract with the HMO (11 R. 70, 1997 regular session, Maryland General Assembly). New York Senate proposed a bill that would create liability for damages on the part of an HMO that delays, disapproves, or denies comprehensive coverage subsequently causing injury, damages, or death (5.3019, 1997 regular sessions, New York Senate). The Virginia General Assembly proposed a bill that would make an HMO a proper party and hold the HMO jointly and severally liable in a medical malpractice action against a health care provider, if that provider is a member of an HMO and is following the HMO's protocol (H.R. 2568, 1997 regular session, Virginia General Assembly). The Missouri General Assembly proposed a bill provided, in relevant part, that an HMO must pay for emergency medical care whenever a "prudent layperson" would have reason to believe that immediate care is needed, even if a managed care administrator might disagree (H.R. 335, 1st session, Missouri General Assembly, 1997). Rhode Island proposed a bill that would create a commission to study the legal liability of HMOs when their policies directly result in inadequate medical care (5.601, 1997 regular session, Rhode Island Senate). New Jersey enacted the Health Care Quality Act, which contains numerous consumer protections but does not establish statutory liability for MCOs under a negligence theory (S. 269. 1st session, New Jersey Senate, 1996).

3. Larson, E. "The soul of an HMO: Managed care is certainly bringing down America's medical costs, but it is also raising the question of whether patients, especially those with severe illnesses, can still trust their doctors," *Time* 147 no. 4 (1996): 44–52.

4. A California jury awarded $3 million to the family of Joyce Ching, who died of colon cancer that went undiagnosed for months while her primary care physicians, under contract to MetLife HMO, ignored her requests to be referred to a specialist. Ching's lawyer, Mark Hiepler, argued that by the time Ching was referred to a specialist, who diagnosed the cancer immediately, the tumor had perforated her colon, reducing her odds of survival from 60 to 80 percent to 11 to 35 percent. (*Ching v. Gaines*, Cal. Super. Ct., Ventura County, No. 137878, 15 November, 1995).

5. SB 386, chapter 88.001(6–9), 75th Legislature, regular session, Texas Senate, 1997. Excluded from the definition of MCOs are pharmacies licensed in Texas and employers purchasing group coverage for affiliated corporations, chapter 88.001(8). In addition, chapter 88 does not apply to workers' compensation insurance coverage, chapter 88.002(h).

6. SB 386, chapter 88.001(6–8), 75th Legislature, regular session, Texas Senate, 1997. Chapter 88 contains an "antiretaliation" provision that prohibits an MCO from removing from its health plan or refusing to renew a provider who advocates on behalf of an enrollee for appropriate and medically necessary health care; chapter 88.002(f). This

duty mirrors that placed on HMOs by the Texas Department of Insurance. See Tax Administration Code title 28, 11.1500, 1997.

7. SB 386, chapter 88.002(f), 75th Legislature, regular session, Texas Senate, 1997.

8. SB 386, chapter 88, Texas Civil Practice and Remedies Code 88.002(g), 75th Legislature, regular session, Texas Senate, 1997. More specifically, chapter 88 prohibits an MCO from entering into a "contract with a physician, hospital or other health care provider or pharmaceutical company which includes an indemnification or hold harmless clause for the acts or conduct of the [MCO]" and declares any such provision in an existing contract void. Importantly, even though its intent is to prohibit provision *requiring a physician to indemnify* an MCO for any liability that arises from the MCO's negligent acts, section 88.002(e) may be sufficiently broad to allow an argument that it prohibits indemnification provisions running in either direction, including those protective of physician providers. If such an argument were to succeed, physicians and other health care providers might be stripped of an important method of protecting against liability arising from the negligence of their counterparts.

9. SB 386, Texas Civil Practice and Remedies Code 88.002, 75th Legislature, regular session, Texas Senate, 1997. Chapter 88 also allows an MCO to request review by an independent review organization, 88.003(c). To do so, the MCO must request review not later than the 14th day after receipt of notice of the patient's intent to file suit. If an independent review is not requested in a timely manner, an enrollee is not required to submit to independent review before filing suit.

CHAPTER 9

Medicare

Marie Oser and Clifford C. Dacso

INTRODUCTION

The successful management of health care, producing positive health outcomes resulting in cost-effectiveness savings, is rooted in the contracting process. This process takes takes place on several different levels and has many different permutations. With Medicare risk contracting, contracts exist between the managed care organization, the federal government through the Health Care Financing Administration (HCFA) in the Department of Health and Human Services, and finally the delivery system. All of these layers come together to determine a plan's ability to operate effectively while attracting and retaining members and maintaining a high quality of care.

Q 9:1   What is a Medicare risk contract?

A Medicare risk contract is between a managed care organization (MCO) and HCFA, whereby the MCO accepts a geographically determined prepayment based on per member per month enrollments for an entire complement of services prescribed by Medicare parts A and B. By this set of relationships, the MCO assumes the insurance risk. Depending on the service area and marketing imperatives, value-added services may be included, such as pharmacy benefits, vision services, and transportation. Copayments vary by service area and plan design.[1] Medicare risk contracts are governed by section 1876 of the Social Security Act, including all congressional amendments, additions, and regulations promulgated by HCFA.

Q 9:2   What are some important strategic aspects of Medicare risk contracting?

It is important that the provider be in a leadership position on the business and financial arrangements. It is axiomatic that the possessor of the data is in a superior position for contract negotiation. The provider should possess clear demographic data on the service area and the eligible population already in the provider's patient mix. Of course, this allows an assessment of how much existing membership is likely to convert to a health maintenance organization (HMO) product if the provider is only performing Medicare indemnity service.

A knowledgeable analysis of the current costs and the impact that participation in a Medicare risk contract will have on the practice and business of the provider organization should be well understood before beginning negotiations with the MCO.

Medicare risk contracting may well have an effect on administrative costs as a result of:

- prolonged record retention
- eligibility determinations
- compliance with all HCFA rules and regulations
- innovative service provisions and value-added services such as DME and pharmacy
- administration of health risk assessments
- an extensive care management program

If the service area is relatively new to managed care, member and provider education will need increased attention. Working with the MCO on creative and appropriate marketing approaches that are in compliance with HCFA and department of insurance regulations is another area that requires a different or new emphasis.

Q 9:3   What characteristics of an MCO are needed to submit an application for Medicare managed care?

The requirements with which an MCO must comply are set forth in the HCFA *HMO Manual*, which can be found on the Internet (http://www.hcfa.gov/medicare/mgdcar1.htm) or ordered from the National Technology Information Service. It is important that the MCO has obtained the most recent application, manual, and other materials relating to the application process—HCFA periodically revises these documents. Each of the requirements is set forth in specific detail based on section 1876 of the Social Security Act and regulations promulgated through the years. Some of the categories include:

- a delivery system able to provide all of the covered services required by Medicare, as well as any value-added services with demonstrable geographic access
- operational policies and procedures, and appeals and grievances as set forth by law (section 1876) and HCFA regulation
- marketing plan and materials
- utilization management plan
- quality improvement plan
- commercial members access plan
- financial reserves and stability
- compliance with a risk management plan
- member services plan and materials

Q 9:4   What are the guiding regulations regarding physician incentives?

Legislative action to regulate physician incentive plans (PIP)[2] was first enacted in the Omnibus Budget Reconciliation Acts (OBRA) of 1986 and 1987. In 1990, these laws were superseded by a new Consolidated Omnibus Budget Reconciliation Act. Statutory authority for this regulation can be found in sections 1876(I)(8), 1903(m)(2)(A)(x), and 1903(m)(5)(A)(v) of the Social Security Act.

A final rule on PIP for Medicare and Medicaid MCOs was published in the *Federal Register* on March 27, 1996. Corrected final rules were published in the *Federal Register* on September 3 and December 31, 1996.

Q 9:5   What aspects of a PIP need to be disclosed to HCFA?

The disclosure requirements apply not only to an MCO's direct contracting arrangements with providers, but to subcontracting arrangements as well. Note that disclosure forms differentiate between physician groups and "intermediate entities." Examples of intermediate entities include individual practice associations (IPAs) that contract with one or more physician groups, as well as physician-hospital organizations. IPAs that contract only with individual physicians and not with physician groups are considered physician groups under this rule. The following pieces of information are required by the regulation:

- whether referral services are covered by the PIP; if only services furnished directly by the physician or group are addressed by the PIP, then there's no need for disclosure of other aspects of the PIP
- type of incentive arrangement (e.g., withhold, bonus, capitation)
- percentage of total income at risk for referrals
- amount and type of stop-loss protection
- panel size and whether enrollees were pooled in order to achieve the panel size; and if the MCO is required by this regulation to conduct a customer satisfaction survey, a summary of the survey results

Q 9:6   What aspects of a physician incentive plan need to be disclosed to Medicare beneficiaries?

At the Medicare beneficiaries' request, MCOs must provide information indicating whether it or any of its contractors or subcontractors use a PIP that may affect the use of referral services, the type of incentive arrangement(s) used, and whether stop-loss protection is provided. If the MCO is required to conduct a survey, it must also provide beneficiary requesters with a summary of survey results.

Q 9:7   What is substantial financial risk (SFR) and why is it important?

According to the final rule, if a PIP puts a physician or physician group at substantial financial risk for referral services:

A. The MCO must survey current and previously enrolled members to assess member access to and satisfaction with the quality of services, and

B. There must be adequate and appropriate stop-loss protection.

Referral risk is defined by the following formula:

Amount at risk for referral services / referral risk =
maximum potential payments

The amount at risk for referral services is the difference between the maximum potential referral payments and the minimum potential referral payments. Bonuses unrelated to utilization (e.g., quality bonuses such as those related to member satisfaction or open physician panels) should not be counted toward referral payments. Maximum potential payment is defined as the maximum *anticipated* total payment that the physician or group could receive. If there is no specific dollar or percentage amount noted in the incentive arrangement, the PIP should be considered as potentially putting 100 percent of the potential payments at risk for referral services.

The SFR threshold is set at 25 percentage of "potential payments" for covered services, regardless of the frequency of assessment (i.e., collection) or distribution of payments. SFR is present when the 25 percent threshold is exceeded.

The following incentive arrangements should be considered as SFR:

- withholds greater than 25 percent of potential payments
- withholds less than 25 percent of potential payments if the physician or physician group is potentially liable for amounts exceeding 25 percent of potential payments
- bonuses greater than 33 percent of potential payments minus the bonus
- withholds plus bonuses if the withholds plus bonuses equal more than 25 percent of potential payments (the threshold bonus percentage for a particular withhold percentage may be calculated using the formula: Withhold % = 0.75 (bonus %) + 25%)
- capitation arrangements: if the difference between the maximum potential payments and the minimum potential payments is more than 25 percent of the maximum potential payments; or the maximum and minimum potential payments are not clearly explained in the physician's or physician group's contract
- any other incentive arrangements that have the potential to hold a physician or physician group liable for more than 25 percent of potential payments

Q 9:8   What happens after SFR is determined?

When SFR as defined above exists, an MCO is required to perform several actions:

1. *Surveys.* When an MCO's physicians or groups are put at substantial financial risk, the MCO must survey its current Medicare enrollees, as well as those who disenrolled in the last 12 months for reasons other than loss of eligibility or relocation outside of the MCO's service area. For further information on surveys, see *Guidance on Surveys Required by the Physician Incentive Regulation and/or Physician Incentive Plan Regulation, 1998 Requirements/Survey Requirements— Additional Guidance.*

2. *Stop-loss protection.* Stop-loss protection must be in place to protect physicians or physician groups to whom substantial financial risk has been transferred. Either aggregate or per patient stop-loss may be acquired. The rule specifies that if aggregate stop-loss is provided, it must cover 90 percent of the cost of referral services that exceed 25 percent of potential payments. Physicians and groups can be held liable for only 10 percent. If per patient stop-loss is acquired, it must be determined based on the physician or physician group's patient panel size, and cover 90 percent of the referral costs that exceed the set per patient limits.

    The institutional and professional stop-loss limits represent the actuarial equivalents of the single combined limits. The physician group or MCO may choose to purchase whatever type is best suited to cover the referral risk in the incentive arrangement.

3. *Pooling criteria.* To determine the patient panel size, you may pool according to the specific criteria stated in the December 31, 1996, regulations. Any entity that meets all five criteria will be allowed to pool that risk to determine the amount of stop-loss required by the regulation:
    - Pooling of patients is otherwise consistent with the relevant contracts governing compensation arrangements for the physician or group (i.e., no contracts can require risk be segmented by MCO or patient category).
    - The physician or group is at risk for referral services with respect to each of the categories of patients being pooled.

- The terms of the compensation arrangements permit the physician or group to spread the risk across the categories of patients being pooled (i.e., payments must be held in a common risk pool).
- The distribution of payments to physicians from the risk pool is not calculated separately by patient category (either by an MCO or Medicaid, Medicare, or commercial).
- The terms of the risk borne by the physician or group are comparable for all categories of patients being pooled.

5. *Enforcement.* As described in 42 C.F.R. section 417.500 (revised), HCFA may apply intermediate sanctions or the Office of the Inspector General may apply civil monetary penalties if HCFA determines that a Medicare plan fails to comply with the requirements of this rule.

Q 9:9   **If a physician is paid a straight capitation without withholds or bonuses, would that still constitute SFR if the physician is at risk for services he or she does not provide?**

Such a compensation arrangement would require a finding of substantial financial risk, because the risk is not limited. If a capitation arrangement places no limit on the referral risk, it essentially requires a finding of 100 percent risk (with potentially greater risk).

Q 9:10   **MCOs that provide services to Medicare and Medicaid patients must also perform surveys. Does HCFA supply a template?**

The final rule did not specify that the plans must conduct a specific survey for this regulation because most plans already administer surveys that meet this regulation's requirements. MCOs may satisfy their requirement for enrollee surveys either by participating in HCFA's national administration of the consumer assessments of health plan study (CAHPS) survey[3] or by conducting their own surveys.

MCOs that became Medicare contractors on or after January 1, 1996, are not included in the 1997 national administration of CAHPS. These MCOs may use CAHPS or another enrollee satisfaction instrument to meet the PIP survey requirements.

The mandatory CAHPS survey will be administered by Barents, a third-party contractor to HCFA, and will survey a random sample of Medicare beneficiaries in each participating MCO for Medicare MCOs with contracts in effect with HCFA on December 31, 1995. The CAHPS survey, which has modules for use with Medicare, Medicaid, and commercial enrolled populations, addresses the basic requirements of the regulation: It includes questions regarding access, quality, and satisfaction.

The CAHPS survey includes a Medicaid version that can be separately administered to Medicaid enrollees. This instrument will yield data that meet the regulation's requirements. Although HCFA will not require that the CAHPS survey be administered for Medicaid MCOs, states will have the option to make such a requirement.

Q 9:11   Is there a survey requirement for those who disenroll from a Medicare MCO?

MCOs that are already gathering information on reasons for disenrollment from their Medicare beneficiaries may continue their current procedures to comply with the disenrollment survey requirements of the PIP regulation. HCFA expects to develop a standardized disenrollment survey for the Medicare population in partnership with the Agency for Health Care Policy and Research that should be ready for implementation in 1999. Until then, HCFA recommends using the disenrollment survey from the Office of the Inspector General (OIG), with the suggested modifications. To obtain this instrument, call (410) 784-1140 or (410) 786-1126, or send a fax to "PIP Disenrollee Survey, S3-19-18" at (410) 786-4005. Please provide your name and address with your faxed request. HCFA will mail a copy of the OIG survey to you. The MCO may also develop its own disenrollee survey if it chooses not to use the OIG survey instrument.

Disenrollment surveys may be conducted either by mail or telephone, preferably within three months of a beneficiary's disenrollment. Where possible, HCFA recommends that MCOs conduct a telephone survey. Plans should attempt to capture at least 75 to 80 percent of their total of disenrolled beneficiaries (excluding the deceased) and obtain a sample of $N = 384$, for a confidence level of 95 percent with a margin of error equal to ± 5 percent.

Q 9:12   Does HCFA provide any standard definitions of terms?

The following list is of some standard terms directly relevant to physician incentives contained within the PIP manual:

- Bonus—a payment a physician or entity receives beyond any salary, fee-for-service payments, capitation, or returned withhold. Bonuses and other compensation not based on referral levels (such as bonuses based solely on quality of care, patient satisfaction, or physician participation on a committee) are not considered in the calculation of substantial financial risk.
- Capitation—a set dollar payment per patient per unit of time (usually per month) paid to cover a specified set of services and administrative costs without regard to the actual number of services provided. The services covered may include a physician's own services, referral services, or all medical services.
- Panel size—the number of patients served by a physician or physician group. If the panel is greater than 25,000 patients, the physician group is not considered to be at substantial financial risk because the risk is spread over a large number of patients. Stop-loss and beneficiary surveys would not be required.
- Physician group—a partnership, association, corporation, IPA, or other group that distributes income from the practice among members. An IPA is a physician group only if it is composed of individual physicians and has no subcontracts with other physician groups.
- Intermediate entities—entities that contract between an MCO or one of its subcontractors and a physician or physician group, other than physician groups themselves. An IPA is considered an intermediate entity if it contracts with one or more physician groups in addition to contracting with individual physicians.
- Physician incentive plan—any compensation arrangement at any contracting level between an MCO and a physician or physician group that may directly or indirectly reduce or limit services furnished to Medicare or Medicaid enrollees in the MCO. MCOs must report on physician incentive plans between the MCO, itself, and individual physicians and groups, and also between groups or intermediate contracting

entities (e.g., certain IPAs and physician-hospital organizations) and individual physicians and groups. The MCO only needs to report the details on physician incentive plans between groups and individual physicians if those physicians are placed at substantial financial risk by the group's incentive arrangement.

- Potential payments—the maximum anticipated total payments (based on the most recent year's utilization and experience and any current or anticipated factors that may affect payment amounts) that could be received if use or costs of referral services were low enough. These payments include amounts paid for services furnished or referred by the physician or group, plus amounts paid for administrative costs. The only payments not included in potential payments are bonuses or other compensation not based on referrals (e.g., bonuses based on patient satisfaction or other quality of care factors).

- Referral services—any specialty, inpatient, outpatient, or laboratory services that are ordered or arranged, but not furnished directly. Situations may arise where services not normally considered referral services will need to be considered referral services for purposes of determining if a physician or group is at substantial financial risk. For instance, an MCO may require a physician or group to authorize "retroactive" referrals for emergency care received outside the MCO's network. The physician or group can experience an increase in bonus (if emergency referrals are low) or a reduction in capitation and increase in withhold (if emergency referrals are high). In these circumstances, the emergency services are considered referral services and need to be included in the calculation of substantial financial risk. Also, if a physician group contracts with an individual physician or another group to provide services that the initial group cannot provide itself, any services referred to the contracted physician or group should be considered referral services.

- Substantial financial risk—an incentive arrangement that places the physician or physician group at risk for amounts beyond the risk threshold, if the risk is based on the use or costs of referral services. The risk threshold is 25 percent.

- Withhold—a percentage of payments or set dollar amounts that are deducted from the service fee, capitation, or salary payment, and that may or may not be returned, depending on specific predetermined factors.

Q 9:13   Where is the full text of HCFA's PIP information sheet available?

The HCFA Web site has the full text and is updated as new information is available. The URL is http://www.hcfa.gov/medicare/physincp/pip-info.htm.

Q 9:14   What is the HCFA application process?

On receipt of the application forms, the MCO sets up an internal process for completion, which generally includes the following steps:

- assembling a project team
- developing a work plan for application completion
- establishing a writer's guide, timeline, and directory of writers
- securing outside consultants for assistance as needed, based on the experience of the MCO with Medicare risk contracting

When the MCO is satisfied that the application is complete and in compliance with HCFA requirements, the application and fee are submitted to the main office in Baltimore. On receipt of the application, HCFA has 30 days to review and respond with requests for any additional information needed. If the application needs additional work to be properly completed, HCFA's regional offices work with the MCO to complete the application and meet the specifications as set forth in the law and regulations. When the application is accepted as complete, a site visit will take place. Following completion of the site visit, a recommendation is sent from HCFA's regional office to its national office. A contract will be awarded after successful completion of the application, a site visit, and recommendation from the regional HCFA office.

Q 9:15   How is an HMO application obtained?

HCFA has published its applications on the Internet. The URL is http://www.hcfa.gov/medicare/mgdcar1.htm#applications.

Q 9:16   What is the timetable for completion of the Medicare risk contracting process?

The internal process depends on the MCO's experience with Medicare risk contracting and its state of readiness in the service area in which it is applying. The typical length of time for internal application processing is 6 to 9 months, assuming that there is a mature delivery system in place. The external process with HCFA varies, but 19 weeks is not an unusual length of time on which to plan.

Q 9:17   Once approved, does a plan have to reapply?

No; however, every two years a monitoring review based on HCFA guidelines, current laws, and regulations is undertaken. HCFA publishes a monitoring review document on a regular basis that can be used to assist MCOs in staying compliant and conducting readiness reviews in anticipation of the monitoring site visits. After the first year of operation, a technical advisory site visit is conducted by the regional HCFA office.

Q 9:18   Should MCOs have delivery system contracting templates?

Yes. The delivery system contracts are critical to the success of any MCO. There are many contract permutations based on community health care economics, MCO business needs, provider sophistication and readiness, and acceptability of managed care by target population—for Medicare risk contracts, the population would be the elderly, over-65 population and those with "special needs," categorized as disabled.

Having contracting templates allows for consistency, straightforward negotiations, and equitable member-friendly management of contracts that are fair and reasonable for both provider and payer. When contracting with HCFA, this further allows for better communication and understanding to ensure compliance with HCFA requirements, as well as with the requirements of the various departments of insurance. Even though contracts may have substitutions, all parties are best served when the process begins with a recognized template on which to build. This heightens the level of trust, which can then lead to a higher quality product and more satisfied members.

Q 9:19   What is an interactive template?

This type of template allows for modifications before it is used. Examples of a model interactive template may contain specifically identified instructions. If the item is applicable, the instructions may then be eliminated. The document is set up in such a way that it can be modified as developed, based on guidelines. This allows the present circumstances to guide the development of the contract based on a common beginning understood by all parties, yet open to negotiations.

Q 9:20   What components are contained in an interactive template?

It is suggested that the interactive template contain the following:

- proprietary and confidentiality statements in contract development (the statements should be agreed on before beginning the contract discussions and using the template)
- user's guide
- definitions
- conditions of the contract
- covered services
- quality management
- obligations of participating physicians
- insurance
- termination, renewals, and renegotiation policy and procedures
- general provisions

Q 9:21   What are the components of the user's guide?

The user's guide will serve as an introduction to the template, describing the document and explaining how it should be used in developing the contract. The user's guide may be divided into two parts: the internal guide and the external guide.

The internal user's guide will explain the contracting process and intent of the language offered in the template to assist the MCO's negotiations in the development of the contract.

The external user's guide will be designed for use by all parties in the negotiations. It will explain the language offered in the template and how the template should be used in developing the contract. The intent of the guide is to further understanding and clarify the purpose and intent of each item in the contract process. Each item should have an intent and purpose section, which is understood by all parties before beginning the discussions. If there is a lack of clarity, it is important that the template be modified to reflect the current understanding of all parties involved in the current discussions.

Q 9:22   What are the components of the definitions section?

It is important to include complete definitions in this section of the template and to have all parties agree on the definitions before negotiations. The template should list as many as possible of the terms that the contracting parties will be using, including federal and state laws, regulatory descriptions, legal terms of the agreement itself, medical codes, and product descriptions. It is essential to be as complete as possible. Assumptions of common understandings should not be made. The definitions will be the guide to mutual understandings.

Q 9:23   What are the components of the section describing the conditions?

Conditions on which the contract will be based, which may be included in the template, are:

- provisions for receipt of the Medicare risk contract from HCFA
- what happens in the event the contract is not awarded
- necessary market conditions
- provisions for successful contracting with other providers for a full delivery system
- services to be provided by the MCO, which may include administration, claims processing, marketing, enrollment, quality management, and utilization management

Q 9:24 **What are the components of covered services for the template?**

This section will include:

- roles, responsibilities, and obligations of contracting parties to deliver covered services
- communication processes for notification of new laws and regulations governing covered services
- compliance procedures
- processes for assessing the impact of changes in covered services on payments structures and how adjustments will be handled
- payment plan for services rendered, including details of the roles and responsibilities for payment of claims, member payments, copayments, and out-of-network payments
- protocols for managing care rendered

Q 9:25 **Which components of quality management should be included in the template?**

Some of the areas of policies and procedures that may be included in the template's area of quality management are:

- roles, responsibilities, and obligations of providers and MCOs in the quality management process
- compliance process and time frames
- rule for failure to comply with quality management
- structure of quality management process
- roles and responsibilities relating to medical records
- MCO and provider communication process
- billing, collection, and copayment and claims payment processes
- retention of records
- credentialing process
- prescription payment process
- member relationship and contacts

- quality improvement process
- care management program based on health risk assessment, completed at the time of enrollment
- quality-of-care complaints and appeals

Q 9:26   What is the purpose of a section in the template on obligations of the participating physicians?

This section may be used to specify the participating physician's obligations above and beyond the other sections, or it may be used to codify the obligations found throughout the contract for the sake of clarity and understanding.

Q 9:27   What are the components of the insurance section of the template?

The insurance section of the template should be used to identify:

- type of insurance coverage, such as errors and omissions or liability
- specific liability coverage that is expected
- the certificate of insurance and instructions on precisely how it is to be maintained

Q 9:28   What are the components of the section on termination, renewals, and renegotiations in the template?

The specific terms for renewal of the contract and of the services of all contracting parties should be stated clearly and with unambiguous language. The specific terms for renegotiations and terminations should also be clearly set forth. The circumstances of bankruptcy or adverse governmental actions should also be addressed in this section.

Q 9:29   What is the purpose of a section on general provisions in the template?

The section on general provisions will include such things as:

- exclusivity boundaries of the agreement
- the use of product names and trademarks

- the use of professional or industry trade confidentialities
- the relationship between the parties
- the governing laws; subcontractor compliance with laws and regulations
- operating structures
- conditions of potential sale of business or transfer of assets
- arbitration rules between parties
- compliance with all provisions required by HCFA and other governmental entities that may have a bearing on the business operations

---

NOTES

1. Health Care Financing Administration, *Coverage Issues Manual* (Baltimore: 1996).
2. Physician Incentive Plan Regulation (PIP) 42 C.F.R. 417.479, 27 March, 1996. *Federal Register* 1996, 61(60):13430–13450. Also: *Federal Register* 1996, 61(171):46384–46385.
3. Health Care Financing Administration, Office of Managed Care, Operational Letter OPL 96.045 (Baltimore: 1996).

CHAPTER 10

Managed Care and Medicaid

Sheryl Tatar Dacso

INTRODUCTION

The U.S. government has been in the health care business since the birth of the Republic. The U.S. Public Health Service was established in 1789 and the government has been responsible for veterans' health in a number of guises as long as there have been wars.

Most elderly beneficiaries (89 percent) have supplemental coverage, either separately purchased private insurance (i.e., "Medigap," 37 percent, employer retiree coverage, 33 percent, Medicaid, 12 percent, or other sources, 2 percent. Since 1988, state Medicaid programs have been required to pay Medicare part B premiums and cost sharing for all qualified Medicare beneficiaries (QMBs) whose incomes are below 100 percent of the federal poverty level and whose assets are below certain levels ($4,000 for individuals, $6,000 for couples in 1995). For those with an income between 100 and 120 percent of poverty, Medicaid pays for their part B premiums only. Individuals must apply for Medicaid in their state to be eligible.[1]

Q 10:1   What is Medicaid?

The Medicaid program is authorized under title XIX of the Social Security Act and is a joint federal-state program supplying health care coverage to low-income, aged, and disabled recipients. Medicaid was established as the counterpart of Medicare to serve the poor but, instead of being a federally mandated and funded program, it relies on the states to set eligibility limits. Thus there is a wide, state-to-state variation in the benefits provided by Medicaid.

Q 10:2   Who is covered by Medicaid?

The Medicaid population is composed of 3.8 million elderly, 5.4 million blind and disabled, 7.5 million adults in families, and 16.9 million children as of 1995.[2]

There is a common misconception that Medicaid is a boondoggle health plan for people who do not work. The state of Texas has collected these 1993 Medicaid statistics to disprove this notion. The relative values have not changed materially to 1998.[3]

- percentage of all Health and Human Services funding in Texas represented by Medicaid: 79 percent
- percentage of Texas's total budget represented by Medicaid (all funds): 26 percent
- percentage of Medicaid expenditure derived from state funds: 13 percent
- Texas's ranking among states on average spending per Medicaid recipient: 48
- Texas's ranking among states on total Medicaid spending: 3
- percentage of Texans living in poverty: 18 percent
- Texas's ranking on percentage of population in poverty: 8
- ratio of Texans in poverty to Texans covered by Medicaid: 58 percent
- Texas's ranking on ratio of Medicaid coverage to poverty population: 42
- percentage of Texas children in poverty: 24 percent
- percentage of Texas Medicaid recipients who are children: 56 percent
- percentage of Medicaid budget spent on children: 25 percent
- total amount spent for Texas Medicaid in 1993: $7.3 billion
- amount of Medicaid funds paid directly to Medicaid recipients: $0
- total payments to nursing homes made by Texas Medicaid: $1.05 billion
- total payments to hospitals made by Texas Medicaid: $2.2 billion

- total payments to intermediate care facilities (ICFs) for the mentally retarded by Texas Medicaid: $536 million
- number of childless, nonelderly, nondisabled, nonpregnant adults eligible for Medicaid: 0
- number of Texans receiving Medicaid in 1993: 2.3 million
- number of Texans on Medicaid with incomes under 20 percent of poverty: 1.26 million
- annual income for a family of three at 18 percent of poverty: $2,256
- federal poverty level for a family of three: $12,320

Q 10:3   How does the Balanced Budget Bill of 1997 (BBA) affect the Medicaid program?

The BBA has the goal of achieving approximately $13 billion in net Medicaid savings over five years while increasing state flexibility for the program's administration and oversight. States will have the ability to provide Medicaid services through managed care without obtaining a federal waiver. The requirement that states pay federally qualified health centers (FQHCs) on a cost basis will be eliminated over a multiyear period. States can use Medicaid payment rates to determine whether cost sharing is owed for QMBs and dual eligibles.

The legislation increases health coverage for children who are uninsured and provides for $24 billion to be spent on children's health care, with more than 7 million of the country's uninsured children becoming eligible for coverage. The Child Health Insurance Assistance Program entitles states to grants to expand health insurance access for eligible children. Many states, such as Texas, have adopted appropriate legislation to enable such funding and match federal funds through a specified formula.

States will also have considerable flexibility on how to spend the money. This includes how they define eligibility—with an income ceiling of 200 percent of poverty for states where current Medicaid eligibility is below 200 percent of poverty and a ceiling of 50 percent above the current ceiling for states with Medicaid eligibility ceilings in excess of 200 percent when the measure is enacted. Options for states include: (1) expanded Medicaid coverage; (2) enrollment of uninsured children in health plans by private health insurers; (3) direct provision of health services to children (including immunizations, well-child care, and services provided by disproportionate share hospitals [DSH]), although no more than 10 percent of the grant money can be used for noncoverage purposes (e.g., administration, outreach, or services); and (4) benefits must include either benefits equal to those provided in a "benchmark" benefits package, those provided by a state-administered program, or those of same actuarial value as one of the benchmark benefit packages and including at least inpatient and outpatient hospital services, physicians' surgical and medical services, laboratory and radiograph services, as well as well-baby and well-child care, including age-appropriate immunizations.

A benchmark benefit package would be either: (1) the standard Blue Cross/Blue Shield preferred provider option service benefit plan offered under the Federal Employees Health Benefits Plan, (2) the health coverage that is offered and generally available to state employees in the relevant state, or (3) the health coverage offered by a health maintenance organization (HMO) with the largest commercial enrollment of the coverage offered by such an organization in the relevant state.

Q 10:4   Who is eligible to receive Medicaid?

The following groups of people are eligible for Medicaid under federal law:

- recipients of Aid to Families with Dependent Children (AFDC)
- recipients of supplemental security income (SSI) or—in states using more restrictive criteria—aged, blind, or disabled individuals who meet more restrictive criteria than those of the SSI program, in place in the state's approved Medicaid plan as of January 1, 1972
- infants born to Medicaid-eligible women. Medicaid eligibility must continue throughout the first year of life, as long as the infant remains in the mother's household and she remains eligible or would be eligible if she were still pregnant.
- children under age 6 and pregnant women who meet the state's AFDC financial requirements or whose family income is at or below 133 percent of the federal poverty level. (The minimum mandatory income level for pregnant women and infants in certain states may be higher than 133 percent if, as of certain dates, the state had established a higher percentage for covering those groups.) States are required to

extend Medicaid eligibility to age 19 for all children born after September 30, 1983, in families with incomes at or below the federal poverty level. This will phase in coverage so that, by the year 2002, all poor children under age 19 will be covered. When eligibility is established, pregnant women remain eligible for Medicaid through the end of the calendar month ending 60 days after the end of the pregnancy regardless of any change in family income. States are not required to have a resource test for these poverty-level-related groups; however, any resource test imposed can be no more restrictive than that of the AFDC program for infants and children and the SSI program for pregnant women.

- recipients of adoption assistance and foster care under title IV-E of the Social Security Act
- certain Medicare beneficiaries
- special protected groups who lose cash assistance because of the cash program's rules, but who may keep Medicaid for a period of time. For example, people who lose AFDC or SSI payments due to earnings from work or increased Social Security benefits, and two-parent, unemployed families whose AFDC cash assistance is limited by the state and who are provided a full 12 months of Medicaid coverage.

Coverage may start retroactively to any or all of the three months before application if the individual would have been eligible during the retroactive period. Coverage generally stops at the end of the month in which a person's circumstances change. Most states have additional state-only programs to provide medical assistance for specified poor people who do not qualify for Medicaid. No federal funds are provided for state-only programs.

Q 10:5   Who else may be eligible for Medicaid?

States also have the option to provide Medicaid coverage for other categorically needy groups. These optional groups share characteristics of the mandatory groups, but the eligibility criteria are somewhat more liberally defined. Examples of the categorically needy for which the states will receive federal matching funds under the Medicaid program are the following:

- infants up to age 1 and pregnant women not covered under the mandatory rules whose family income is below 185 percent of the federal poverty level (the percentage to be set by each state)
- certain aged, blind, or disabled adults who have incomes above those requiring mandatory coverage, but below the federal poverty level
- children under age 21 who meet income and resources requirements for AFDC but who otherwise are not eligible for AFDC
- institutionalized individuals with income and resources below specified limits
- people receiving care under home-based and community-based services waivers
- recipients of state supplementary payments
- tuberculosis-infected people who would be financially eligible for Medicaid at the SSI level (only for tuberculosis-related ambulatory services and tuberculosis drug therapy)

Q 10:6   What is Medicaid coverage for the "medically needy"?

The option to have a "medically needy" program allows states to extend Medicaid eligibility to additional qualified people who may have too much income to qualify under the mandatory or optional categorically needy groups. This allows them to "spend down" to Medicaid eligibility by incurring medical or remedial care expenses to offset their excess income, thereby reducing it to a level below the maximum allowed by that state's Medicaid plan. States may also allow families to establish eligibility as medically needy by paying monthly premiums to the state in an amount equal to the difference between family income (reduced by unpaid expenses, if any, incurred for medical care in previous months) and the income eligibility standard.

Eligibility for the medically needy program does not have to be as extensive as for the categorically needy program. However, states that elect to include the medically needy under their plans are required to include certain children under age 18 and pregnant women who would be eligible as categorically needy except for income and resources. States may choose to provide coverage to other medically needy people: aged, blind, or disabled people; certain relatives of children deprived of parental support and care; and certain other financially eligible children up to age 21.

Q 10:7   Are there any other Medicaid eligibility criteria?

Medicaid does not provide medical assistance for all poor people. Even under the broadest provisions of the federal statute (except for emergency services for certain people), the Medicaid program does not provide health care services even for very poor people unless they are in one of the designated groups. Low income is only one test for Medicaid eligibility; assets and resources are also tested against established thresholds. Categorically needy people eligible for Medicaid may or may not also receive cash assistance from the AFDC or SSI programs. Medically needy people who would be categorically eligible, except for income or assets, may become eligible for Medicaid solely because of excessive medical expenses.

States may use more liberal income and resource methodologies to determine Medicaid eligibility for certain AFDC-related and aged, blind, and disabled individuals under section 1902(r)(2) of the Social Security Act. The more liberal income methodologies cannot result in the individual's income exceeding the limits prescribed for federal matching (for those groups subject to these limits).

Significant changes were made in the Medicare Catastrophic Coverage Act (MCCA) of 1988 that affected Medicaid. Although much of the MCCA was repealed, the portions affecting Medicaid remained in effect. The law also accelerated Medicaid eligibility for some nursing home patients by protecting more income and assets for the institutionalized person's spouse at home. Before an institutionalized person's monthly income is used to pay for the cost of institutional care, a minimum monthly maintenance needs allowance is deducted from the institutionalized spouse's income to bring the income of the householder spouse up to a moderate level.

Q 10:8   What is the current Medicaid beneficiary profile?

In 1995, Medicaid provided health insurance coverage to approximately 35 million beneficiaries (almost 13 percent of the U.S. population) at a cost of about $150 billion. Of the eligible beneficiaries, about 17 million were children in low-income families, 8 million were adults in low-income families, 6 million were disabled, and 4 million were elderly.[4] Of these eligible Medicaid beneficiaries, almost 5 million qualified for Medicare because of age or disability.

The spending and service use among these populations also varied, with most money being spent on disabled and aged beneficiaries. According to the 1997 Kaiser Commission Report, average per capita spending for low-income children was about $1,500, whereas average per capita spending on the disabled and elderly beneficiaries was $8,700 and $10,100, respectively.[5]

Q 10:9   What are the states doing to address this disparity in the Medicaid program?

Many states have taken steps to restructure their Medicaid programs by using managed care. To date, 42 states have waivers of certain Medicaid rules that permit them to require enrollment in managed care plans. Most states have concentrated on low-income children and adults; however, as discussed in Q 10:13, other states have established pilot programs for dual eligibles either with or separate from the federal Medicare program.

Q 10:10   Do all people eligible for Medicaid enroll as beneficiaries?

Some people who are eligible for Medicaid benefits do not enroll. According to the General Accounting Office, an estimated 3 million out of 14 million Medicaid-eligible children were neither enrolled in Medicaid nor covered under any other insurance program. These Medicaid-eligible uninsured children accounted for 30 percent of all uninsured children in the 1994 study.[6]

Q 10:11   What services must the states offer?

Although services covered by Medicaid vary by state, federal law requires the provision of hospital and physicians' services; laboratory and radiology services; nursing home and home health care; and early and periodic screening, diagnosis, and treatment (EPSDT) for children under age 21. Title XIX of the Social Security Act requires that to receive federal matching funds, the following basic services must be offered to the categorically needy population in any state program:

- inpatient hospital services
- outpatient hospital services
- physician services
- medical and surgical dental services
- nursing facility services for individuals aged 21 or older
- home health care for people eligible for nursing facility services
- family planning services and supplies
- rural health clinic services and any other ambulatory services offered by a rural health clinic that are otherwise covered under the state plan
- laboratory and radiology services
- pediatric and family nurse practitioner services
- federally qualified health center services and any other ambulatory services offered by a federally qualified health center that are otherwise covered under the state plan
- nurse-midwife services
- EPSDT services for individuals under age 21

If a state chooses to include the medically needy population, the state plan must provide, as a minimum, the following services:

- prenatal care and delivery services for pregnant women
- ambulatory services to individuals under age 18 and individuals entitled to institutional services
- home health services to individuals entitled to nursing facility services

If the state plan includes services either in institutions for mental diseases or in ICFs for the mentally retarded, it must offer either of the following to each of the medically needy groups: (1) the services contained in 42 C.F.R. sections 440.10–440.50 and 440.165 (to the extent that nurse-midwives are authorized to practice under state law or regulations); or (2) the services contained in any seven of the sections in 42 C.F.R. sections 440.10–440.165.

States may also receive federal funding if they elect to provide other optional services. The most commonly covered optional services under the Medicaid program include:

- clinic services
- nursing facility services for the aged in an institution for mental diseases
- intermediate care facility services for the mentally retarded
- optometrist services and eyeglasses
- prescribed drugs
- tuberculosis-related services for people infected with tuberculosis
- prosthetic devices
- dental services

States may provide home- and community-based care to those who are either medically needy or eligible for Medicaid due to receipt of SSI benefits; have limitations in specified activities of daily living (for example, toileting, transferring, and eating); and are at least 65 years of age. The services to be provided to these people may include personal care services, chore services, respite care services, adult day care, homemaker or home health aide, training for family members, and nursing services.

Q 10:12   What is the role of Medicaid as a benefit program?

Today, Medicaid assists more than 35 million low-income families as the safety-net health insurance program for the poor, as a Medigap policy for the poor elderly and disabled Medicare beneficiaries, and as a long-term care program for the disabled and elderly. Medicaid finances care for one in eight Americans and one in four children, and pays for 40 percent of the nation's births and half of all nursing home care. As an entitlement program, Medicaid pays for medical services to as many as 37 million low-income people who are blind, aged, disabled, or members of families with dependent children. It has three distinct features: (1) joint federal-state financing, (2) state administration consistent with broad federal standards, and (3) eligibility tied to standards for other cash benefits. Although federal law defines general eligibility and coverage, states design and administer the programs at the state level.

Q 10:13   What are the unique challenges facing federal and state policy makers under Medicaid?

Medicaid poses different challenges to regulators than does Medicare. The federal government pays more than one half of the expenditures for people eligible for Medicaid. This has caused federal regulators, and in response, state regulators, to control spending under the Medicaid program. The federal government seeks to reduce federal spending and limit its liability for Medicaid costs. States also seek to curb Medicaid spending, which usually makes up a substantial portion of the state's budget. A major tension in Medicaid comes from the pressure to maintain and expand services to the poor, elderly, and disabled while constraining the cost of the program's safety-net role and its impact on federal and state budgets.

Another challenge is the continued growth in enrollment. As insurance coverage for the nonelderly population has been eroding, Medicaid has become the major vehicle for the low-income population, particularly poor children and pregnant women. This, along with the increased number of elderly and disabled beneficiaries whose per capita costs account for a greater share of the spending increases, has escalated over the past few years.

Of particular concern are those beneficiaries who receive both Medicare and Medicaid benefits. The challenge is to coordinate between two different federal programs and involve states in the process. Any modification to these programs must take into consideration the unique status of these beneficiaries. Several states in New England are working together to design and develop a managed care model for integrating the financing and delivery of health care services to seniors and people with disabilities who are dually eligible for Medicare and Medicaid benefits. Under the proposed model, an integrated service network would manage all services, possibly under a shared-risk arrangement.

Q 10:14   How does the growth rate in Medicaid expenditures compare to national health care expenditure rates?

In 1995, the growth rate in Medicaid expenditures was about 9 percent, with state and federal Medicaid spending accounting for nearly 14 percent of total national health expenditures.[7] Although growth rates experienced extremely high levels in the late 1980s, the growth rate has slowed down greatly since 1992 when it was increasing at 22.4 percent per year.[8] Between 1992 and 1995, Medicaid spending grew only 9.5 percent annually and although it is expected to continue to grow, future projections place average annual increases at 7.7 percent until 2002 based, in part, on lower projected growth in enrollment.[9]

Q 10:15   What is the effect of recent welfare reform legislation on Medicaid?

The federal welfare reform legislation—Public Law 104-193—gave states the ability to unlink Medicaid eligibility from their new public assistance programs while retaining the old AFDC standards. The law eliminates the AFDC program but replaces it with a new block grant program called Temporary Assistance for Needy Families (TANF). Those previously eligible for AFDC retain Medicaid eligibility automatically. States are permitted to modify or simplify Medicaid eligibility standards as long as the 1996 Medicaid rules are treated as minimum standards. Consequently, some individuals will be eligible for Medicaid even though they are not eligible for TANF.[10,11] Other provisions of the new welfare reform law may result in fewer people receiving Medicaid benefits. Tightened eligibility scrutiny for coverage of disabled children under SSI could result in loss of coverage. Also, states will not receive federal matching funds for coverage provided to legal immigrants within five years of their entering the country. Legal immigrants already on Medicaid will not lose their eligibility.

MANAGED CARE SOLUTIONS

Q 10:16   What are the models of Medicaid managed care?

The guiding principle of Medicaid managed care is to achieve cost reduction by controlling utilization and providing incentives to the providers to control patient care. There are three major forms of Medicaid managed care arrangements:

Primary care case management (PCCM). This is the most loosely controlled Medicaid managed care product. It establishes the relationship between a primary care physician and a Medicaid client in which the provider agrees to provide gatekeeper services for a fixed fee per month per client. The contractual relationship exists, usually, between the state and the provider. The PCCM approves and monitors all services provided to the client and is accessible for emergencies 24 hours a day, seven days a week.

Prepaid health plans (PHPs). A state Medicaid agency can contract with a PHP for a specific range of services and limited risk, which the PHP can then contract to individual providers or clinics.

HMOs. The state can contract with HMOs to provide the full range of services to Medicaid clients, thus bearing the entire risk. In an HMO contract, all the providers are part of the same plan. The state may contract for multiple HMOs in a provider area. Another variety of this type of risk plan involves a health insuring organization, which takes full risk as a fiscal intermediary.

Q 10:17   How have states approached implemented Medicaid managed care?

States implementing Medicaid managed care have taken a number of different approaches, which have been studied by the National Academy for State Health Policy, the Commonwealth Fund and Henry Kaiser Family Foundation, and the General Accounting Office.[12-14] Those program elements that vary the most from one state to the other include eligibility and enrollment, disenrollment, marketing, use of enrollment brokers, selection of plans, and capitation payments to plans.

Q 10:18   What has been the effect of Medicaid managed care on enrollment and spending?

The Physician Payment Review Commission estimates that total Medicaid enrollment in managed care for June 1996 was about 12.8 million, or 38.6 percent of all beneficiaries. Enrollment in plans that are at full risk for the cost of services was about 8.8 million in 1996 (26.5 percent of all beneficiaries).[15] Although Medicaid programs have enrolled many beneficiaries into managed care programs, the impact on Medicaid spending has not been substantially affected. This is attributed to the particular problems with the disabled and elderly beneficiaries.

Q 10:19   What has been the impact of Medicaid HMOs on the academic medical centers?

In 1994, Tennessee created a giant Darwinian experiment in managed care. TennCare included 25 percent of the state's population and a substantial proportion of its indigents in one health care system. The inauguration of TennCare was marked by general chaos. Meyer and Blumenthal[16] identifies four "critical challenges" arising for the academic medical centers from the TennCare experience:

1. Decreased payments for services. Tennessee Medicaid was a generous supporter of medical care in academic medical centers and of graduate medical education itself. After TennCare, there was a general and severe decline in the revenues of academic medical centers largely as a result of reduced payment, high cost structure, and the inability to cost shift.
2. Decreased volume of clinical services. Managed care works by decreasing the amount of inpatient use. Academic medical centers, however, saw a painful reduction in the volume of patients and a shift to higher risk and higher intensity patients. Additionally, the academic medical centers caring for a large population of indigent and Medicaid patients have a general inability to cost shift.
3. Academic medical centers suffer from adverse selection. Although every physician and hospital will claim that its patients are sicker, the data on TennCare seem to show that the high-risk and resource-intensive patients did indeed stay with the academic medical center. This is not restricted to pregnancy—Vanderbilt has seen an increase in patients with acquired immune disease syndrome (AIDS), cystic fibrosis, and women who deliver low birth weight infants.
4. Decrease in graduate medical education funding. Despite assurances to the contrary, academic medical centers have seen a substantial decline in funding for graduate medical education as a result of inefficiency of collections of premiums on the part of the payers and discontinuation of disproportionate share payments by the federal government.

In response to the obvious financial problems for the academic medical centers engendered by TennCare, Tennessee restored funding and extracted some concessions regarding the training of primary care physicians.

Q 10:20   What types of organizations provide managed care to Medicaid recipients?

Many organizations that provide managed care to Medicaid recipients are the same as commercial managed care organizations. There is an increasing trend for community-based programs to become Medicaid providers under the theory that they best understand the needs of the clients. CalOptima was formed in Orange County, California, for the purpose of supplying managed care services throughout the county. CalOptima is designated as a county organized health system and contracts with physicians, physician/hospital organizations, and managed care organizations to provide services to county citizens eligible for MediCal. Because patient satisfaction is so closely linked to remaining with a patient's provider, CalOptima made a strong effort to involve the public by way of hearings and to enroll traditional MediCal providers. In April 1996, CalOptima had enrolled 255,000 patients in Orange County and had contracted with 8 HMOs and 28 physician/hospital consortiums.

Q 10:21   What role does a FQHC play in servicing care of indigent and Medicaid populations?

FQHCs were created under the Omnibus Budget Reconciliation Act (OBRA) of 1989 and are health care delivery units located in medically underserved areas. They are paid on a cost-based reimbursement at 100 percent, and may require the same of HMOs. Except in states where mandatory HMO programs exist, HMOs are not required to contract with FQHCs; however, FQHCs may contract with the state as an HMO or PHP.

Q 10:22   What is the present status of Medicaid reform?

Over the years, Medicaid has expanded to fulfill various social agendas and now plays a role as a significant payer. Medicaid payments and eligibility vary state to state. The federal contribution is determined largely by the number of eligibles. DSH compensates those hospitals that are the major Medicaid providers in their areas. Medicaid has historically been a low-paying indemnity provider with a small number of physicians seeing a large number of the patients. Because of its payment structures, Medicaid has had a tendency to be victimized by unscrupulous physicians, pharmacists, and other health care providers. They have created Medicaid "mills" that churn patients through, generate invoices, and give rudimentary care, at best. Thus, in the eyes of many managed care providers, Medicaid is rather unsavory.

As Medicaid becomes increasingly restrictive and a poor payer, Medicaid managed care has sparked interest in the provider community. Several pilot programs have been authorized by the Health Care Financing Administration (HCFA) to allow the states to try new ways of delivering medical care to Medicaid beneficiaries. The availability of managed care plans has sparked a major growth in this segment of the Medicaid market.

The states accomplish changes in their Medicaid structure primarily by means of waiver mechanism. Sections 1915 and 1115 of the Social Security Act allow the states to apply to HCFA for waivers of access or eligibility requirements. The section 1915 mechanism is primarily for defined pilot programs and the section 1115 mechanism is for state programs.

There is increasing enthusiasm for block grant legislation at the federal level. The proposal of Congress for block grant legislation would allocate funds to the states for support of the Medicaid program. Grants would reflect the Medicaid activity current in the state. A Medicaid block grant program takes the differences that already exist among the states and freezes them at current levels. Thus, under proposed block grant legislation, federal payments to the states could range from $846 for a West Virginian to $227 for a Nevadan. The average payment would be $464.[17]

Q 10:23   What is EPSDT?

EPSDT is a federally mandated program and in a managed care setting is required of the plan with the Medicaid contract. In 1989, OBRA expanded EPSDT and required the states to provide all medically necessary allowable services to eligible children. This can include even services that may be optional for others under a state's Medicaid program. EPSDT compliance once depended on the interaction between the physician and the parent of the beneficiary. Under managed care, it is a requirement for the plan.

Q 10:24   What role have Medicaid demonstrations played in reforming Medicaid at the state level?

Many states have sought section 1115 waivers to develop innovative demonstration, experimental, or pilot projects consistent with the broad goals and objectives of the Medicaid program. HCFA has approved demonstrations in Florida, Hawaii, Kentucky, Ohio, Oregon, Rhode Island, and Tennessee. HCFA has also granted an extension to the Arizona Health Care Cost Containment System. An application has been approved, in principle, in South Carolina, subject to the fulfillment of specified conditions. There are applications pending for nine other states, and several states are in the application process. States are increasingly turning to this waiver authority to expand Medicaid eligibility for acute care services to low-income, uninsured people; enroll Medicaid and newly covered beneficiaries into managed care; contain Medicaid costs; and gain flexibility in meeting federal program requirements. Whether or not these demonstrations have achieved all the goals and objectives of their proponents remains to be seen. For example, the Tennessee demonstration has shown lower beneficiary satisfaction than existed under the original state program. In a study conducted by William F. Fox and William Lyons in 1994, slightly less than two thirds of the beneficiaries were satisfied with the demonstration while over 80 percent were satisfied with Medicaid.[18]

The common characteristics of these demonstrations are:

- Expand Medicaid coverage to previously uninsured populations and use mandatory managed care arrangements for health care delivery.
- Focus on preventive and acute care coverage, usually for children and adults (except elderly and disabled).
- Exclude nursing home and institutional care for the mentally retarded.

The design of these programs varies from one state to another.

Q 10:25 What are the requirements of the Medicaid program for HMOs, health insuring organizations, and PHPs?

Risk-based contracts for specified health services are limited to federally qualified HMOs or those entities meeting two accessibility and fiscal solvency requirements. An exception is provided for certain prepayment plans that are not HMOs. All contracts and subcontracts under the Medicaid program must:

- Include provisions that define a sound and complete procurement contract.

- Identify the population covered by the contract.
- Specify enrollment and reenrollment procedures.
- Specify the amount, duration, and scope of services to be provided.
- Allow the state Medicaid agency and the Department of Health and Human Services to evaluate the quality, appropriateness, and timeliness of services performed under contract.
- Specify procedures and criteria for terminating the contract, including promptly supplying all information necessary to reimburse any outstanding Medicaid claims.
- Require the contractor to maintain an appropriate record system for services to Medicaid enrollees.
- Provide that the contractor safeguards information about recipients.
- Specify contractor activities that are related to third-party liability requirements.
- Specify which functions may be subcontracted.
- Provide that any subcontracts will be in writing and will be fulfilled as delegated.[19]

Q 10:26   What is the benefit of Medicaid reform to the federal government?

There are several benefits that could accrue to the federal government from Medicaid reform. The failure of meaningful health care reform in Congress did not change the fundamental pressure that drove it. The costs of caring for the sick of this country continue to grow at a rate exceeding inflation. Managed care of some sort appears to be the only mechanism by which costs can be controlled. Maintenance of a balanced budget requires payment reform. Because of the vast proportion of the budget consumed by entitlements, changes in Medicaid to reduce costs could have a profound influence on the budget balancing effort. The block grant mechanism is widely viewed as a mechanism for controlling the federal government's exposure to higher costs. Even in the absence of block grants, HCFA needs a credible alternative to the DSH (or "Dispro") program.

The present political atmosphere is likely to favor incremental health care reform and Medicaid is a likely target. This is consistent with a move to increase states' autonomy in health care systems and may include changes in federal regulations such as the Employee Retirement Income Security Act (ERISA).

Q 10:27   Can HCFA require cost sharing for Medicaid recipients?

Cost sharing is the shifting of some of the cost of the care to the recipient of the care. This can be accomplished by instituting copayments or requiring coinsurance. Coinsurance can be either a separate policy that pays for deductibles or a percentage of the cost paid directly by the beneficiaries. Federal law prohibits requiring cost sharing from Medicaid recipients for certain defined services. No cost sharing can be required from any person under 18 or 21 (state's option), for HMO services, for hospice services or services provided in institutions where beneficiaries apply their own income, or for family planning or emergency services. When cost sharing is applied, it typically is for pharmacy benefits and physician visits. Under a section 1115 waiver, cost sharing can be implemented within the defined expansion program. Because eligibility caps in many states are very low, any cost sharing may represent an unacceptable barrier to seeking care. When cost sharing is applied, the amount can be so low as to be more expensive for the state to collect than the revenue it produces.

Q 10:28   Will cost sharing decrease utilization?

Cost sharing may certainly pose a barrier to utilization. Requiring a copayment can decrease unnecessary use of services; however, for the very poor who are the recipients of Medicaid, copayment may force them to forgo preventive services or early treatment, which may avoid a more expensive hospitalization or episode of illness. Clear examples of the efficacy of prevention include childhood immunizations and prenatal nutrition. Decreasing access to these types of services would not be in the best interest of the health care system.

Q 10:29   What are the "macro" issues in health care that are likely to affect Medicaid program innovation?

The penetration of highly controlled and managed systems of care is variable throughout the United States. This creates an arbitrage opportunity for nationwide systems that see profits in being able to charge different rates for identical services in different parts of the country. With millions of Americans uninsured or underinsured, any expansion of eligibility of title XIX programs would disproportionately benefit managed care organizations. These organizations, therefore, are anxious to participate in Medicaid programs that they once shunned as too low paying. Further, since Medicaid is a joint state-federal program, it provides an opportunity for the commercial managed care organizations to access reasonably secure sources of funding. Because Medicaid is an entitlement program like social security and food stamps, the states alone cannot limit enrollees, for the most part.

Q 10:30   What has been the effect of Medicaid managed care on the quality of care for Medicaid recipients?

Because quality is such a nebulous value, it is difficult to assess, even in a program as large as Medicaid. There have been several systematic efforts at assessing quality in Medicaid programs.

Medicaid has been managed in Arizona since 1982. Prior to that time, Arizona did not participate in the Medicaid program. The Arizona Health Care Cost Containment System (AHCCCS) was created to enroll Arizona's poor in a managed care program. In 1989, long-term care was added through the Arizona Long Term Care System. The Kaiser Foundation[20] has studied the outcomes of AHCCCS. Patients enrolled in the system had the same or better access to medical care than did the comparison group in neighboring New Mexico, and the quality of care given to children was better. Prenatal care and nursing home care, however, was not as good. The Kaiser Foundation found AHCCCS to have saved a lot of money in its lifetime, perhaps more than $500 million; yet, the administrative costs were higher than comparable indemnity-like Medicaid programs, largely as a result of managing the care and providing the necessary information system.

The General Accounting Office released a 1996 report that was very critical of Medicaid. Commissioned by the House Ways and Means Committee, the report identifies three major problems with HCFA health care quality improvement program:

- HCFA does not determine if HMO quality assurance programs are operating effectively.
- HCFA does not systematically incorporate the results of the peer review organization review (PRO) of HMOs or use PRO staff expertise in its compliance monitoring.

- HCFA does not routinely collect utilization data that could most directly indicate potential quality problems.

The HCFA administrator has responded that this report unfairly emphasizes past events and does not recognize continuous improvements in quality monitoring. The report makes several recommendations that are useful for managed care organizations engaged in Medicaid managed care or contemplating entering that market:

- Build on existing federal, state, and private efforts.
- Use multiple strategies to evaluate care (certification, patient satisfaction survey instruments, and outcome measures).
- Encourage continuous quality improvement.
- Make information about providers available to beneficiaries in a useful and understandable way.

A major study examining the quality of care of Medicaid recipients is underway in New York City, conducted by the New York Consortium for Health Services Research. This three-year project examines questions related to quality and outcome of Medicaid, including:

- How does Medicaid managed care affect patterns of health care, utilization, and health outcomes?
- What is the impact on quality of care?
- Which Medicaid managed care plans are successful and why?
- What is the impact of Medicaid managed care on the financial condition of essential community providers, who have traditionally met the needs of Medicaid patients?
- How does Medicaid managed care affect the growing number of uninsured?

Q 10:31   Does Medicaid managed care actually save money?

In 1984, the combined federal and state expenditure from Medicaid was $36.7 billion. In 1994, this had increased to $135.5 billion and, without controls, is expected to be $262 billion by 2002. Although the costs for caring for a Medicaid beneficiary are less than for a commercial one, the increase in the number of Medicaid eligibles, coupled with the expected increase in the number of indigent and uninsured, is expected to put a tremendous stress on the system. It is expected that managed care will provide at least a partial solution. As important as Medicaid is at the federal level, the impact is even more at the state level. Between 1987 and 1994, the proportion of state general fund spending allocated to Medicaid increased from 8.1 percent to 13.3 percent.

The AHCCCS study indicates that there have been significant savings in Arizona since the inception of Medicaid managed care. Twelve studies that examined the impact of managed care on Medicaid costs found mixed results. Seven reported a decrease in costs to state Medicaid agencies, two reported cost increases, and the remainder showed unchanged, variable, or ambiguous results.[21]

A reasonable fear is that commercial managed care programs will avoid, if possible, covering those beneficiaries that cost the most: the frail elderly in nursing homes, those with AIDS, and the disabled.

Q 10:32   What is the impact of fraud and abuse in Medicaid?

It has been estimated that 10 percent of the estimated $1 trillion spent in the United States on health care is spent on providers who fraudulently bill public programs and private providers.

Q 10:33   What are the major types of fraudulent activities affecting Medicaid?

Fraudulently organized clinics. Because of the state-specific complexities in billing Medicaid, the opportunities for fraud are virtually infinite. California, for example, provides a differential payment for urban versus rural clinics, thus encouraging clinics to enroll patients from the rural areas. Similarly, in the indemnity model, there is a temptation for clinics to provide a large menu of services to patients, and to profit from them. Managed care, of course, promises to control this type of activity by paying a capitation rather than fee-for-service.

Durable goods. Fraud occurs here by unscrupulous vendors disassembling equipment and repackaging it to bill Medicaid at a higher price. Other schemes abound.

Home health. Typical fraudulent schemes include billing Medicaid for more hours than were provided or even billing for services provided when the alleged beneficiary was deceased.

Number brokers. Medicaid numbers have been sold to unscrupulous providers to bill for services never rendered.

Pharmacists. A common scheme is to bill Medicaid for more expensive drugs than were supplied.

Psychiatrists. Unbundling, overstating codes, billing for individual therapy when the patient is part of a group, and billing physician rates when a nonphysician provides the service are common fraudulent practices.

Dentists. Fraudulent procedures include billing for services not provided or unnecessary procedures.

Physicians. Physician fraud includes most of the other types of fraudulent practices identified above such as billing for services not performed, improper use of procedure codes, billing for unnecessary services, and self-referral. A 1994 settlement involving Caremark, Inc. involved payments made to physicians for referrals to Caremark facilities.

Transportation. Common frauds involve unbundling and charging for services not provided.

Problems with fraud cannot be expected to disappear with the advent of managed care. Because capitated payments will be made to managed care organizations to care for panels of patients, the fraud opportunities will come from overstating the number of enrollees, providing inadequate or less than mandated services to them, or providing substandard medications and equipment.

Q 10:34   What are the appropriate steps in assessing a Medicaid risk contracting opportunity?

North Western National Life Health Management Corporation of Minneapolis, Minnesota, has identified 10 major steps for entering into a risk arrangement:[22]

- Evaluate potential risks and benefits specific to the provider.
- Collect experience data to assess rates.
- Evaluate the balance of the network regarding hospitals, specialists, and primary care in the context of the Medicaid population.

- Establish a utilization monitoring function to ensure appropriate utilization within the confines of mandates.
- Consider a partner for capitation management.
- Establish management information systems links among providers (eligibility verification capability is required for Medicaid).
- Obtain stop-loss coverage.
- Develop a marketing plan specific to the Medicaid clientele.
- Monitor outcomes using a measurement of real time as much as possible.
- Align incentives.

There are several key issues that must be evaluated by anyone considering participating in the delivery of health care services covered under the Medicaid program.

Extensive regulations for eligibility and compliance. The regulations are extensive and somewhat onerous at the outset, suggesting the common concern of whether there is too much regulation to make it attractive business for managed care organizations (MCOs) and HMOs.

Broad scope of services. Coverage is broader than generally available under commercial plans with no copayment requirement. Although it is more difficult to establish appropriate incentives within the Medicaid populations, it has been shown that a managed care approach to the provider network can achieve significant savings without imposing substantial barriers to access. Because of the fixed dollar limitation and the regulatory restrictions of the program, HMOs and other MCOs competing for Medicaid enrollees will have to compete on the basis of benefits rather than price.

Marketing restrictions. The regulations require prior approval of marketing for enrollment. The confidentiality requirements of the regulations may pose a barrier to effective marketing. There has historically been a high turnover in enrollment because of the traditional eligibility requirements.

Enrollment and disenrollment. The regulations foster a "freedom of choice" and voluntary disenrollment is often on demand absent a state obtaining a waiver. There is no limited period during which the enrollees must remain enrolled, although loss of eligibility results in automatic disenrollment.

Provider network. There has been a problem, historically, in getting providers to serve the Medicaid populations. To the extent a program is risk based, there may be problems recruiting qualified providers.

Controlling utilization. One of the major problems identified in the Medicaid program is the lack of control over utilization because the traditional Medicaid program has no disincentives for utilization and a participant could, effectively, spend the entire day going from one physician to another without any controls. Medicaid eligible individuals have often misused the hospital emergency department as a "clinic" in the absence of physicians willing to accept the low levels of reimbursement. An advantage of a managed care model is the ability to direct enrollees to a network of providers.

Profitability. Although Medicaid has traditionally been the lowest level payer of all programs, in an efficiently run managed care model, there may be potential profits to MCOs and HMOs through effective management of marketing activities, voluntary disenrollment, and utilization controls. Some carve-outs of high-risk cases related to drugs, AIDS, neonatal care, and long-term care can be profitable for MCOs and HMOs.

Q 10:35   How does Medicaid compare to Medicare in physician reimbursement levels?

The answer to this question varies by state as the states' contributions vary. Table 10–1 shows physician payments by Medicaid as a percentage of Medicare reimbursement.

Q 10:36   What has been the state-level response to the demise of a national health care reform program?

After the demise of the various proposals in 1994 to revamp the American health care system, many states undertook ambitious plans to extend health insurance to more people. Of the states with universal coverage legislation, only Hawaii has implemented and expanded its 20-year-old program. One approach being taken by the states is to obtain waivers for expanded Medicaid programs for low-income people using a managed care model.

Table 10–1 State Medicaid Payments to Physicians as a Percentage of Medicare

State	%	State	%	State	%
Alabama	76–86	Kentucky	100–108	North Dakota	85
Alaska	74–220	Louisiana	85	Ohio	61
Arizona	112	Maine	58	Oklahoma	79
Arkansas	119	Maryland	55	Oregon	76
California	63	Massachusetts	87	Pennsylvania	57
Colorado	71	Michigan	69	Rhode Island	42
Connecticut	74	Minnesota	105–127	South Carolina	75
Delaware	76	Mississippi	81	South Dakota	111
DC	64	Missouri	49–55	Tennessee	93
Florida	78	Montana	95	Texas	92
Georgia	113	Nebraska	95	Utah	82
Hawaii	85	Nevada	96	Vermont	68
Idaho	91	New Hampshire	84	Virginia	90–92
Illinois	66–73	New Jersey	36–38	Washington	76–83
Indiana	99–101	New Mexico	82–83	West Virginia	98
Iowa	82–86	New York	31	Wisconsin	77–104
Kansas	67	North Carolina	98	Wyoming	121

Q 10:37   What has motivated state governments to consider managed care programs to meet their Medicaid program needs?

The primary reason that many state governments are turning to managed care to meet their Medicaid program needs is fiscal. Most states are experiencing dramatic increases in their Medicaid budgets that are creating major problems for state budgeting. In addition, most Medicaid programs are not well managed because there are no restrictions on a patient's ability to access a provider. Finally, many states are not accessing all the funds available under the federal matching program because of inefficiencies in the system.

NOTES

1. Adapted from: National Academy on Aging, *Facts on . . . Medicare: Hospital Insurance and Supplementary Medical Insurance* (Washington, DC: 1995).

2. National Academy on Aging, *Facts on . . . Medicare: Hospital Insurance and Supplementary Medical Insurance.*

3. Kaiser Commission on the Future of Medicaid, *PPRC Report, Medicaid Facts: The Medicaid Program at a Glance* (Washington, DC: 1997). Within "Physician Payment

Review Commission Annual Report to Congress: Medicare and Medicaid Guide," *CCH* 955 (11 April, 1997): 187.

4. Kaiser Commission on the Future of Medicaid, *PPRC Report, Medicaid Facts: The Medicaid Program at a Glance.*

5. Kaiser Commission on the Future of Medicaid, *PPRC Report, Medicaid Facts: The Medicaid Program at a Glance.*

6. *Health Insurance for Children: Private Insurance Coverage Continues To Deteriorate,* HEHS-96-129, PPRC Report (Washington, DC: 1996), 14. Within "Physician Payment Review Commission Annual Report to Congress: Medicare and Medicaid Guide," *CCH* 955 (11 April, 1997): 187.

7. K.R. Levit et al., "National health expenditures, 1995," *Health Care Financing Review* 18, no. 1 (1996): 175–214.

8. J. Holahan and D. Liska, "The slowdown in Medicaid spending growth: will it continue?" *Health Affairs* 16, no. 2 (1997): 157–163.

9. "The Economic and Budget Outlook: Fiscal Years 1998–2007," (Washington, DC: Congressional Budget Office, January 1997).

10. Health Care Administration Agency, "Link between Medicaid and Temporary Assistance for Needy Families, Fact Sheet # 1" (Washington, DC: 1996).

11. An analysis of the AFDC-related Medicaid provisions in the new welfare law, unpublished memorandum, 19 September, 1996, Center for Budget and Policy Priorities, Washington, DC; Impact of the new welfare law on Medicaid, Issue Brief no. 697, National Health Policy Forum, Washington, DC, 7 February, 1997. Referenced in "Physician Payment Review Commission Annual Report to Congress: Medicare and Medicaid Guide," *CCH* 955 (11 April, 1997): 416.

12. M. Gold et al., "Medicaid managed care: lessons from five states," *Health Affairs* 15, no. 3 (1996): 153–166.

13. J. Horvath and N. Kaye, eds., *Medicaid Managed Care: A Guide for States,* 3d ed. (Portland, ME: National Academy for State Health Policy, 1997).

14. *Medicaid States' Efforts To Educate and Enroll Beneficiaries in Managed Care,* HEHS-96-184 (Washington, DC: September 1996). Within "Physician Payment Review Commission Annual Report to Congress: Medicare and Medicaid Guide," *CCH* 955 (11 April, 1997): 439.

15. Physician Payment Review Commission Annual Report to Congress, "Medicare and Medicaid Guide," *CCH* 955 (11 April, 1997): 427.

16. G.S. Meyer and D. Blumenthal, "TennCare and academic medical centers," *Journal of the American Medical Association* 276 (1996): 672–676.

17. C. Mann, "Inside Medicaid: under fire from all sides," *Inside Medicaid Managed Care* (1996).

18. *Medicaid Facts: The Medicaid Program at a Glance. Fact Sheet from Kaiser Commission on the Future of Medicaid.* Within "Physician Payment Review Commission Annual Report to Congress: Medicare and Medicaid Guide," *CCH* 955 (11 April, 1997): 187.

19. Title XIX, Social Security Act; 42 C.F.R. § 434.6.

20. N. McCall, *The Arizona Health Care Cost Containment System: Thirteen Years of Managed Care in Medicaid* (Menlo Park, CA: The Henry J. Kaiser Family Foundation, July 1996).

21. D. Rowland et al., *Medicaid and Managed Care: Lessons from the Literature* (Washington, DC: Kaiser Commission on the Future of Medicaid, March 1995), 18.

22. Adapted from "Capitated Medicaid: 10 tips for a smoother transition," *Inside Medicaid Managed Care* (1996).

CHAPTER 11

Direct Contracting and Group Purchasing: An Employer and Regulatory Perspective

Marc B. Samuels

INTRODUCTION

Traditionally, employers have aligned themselves with managed care to achieve greater cost savings and administrative efficiencies than currently exist in fee-for-service medicine. To the employer, there is also often the appeal of control over quality. Managed care—health maintenance organizations (HMOs) in particular—offers the employer the important certainty of cost exposure. That is, a purchaser of an HMO product has shifted the responsibility of allocating medical care provision to another entity that is assuming the risk for it.

During the past year, however, employee and political concerns about the quality and accountability of managed care plans have made health care purchasers wary of their relationships. Although employees appreciate the cost savings attendant to HMO care, they resist the restrictions in choice and other burdens associated with a managed care product.

Employers in 28 states and at the federal level are being pulled into political battles over proportionate liability extended to managed care plans, the most threatening of which does away with protections afforded large employers who self-insure company health plans under the Employee Retirement Income Security Act (ERISA). This political climate, coupled with almost certain double-digit spending increases for employers, makes direct contracting between employers, physicians, and providers a strategy for businesses to explore.

Q 11:1   What is direct payer-provider contracting?

Simply put, direct contracting is a strategy by which physicians and other providers of health services contract directly with employers as payers for those services to deliver health and medical services to their employees. Under such an arrangement, an employer agrees to mandate or to provide financial incentives to employees to use specific physicians and providers while the physician or provider is issued incentives through a prepaid or other financial arrangement. If the contracting arrangement involves prepayment, most states will require the contracting arrangement to be made through an HMO that is regulated under state law. More often than not, however, direct contracting arrangements are not structured through HMOs, but instead involve an insurer or like company acting as a third-party administrator, or providing administrative services only (ASO).

Although this activity is also often regulated, it generally does not require the same stringent financial security of an HMO.

Q 11:2   Why is there an increased interest in direct contracting?

Perhaps the best reason for increased employer interest in direct contracting is the political and economic climate. Health care costs are rising once more; some experts say in the double digits. Congress has approved limited direct contracting in the Medicare program in the recently enacted Balanced Budget Act. The employer is looking for economic certainty.

Apart from the political and economic realities, certain limitations are being experienced in the employer's traditional relationship with managed care companies that make direct contracting an appealing alternative strategy for many employers. These limitations include:

Lack of control. When an employer contracts with an HMO, it places the responsibility for its employees' medical care in the hands of a third party that has accepted this responsibility in return for financial rewards dictated by contractual obligations. Although the employer may well have dictated the terms and characteristics of the health plan at the time of the negotiation, its actual day-to-day control is limited. Nonetheless, the contracting department of the employer, usually human resources, is the focus of employee malcontent (if it is present) with the health plan.

Lack of flexibility. For health plans, contractual terms are usually established annually at the time of contract renewal. Thus, alterations in an employer's financial status, employee relations, or business standing can not be reflected in the health plan in a meaningful time frame.

Lack of accountability. Once again, the relationship between the employer and the health plan is dictated contractually. The employer, however, is more directly accountable to its employees' health as a result of day-to-day contact.

Lack of trust. This problem stems from the fundamental lack of alignment among the participants in the employer-health plan-provider triangle.

Q 11:3 What is meant by "lack of control, flexibility, accountability, and trust"?

Employers today are more concerned about receiving value for their capital investment than in years past. A few years ago, cost was the benchmark by which employers chose health plans for their employees. As long as increased cost was accompanied by an increase in quality or accountability, the employer was happy. Today, employers want value for their health care investment dollar, expressed in quality outcomes rather than goals or cost saving strategies, and predictable, reasonable pricing, rather than the least costly physician, provider, or health plan.

From a service quality standpoint, many employers are becoming increasingly dissatisfied with their managed care plans. Companies are asking for increased control in the development, administration, and credentialing of contracted physician networks. HMOs and preferred provider organization (PPO) plans also upset many over the lack of flexibility in plan offerings. Still others are weary of their lack of control or input into plan modifications, claims adjudication, or the complaint resolution process. Indeed, the latter concern is the catalyst that sparked state medical association efforts over "patient protection" and proportionate liability for denial of medically necessary treatment(s) by HMOs.

Perhaps the greatest employer concern is the power of HMOs in the negotiating process and delivery of care. In some instances, HMOs download risk to physician and provider organizations without a perceived equitable sharing of the resultant rewards. There is also widespread perception that HMOs are unreasonably and unfairly profiting at the expense of employers and consumers. Finally, employers are most concerned about the unwillingness of HMOs and PPOs to share data on quality of care or internal operating costs and procedures—even with employers offering blanket confidentiality agreements.

Q 11:4   Why are physicians and providers interested in direct contracting?

On the physician and provider side, direct contracting is a valuable strategic asset, as well as a means to increase reimbursement by, in most cases, cutting out the middleman. If physician, provider, and purchaser are happy, a direct contracting relationship with a large company can ensure a physician practice or hospital system a solid income, as well as bring them closer to the patients they serve, the company employees, and their families. Physicians and providers, like many employers, also believe that managed care plans—especially HMOs—are too profitable at the expense of providing care. Rather, many physicians and providers believe that HMOs merely manage cash, not care.

Physicians and providers also believe that they must regain ground lost to HMOs during the past years. Some believe they have become nothing more than vendors in the new health care delivery system. Finally, like many employers, physicians and providers believe that managed care plans do not share any "savings" with employers or providers. In fact, physicians and providers believe that direct contracting may enable them to align their incentives with the downward reimbursement trends occurring in both the public and private markets. Direct contracting allows physicians and providers to align their financial gains with the provision of care in their local communities, rather than gain significant advantages from keeping patients out of their offices and hospitals.

Public programs such as Medicare and Medicaid have begun to explore new means to achieve financial savings and continue to push responsibility for funding and control to the states. As this has occurred, physicians and providers have come to believe that direct contracting is a better means of interacting with government purchasers and find this preferable to serving as mere providers under contract to selected HMOs. Quality and reimbursement concerns in many state Medicaid programs may give physicians and providers the competitive edge they need to compete effectively with managed care for such business.[1]

Q 11:5 What market conditions are needed for viable direct contracting?

The best market conditions in which employer direct contracting can work efficiently and effectively are:[2]

- large, urban settings
- low managed care penetration
- few organized managed care plans
- strong physician and provider relationships with business, including community participation
- local, community-based decision makers
- broad offerings and scope of services
- physician and hospital commitment to the employer and employee

Q 11:6 Why are employers moving away from the standard HMO model?

Many employers are concerned with the increasing costs of managed care and the reemergence of strong physician/provider groups or integrated systems. Employers want to share in the tremendous profits garnered by HMOs in the past years, and realize the only way to achieve efficiencies for their boards and management is through dealing directly with providers in purchasing care. These sentiments are being echoed throughout the employer community: large or small, self-insured or fully insured, ERISA or non-ERISA.

Q 11:7 Which companies would consider direct contracting?

Any business that sponsors its own employee health care plan(s) is a candidate for direct contracting. Typically, major employers (e.g., Delta Airlines, American Airlines, Dow Chemical, U.S. West, Mobil Oil, Weyerhaeuser, Brown and Root, or International Paper) have the number of employees to achieve the administrative efficiencies and quality outcomes sought by employers. On the other hand, many small companies are

finding means to collectively contract directly through purchasing coalitions and cooperatives. Since the early 1980s, businesses have created
more than 135 employer-led health care coalitions in the United States. As
many as 95 of them are members of the National Business Coalition on
Health, an umbrella group of state and local employee coalitions involved
in group purchasing efforts and the quest for value and accountability in the
health care system. Direct contracting and its value and accountability
underpinnings have also been the springboard for several business, physician, provider, and health care vendor industry coalitions, the purpose of
which is to study outcomes and accountability of players in the health care
game. Some of the more prominent groups include the Foundation for
Accountability, the North Central Texas Health Plan Employer Data and
Information Set Coalition, the Washington Business Group on Health, a
new institute founded by Sean Sullivan of the National Business Group on
Health, and the National Association of Managed Care Physicians.

Q 11:8   For which services do companies typically contract?

Typically, targeted medical and health services such as acute care
hospital service, laboratory, home health, skilled nursing care, physician,
prenatal and maternity care, prescription drug benefits, and mental health
programs are service targets of employer direct contractors. In several
instances, ERISA employers are moving toward contracting for such
services on a prepaid or "capitated" basis, asking to share or shift the risk
to physicians and providers to the extent allowable under state law.

**Q 11:9   What financing mechanisms do employers use when direct
contracting with providers?**

In several states, the development of these risk contracts may be in
conflict with state insurance regulations, prompting employers to engage
an insurance partner to act as an ASO. Physicians and providers would then
work through the ASO, making the deal legal. Employees, physicians, and
providers often find themselves in strong policy debates with state regulators over what is "allowable," and several employer-provider coalitions
have formed at the state level—often with resistance from the managed
care industry—to push for relaxed direct contracting regulations.

Contracts entered into in tough regulation states are often consummated on a negotiated fee-for-service basis or using some form of legal financial incentive scheme. With physicians, fee-for-service to generalist physicians and financial incentives to specialists seems to be the emerging trend. With hospitals, per diem arrangements are still the most popular since they are easy to calculate and negotiate for the employer.

Q 11:10   Which direct contracting models are most employed by companies?

Each marketplace has its own unique direct contracting model based on political and health care physician and provider demographics, managed care market penetration, and employer size and participation in group purchasing arrangements. The four models most used by employers are:

Single service or "carve-out" model. In this model, coalitions use their collective purchasing power to jointly consider such programs as prescription drug benefits, mental health care services, utilization review, outpatient laboratory tests, drug testing, or specialty and postacute care. Coalitions in Kalamazoo, Michigan; Nashville, Tennessee; and Tampa, Florida, are examples of this approach. Employers receive value for their collective union by receiving lower unit prices for these services.

Group purchasing and evaluation of HMO services. In this model, a single request for proposal is offered to competitive bidding by interested HMOs. As a part of the selection process, coalitions usually include product and patient satisfaction tools. The results of these surveys are used in the rate negotiations and are usually published and shown to the employees, as well as the managed care plans. This approach is best employed in mature managed care markets. As a result, it is most widely used in California by the Pacific Business Group on Health. It is also popular in the Midwestern market, and is employed in Missouri by the Gateway Purchasing Alliance. To some extent, the "big 10" coalition of employers, including Sears and American Express, used this model when they created a single request for proposal for collective employer bargaining in 1995. In that case, employee benefits consulting giant Mercer designed and implemented the study and the model.

Employer-provider cooperative model. Under this scenario, a group of employers in a particular community band together, design a plan, and invite providers to bid. This approach has been successful in the Midwestern market in Minneapolis and Minnesota. It is usually a tough sell to employers because it affords the companies little control over the product or plans.

Provider-sponsored network model. Several coalitions have increasingly contracted directly with individuals and networks of physicians and providers. This model has been employed in Denver; Madison, Wisconsin; Memphis, Tennessee; and Houston. The Houston Health Care Purchasing Organization (HHPO) contracts directly with more than 55 hospitals and 4,500 physicians in the Houston and surrounding market. Although Denver has a competitive pricing approach to its model, the HHPO initially priced its physician and provider contracts on a uniform basis, meaning that the service and unit price provided in an out-of-medical-center hospital is the same as that provided in a medical center facility. The hospital pricing is based on diagnosis-related groups (DRGs); thus, the overall control and responsibility for utilization is with the physicians and the providers rather than a third-party administrator. Physician contracts are structured on a similar basis, except they are negotiated on a fixed fee basis. The HHPO does not have a common plan design or claims payer, and employees maintain that responsibility. The HHPO maintains responsibility for negotiating contracts, repricing resultant claims, and administering the quality analysis reviews of network physicians and providers. As part of their contract with the HHPO, network physicians and providers have agreed to submit data to the HHPO for quality and analysis review for all patients—not simply for HHPO patients. The format for the data is the Uniform Billing Form (UB 92), established by the National Uniform Billing Committee. None of the HHPO contracts are currently capitation based because Texas requires that a prepaid contract be administered solely through HMOs, or certified nonprofit health care corporations (5.01(a)s).

Contracts between one medical group/one hospital and one employer. This type of relationship is best where the provider is a multispecialty group or independent practice association offering a wide variety of services. Such an arrangement will reduce the employer's overall administrative burden and costs associated with contracting multiple provider relationships. Medical groups that offer fewer, less comprehensive services are at a competitive disadvantage with one employer or employer group, but may seek to competitively align with employers as a mechanism to achieve certain business objectives. For such groups, independence is the primary motivation for the medical group and facility, while simplicity is the primary motivation for the employer. For larger medical groups, this type of arrangement allows for hiring or contracting new physicians (depending on the state) to "fill in the gaps" and attract other business arrangements.

Contracts between several medical group/hospital facilities and one employer. This approach, similar to the HHPO model above, involves an agreement between several medical groups and hospital facilities and one very large employer. In some states, the physicians or physician groups and hospitals may form a physician-hospital corporation or some other joint venture arrangement. This arrangement provides the same incentives for the employer as the first model described, with the additional diminution of unit prices.

Q 11:11 What risks do providers feel are associated with direct contracting arrangements?

Many physicians and hospitals are concerned that entering into direct contracting relationships with employers will damage, perhaps to their economic detriment, their relationships with managed care plans. Some providers even believe that vindictive HMOs may alter their patient flow, renegotiate their financial incentives, or worse, terminate their relationship. These concerns should not prevent physicians and providers from exploring direct contracting relationships. Hospitals may have the most to lose as their capital base is derived completely from factors beyond their control: physician referral patterns, HMO contracting patterns, demographics, and technological innovation. For hospitals, loss of managed care business may be damaging, but more important, it may be "life threatening"; however, because of favorable congressional activity on the "provider sponsored network" issue in Medicare, hospitals, especially, should not deter themselves from direct contracting relationships. In fact, in a well-penetrated market, or in markets with sophisticated purchasers, managed care plans, physicians, and providers may all benefit from collaboration and sharing product offerings.

Q 11:12 What is the effect of the trend toward integrated delivery systems on direct contracting?

The trend toward integration in the health care services sector is consistent with employer direct contracting. Some posit that physician, provider, and health care organization integration is a necessary prerequisite for direct contracting to occur effectively.[3]

The incentives aligned with physician and provider integration are consistent with the incentives for employers and providers entering into direct contracts: cost efficiencies, consolidation of services, increased market leverage through increased provider and consumer contact and larger geographic access, and increased market share commensurate with lower per diem costs. Fully integrated provider networks are optimally aligned to gain through direct employer contracting arrangements because the "one-stop shopping" they offer is consistent with the employer's search for value, regardless of employer size. Integrated systems also are perceived as less of a threat on the part of HMOs and other managed care plans because these plans need large, integrated systems to make themselves appealing to employer groups and coalitions, especially self-insured, large ERISA employers.[4]

Q 11:13   By what means can employers and providers maintain effective direct contracting relationships?

Employers, physicians, and providers can keep effective direct contracting relationships moving in a positive direction by employing such directives as: a continuous quality improvement council or mechanism; consultation on strategy among all parties to the contract and between employers and employees; and structuring the original arrangement to include a "buy in" by all parties so that the parties do not take the relationship for granted in the future.

These strategies will afford all parties the transaction stability, predictability, and "value" in their arrangement, and will help ensure lasting relationships.

Q 11:14   What financial risks are present for employers and providers in direct contracting relationships?

Failure to align medical management responsibilities with existing financial risk. In certain instances, physicians and providers may not be ready to accept such large insurance risk from business or employer coalitions. Such an event may lead to the acceptance of "bad risk" by providers, and will result in employees going out of network to receive contracted services. To ensure that this pitfall does not occur, business negotiators should consider using a third party or provider-sponsored insurer to accept hospital risk, while waiting to fully consummate a contract with some or all physician groups until they are capable, both from a business and personal perspective, to accept insurance risk.

Failure to research insurance or provider partner(s). Many employers and providers feel it necessary to "jump into" direct contracting relationships when first presented with the opportunity. When this event occurs, negative consequences may result. Physicians and providers may enter into contracts for the wrong reasons, such as lack of alternative business opportunities or lack of alternative provider network partners. In addition, employers searching for value need access to patient provider data. In haste, employers may contract with providers that lack a proven track record in collecting or providing data. On the other hand, many providers may expect greater financial incentives in return for their services than employers are willing to give. Failure on the part of employers to rationalize to providers their reimbursement scheme down to the lowest common denominator may immediately lead to credibility problems with providers. In order to remedy this scenario, all partners to the agreement must evidence proof of commitment at the front end. If either party cannot find a way to track necessary data, whether outcomes or cost, the item or items should be eliminated from the contract between the parties, or risk should be shifted accordingly between the parties.

Inadequate fee schedule. Traditional arrangements favor capitating generalist physicians and paying fee-for-service to specialist providers. This mode of reimbursement, however, is not consistent with demographic, technological, and market health care trends. Employers should consider paying fee-for-service rates to generalist physicians and capitating specialists, so as to thwart the possibility of unequal profits and losses among various network providers leading to adversity to the direct contracting relationship. Perhaps the easiest answer is to have a common fee schedule (such as Medicare DRG rates) going into the contract among the various physician and provider groups/networks. Another issue to watch for is the adequacy of the withholding or reserve fund for noncapped physicians and providers. Without a financial cushion, unanticipated utilizations may lead to undesired financial circumstances.

Lack of adequate stop-loss insurance. The adequacy of stop-loss insurance is critical to the success of the employer/provider direct contracting relationship. Employers should shop carefully, as rates vary widely. Employers should seek advice from an ASO or other insurance knowledgeable consultant in setting up stop-loss coverage.

Marketplace issues. Make sure prior to finalizing any contract that all physicians and providers in a given network can participate in the employer plan or employer and HMO contracted plan. Often, physicians and providers enter into noncompete or exclusivity arrangements with HMOs and other managed care plans in exchange for more favorable financial incentives. Consequently, physicians and providers may be putting themselves at financial and business risk by entering into certain direct contracts, while employers will not be receiving all they bargained for.

Q 11:15   What are the business issues that concern employers entering into a direct contracting relationship with providers?

When making the decision to commit to direct contracting, employers must think through whether they will purchase existing products or design a product of their own. Second, members within an employer coalition need to compare a collaborative strategy to a competitive one. Third, the employers need to decide if the number of physicians and providers should be limited, or if the plan should be designed to include "any willing participant." Employer coalitions need to decide whether common design elements will work for all employers in the coalition or the community. Finally, employers need to decide how to gauge, employ, and use quality and accountability data to attain the value in purchasing that is the cornerstone of the direct contracting rationale.

Q 11:16   What about provider concerns?

Providers are generally supportive of direct contracting relationships. As in many managed care settings, generalist physicians may at first appear more easygoing than specialists about entering into such contracts. Many state medical associations are gaining great leeway in their ability to contract directly with employers at various levels of insurance risk. Physicians are concerned most about the one element that is nonnegotiable to most employer coalitions: data. Employer desire for patient and physician identifiers and encounter data worries physicians on several levels. To create and maintain a responsive health care economy, physicians and employers will have to negotiate and come to terms on the data issue, as they are still accountable to the purchaser(s) for quality of provided care.

Q 11:17   What about hospital concerns?

Hospitals are key players in the regulatory battles over direct contracting being waged at the state level; however, they seldom want to engage the issue. With the exception of federal legislation governing provider-sponsored organizations, nary a peep has been heard from many state hospital trade associations over the impediments being constructed against their autonomy and competitiveness by the insurance industry. Central to the hospital case should be that healthy competition or collaboration between providers and HMOs is valuable to the health care system. It aligns incentives and may lead HMOs to play new roles necessary for their future survival as the pendulum swings back toward healthy communities and more personal delivery of needed health care services.

NOTES

1. E.P. Gee and A. Fine, *Health Systems Review* (March/April 1997): 70–74.
2. A. Fine, Conceptual rationale and practice imperative for direct contracting, Second Annual Direct Contracting Forum: Direct Contracting '96 The Future of Managed Care, ICM, Chicago: 30 September, 1996.
3. Fine, Conceptual rationale and practice imperative for direct contracting.
4. Fine, Conceptual rationale and practice imperative for direct contracting.

CHAPTER 12

Corporate Compliance Issues in Health Care Delivery

Cyndi M. Jewell

INTRODUCTION

A landmark of sorts occurred in 1997 and 1998 when academic medical centers came under closer scrutiny by the Health Care Financing Administration (HCFA) than ever before. Signaled by the action against the University of Pennsylvania to settle claims for overcharging Medicare that amounted to $30 million including penalties, academic centers nationwide prepared for similar disasters. Some centers voluntarily disclosed overcharges and paid a lesser penalty. The magnitude of the compliance with billing audit can be demonstrated by the March 1998 ruling, noting that the University of Pittsburgh School of Medicine agrees to pay $17 million to settle Medicare and Medicaid billing disputes. In fact, the industry of consultants that formerly focused on "revenue maximization" and recommended unbundling of codes and other measures to squeeze more money out of payers are now consulting on "compliance" and rigid observation of the rule book. This is certainly not limited to the academic medical centers, although these institutions have the additional exposure of the supervision of clinical activities by the teaching physician. The result is confusion on the part of HCFA when it is billed under part B for a clinical service provided by a trainee supported by Medicare educational payments to the hospital.

Formerly the province of large industries, the phrase "corporate compliance" is gaining recognition in health care circles, particularly those dealing with the direct delivery of health care, including those organizations that employ or contract with physicians. In general, compliance can be defined as a comprehensive strategy to ensure that the organization consistently complies with the applicable laws relating to its business activities. For health care, those laws are increasingly being redefined, specifically by several recent sentinel legislative initiatives: the Healthcare Insurance Portability and Accountability Act of 1996 and the Balanced Budget Act of 1997.

Q 12:1   What activities of managed care organizations (MCOs) and health maintenance organization (HMOs) are subject to health care fraud?

Health care fraud enforcement activities arise under several provisions of federal law and under state law. These activities include false claims and other fraudulent billing practices, illegal referrals under the Medicare and Medicaid antikickback statute, and physician self-referral practices proscribed under federal and state law. With respect to MCOs, any time an arrangement directs the flow of health care to any specific provider, or any one party exercises undue influence over a patient's health care decision, there is the potential for violation of these laws.

Medicare fraud and abuse (F&A). Managed care arrangements are subject to scrutiny under federal and state antikickback laws. In the context of Medicare and Medicaid, F&A laws prohibit arrangements that encourage or influence referrals of patients.[1] In the case of *U.S. v. Greber*, 760 F.2d 68 (3d Cir.), *cert. denied*, 474 U.S. 988 (1985), the court adopted a broad test that provided that even if one purpose of the arrangement was to induce referrals, the statute was violated.

Billing fraud. In addition, the F&A Act defines two general categories of conduct as potentially violate of its provisions. The first is filing false claims and the second is giving or receiving payment for referrals. Such violations can result in criminal penalties if performed willingly and knowingly and can result in civil monetary penalties and program exclusion even in the absence of intent.[2]

Illegal referral restrictions. Under legislation commonly referred to as the Stark Laws, a physician or immediate family member may not make patient referrals to an entity for furnishing Medicare- or Medicaid-reimbursed designated health services if the physician or a family member has an ownership or investment interest in, or a compensation arrangement with, the entity.[3] An ownership or investment interest may involve equity, debt, or other means, and includes an interest in an entity that holds an ownership or investment interest in an entity providing designated health services. Designated health services include (1) clinical laboratory services; (2) radiology services; (3) radiation therapy services; (4) physical and occupational therapy services; (5) durable medical equipment and supplies (DME); (6) parenteral and enteral nutrients, equipment, and supplies; (7) prosthetics, orthotics and prosthetic devices, and supplies; (8) outpatient prescription drugs; (9) home health services; and (10) inpatient and outpatient hospital services.

Q 12:2   Is health care fraud important to the federal government?

The federal government announced that health care fraud is the number two enforcement priority. The volume of health care fraud is estimated at $100 billion, of which $23 billion is fraud perpetrated on Medicare. With the contraction of funding available for Medicare payment, the government does not perceive that it can lose this amount of money. For example, although the False Claims Act has been in existence since the Civil War, recently it has been amended and its use has resulted in more than $1 billion in recovery since 1986.

Q 12:3   Does Medicare regulate physician incentive arrangements under managed care?

Yes. On December 31, 1996, HCFA published final rules amending its earlier rules governing physician incentive plans operated by federally qualified HMOs and competitive medical plans (CMPs). The objective of the rule was to prohibit the use of physician payments to limit or reduce necessary services to enrollees. In addition, the rule imposes certain disclosure and stop-loss requirements on HMOs when payments put physicians at substantial financial risk for referral services. Plans with direct contracting and subcontracting arrangements that shift substantial risk must disclose the following information on an annual basis:[4]

- whether referral services are covered by the incentive plan
- the type of payment arrangement used (e.g., withhold or capitation)
- the percentage of total income at risk for referrals
- the amount and type of stop-loss coverage
- the number of enrollees and whether enrollees were pooled to achieve the total

- for capitated physicians, the previous year's percentage of payment that was for primary care services, specialty referral services, hospital services, and other types of providers
- a summary of enrollee surveys results

Physician groups that do not transfer substantial risk to their own physicians are not required to disclose this information. Intermediaries such as independent practice associations (IPAs) are required to report their incentive arrangements, regardless of the risk transferred.

Q 12:4   What activities of a managed care entity could constitute fraud as defined in the F&A Act?

Fraud includes any intentional deception or misrepresentation that an individual knows to be false and that could result in an unauthorized benefit to himself, herself, or some other person. Examples of such activities include:

- billing for services not rendered
- misrepresentation of services rendered
- kickbacks
- deliberate application for duplicate reimbursement
- false or misleading entries on cost reports

Q 12:5   What type of activities involving a managed care entity could be deemed abusive under the F&A Act?

Incidents or practices that may directly or indirectly cause financial losses to government health programs or to beneficiaries or recipients (which is almost anything a government agent considers unacceptable, but does not rise to the level of actionable fraud) include:

- unnecessary services
- breach of assignment agreement
- gang visits (in which a physician charges for multiple patients during a single encounter)

- improper billing practices
- routine waiver of coinsurance and deductibles
- failure to maintain adequate records or accounting to substantiate costs
- excessive compensation to owners, administrators, or owner-related employees

Q 12:6   How do Medicare and Medicaid reimbursement rules apply in managed care arrangements?

For managed care organizations, the most significant reimbursement issues arise under the related organization principle and the prohibition on assignment and reassignment of Medicare and Medicaid payments. These include:

Cost of related organization principle. When a provider is paid on a cost basis, it is subject to a limitation on costs applicable to services, facilities, and supplies when they are furnished by organizations related by ownership or control. Costs for items furnished by a related party are limited to the cost to the related organization and may not exceed the price of comparable items or services that could be purchased elsewhere. In the context of an integrated delivery system (IDS), if a management services organization (MSO) buys services from the hospital that formed it, the principle applies unless the MSO qualifies under this exception to the principle as follows:

1. The supplying organization is a bona fide separate organization.
2. A substantial part of the supplying organization's business activity of the type carried on with the provider is transacted with other organizations not related to the provider and the supplier by common ownership or control, and there is an open, competitive market for the type of services or supplies furnished.
3. Institutions such as the provider typically obtain services, facilities, or supplies from outside sources rather than producing them internally.
4. The charge to the provider is in line with the charge for similar items in the open market and no more than the charge made under comparable circumstances to others by the supplying organization.

Restrictions on assignment or reassignment. Under Medicare part B, payment for physician services and other medical and health services may be made either to the beneficiary or directly to the provider of services under an assignment agreement. Although a beneficiary can assign his or her rights to payment to the physician or supplier, these parties are prohibited from reassigning rights to receive payment to others absent certain exceptions, such as payment to an employer as a condition of employment or payment to an agent who provides billing and collection services. In the context of a managed care entity, the mechanism for billing Medicare or Medicaid must consider these prohibitions against reassignment.

For fully integrated systems, such as those that employ the providers, there is greater protection under the existing statutory exceptions and under applicable safe harbor regulations for violating any federal or state antireferral laws or regulations. To analyze the potential liability of any provider organization or its activities under federal antifraud and abuse laws and regulations, each structure has to be evaluated in the context of each activity in which it is engaged. For example, an IPA is far less at risk for fraud and abuse than an MSO because of its limited function as a provider organization that facilitates contracts.

Q 12:7   What is the antikickback statute and how does it affect managed care arrangements?

The antikickback statute prohibits the knowing and willful solicitation, receipt, offer, or payment of any remuneration directly or indirectly, overtly or covertly, in cash or in kind, in return for (a) referring an individual to a person for the furnishing or arranging for the furnishing of any item or service for which payment may be made in whole or in part by Medicare or Medicaid or (b) purchasing, leasing, ordering, or arranging for or recommending purchasing, leasing, or ordering any good, facility, service, or item for which payment may be made in whole or in part by Medicare or Medicaid.[5]

Penalties for violation range from civil monetary penalties of up to $25,000, incarceration for a period up to five years, and exclusion from Medicare and Medicaid programs. With the recent holding in the case of *Hanlester Network v. Shalala*, 51 F.3d 1390 (9th Cir. 1995), there is now

some clarity to the scope of the "one purpose" test because of the requirement that there be some element of intent to violate the statute.

Q 12:8   What are the laws that regulate physician referrals?

Under the Ethics in Patient Referrals Act (also known as the Stark Bill),
referrals by a physician to a clinical laboratory in which or with which the
physician has a financial interest or relationship are expressly prohibited.
When enacted in 1989, this act did not apply to services provided directly
by a physician (or under the physician's direct supervision) or to non-
Medicare covered services. Effective December 31, 1994, however, under
an amendment to the Stark Bill, the prohibition was extended to cover not
only clinical laboratory services, but also physical therapy services; occupational therapy services; radiology or other diagnostic services; radiation
therapy services; durable medical equipment; parenteral and enteral nutrients, equipment, and supplies; prosthetics, orthotics, and prosthetic devices; home health services; outpatient prescription drugs; and inpatient
and outpatient hospital services. Proposed amendments to the law will
extend beyond Medicare-covered services to include all services for which
payment is made with federal funds (e.g., Medicaid). Penalties for violating the Stark Bill include not only nonpayment for services subject to
prohibited referrals and program exclusion, but also civil monetary penalties of up to $15,000 per service, civil monetary penalties for each day that
a required disclosure is not made, and up to $100,000 for participation in
any circumvention scheme.

There are a number of general exceptions to the prohibitions in the Stark
Bill. The most important is the medical group practice exception. Under
this exception, each physician must provide most of the services; the group
provides, bills, and collects for the services; the expenses and income are
allocated by the existing system; there is no compensation for volume or
value of referrals; and 75 percent of the patient encounters are conducted
by group members. This exception does not apply to the offering of durable
medical equipment (other than infusion pumps) or parenteral or enteral
nutrients, equipment, or supplies.

There are published exceptions for ownership in publicly traded securities: ownership and investment in services provided by hospitals located in
Puerto Rico, by rural providers, and when the physician is authorized to

perform the services and the investment or ownership interest is in the hospital itself and not merely a subdivision thereof. Other exceptions exist for prepaid plans or other HMOs as defined by statute, rental of office space or equipment, hospital employment and service arrangements, physician recruitment, other service arrangements, and other isolated financial transactions.

The self-referral ban does not apply to *bona fide* employment relationships where the employer is paying the employee for the provision of designated services; however, the test for a *bona fide* employment relationship will require a finding that:[6]

1. the employment is for identifiable services
2. the remuneration is consistent with the fair market value of the services and is not based on the volume or value of referrals
3. the remuneration is provided under a commercially reasonable agreement
4. such other requirements as the Secretary of the Department of Health and Human Services (HHS) may impose

Productivity bonuses are allowed provided they are based on services performed personally by the physician. This is more restricted than the productivity bonus available under the group practice exception.

Q 12:9   Do managed care arrangements using IDSs and MCOs create any risk for violating laws that regulate physician referrals?

Yes. Because the statute defines "financial relationship" to include both ownership/investment as well as compensation arrangements, the provisions of the Stark Bill must be taken into consideration when structuring the various provider organizations for participation in managed care arrangements. Activities of HMOs, MCOs, and IDSs are subject to scrutiny under both the antireferral and the antikickback laws, regardless of the existence of a specific Medicare or Medicaid contract, because the laws apply to any payments made by Medicare or Medicaid. Because Medicare is often a secondary payer to employer group health plans, each contract executed by an HMO with an outside provider, physician, or supplier will involve providing an item or service to a Medicare beneficiary.

Antikickback issues. There are several arrangements that are fundamental components of an MCO, HMO, or IDS that are within the scope of the antikickback laws but do not fall within any current safe harbor. These include:

1. incentives to encourage use of a provider panel
2. incentives to encourage preventive care
3. provider discounts
4. part B coinsurance discounts under Medicare Select

Self-referral issues. Provider integration is a natural end product of the evolution of the health care system as it moves toward increased cost-effectiveness. Vertically integrated structures will own or control their ancillary services such as laboratory and radiology facilities. Such organizations may offer physicians a financial stake in the cost-effective practice of medicine through ownership interests in the entity. Although there is no motive in the structure to "over-refer" for profit, under the Stark Laws, any physician ownership in an entity (except those qualified under section 1876 as cost risk contractors or as federally qualified HMOs) will subject the entire arrangement to regulatory scrutiny. With the sunset of employer mandates to offer federally qualified HMOs, there will be less incentive for HMOs to seek federal qualification unless they intend to service the specific Medicare and Medicaid programs. Even the contractual arrangements with physicians can create a problem under the Stark regulations.

Physician incentives. To respond to fears surrounding increased use of managed care in government programs, HHS has issued new regulations that place limitations on incentive arrangements that may influence a physician's care decisions. Final rules were published on March 27, 1996, and apply to physicians providing medical care through HMOs, CMPs, and health insuring organizations.[7] Key provisions include:

- prohibitions against making specific payments for limiting or reducing medically necessary services
- defining a medical group as having "substantial risk" if more than 25 percent of its potential payment is at risk for services it does not provide
- providing for adequate stop-loss insurance for physicians at substantial risk

- availability of annual beneficiary surveys of enrollees and disenrollees on indicators of satisfaction, quality, and access to services for the physicians who are at substantial risk

Q 12:10   What are the sources of "leads" that trigger a health care fraud investigation?

Statistical aberrations. Statistical aberrations can be detected by using claims data—there is an expected distribution of charge levels by specialty. An internist, for example, can be expected to generate charges in all levels of service. Should an internist's services be skewed disproportionately to a higher level of charge, it may trigger an investigation.

Office of the Inspector General (OIG) audits. These audits and referrals occur when the OIG has reason to believe that systematic overcharging is taking place. This is the situation that generated the actions and the settlements with the academic medical centers, a saga whose final chapter has not yet been written.

Competitor complaints. Competitor complaints occur when one party in a competitive situation believes that another party is overbilling or is billing for services not rendered. Such complaints may trigger an investigation.

Employee complaints. Disgruntled former employees are common sources of complaints.

Whistleblower complaints. Qui tam actions include the so-called "whistleblowers." These people stand to reap profit from any recovery generated from their identification of overbilling and thus they are highly motivated to report such items. Recent legislation smoothes the access for *qui tam* actions by providing ease of access, such as toll-free numbers.

Undercover operations. Some agencies will engage undercover agents to infiltrate a company and obtain information that will be used in a claim.

Electronic surveillance.

Q 12:11   What are the major features of the False Claims Act?

The False Claims Act imposes liability on those who:

- knowingly present or cause to be presented a false or fraudulent claim for payment to the U.S. government
- knowingly use a false record or statement to obtain payment on a false or fraudulent claim paid by the U.S. government
- engage in a conspiracy to defraud the U.S. government to obtain allowance for or payment of a false or fraudulent claim

Q 12:12   How does the False Claims Act define "intent"?

The False Claims Act defines "knowing" or "knowingly" as having actual knowledge of the falsity of the claim, acting in deliberate ignorance of the truth or the falsity of the claim, or acting in reckless disregard of the truth or falsity of the claim. Specific intent to defraud is not required.

Q 12:13   What are the penalty provisions of the False Claims Act?

The False Claims Act prescribes civil monetary penalties for violation. These penalties range from $5,000 to $10,000 per claim. Treble damages apply under the Act so that actual payment to the U.S. government can vastly exceed the actual amount of Medicare overbilling. Even more important, for the purpose of health care, a claim is defined as each HCFA 1500 form submitted for payment. Because payment for physician services under Medicare requires such a form, it is clear that the exposure for fraudulent billing is immense.

A further prescribed penalty, sometimes referred to as the "neutron bomb," is possible exclusion from the Medicare and Medicaid programs. For virtually all disciplines with the possible exception of cosmetic surgery, this would be crippling.

Q 12:14   Is there a statute of limitations on False Claims Act causes of action?

The statute of limitations for a False Claims Act action is six years; however, there is a "discovery rule" that may be tallied three years from the point at which the government or relator knew or should have known of the alleged fraud. This broad coverage of the False Claims Act has been a source of contention in application of the law. An additional contention is that the law was designed to prosecute fraudulent procurement practices during the Civil War rather than claims for payment for health care services.

Q 12:15   What defines a "whistleblower"?

A private individual can initiate a False Claims Act action on behalf of the federal government. This person is known as a *"qui tam* plaintiff," "relator," or "whistleblower." A relator may receive a percentage of the government's recovery.

Q 12:16   What can MCOs, IDSs, and HMOs do to reduce their regulatory risk for violating the antikickback and antireferral laws?

There is no simple solution and each arrangement must be analyzed based on its own unique facts and circumstances. In the area of mergers and acquisitions, which is a common component of developing an IDS or other arrangement, however, Alice Gosfield, JD, an expert in managed care and IDS arrangements, suggests the following as a checklist of suggestions:[8]

Choose your advisors carefully. Securing a qualified health care attorney and consulting expert is critical to any proposed merger or acquisition.

Recognize the trouble spots in advance. Practice purchase arrangements pose the greatest challenge because the regulatory focus will be on whether you are paying or receiving a portion of the valued assets as an inducement for future referrals.

Do not overvalue goodwill. The value of goodwill is usually the first target of a fraud and abuse investigation. Using a reputable third-party valuation expert is crucial to the necessary documentation of value.

Check out the billing arrangement in advance. To avoid assuming any false claims liability, determine how billings will be handled in advance. Even if you have just assumed the accounts, there is *respondeat superior* liability of the principal for its agent. The same applies where outside billing firms are used.

Scrutinize intragroup referrals for medical and ancillary services. Does the entity meet the definition of a group under the Stark II amendments? How is the compensation formula structured and does it offer incentive for such referrals?

Caution if upcoding. Upcoding can be another source of false claims; for example, where you use the more remunerative code or when other services are performed but not needed.

Be aware of the safe harbors; there are no loopholes. There is no safe harbor for a hospital purchasing a physician's practice. Although the safe harbor provisions in the antikickback statutes are more amenable to good faith interpretation and falling outside does not mean there is a *per se* violation, there are no loopholes in either the safe harbor regulations or in the antireferral exceptions.

Avoid anything that looks like a kickback. As suggested by the case involving kickbacks against National Medical Enterprises, which agreed to pay $379 million in criminal fines, civil damages, and penalties in July 1994, any financial relationship with a hospital may be suspect.

Q 12:17   What are the differences between the Medicare and Medicaid antikickback statute and the Stark Laws?

Both of these laws attempt to eliminate fraudulent referral and billing practices by providers—particularly physicians—based on conflicts of interest. Compliance with both is necessary to avoid significant penalties, although compliance with one does not automatically mean compliance with the other. Stark Laws are not criminal in nature, whereas Medicare and Medicaid antikickback statutes include criminal sanctions. Evidence of corrupt intent is critical to a violation of antikickback statutes but does not apply to the Stark Laws.

Q 12:18   What are the new developments in fraud and abuse, self-referral, and false claims law?

There has been increasing attention given by federal agencies, particularly the HHS, to curbing waste, fraud, and abuse in the health care industry. Stepped-up agency activity is reflected in the investigations by the OIG of large systems such as Columbia/HCA.

Of note are the fraud and abuse provisions of the Health Insurance Portability and Accountability Act of 1996 (HIPAA), the availability of advisory opinions for business arrangements, negotiated rule making for managed care exception to the antikickback statute, the administration's fraud and abuse proposals, corporate compliance, and Stark Regulations.

Fraud and abuse provisions of HIPAA

- fraud and abuse control program
- new resources for OIG, the Federal Bureau of Investigation, and intermediaries and carriers through direct funding
- a bounty system to encourage reporting
- application to private health plans
- advisory opinions
- antikickback managed care exceptions established for entities at substantial financial risk
- new prohibited practices include (1) upcoding, (2) unnecessary services, (3) payment to beneficiaries, and (4) home health certification
- new category of federal crimes: "Federal Health Care Offenses" for federal and private health plans including (1) health care fraud, (2) theft or embezzlement, (3) false statements, (4) obstruction of an investigation, and (5) money laundering
- amends exclusion authority of OIG to enhance ability to exclude
- imposes minimum three-year exclusion
- allows for a "guilt by association" permissive exclusion for those without culpability
- criminalizes disposal of assets in order to become eligible for Medicaid

Advisory opinions

- will cover specified matters related to remuneration and business activities
- case-specific safe harbors available
- disclosure of identities required

- no immunity for information provided
- limited protection from obtaining advisory opinion
- not precedential; therefore, subject to challenge and not applicable to other similar facts
- OIG will charge fees ($100/hour) for preparing opinions
- 60-day turn-around
- opinions will be public
- OIG can change its position

Negotiated rulemaking for managed care exception to antikickback statute voluntary corporate compliance

OIG is encouraging model compliance programs and corporate integrity agreements to include the following elements:

- written standards of conduct for employees
- written policies that promote the entity's commitment to compliance, addressing specific areas of potential fraud such as billing, marketing, and claims processing
- designation of a chief compliance officer to operate the program
- education and training programs for employees
- use of audits and other evaluation techniques to monitor compliance
- disciplinary actions against employees who violate compliance policies or laws
- investigation and remediation of compliance problems
- use of compliance as an element in evaluating supervisors and managers
- policies to fire and not hire sanctioned individuals
- hotlines to receive anonymous or confidential complaints without retaliation against "tipees"
- documentation of compliance activities and retention of such records

Q 12:19   What are the major foci of the OIG regarding compliance?

The OIG has a number of areas in which it is accomplishing intensive and focused review. These include:

- evaluation and management services
- audits of physicians at teaching hospitals
- new laboratory codes in chemistry and hematology (special attention is focused on panels and profiles)
- procedures performed in conjunction with visits (modifier-25)
- physicians with excessive nursing home visits
- physician certification of durable medical equipment
- diagnosis code validation
- hospital ownership of physician practices
- multiple hospital discharge billing on single stay
- critical care billing review
- physician billing for services rendered by a physician assistant
- anesthesia services "personally performed"
- improper billing for psychiatric services

Q 12:20 How does HIPAA relate to compliance?

HIPAA explicitly makes health care fraud a federal crime. In addition to direct fraud perpetrated against the federal government, HIPAA also includes private insurance. HIPAA expands the roles of the OIG, Federal Bureau of Investigation, and the Department of Justice in terms of investigation of allegations regarding health care billing fraud. HIPAA specifies fraudulent billing procedures, and it also has applications to cover theft or embezzlement. Additionally, HIPAA extends to false statements and concealing information as well as to obstruction of an investigation.

Q 12:21 What are the major components of HIPAA?

HIPAA creates four programs to implement federal fraud enforcement priorities. These are:

Fraud and Abuse Control Program. The fraud and abuse control program coordinates federal, state, and local law enforcement and issues fraud alerts. It authorizes 200 prepayment audits per state.

Medicare Integrity Program. This program allows for self-reporting of possible fraud to the government in exchange for reduced liability.

Beneficiary Incentive Program. This program pays cash rewards to *qui tam* plaintiffs.

Health Care Fraud and Abuse Data Collection Program. This program establishes a national database for the reporting and disclosing of final adverse actions taken against health care providers, suppliers, and practitioners. Final adverse actions include federal or state civil judgments; criminal convictions; actions by agencies responsible for licensing and certification; and exclusion from participation in any federal or state program related to the delivery of a health care item or service.[9]

Q 12:22   What are the penalties associated with violation of regulations mandated by HIPAA?

HIPAA requires a 10-year or more exclusion from the Medicare program for one previous health care offense conviction and mandates permanent exclusion for multiple previous convictions. It also allows exclusions of directors, officers, and managers of health care companies that are convicted of fraud or excluded, even if those people had no direct knowledge of the wrongdoing. HIPAA, therefore, extends the government's reach through the corporate veil to individuals. Obviously, this means that officers and directors of corporations engaging in the business of health care delivery have a strong personal interest in establishing a powerful corporate compliance program.

Q 12:23   What are the compliance issues of the Balanced Budget Act of 1997 (BBA)?

The BBA is a far-ranging piece of health care legislation whose impact is just beginning to be felt in the HMO arena. In addition to providing for newer vehicles for health care delivery such as provider service organizations, the BBA has some specific compliance provisions. It augments the government's fraud and abuse investigation capability by providing a large funding war chest of many million dollars. It also augments the Medicare Integrity Program by adding 2,000 random prepayment audits per state to increase the fraud and abuse arsenal.

Q 12:24   What role do the federal sentencing guidelines play in the development of a compliance program?

The sentencing guidelines, interestingly enough, are the starting point for the development of any compliance program. The guidelines outline a "culpability score" that ascribes the degree of guilt to parties found to be in violation of a federal regulation. Corporations that have an effective plan to prevent and detect violations of the law are entitled to a three-point reduction in the "culpability score." Programs must be reasonably designed, implemented, and enforced so that they will be effective.

Q 12:25   What are the elements of an effective compliance plan?

- written compliance standards established and disseminated throughout the organization
- top-down oversight demonstrated (ideally, this is shown through decision making at the level of the governing body)
- those with discretionary authority have to be scrutinized
- employees throughout the organization must participate in educational programs about corporate compliance and this must be documented
- documented communication of the organization's commitment to a compliance program and the necessary steps involved in the program
- compliance as a dynamic program; explicit programs in place to monitor compliance, audit compliance, and record the steps taken in response to information uncovered
- standards investigated and enforced throughout the organization
- discovered departures from the standards have to be corrected and measures introduced to prevent recurrence
- written policies developed and disseminated
- compliance demonstrated as a criterion for promotion
- a hotline established and announced for a rapid and anonymous reporting route
- measures implemented to guard against retaliation directed toward an employee who exposes compliance violations
- policies developed and adhered to regarding record creation and retention

Q 12:26   Which characteristics of billing forms can help practitioners?

- Forms and templates can be developed by specialty—many specialty societies and the American Association of Medical Colleges have developed acceptable billing forms.
- Forms should be carefully examined to ensure that no wording exists that could be construed to constitute a misrepresentation of services that were furnished.
- All levels of coding should be listed and *not* just the higher level codes.

Q 12:27   What are the benefits of a corporate compliance program to the organization?

An intact and vibrant corporate compliance policy:

- Demonstrates an organization's commitment to quality and excellence.
- Sends a strong message and enhances employee awareness of conduct that is unacceptable.
- Identifies problem areas early and promotes intervention.
- Reduces the organization's exposure to civil and criminal liability.

Q 12:28   What is a compliance committee's responsibility?

A compliance committee is established at the direction of the organization's governing body. It provides oversight and leadership to the compliance activity and ensures reporting and accountability to the governing body. The committee serves as an advisory body for employees who request reviews or those who make complaints. Finally, the committee is intimately involved in fashioning corrective actions when departures from compliance policies are observed or reported. A compliance officer appointed by the organization's governing body works with the compliance committee and is responsible for educating the committee and monitoring its work. Figure 12–1 illustrates the typical structure of a billing compliance program.

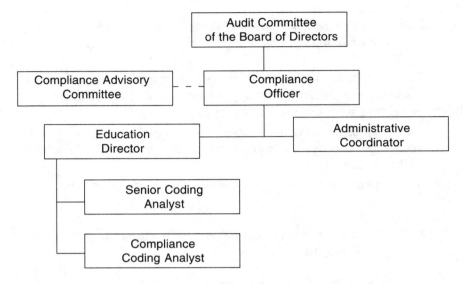

Figure 12–1 The Typical Structure of a Billing Compliance Program

---

NOTES

1. 42 U.S.C. §§ 1320a-7, 7a, and 7b.

2. 42 U.S.C. § 1320a-7b.

3. 42 U.S.C. § 1395nn.

4. Office of Managed Care, *Operational Policy Letter #96.045* (Washington, DC: 3 December, 1996) and 61 Fed. Reg. 13430, *PPRC Report* 242 (27 March, 1996).

5. 42 U.S.C. § 1320a-7b.

6. 42 U.S.C. § 1395nn(e) (2).

7. 61 Fed. Reg. 13430–13450, 27 March, 1996. 42 C.F.R. §§ 417.479, 714.500, 434.44, 434.67, and 434.70. The rules were promulgated in 61 *Federal Register* 13430–13450 and codified at 42 C.F.R. §§ 417.479, 714.500, 434.44, 434.67, and 434.70. These rules require any HMO or other covered managed care plan that has an incentive arrangement with physicians to disclose these arrangements to HHS, and make such disclosures to every Medicare beneficiary or Medicaid recipient.

8. A. Gosfield, *Physician's Management* (December 1994).

9. Health Care Fraud and Abuse Data Collection Program: Reporting of Final Adverse Actions. Department of Health and Human Services, Office of the Inspector General, 45 C.F.R., part 61. *Federal Register*, 30 October, 1998; 63(210): 54341–7.

CHAPTER 13

Network and Integration Strategies

Clifford C. Dacso and Sheryl Tatar Dacso

INTRODUCTION

Five years ago, the accepted view of provider networks was that they should be as vertically integrated as possible. Such integration seemed to offer control over quality and use of resources. Today it is clear that cost-containment can be achieved without complete vertical integration and that providers often function better in more flexible arrangements. That is not to say that integration is not essential. Legal and functional integration of delivery systems is still necessary for economic and operational efficiency. But other integration options are emerging that are less resource intensive. They use horizontal, functional, and virtual integration techniques to create organized delivery systems that can share risk and reward from payer contracts or become provider sponsored organizations (PSOs). Even the Kaiser Health Plan and system of hospitals and medical groups are moving from a vertically integrated, ownership model into an affiliated model.

The experiences of the older integrated delivery systems did identify several crucial elements. These "critical success factors" include the facilities, the physicians, the network, the ability to accept risk, information system networks, and standardization of practices and protocols. By focusing their efforts on these key areas, the new systems can allocate their resources to those capabilities that will yield the best returns.

Because there is no one successful model, this chapter outlines the advantages and disadvantages of a variety of integration vehicles, many of which developed in response to the Balanced Budget Act of 1997. Barriers to integration, governance issues, legal issues, and strategies that are appropriate for the level of risk accepted and the level of development of the market are all discussed.

Q 13:1   Why are health care providers forming provider organizations?

Health care providers are responding to a changing economic market, legal system, and expansion of managed health care benefit products that are placing greater emphasis on lower cost, higher value, greater access, and improved quality of care. With many states enacting legislation designed to control costs and increase access, market forces are driving health care providers into organizations that can accommodate coordinated care and shared reimbursement. To effectively compete with the various types of managed health care benefit products being developed by employers, insurers, and others, health care providers are seeking to arrange themselves into various legal and operational structures that will allow them to accept and share risk.

Events driving integration include increased

- managed care contracting and the need to accept risk in return for increased volume
- demand for efficiency in cost and service
- legal and regulatory restraints inherent in the health care industry
- competitive environment among providers under managed care

The successful provider organization will be able to accept capitation and risk and attract payers because of vertical integration, geographic coverage, low cost, and high quality as measured by good outcomes and patient satisfaction.

Q 13:2   What is integration?

Webster's Ninth New Collegiate Dictionary defines integration as "a process by which activities are formed, coordinated or blended into a functioning or unified whole." It is a whole made up of distinct parts that function as a "confederacy," or it can be a unified organization that functions in a very centralized fashion. Integration for a health maintenance organization (HMO) generally refers to the conflation of disparate components of the care delivery system under one body of governance.

Q 13:3   What are the strategic issues and preliminary considerations of an integration plan?

The optimal organized delivery system is both legally and functionally integrated. If legal or structural integration is not feasible because of laws or regulations, functional integration is essential to achieve the necessary economic and operational efficiencies. Some of the advantages of integration include:

- reduced regulatory risks to providers (e.g., antitrust)
- reduced competitive and duplicative services
- increased operating efficiencies
- increased efficiency in strategic planning and marketing
- improved contracting position with payers
- aligned economic incentives (risk and reward systems)
- expanded delivery systems that can be seamless
- improved and common information systems
- improved outcomes management and case management programs
- enhanced geographic market

The consideration of any type of integration strategy should first include a determination of the primary goals and objectives for developing an integrated structure. Is the goal to develop a new product in the market, or is it intended to leverage a provider organization in its managed care contracting?

The next step is to determine the appropriate organizational structure. Will there be a single organization or multiple organizations? What are the advantages and disadvantages of each structure as it relates to the goals and objectives?

The third step is to decide on the degree or level of integration. Will it be a contractual relationship among providers, or will it be a provider organization? Will the organization be an expanded delivery system or network?

The next decision concerns the most appropriate legal entity for the organization. Should it be structured as a joint venture or partnership, or should it be a corporate entity? If it is to take a corporate structure, should it be a general corporation or a nonprofit corporation? If a nonprofit corporation, should it be tax-exempt or taxable? If a proprietary organization, who will be eligible to invest? The physicians? Hospitals? Insurers or other payers? Which structure do payers in the market prefer?

The type of relationship between the entity and the physicians, hospitals, and payers must also be determined. What relationship will be most effective to increase market position? Which option will be acceptable to other providers? Other payers? Prospective partners? Will the physicians be employed by the organization or will they be independent contractors?

Finally, the capital requirements must be determined for each option. How much financial risk can be taken? How will capital be accessed?

Q 13:4   What are the traditional integration vehicles for provider organizations?

Historically, preferred provider organizations (PPOs), independent practice associations (IPAs), physician-hospital organizations (PHOs), and management services organizations (MSOs) were the predominant organizations used in networks as provider organization models. It is helpful to differentiate those models that represent the integration of physicians or other licensed individual providers (such as the IPA or single and multispecialty medical group practice arrangements) from those models that include hospitals (such as the PHO and the medical foundation model). The provider-based PPO was one of the earliest models to bring together providers in order to obtain payer contracts on an indemnity or discounted fee-for-service basis. The MSO is often used to facilitate and integrate these various provider organizations, or it may be the entity that brings a network of providers to a payer relationship.

Q 13:5   What are the barriers to achieving effective integration?

Physicians want the benefits of being included in managed care contracting but do not want to give up autonomy or control. Hospitals see themselves as losing control over the continuum of health care, but they have access to capital. Payers want the ability to contract at a single source without having to administer a network of providers. Converting from a fee-for-service reimbursement system to one based on capitation poses the greatest difficulty to an individual provider and is the most important challenge to the survival of hospitals and physicians who want to move toward integration. This conversion requires reengineering the physician mix and compensation structure with increased emphasis on developing a primary care focus. The capital costs associated with building these networks can be in the millions. It has been estimated that to build a 100-

physician network may require from $10 million to $16 million in start-up capital. Ongoing maintenance costs may be at similar levels.[1]

Q 13:6   What are the governance issues associated with developing a provider organization?

Whenever separate individuals or organizations are merged into a single organization, there are internal and inherent conflicts of interests, often associated with control. One of the most important steps in the provider integration process is to define, design, and develop the governing body of the newly integrated organization to view the organization as a new, unified, and unique entity rather than an organization made up of multiple parts. In determining a governance structure, an organization must consider four key issues:

1. control
2. structure
3. function
4. composition

The characteristics of these four issues will determine much of the governance structure of the organization.

The governance structure's objectives should be to facilitate effective decision making and ensure representation of interests. Sometimes, the parties' desire to maintain equal representation on the governing board and on all committees can undermine effective integration. The use of "supermajority" voting or reserved voting rights may be considered less objectionable than having unequal board representation; however, these ploys generally protect the minority stakeholder and can paralyze the board from effective decision making and action. Too often, effective integration strategies fail because the group dynamics are not addressed or resolved at the organizational stage. This can occur even if the documentation is perfect and the economics of the arrangement are ideal.

Q 13:7   What are some of the major challenges associated with establishing an organized delivery system?

In addition to the governance issues, the most common problems encountered in the development and operation of an integrated delivery system (IDS) include:

- access to capital
- moving money around the system
- systemwide credentialing and accreditation
- managed care contracting

Whenever one attempts to integrate or affiliate different organizations, there must be a careful planning process and anticipation of the potential problems that can arise. Sometimes, problems affect the parties equally and they can collectively respond. Other times, problems affect one of the parties, which can adversely affect the others. The structure and documents should anticipate a number of potential problems, including changes in the law, and allow for midcourse adjustment in the structure and relationships. Building in the ability to terminate and unwind the relationship is prudent.

Q 13:8   What are the most effective strategies for providers seeking to develop a fully integrated delivery system?

Because integration occurs at a number of levels, one must distinguish between those strategies that involve the development of entry models such as IPAs, PHOs, and PPOs, and those that have actually achieved the more effective level of integration as a provider organization. Between the entry models and the more integrated models, there are transitional models designed to allow the system to evolve to the next higher level. From the perspective of the hospital and physician seeking integration, there are several models to consider.

Entry Model. The most common entry models are structures such as the following:

- A physician office management service bureau, which usually involves a hospital providing or arranging for the provision of basic office services such as billing, collection, information systems, and group purchasing.
- A group without walls, which brings together a number of previously independently practicing physicians in a common legal or operational structure.
- The open PHO, which establishes a contracting vehicle with shared governance between the hospital and physicians to jointly engage in managed care contracting.

Transitional Model. The common characteristic of a transitional model is its use of a selection and monitoring process to ensure that the appropriate mix of providers is maintained in response to the needs of prospective payers. A PHO that uses stringent selection and deselection criteria for its participating providers and maintains a specific size and composition (referred to as a closed PHO) will be far more competitive than an open PHO. The MSO is often an important part of the transitional model, because it can facilitate the selective integration process, provide access to capital during the start-up and transition period, and directly administer the managed care contracting on behalf of the provider organization.

Integrated Model. Although many IPAs, closed PHOs, and MSO-managed groups can function almost as effectively as a foundation model, staff model, or equity model, the latter structures still have increased efficiency. The major distinction between the foundation model and the staff model is the manner in which the physicians relate to the entity and are paid. In a foundation model, the relationship between the foundation and the physicians is contractual. This continues, to some degree, the inherent conflict and adverse interests of the parties to the system. The staff model, however, places the physicians in an employment relationship to the clinic or entity. This model may not be available in states that prohibit the corporate practice of medicine. Finally, the equity model achieves several advantages over the other two models, the most important being its ability to recruit and retain physicians because of the ownership opportunity, allowing both voice and equity. Another advantage is its focus on the physician rather than the hospital. The equity model reflects the acceptance of a hospital as a cost rather than revenue center and structures its contracts accordingly. However, the equity model is the most capital-intensive.

Q 13:9   Where does physician integration fit in developing an IDS or network?

A discussion of provider integration cannot be complete without focusing on the alternate forms of physician integration. The organization of physicians into groups is key to the success of any integration strategy except the staff model, in which all physicians are employed by the entity.

Independent Practice Association. The IPA is a practitioner-controlled legal entity that acts as a vehicle for managed care contracting on behalf of its members, who are generally independent practitioners. Except for risk sharing in managed care contracting, there is little sharing of economic risk or practice.

Medical Group Practice. Some medical groups begin their integration process through more loosely structured arrangements, such as those involving individual practitioners and group practices with shared overhead arrangements. The progress toward integration of physicians into group practices can be further facilitated by MSOs, which provide business management and contract administration to individual or group practices. An example of a partially integrated practice is the group without walls (GWW), a form of partially integrated medical group practice that involves physicians who maintain separate practice sites but come together to form a single professional organization with shared economic risk while treating overhead, profit, and loss as if still in separate practices. This can mature into a fully integrated medical group practice (FIMG), which is characterized by more complete operational and economic integration into a single, more powerful organization. Characteristics of an FIMG include centralized governance and control and medical records and operational policies and procedures, uniform and consolidated managed care contracting with all participants as providers, formal quality assurance and utilization management programs, and income allocation systems rewards according to group and individual performance.

Q 13:10   What should be the goals of integration?

According to John D. Cochrane, editor of the *Integrated Healthcare Report*, the ultimate goal of integration is to create a comprehensive, geographically dispersed, yet efficient and fully coordinated system of physician, acute hospital, outpatient, home care, prevention, and wellness services that can assume and effectively manage the full risk for delivering those services for a fixed payment. When full integration is achieved, an individual using the services can move from the physician's office to a hospital, to a transitional care service, to a home care service with ease of admission and coordinated records and can expect to receive the same quality of care throughout. Cochrane further describes an integrated system as including a comprehensive service continuum, one management and administrative support structure, and an information network that connects all parts of the system. Although geographically dispersed, it is coordinated, and physician, hospital, and insurance incentives are aligned.

The system's costs and value are continuously measured, and it is highly competitive in cost, quality, and access.[2]

Q 13:11   What are the desirable features of integration?

In evaluating the various integrated delivery systems, a number of desirable features should be considered. The system should be customer-oriented with a commitment to quality, community-based, and highly accessible through primary care sites close to patients' homes and places of business. It should provide efficient, high-quality care and focus on a specific patient population in a defined geographic area. Resources should be determined and distributed. An integrated health care delivery system requires physician leadership. It should use a unified patient data system and a variety of innovative financing arrangements and partnerships. Its availability should extend to the entire community. Finally, the system should be able to manage medical costs without cost shifting.

Gerald R. Peters describes two basic types of integration from a business perspective: structural and operational integration.[3]

Structural Integration. Structural integration refers to the consolidation of separate businesses into either a single organization or a group of affiliated organizations under common ownership and control. For example, a hospital and physician group practice creates a holding company and each transfers control over their respective organizations to the new company. This is why entities such as PHOs and IPAs are not structurally integrated. These represent ancillary structures to the participants' existing but separate businesses. Structural integration does not, however, require that the participants operate as a single enterprise.

Operational Integration. Operational integration involves the consolidation of previously separate business operations such as planning, staffing, and operational systems. Peters outlines the following characteristics of operational integration:[4]

- operating all lines of business (hospital, medical practice, ancillary services) under a consolidated budget
- unifying governance and management responsibilities to coordinate all lines of business
- coordinating and making compatible all operating systems (accounting, billing, collections, data processing)
- sharing vision and common goals

- unifying strategic planning and marketing
- providing single-payer contracting

Q 13:12   What role are employers and businesses playing in the trend toward integration of health care providers?

This trend is driven by the increasing demands placed on the health care delivery system by those responsible for paying for health care services. As businesses seek to control health care expenses, as business communities develop coalitions, and as federal and state governments focus on legislating health care reform, several common themes appear in these proposed plans: cost control, access, and quality. The provider models developed in response to these trends seek to redefine managed care, which was previously described as something someone from the outside does to providers.

Q 13:13   Is there a generic definition of an integrated delivery system?

The affiliation of physicians or medical groups with hospitals represents one level of integration. This can occur either through the facilitation efforts of an MSO or through a provider structure such as a PHO. The PHO is similar to the IPA, except that the hospital or institutional provider is included in the contracting entity and participates in managed care contracts with the physicians. In some communities, hospitals and physician groups are organizing integrated health care organizations (IHOs), which achieve the vertical integration of hospitals with medical practices. The characteristics of an IHO include:

- one organization owning the medical practice, the hospital, and ancillary services
- a global contract by the IHO for both medical and hospital services with payers
- a single governing body
- single management
- employed or independent contracting physicians
- common consolidated capital and operating budgets
- a common data and information management system
- a common business focus

In contrast, the traditional IDS usually consists of a parent holding company that owns or controls subsidiary organizations that provide the delivery system's separate and discrete health care services. A common example of an IDS is the medical foundation, which is generally structured under a state's nonprofit corporation statutes as an entity that may have a hospital or health system as its corporate member that qualifies as a provider of care that can employ or contract with physicians to provide medical care to the foundation's patients. In states that strongly prohibit the corporate practice of medicine, such as Texas and California, the foundation model allows the clinic to control the managed care contracts and contract with either physicians or medical groups for medical services. In states without strict corporate practice restrictions, the foundation can employ physicians.

Q 13:14   What are the major considerations in a provider sponsored organization (PSO) strategy?

In developing a PSO, there are several strategic observations and considerations. Experts have suggested the following:[5]

- A PSO must be majority owned by health care providers.
- A PSO can be owned by any individual category of provider (e.g., hospital, physician, or allied health professional).
- A PSO must arrange for a substantial portion of the covered benefits to be rendered by providers who are at substantial financial risk.
- A PSO may offer a variety of benefit options ranging from HMO to point-of-service products.
- A PSO may become licensed under state law to bear insurance risk, or, under certain circumstances, may seek a federal waiver of state licensure for up to 36 months.
- A PSO must meet solvency standards as promulgated by the Health Care Financing Administration (HCFA) and otherwise satisfy all other PSO standards.

HCFA began receiving PSO applications in June 1998.

Q 13:15   What are the critical success factors for an effective organization?

A streamlined governance organization and process for decision making is critical to the effectiveness of an organization. Management must be redefined and more responsive to the newly integrated system. Finally, physician leadership is a critical component to an organization's success. Because health care is a dynamic industry, an effective organization should be capable of making regular adaptations as the organization moves forward.

Q 13:16   What is the difference between integration and re-engineering?

Reengineering a health care organization becomes part of the integration process. As described by Stephen Shortell in his book *Remaking Healthcare in America*, the primary objective of reengineering is to develop an organized delivery system out of a system of individual providers, or a merged system of systems.[6] Before an organization can become truly organized, it must first become functionally integrated across institutions and then integrated with its physicians. Only when the system-physician integration occurs can there be clinical integration.

Functional integration involves coordination across operating units of the health system. Physician integration occurs when the physicians become economically tied to the system and are actively involved in essential management and decision-making roles. Clinical integration is the goal and, like the quality improvement process, is never perfected. It is achieved through the development of a seamless process of patient care that requires a high level of communication among caregivers, excellent information system technology, and the ability to use standardized protocols in important clinical areas. The focus becomes one of patient care.

Q 13:17   What are the characteristics of a mature clinically integrated system?

According to Dr. Shortell, a mature clinically integrated system

- knows the health needs of its community
- knows the resources required across the continuum of care to address these needs

- knows what it can provide, and what it must provide through others in partnership with it
- knows its work
- "knows that it knows"; it is a self-aware organization
- knows how to adapt and improve
- invests in its human capital
- can meet stakeholder expectations

Q 13:18   What are the consequences to providers in markets where effective integration is not obtainable?

There will always be people who will want to select their health care providers—even at personal expense—even if the providers are unable or unwilling to participate in a provider network and will have reduced access to revenue associated with health benefit products. As payers seek contracts with more fully integrated delivery systems and networks, those that are not already within the system will have to seek subcontracts with systems holding the primary contract in order to have some access to patients and contract revenue.

Q 13:19   Where does the community fit into the organized delivery system?

There have been recent studies that highlight the importance of local, community-based partnerships as a means of identifying community health needs that can be addressed through innovative community health plans. These organizations can evolve into cooperatives or, as in Texas, a statewide rural health plan.

Three primary governance issues emerged from a study conducted by the Community Care Network Demonstration under the auspices of the American Hospital Association's Hospital Research and Educational Trust, the Catholic Hospital Association of the United States, and the Voluntary Hospital Association, Inc., with grant support from the Duke Endowment and the Kellogg Foundation. The three governance issues are:

1. managing turf issues among partner organizations
2. defining and incorporating community accountability into the governance process

3. coping with the competing demands of partnership growth and development[7]

Q 13:20   What are the major legal issues associated with the development of integrated health care delivery systems and networks?

The potential legal issues associated with developing an integrated network of provider arrangements depend on the type and extent of responsibilities of the integrated entity. The legal and regulatory considerations associated with the activities of the various integration models include:

- antitrust issues
- licensing and corporate practice of medicine issues
- personnel and benefit issues
- choice of entity
- state certificate of need or rate regulation laws
- credentialing and peer review of participating providers
- licensing and certification
- Medicare and Medicaid requirements
- physician referral restrictions
- insurance risk bearing and sharing
- tax issues

The legal and regulatory issues that apply most often to the development and operation of networks and PSOs are included in the paragraphs that follow.

Antitrust. Federal and state antitrust laws regulate competition and, in general, prohibit certain unreasonable restraints on trade. Any antitrust analysis should include assessing the risks of both developing a network or PSO that involves merger of providers and operating it without creating market dominance and incurring antitrust risk associated with such a market position. Issues to be considered in analyzing the antitrust risk of a network or PSO include the following:

- Does the formation of the network or PSO create too much market dominance or power?

- Are the physician relationships exclusive? If so, are other competitor organizations foreclosed from effectively competing because the physicians are tied to a particular organization?
- Does the network or PSO agreement preclude its members or participants from dealing with its competitors?
- Does the network or IDS payer contract tie the purchase of a separate service (e.g., hospital services) to the one being sought by the payer (physician services)?
- Have the physicians and hospital engaged in any illegal pricing discussions prior to actual formation?
- Has the merger of participating providers been done in compliance with antitrust statutes, including premerger guidelines?

Personnel and Benefits Law. In addition to standard employer liability issues for employed providers, two essential benefit law concepts could affect network participants and their employees. The first concerns the tax treatment of each participant's employee benefits plan on the basis that the entity's structure does not discriminate against non–highly compensated employees in favor of more highly compensated employees. The second benefit law concept focuses on the application of nondiscrimination tests to organizations related by common ownership or control, or on the basis of the services provided in determining whether they should be treated as a single employer.[8]

Licensing and Corporate Practice of Medicine. Whenever an organization seeks to employ or contract with a licensed professional or institution or seeks to engage in a regulated activity, it is important to determine whether any licensing laws apply or whether the corporate practice of the licensed activity is prohibited. Because the scope of the corporate practice doctrine varies among states, it is important to analyze each state's laws as part of developing a network or PSO. For example, if a state has a strong corporate practice of medicine doctrine, it is likely that absent specific exceptions in the law, a true network or IDS will not be possible (unless it is owned by physicians and licensed as a medical practice entity). Under such circumstances, an MSO can be used to coordinate among the institutional and licensed professionals in obtaining the efficiencies through contract and operation rather than structure.

Choice of Entity. Although a corporate structure is most common, the choice of entity depends on many factors of a business and tax nature, as well as regulatory considerations. Partnerships allow flexibility in operations and "pass through" taxable income and losses. Corporations, limited liability partnerships, and limited liability companies allow limited liability for owners, centralized management, and ease of transfer of ownership interests. Nonprofit corporations may be preferred because of tax-exempt issues. States also regulate the types of entities that can contract on a risk basis for medical or health care services. For example, a state department of insurance may restrict a provider to accepting risk only for its own services and preclude "downstream" subcontracting for covered services. Other states may allow a provider organization to control a risk contract for both institutional and professional services. A thorough review of a state's HMO and insurance regulations is essential to the development of a network or PSO.

Insurance Law and HMO Regulation. State insurance laws will determine whether a risk-sharing organization such as a PSO or network can enter into a particular risk-sharing arrangement, the nature and extent of risk it can bear, and whether the organization will require HMO or insurance licensure. Most HMO statutes define an HMO as "any person who undertakes to arrange for the provision of healthcare services to subscribers and enrollees, or to pay for or reimburse any part of the cost of such services, in return for a prepaid or periodic charge paid by or on behalf of such subscribers or enrollees."Absent an exception for certain types of provider organizations that are allowed to accept business risk for services they provide as licensed providers, HMO licensure may be required.

Illegal Remuneration Laws. A network or PSO should be organized with careful attention to state and federal illegal remuneration laws that prohibit the payment or receipt of anything of value to induce, or in return for, referrals of patients. There are no safe harbors applicable to the purchase of a physician's practice by either a hospital, another physician group, or a network or PSO where the physician is to remain in the practice. Important issues in the analysis of network or PSO formation include valuation of the assets and the nature of the assets to be purchased. The essential consideration is that there can be no hidden payment for an asset. In fact, goodwill, ongoing business value, and payments for exclusivity or noncompetition could be suspect as inducements for future referrals.

Medicare and Medicaid Rules. Medicare and Medicaid rules pertinent to network or PSO arrangements include reassignment rules and physician incentive plan rules.

- Reassignment rules prohibit a physician from reassigning payment to another entity except where payment is made to the physician's employer under a contract or if the service is being provided in a hospital or rural primary care facility. Therefore, in a practice acquisition by a network or PSO, the physician may not be able to assign his or her Medicare or Medicaid accounts receivable to the network or PSO as part of the acquisition. Also, if the physician is an independent contractor rather than an employee, he or she may not be able to assign the right to receive payment to the network or PSO for the services provided.

- Physician incentive plan rules apply to managed care arrangements that make a specific payment of any kind to a physician or physician group as an inducement to reduce or limit medically necessary services. These rules require an entity that operates a physician incentive plan that places physicians at substantial financial risk to conduct annual beneficiary surveys, disclose information about the plan to regulatory authorities and beneficiaries, and ensure that all physicians subject to such plans have specified stop-loss protection.

Certificate of Need/Rate Setting. Many states have certificate of need (CON) laws that govern the establishment and expansion of health care facilities and services to manage health care resources and control costs. Although most of these laws apply to expenditures related to facilities and expensive equipment, some extend to new services. Most CON laws exempt physician services. West Virginia is one of the only states that has retained a law that prohibits a hospital from discounting below its reported costs. Hospitals are required to report costs to the state on an annual basis. These costs become the floor for any change in charge that the hospital may make. To discount below the reported cost will result in penalties to the hospital.

Self-Referral Prohibitions. Federal laws and many state laws prohibit a physician from referring a patient to an entity for "designated health services where the physician or a member of the physician's family has a financial relationship with the entity." Financial relationship can mean ownership or compensation arrangements.

Tax Exemptions. Where a tax-exempt institution is involved in the development of a network or PSO, there are compelling reasons to seek tax-exempt status for it. Most important is the avoidance of inurement to the exempt institution that is seeking to develop and participate in the PSO or network. The more difficult issue, however, is the ability of the PSO or network to obtain a tax exemption from the Internal Revenue Service (IRS) given the strict guidelines it uses to determine whether such organizations serve an exempt purpose.[9]

PROVIDER INTEGRATION MODELS

Q 13:21   What are the structural choices for provider integration?

The fundamental structural choices for provider integration include IPAs, GWWs, consolidated medical group practices, MSOs, PHOs, medical foundations, and fully integrated systems.

Q 13:22   What are the basic components of an integrated delivery system?

The components can be broken down into the physician organizations—made up of IPAs and integrated medical groups—and the institutional component that includes the facilities (e.g., hospital, clinics, ancillary services providers). The linking organizations developed to integrate the physician organizations and the institutional component include the PHO, MSO, and other organizations that exist for either contracting or operating purposes.

INDEPENDENT PRACTICE ASSOCIATIONS

Q 13:23   What is an IPA?

The IPA is the simplest form of physician organization and is composed of individual practitioners who partially integrate their practices through sharing risk in managed care contracting. An IPA contracts with payers to arrange for the provision of medical services and with individual physicians to provide services under those payer contracts arranged by the IPA. Because the IPA is nominally capitalized, it is attractive to physicians who have no prior experience with managed care or practicing as a group.

Developed more than a decade ago, the IPA offers a vehicle for physicians and other health care professionals to participate in managed care contracting as an effective alternative to the full-time multispecialty group practice. IPAs perform a dual function in managed care: They can facilitate direct fee-for-service contracting through messenger arrangements, and they can act as an integrated group for purposes of accepting economic risk through capitation. IPAs commonly contract with HMOs and managed care plans to deliver the services desired by the plan for its subscribers on either a capitated or other risk basis. The IPA in turn contracts with individual providers to provide the services, either on a capitated or fee-for-service basis. Examples of various IPA structures are shown in Figures 13–1 and 13–2 (see Q 13:24). Figure 13–1 represents a standard IPA structure and its contractual relationships with other providers (e.g., hospitals) and payers. Figure 13–2 represents a second generation IPA that accommodates fee-for-service and risk-taking providers through shared-risk arrangements. To the extent that the IPA can legally assume full or global risk, it may assume management functions such as utilization management, quality assurance, and credentialing from the payer, as well as administration of the risk pools on behalf of its downstream contractors.

Q 13:24   What dictates the various forms that IPAs can take?

The form of an IPA arrangement is usually dictated by the local market, the role (if any) of the hospital in associating with the IPA, and the number and practice specialties of physicians choosing to participate; however, these can be hospital affiliated or can be part of a network of IPAs under the umbrella of a super-IPA. The contemporary IPA often functions as a part-time group practice for physician participation in various managed care arrangements.

Q 13:25   What are the general characteristics of an IPA?

Most IPAs are organized as corporations made up of individual or small groups of physicians. Some are set up as not-for-profit corporations, and others are organized as professional corporations, partnerships, or associations. Common characteristics of most IPAs include:

* partial integration; physician-owned or sponsored
* contracts on a fee-for-service or capitated basis
* physicians remain independent competitors

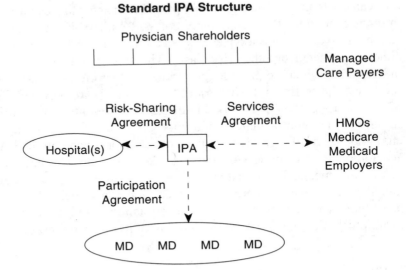

Figure 13–1 Standard IPA Structure and Its Contractual Relationships

- contracting physicians may be owners or members, but this is not a requirement

Most IPAs have a simple and efficient method of governance, flexibility in the increasingly competitive and dynamic managed care market, equal distribution of economic benefits and burdens, and minimal income tax liability.

Q 13:26   What are the advantages of the IPA?

The IPA is a flexible model that does not compromise practice autonomy. Most IPAs are formed for the purpose of contracting with one or more HMOs, health care plans, or managed care organizations. The IPA's attractiveness to HMOs and other managed health care organizations is its ability to provide a large panel of participating providers and accept payment on a capitated basis over a broader geographic area than that which is available through individual physician practices or groups. Most

Risk-Sharing IPA

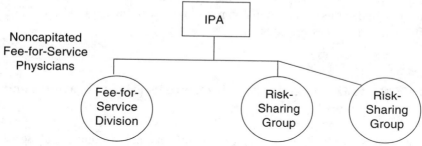

Figure 13–2 Second Generation IPA: Fee-for-Service, Risk-Taking Providers

IPAs also perform peer review, quality assurance, utilization management, and review of outcomes data, which are required by most HMOs and managed care companies.

For physicians, the IPA structure offers the ability to maintain practice autonomy while electing to participate on a capitated or fee-for-service payment basis. For physicians who are willing to accept capitation, the IPA can capitate those physicians' services through its provider agreements. For physicians who do not wish to accept capitation payments, the IPA can accept capitation and pay the participating physicians on a fee-for-service basis.

Q 13:27   What are the disadvantages of an IPA?

As with any of the less than fully integrated models, physician practices under this structure do not benefit from group efficiencies, and therefore practice expenses are not significantly reduced. Except for IPA contracts, the physicians remain independent competitors, which can be divisive and also subject to antitrust risks. Further, the presence of an IPA in a hospital that has an existing PPO may cause divisiveness among the medical staff because it will directly compete with the physicians comprising the PPO. Other potential concerns with the IPA model are its operational expenses, which, coupled with its members' financial exposure under capitated contracting and the increased liability exposure associated with improper credentialing of participating providers, may be too much for physicians, who are generally averse to risk. Depending on the legal structure, there may be potential problems with the participating providers' protection of the qualified status of their pension plans in view of the application of IRS-affiliated service group rules.

Q 13:28   What can an IPA do to enhance its value to providers and payers?

Where possible, the IPA should secure exclusive contractual agreements with physicians—this reduces the effect of HMOs playing one IPA off another using different reimbursement rates to attract common physician participants. IPAs should use incentives to increase physician loyalty such as risk-pool-surplus participation or equity positions in the IPA or affiliated MSO. Smaller boards allow an IPA to make decisions efficiently and effectively. This includes an expedited process for the discipline and termination of outlier physicians. Finally, the IPA should have access to capital to meet funding requirements that may arise in risk contracting arrangements. Many IPAs that go into risk arrangements are ill prepared to manage the exposure.

Q 13:29   How does the hospital-affiliated IPA differ from the physician-sponsored PPO?

During the early days of managed care, when most plans offered a preferred provider option using discounted fee-for-service products, hospitals and their medical staffs developed PPOs made up of the hospital and open to its medical staff. Because of the political considerations and the legal structure of the PPO, its ability to participate effectively in the more modern managed care plans and products is substantially limited by its loose, inefficient structure. In addition, its lack of sufficient integration made it an easy target for antitrust challenges.

The hospital-affiliated IPA developed as an effective alternative for more selective physician participation in managed care contracting, particularly in capitated arrangements. Some hospitals have both PPO and IPA models in place. The presence of these two arrangements in the same hospital may result in competition between the PPO and the IPA for the same physician services component of a managed care contract. The preferred approach is one that has the hospital affiliated with a single physician organization under an arrangement that is flexible enough to allow for a broad range of managed care contracting options for both the hospital and its affiliated physicians.

GROUP WITHOUT WALLS

Q 13:30   What are the general characteristics of a GWW?

A GWW is a group medical practice that takes one step toward structural integration of multiple individual practices under a single medical practice organization. This form of group practice is a partially integrated medical group organization that consolidates staffing, billing, and collection functions under a single organization that has a single provider identification and tax number, but leaves each individual practice in its original location, with the same staff, patient records, and often, practice style. Some physicians also attempt to retain their individual professional revenues and expenses. Physician compensation may be structured as either practice revenues less local office expenses, less proportional share of central office expenses, or through pooled revenues and expenses at all sites. Of these two options, the latter more clearly reflects integration.

Q 13:31   What is the difference between a GWW and a traditional medical group practice?

A GWW represents a level of integration among independent group practices without full merging of the separate practices. The major distinction is the degree of integration among the physicians' medical practices and with the medical practice organization with respect to risk sharing and pooling of revenues and expenses, as well as common central services, billing, and collection. These may appear the same, but they are functionally quite different.

Q 13:32   What are the advantages of a GWW?

The GWW structure provides many of the benefits of a fully integrated group practice—such as cost efficiencies and pooled working capital—

with limited up-front capital investment and without mandating a single site. It also gives the physician greater autonomy and allows primary care and specialty physicians to achieve the benefits of a multispecialty group practice. This structure enhances managed care opportunities because (1) some contracts are available only to large physician groups, (2) multiple sites may be attractive to managed care payers, and (3) the financial risk may be spread among several physicians. The GWW provides physicians with increased leverage in negotiating with hospitals and payers for inpatient risk pools. The group practice attribute also facilitates the sale of physician practices upon retirement.

Q 13:33   What are the disadvantages of a GWW?

The GWW model affords no integration between hospitals and the physicians except where an MSO is involved. In addition, many existing models have experienced a high level of physician dissatisfaction, which has been attributed to the compensation structure and absence of physician commitment to a group practice philosophy. There is also increasing risk that the regulators will view this arrangement as a sham and will deem that the referral and compensation arrangements violate antireferral laws. This, in addition to the inability to centralize ancillary services on behalf of its members consistent with the recently enacted extension of the Stark Amendment, makes the structure potentially unworkable under current Medicare reimbursement regulations.[10]

Multiple independent practice sites hamper efficiencies of scale, and therefore the group may not be competitive with more fully integrated practices. Additionally, because of the multiple scattered sites, governance and decision-making bodies may be disjointed and in conflict. Finally, some physicians will not adjust to a group practice style of medicine, and therefore the GWW model must provide for the departure of incompatible physicians.

MEDICAL GROUP PRACTICE

Q 13:34   What are the general characteristics of a medical group practice?

The fully integrated group practice formally consolidates physicians into a single cohesive entity. The entity has a single tax and provider number, and all revenue and expenses flow through the group practice. All professional staff members are employed by the practice, although if there is a management arrangement with an MSO, the MSO may employ the lay administrative staff. Generally, there is a group compensation system that may be fixed or production-based. These models can be either primary care or specialty practice, although some are multispecialty group practices.

Q 13:35   What are the advantages of a medical group practice?

Full integration guarantees physician oversight and involvement in practice decisions while maximizing the ability to contract, compete, and gain access to capital. A greater degree of integration also increases the financial advantages achieved through economies of scale. Because the physicians' interests are aligned, much of the conflict and confusion otherwise present are eliminated. By spreading risk for capitated contracts among all physicians, the financial risk, as well as antitrust risks associated with price fixing among competitors, is greatly reduced. An integrated medical group practice also eliminates capital obstacles for new physicians in practice start-up, management, recruitment, and retention.

Q 13:36   What are the disadvantages of a medical group practice?

The most obvious disadvantage is the loss of autonomy physicians may feel that could cause them to refuse to devote maximum efforts to the group. Moreover, as a result of the level of detail involved, full integration involves greater start-up time and costs, as well as greater capital outlay if a practice acquisition strategy is involved. There are legal and tax issues associated with buy-in/buy-out situations involving new or retiring physicians.

MANAGEMENT SERVICES ORGANIZATION

Q 13:37   What is an MSO?

A management services organization is a business that provides management services to physicians and physician groups. The MSO can be hospital affiliated, physician owned, jointly owned, or investor owned. Most MSOs own the facilities, equipment, and supplies used in a medical practice. MSOs developed out of the perceived need for separating the business and management functions from the medical practice. Growing out of the medical management services bureau, the MSO can provide a broad range of services, facilities, equipment, and support to a variety of provider entities such as individual physicians, medical groups, IPAs, PHOs, medical foundations, and related entities on a contract basis. The MSO often functions as an administrator of managed care contracts on behalf of its managed entities, in addition to the more common MSO services such as furnishing facilities, staff, and support services.

The MSO may acquire the tangible assets of a medical practice or acquire new assets and then lease the assets to the medical practice under the management services agreement. The physicians remain the providers of care, operate all clinical aspects of the practice, and own the medical records and any HMO or PPO contracts. Physician bonding can be achieved through asset purchase paid out over time, deferred compensation, and restrictive covenants.

Figure 13–3 (see Q 13:38) reflects the general structure of a free-standing MSO. Figure 13–4 shows a hospital-affiliated structure. Finally, Figure 13–5 depicts a joint venture MSO.

Q 13:38   What is a physician practice management company (PPMC)?

A PPMC is an organization that provides a variety of assets and management to one or more medical practices. They are designed to

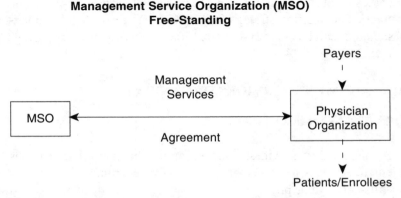

Management Service Organization (MSO)
Free-Standing

Figure 13–3 General Structure of a Free-Standing MSO

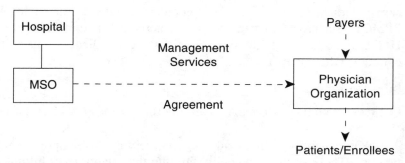

Figure 13–4 General Structure of a Hospital-Affiliated MSO

acquire the tangible assets of the medical practice and lease them back to the practice as part of a management services agreement. Sometimes, PPMCs acquire new assets and lease them to the practice. Occasionally, they provide support services to other organizations such as hospitals. PPMCs are management services organizations. Some PPMCs focus on specialty care networks, while others concentrate on primary care prac-

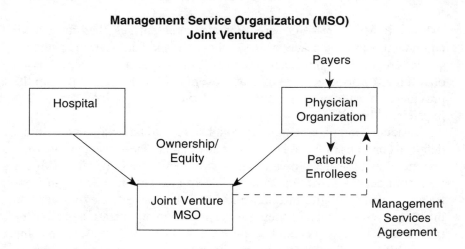

Figure 13–5 General Structure of a Joint-Ventured MSO

tices. A PPMC is not a provider of health care services, but it often affiliates with physician groups, negotiating and even executing managed care contracts on behalf of the contracted groups. Some of the larger PPMCs—such as MedPartners—have entered into national alliances with HMOs and other payers to make their affiliated medical groups parties to contracts with payers on a national basis.

Q 13:39   What services are available through a PPMC or MSO?

MSOs can provide a broad range of services to support a medical practice. These services generally fall into the categories of billing, practice management, network administration, and medical outcome management.

The PPMC or MSO bills and collects for medical services on the physicians' behalf and may negotiate and administer managed care contracts on behalf of the physicians as attorney-in-fact. Nonclinical employees of the medical practice may become employees of the PPMC or MSO, adding employee benefits and taxes to the PPMC's or MSO's responsibilities.

Q 13:40   What are the general characteristics of a PPMC or MSO?

Most PPMCs or MSOs are separate legal entities that furnish all equipment, supplies, practice sites, personnel, and administrative support services required by physician practices. Compensation typically is based on a fixed fee or percentage of gross revenue. The physicians remain the providers of care, and the PPMC or MSO bills and collects on the physicians' behalf.

Physician bonding is achieved through asset purchase payout over time, deferred compensation, and restrictive covenants. The physicians own and operate clinical aspects, own the medical records, and hold the HMO or PPO contracts. The MSO may negotiate and execute managed care contracts on behalf of the hospital and physicians as attorney-in-fact and maintain exclusive management for the physician organization or have the right of first refusal to capitalize and manage new clinic sites. Ownership of the MSO may be solely by the hospital or jointly with physicians,

HMOs, entrepreneurs, and so on. The MSO is a taxable entity (a general or membership corporation or a general or limited partnership).

Q 13:41   What are the advantages of a PPMC or MSO?

The principal benefit to each physician in a PPMC or MSO setting is the ability to retain his or her practice autonomy while eliminating management headaches. Additionally, physicians who are managed by a common PPMC or MSO can benefit from reduced overhead resulting from economies of scale, the PPMC's or MSO's management expertise, and increased access to managed care plans. The PPMC or MSO allows physicians to recover the equity from their medical practices by selling the tangible assets to the PPMC or MSO and to assign liability by transferring overhead and practice responsibilities to a business that specializes in practice management. For physicians who practice in a state where the corporate practice of medicine is prohibited, PPMCs or MSOs offer unlicensed entities the ability to participate in the management of a medical practice as long as clinically related decision making is not affected. Even in states that do not prohibit the corporate practice of medicine, PPMCs or MSOs are viable to physicians as an alternative to selling one's practice to a hospital or other entity and becoming an employee of someone else's business.

The PPMC or MSO can bring added value to a physician practice through centralized marketing and management services and the collective purchasing power of its several managed entities. A PPMC or MSO offers one-stop shopping to patients, flexibility in the range of services and number of physicians, and a vehicle for physician recruitment, network development, and practice acquisition.

Q 13:42   What are the disadvantages of a PPMC or MSO?

Because of the regulatory restrictions on PPMC or MSO activities that preclude control of patients and referrals, there is a financial risk associated with the potential for a runaway medical group that is either recruited from under the contracted medical group or terminates the contract with the PPMC or MSO and enters into direct competition with it. In view of the significant capital investment required of most PPMC or MSO operations, these risks can be significant to the PPMC's or MSO's economic viability.

The PPMC or MSO model offers limited opportunity for the operational integration of providers who are not already in one group practice. Because physicians continue to practice separately, their economic interests are not necessarily aligned, and they potentially could compete against each other.

Removing control over the practice management from the physicians themselves may be perceived as a loss of control and autonomy, even if the physicians retain MSO ownership. There is an inherent conflict of duties that arises when physicians as MSO owners have different objectives than they would as the owners of their own medical group. There is increased bureaucracy in a business organization such as an MSO, which increases as it takes on the management of more than one group.

Q 13:43   What makes a PPMC or MSO attractive to physicians?

Physicians who accept PPMC or MSO arrangements are usually specialists who see that their hard work results in less income as managed care and overhead take a larger bite out of their gross practice revenue. Many also see the advantage of having a collaborative rather than competitive relationship with other physicians and hospitals. As resources shrink and cost containment becomes more important, physicians are seeking management services that will make their practices both successful and economically viable. Finally, many physicians realize that sustained growth in today's economy will be difficult to accomplish without the support of a larger player with which to collaborate.

PHYSICIAN-HOSPITAL ORGANIZATIONS

Q 13:44   What is a PHO?

A PHO is a form of joint venture managed care contracting organization that has the following characteristics:

- Functions as a negotiating vehicle for managed care contracts on behalf of hospital(s) and physicians.

- May perform utilization review, management, and credentialing functions.
- Does not assume direct contract responsibility for services.

The PHO evolved from the earlier PPO structures as an organization that can offer to HMOs and managed care contractors both inpatient hospital and professional health care services on a risk basis. A PHO is similar to an IPA for contracting purposes, but it represents a slightly broader group of providers. The PHO brings together the hospital, physicians, and possibly other ancillary providers, with shared governance among all, and may have either open or closed physician membership.

Q 13:45   How is a PHO structured?

The most common structure includes a hospital organization and a physician organization. However, there are many different levels of integration. Some PHOs are structured as mere contractual arrangements between a hospital and its affiliated physicians (or affiliated-physician organization or IPA). Others take the form of a separately organized legal entity made up of equal ownership and representation by the hospital and its affiliated physicians (or physician organization or affiliated IPA). The latter description is the most commonly used because of the legal and operational realities of managed care contracting. PHOs can be organized as for-profit business corporations or nonprofit (usually taxable) entities. Figure 13–6 (see Q 13:46) reflects the generic PHO structure.

Q 13:46   What are the general characteristics of a PHO?

Most PHOs have joint ownership or board membership by the hospital and its affiliated physicians and may be capable of contracting on a risk basis for inpatient hospital and professional services (depending on the various state laws related to risk-bearing activities). PHOs may be open or closed membership organizations. Open membership permits all physicians with basic credentials to participate. Closed membership is typically chosen if a sufficient number of primary care physicians are members. Physician participation may be through an IPA structure, separate physician organization, or independent contractors.

Physician-Hospital Organization

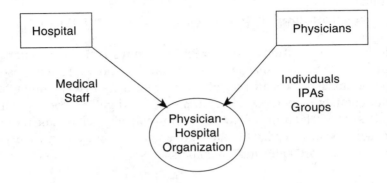

Figure 13–6 Generic PHO Structure

The PHO operates as a contract broker and facilitates negotiations with payers by bringing a complete package of providers to the negotiating table subject to limitations imposed by recent antitrust reviews of PHOs.

Q 13:47   What are the advantages of a PHO?

The PHO integrates the physicians with the hospital in a separate and distinct legal and contracting entity. Hospitals and physicians share ownership and control of the legal entity with less up-front capital investment. Because of the separation of the PHO from the more adversarial, traditional hospital-physician relationship, the PHO can arrange for managed care and HMO contracting on behalf of its hospital and physician members. PHOs can receive compensation under a variety of methods ranging from fee-for-service and discounted fee-for-service to capitation, case rates, or *per diem* rates as well as a variety of other risk-shifting payment mechanisms. This is subject to the insurance law considerations.

A PHO builds teamwork and trust by means of a shared decision-making structure, through which the providers can present themselves to payers as a single voice. Shared resources and contracting efforts often improve cost effectiveness and lessen physicians' contracting hassles. There is flexibility in the PHO model although it increases its participants' awareness of joint cost-control measures and patient care concerns in managed care settings.

Q 13:48   What are the disadvantages of a PHO?

The PHO model produces only a partial integration of the hospital and physicians. This increases the risk of antitrust scrutiny. In addition, because of state insurance laws that regulate the business of insurance and require licensure of HMOs, many PHOs are limited to discounted fee-for-service or direct contracting arrangements on a global fee basis. Capitated arrangements require careful structuring of the PHO contracting arrangement to avoid functioning as an unlicensed insurance company or HMO.

Most PHO provider panels are not selective enough to exclude inefficient providers. The hard choices of excluding practitioners with whom they have practiced for years cause most PHO participants to be overly inclusive, thereby diminishing the ability to control cost through effective use.

Until recently, it was possible to establish minimum reimbursement rates in contract negotiations. Because of recent increased scrutiny by the Federal Trade Commission (FTC) under its antitrust enforcement role, many PHOs have lost some leverage and economies of scale in price negotiation terms. As with many managed care provider organizations, there is a potential for high overhead since some system is required for tracking utilization, costs, and patient outcomes. The PHO must have expertise in contract negotiations and management.

MEDICAL FOUNDATION

Q 13:49   What is a medical foundation?

The medical foundation was originally developed in California pursuant to a state statute that allowed tax-exempt nonprofit medical foundations to provide medical care without violating the prohibitions against the corporate practice of medicine.[11] Rather than the physicians or medical group, the foundation holds the patient relationships and managed care contracts. This contrasts with the MSO, which does not provide patient care but rather provides services to the entity that provides care.

Not to be confused with the California medical foundation model is the nonprofit health corporation, which, in Texas, permits the practice of medicine through a nonprofit corporation certified under section 5.01(a) of the Medical Practice Act.[12] This organization can achieve a level of vertical integration by having as its sole corporate member a hospital or other nonphysician entity, provided the 5.01(a) organization's board is composed solely of licensed physicians. This should not be confused with the MSO arrangement that involves a professional medical corporation or other equity structure that is managed by and leases space and equipment from a management services organization.

Q 13:50   What are the general characteristics of a medical foundation?

The medical foundation model is most often structured as a nonprofit tax-exempt corporation affiliated with a hospital or health system through a common parent organization or as a subsidiary of a hospital or health system. The medical foundation functions like a consolidated medical practice group and MSO to provide medical care to patients, hold HMO and PPO contracts, bill and collect in its own name for medical and ancillary services, own patient medical records and accounts receivable, and either employ or contract with physicians or medical groups for services to foundation patients.

Q 13:51   What are the advantages of a medical foundation?

If the foundation qualifies for tax exemption as a nonprofit medical foundation, the advantages include exemption from federal and state income taxes and from property taxes, availability of charitable deductions for contributions to it, and access to tax-exempt financing. The foundation also may be more acceptable to physicians if the medical group remains a separate contracting entity.

The 5.01(a) organization offers tremendous flexibility since it can function as a medical practice organization and can contract for medical services on a full-risk basis in direct contracts with payers. If the 5.01(a) organization is contracted to a state-licensed HMO, it can accept full or global risk for both institutional and medical services.

Q 13:52   What are the disadvantages of a medical foundation?

Most disadvantages from the perspective of the physician mirror those for medical group practices (see Q 13:34, Q 13:35, and Q 13:36). Like the MSO, this model is capital-intensive and expensive to operate. Also, as a nonprofit corporation, it cannot dividend money to its owners. Profits can only be extracted through contractual arrangements.

FULLY INTEGRATED SYSTEM

Q 13:53   What is an IDS?

Broadly defined, the integrated health care delivery system is a group of affiliated organizations that provides comprehensive health care services to patients. At a minimum, the IDS provides hospital, physician, and related ancillary services. More sophisticated systems coordinate care to patients and may also provide home health, hospice, skilled nursing, preventive medicine, mental health, rehabilitation, long-term care, and other programs representing the full continuum of care. An IDS may be a single organization or a group of affiliated entities under common control or management. The affiliated groups are organized into a comprehensive delivery system that can offer a variety of provider arrangements to payers and other health plans—including HMOs—and to employers under direct contract. This represents the integration of alternative structures into a health care delivery system that can be responsive to a variety of managed care arrangements, including both capitated and discounted fee-for-service health plans.

Most integrated health care delivery systems are provider organizations that do not include the insurance component. Comprehensive systems such as Kaiser, which includes the Kaiser hospitals, the Permanente Medical Group, and the Kaiser Health Plan, are not the trend. Some of the large insurers are using both the MSO and direct acquisition of medical practices to integrate providers with health plans and products in response to health care reform pressures.

Q 13:54   What are the major issues that arise in structuring an IDS?

The process of integrating providers with different backgrounds can prove to be a challenge; however, according to Gerald R. Peters, the following are the four major issues:[13]

Structure. The IDS can be housed in a single organization or developed as a subsidiary of a hospital or as a parent holding company that is the sole owner of both the hospital and the physician or medical practice organization.

Mission. The participants in the IDS must determine its mission and purpose, including whether it will be nonprofit or for-profit.

Control. Whether the IDS will be under shared control or under the control of any one of the participants must be determined at the outset.

Physician relations. In the physician or medical practice organization, whether the physicians will be employees or independent contractors must be evaluated.

Q 13:55   How does the MSO facilitate IDS integration?

An MSO is not itself an integrated delivery system. It is a business organization that facilitates the integration of the delivery system by funding the development or start-up of the physician group practice. By facilitating physician integration, the MSO can provide the essential coordination of functions with the hospital to allow for the possible development of either a network or IDS.

PAYER-PROVIDER INTEGRATION

Q 13:56   What role do employers, businesses, and insurers play in the trend toward integration of health care providers and payers?

The trend toward integration is being driven by the increasing demands placed on the health care delivery system by those responsible for paying for health care services. As businesses seek to control health care expenses, as business communities develop coalitions, and as federal and state governments focus on legislating health care reform, several common themes appear in these proposed plans: cost control, access, and quality. When developing an IDS or provider network, the payer's relationship may range from a purely contractual association to a joint venture system or MSO. Many of these ventures are being sought as a response to increased competition.

Q 13:57   What are the characteristics of payer-provider integration?

In several parts of the country, HMOs started out using a staff model of employed physicians. In California and Arizona, HMOs such as FHP used the staff model extensively. In Southern California, the IPA model developed as a contractual means for an HMO to access provider services. In Texas, exclusive contractual relationships between medical groups and insurers (MacGregor Medical Association and Prudential Insurance) developed for the same reasons. Then, in response to Medicare and Medicaid managed care initiatives, many provider organizations applied for and obtained certificates of authority to operate an HMO. All of these arrangements involved either the HMO accessing provider services or the provider assuming the ability to function as an HMO.

Although there is no single model, the basic approach to payer-provider integration ranges from purely contracting relationships and alliances to shared equity models to fully merged organizations. In the contracting model, payers use exclusive and risk-sharing arrangements to achieve alignment of interests with providers at a preintegration level. In developing structures that allow shared equity, some payers and provider systems may jointly venture a managed care product (for example, an HMO). Others may enter into equity arrangements in which payers acquire, employ, and control providers, or providers acquire and control payers. In the fully merged model, the payers and providers merge.

There are innovative arrangements associated with the desire of provider organizations to partner with insurers and other vendors to offer products and services to all forms of payers: self-insured, government, and fully insured. The PSO represents the organization most likely to reflect payer-provider integration strategies. The PSO represents the ultimate integration of providers with insurers or assumption by providers of insurance functions on a vendor basis.

Q 13:58   What are the advantages of payer-provider integration?

From the provider's perspective, the advantages of aligning with a single payer include:

- revenue increases because of removal of the "intermediary"

- participation in the design and structure of the managed care arrangement increases
- ability to use the payer's expertise and resources
- cost control and access to capital
- time frame to market entry shortens

From the payer's perspective, alignment with a provider (or provider network or IDS) removes a potential competitive threat in a particular market. It also makes available to the payer a group of dedicated providers, including some that might not otherwise contract. There are distinct market advantages to such alignment, because access to a network facilitates early market entry and enhances the marketability of the product.

Q 13:59   What are the disadvantages of payer-provider integration?

Many providers, provider networks, or PSOs may be reluctant to commit to a single payer, as attractive as it may seem. Even if the relationship is not exclusive, its existence may foreclose the ability of the network or PSO to have contracts with other payers. Another concern may be the differing interests of the parties, with the providers more focused on local health care issues and the payers focused on a larger agenda.

From the payer's perspective, there may be inherent conflicts in the goals of payers and providers. Providers are far more concerned about revenue enhancement, which may at times be inconsistent with the use controls imposed on the network or PSO. Like the providers, payers may be reluctant to pick one horse to ride, at the risk of losing opportunities to work with other desirable networks or PSOs.

PROVIDER SPONSORED ORGANIZATIONS

Q 13:60   What is a PSO?

A PSO is a local health care delivery system created through formal affiliations among health care providers. Sometimes called a provider sponsored network (PSN), these entities can be physician-based, hospital-based, or IDS-based, encompassing other ancillary health service providers such as home health and long-term care providers. At the lowest level of integration, a PSO could be a loose affiliation of physicians or a joint venture between a hospital and several physician groups. At a higher level of integration, PSOs have a defined legal and governance structure that brings providers together under common medical and financial management, and encourages coordination of various clinical and business functions of the organization.

Q 13:61   What are the characteristics of a PSO?

A PSO is not subject to a simple definition. At best, it should have

- a provider network or organization such as a PHO that includes a broad range of health care providers
- an MSO capability
- an IDS

The definition of a PSO cannot precisely address the foregoing characteristics because they can exist along a continuum of integration as shown in Exhibit 13–1 (see Q 13:60); therefore, many organizations may be PSOs based on the existence of these characteristics. PSOs, however, can also be characterized by such other variables as size, age, financial status, and types of provider relationships.

Under the Medicare+Choice program (M+C), a PSO is one of the M+C coordinated care plans defined in 42 C.F.R. part 400, et al., as an entity established by health care providers for the purpose of participating directly in the Medicare program on a risk basis.

Q 13:62   Can a PHO be a PSO?

A PHO, without the other characteristics in place, would not be a PSO. It is suggested that a PHO could be a start-up organization for providers intending to move toward a more integrated delivery system, which is essential to taking risk under capitated arrangements.[14] Most PHOs, how

Exhibit 13–1 Continuum of Integration for PSOs

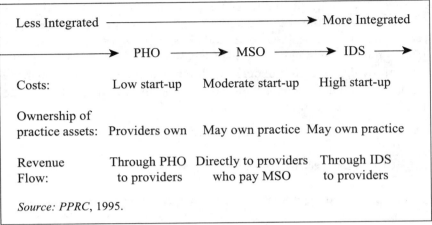

Less Integrated ⟶ More Integrated			
⟶ PHO ⟶	MSO ⟶	IDS ⟶	
Costs:	Low start-up	Moderate start-up	High start-up
Ownership of practice assets:	Providers own	May own practice	May own practice
Revenue Flow:	Through PHO to providers	Directly to providers who pay MSO	Through IDS to providers

Source: PPRC, 1995.

ever, are new organizations that do not have the size and financial capability to undertake the role of a PSO without substantial capital investment. Another problem with the PHO as a foundation for the PSO is its lack of integration. Most PHOs cannot accept risk either operationally or legally because of this factor.

PHOs are limited in their effectiveness because of their structure. Often, they are specialist-dominated and do not have sufficient integration to allow for effective quality management and utilization controls. There are significant legal barriers to PHOs because they are subject to antitrust scrutiny and can pose problems under Medicare fraud and abuse as well as inurement issues for tax-exempt organizations.

Q 13:63   What role can a management services organization play in a PSO?

MSOs are entities that may do as little as furnish billing, recordkeeping, office administration, and contract negotiation assistance—or they may play the more sophisticated role of purchasing physical assets of physician practices and renting them back with the assumption of all business functions for the practice. MSOs often have access to much needed capital to acquire the medical information systems for effective management of funds and services.

Q 13:64   What is the difference between a PSO and an IDS?

The term *integrated delivery system* refers to an entity that incorporates provider organizations with the management services capability and adds a level of clinical integration that allows the organization to function as a unified provider of care. An IDS may be organized around a medical foundation, a staff or affiliated medical group, or equity model organization. In a foundation model, an entity (usually a hospital) establishes an affiliated foundation that acquires the assets of physician practices and enters into exclusive contracts with the physicians or groups to provide professional medical services. The physicians are paid by the foundation for their services. The staff model employs physicians directly. Under the equity model, the physicians own a part of the IDS with the hospital and share in its financial success or failure.

A PSO can be an integrated delivery system. The Balanced Budget Act of 1997 (BBA) provides the defining characteristics of a PSO.

Q 13:65   What are the advantages of a PSO that is an IDS?

An IDS can take advantage of both horizontal and vertical integration. Horizontal integration allows the organization to increase its service area geographically. Vertical integration allows the IDS to more effectively move patients along a continuum of care without loss of revenue. If an IDS is an organized delivery system, it can effectively function via clinical integration even if the legal structure is not fully integrated on a vertical or horizontal basis.

Q 13:66   Do PSOs have to be licensed as HMOs?

Whether a PSO must be licensed as an HMO depends on what it does and whether state law applies to regulate its activities. On March 5, 1998, the federal Negotiated Rulemaking Committee on PSO Solvency Standards reached agreement on proposed solvency standards for PSOs. These standards are contained in Appendix A. The standards set the minimum requirements for PSO solvency and must be evaluated against each state's solvency standards to determine whether waiver under the M+C program is appropriate or even applicable. These determinations must be guided by each state's commissioner of insurance because certain requirements may be discretionary or may be waived at the state level.

The American Medical Association (AMA) reviewed the solvency standards for all 50 states and compared them to the PSO solvency standards developed through the Negotiated Rulemaking Committee. Based on information obtained by the AMA through June 1998, it appears that the federal PSO standards are *less* rigorous than the standards in 11 states.[15] They are equivalent to the standards in nine states.[16] They appear less rigorous in nine states than the state statutory standards, pending receipt of information on whether the state required prefunding of losses.[17] In nine states, the federal standards were more rigorous than the state statutory standards, pending receipt of information on whether losses are prefunded.[18] Finally, for 12 states, the federal standards were actually *more* rigorous than the state standards.[19]

Q 13:67   How are PSOs regulated?

Many states do not have specific regulations for entities that call themselves PSOs because they evolved outside the scope of existing state regulations. In analyzing their status under state law, the states will look at what the PSOs do rather than what they claim to be. States regulate health care providers and insurers in a number of ways. Health care providers are often subject to licensure to engage in a field of medical practice or to operate health care facilities. The business of insurance, including HMOs, is subject to licensure or certification by the state. Consequently, states will need to ascertain whether the PSO is a provider, an insurer, or other health care organization subject to state regulation. Key considerations include whether the entity is assuming a business risk or an actuarial risk, and whether the entity is involved in the business of insurance (which may include certain forms of provider risk sharing). For purposes of the M+C program, PSOs must be capable of participating in the Medicare program on a risk basis.

Q 13:68   What are the major concerns that regulators have with PSOs?

Most of the concerns that state regulators and legislators have with PSOs relate to their ability to accept financial risk. State regulators want risk-bearing entities to be licensed and subject to consumer protection requirements. Based on a 1995 survey of state regulators by the Group Health Association of America, most states require PSOs to obtain HMO licenses if they accept full risk.[20] This issue becomes less clear when PSOs have direct contracts where they take partial risk by sharing risk with an employer, or where the risk is through a downstream risk arrangement with a licensed HMO.

Some states still require HMO licensure even if the risk taking is partial; however, where the PSO is merely passing risk down from a licensed HMO, other states have taken the position that a license is not required since a licensed HMO is involved in the arrangement. The issue becomes more complicated where the arrangement is subject to an Employee Retirement Income Security Act arrangement. In a bulletin sent by the National Association of Insurance Commissioners (NAIC) to all state insurance commissioners in 1995, there was an attempt to clarify this situation with the statement that if PSOs accept risk on a prepaid basis, they should be licensed in some manner. Where the entity accepts downstream risk from a licensed HMO, however, there should be an exception to licensure.

Where states regulate PSOs under existing HMO statutes, HMO solvency requirements will apply to the PSOs; however, where states have developed specific statutes for regulation of PSOs, there may be less rigorous solvency requirements. For example, California issues a limited license to PSOs engaged in downstream risk arrangements with HMOs. On the other hand, Maine has licensed its only PSO under its preferred provider organization statute.

Q 13:69   What approaches have states taken with respect to licensing PSOs?

States have taken one of three approaches with respect to PSOs. These are summarized from the Physician Payment Review Commission Report as follows:[21]

1. License PSOs under existing laws as
   * health maintenance organizations
   * limited health maintenance organizations
   * indemnity health insurers
   * health service corporations

- preferred provider organizations
- health care service contractors

2. License PSOs in a new regulatory framework under
   - a separate licensing category
   - a category that covers all risk-bearing entities

3. Require no license for PSOs

Most states have taken the position that existing laws and regulations may be applied without the need to create new laws and regulations. Others have either devised a new regulatory framework or established different forms of licensure.

The NAIC has undertaken an initiative called the "consolidated licensure for entities assuming risk" or "CLEAR" as a means of consolidating the licensure of risk-bearing entities or activities. It bases the initiative on seven standards intended to make the various model acts consistent in the areas of credentialing, quality assessment and improvement, utilization review, grievance procedures, provider network adequacy and contracting, consumer disclosure, and data reporting.

Q 13:70   What effect has the BBA had on PSOs and their ability to directly contract with Medicare?

Under the BBA, Pub. L. No. 105-33, H.R. 2015 (BBA), a PSO is now eligible to contract directly with the Medicare program on a risk basis provided it meets the definition stated in the BBA as being a public or private entity

- that is established or organized and operated by a "health care provider" or group of "affiliated health care providers"
- that provides a "substantial proportion" of health care items and services through the provider or affiliated group of providers
- in which the "affiliated" providers share, directly or indirectly, substantial financial risk with respect to the provision of such items and services and have at least a majority financial interest in the PSO entity[22]

Q 13:71   What types of entities are eligible to become Medicare risk PSOs under the BBA?

The definition of a PSO is broad enough to encompass a broad spectrum of MCOs. The essential terms include "health care providers" at "substantial financial risk" who provide a "substantial proportion" of the covered benefits. It is likely that entities such as IDSs, PHOs, hospital systems, medical groups, PPOs, and IPAs could be eligible provided they meet the definition and satisfy the standards to be a PSO as set forth in the M+C rules.

Q 13:72   What legal structure is appropriate for a PSO?

There are no limitations on the form of entity for a PSO; PSO organizations can take a variety of legal forms. They may be public or private entities, for-profit or nonprofit, or pass-through structures such as limited license corporations, limited partnerships, or limited liability partnerships. As long as providers establish, organize, and operate the PSO and own a majority financial interest in the PSO, the choice of entities is not limited. In fact, a PSO can operate as a "line of business" or division of another entity that otherwise satisfies these minimal requirements.

Q 13:73   How does a PSO qualify as a Medicare+Choice organization?

PSOs must go through two regulatory approvals. The first involves either state licensure or federal waiver. The second requires the PSO to show evidence of compliance with federal contracting requirements as a condition to enter into a Medicare risk contract.

Licensure or Waiver. Although the BBA provides that the M+C organization be licensed and organized under state law as a risk-bearing entity eligible to offer health insurance or health benefits coverage, the BBA directs the Secretary of Health and Human Services (HHS) to waive state licensing requirements if

- The state has failed to complete action on the PSO's licensing application within 90 days after the state's receipt of a substantially complete application.
- The state has denied the PSO's licensing application *and* as a condition for approval of the application, the state imposed material requirements upon the PSO (other than solvency requirements) that generally are not applicable to other entities engaged in a substantially similar business as the PSO; *or* as a condition for approval of the application, the state required that the PSO offer any product other than an M+C plan.
- Where an application is filed on or after the date that federal financial solvency and capital adequacy standards for PSOs are established by HHS, the state has denied the PSO's licensing application based on the PSO's failure to meet the state's solvency requirements *and* such requirements are not the same as the federal standards established by HHS; *or* as a condition for approval of the application, the state imposed documentation or information requirements relating to solvency or other material requirements, procedures, and standards relating to solvency that are different from the federal requirements, procedures, and standards applied by HHS to PSOs.

PSOs must file applications for a waiver from state licensing requirements with HHS by November 1, 2002. The Secretary of HHS must grant or deny a waiver application within 60 days after the date he or she determines that a substantially complete waiver application has been filed. If granted, the waiver is good for a period of only 36 months and cannot be renewed. PSOs that receive a waiver from the Secretary will still have to meet all consumer protection and quality standards applicable to PSOs that are state licensed, with the exception of standards applicable to (1) benefit requirements, (2) requirements relating to inclusion or treatment of providers, or (3) coverage determinations (including those related to appeals and grievance processes). This will also apply to other M+C organizations operating in the state.

Under the PSO standards, PSOs seeking to offer M+C plans must have at least 1,500 individuals (500 for rural or nonurban areas) who are receiving benefits through the PSO before contracting with the Medicare program, whereas other M+C organizations must have at least 5,000 individuals (1,500 for rural or nonurban areas) who are receiving benefits through the organization before contracting with the Medicare program. The Secretary may waive these minimum enrollment requirements during the first three contract years with respect to any M+C organization.

Contracting Standards. A PSO must enter into a contract with HCFA to offer an M+C plan to Medicare beneficiaries. These extensive standards are set forth in the recently published "mega-regs" that address (1) service area requirements, (2) beneficiary protections, (3) quality assurance or quality improvement, (4) provider issues, (5) preemption of state law, (6) risk adjustments to payment, and (7) other compliance requirements.[23]

Q 13:74   What is the status of the PSO under current antitrust law?

Antitrust issues applicable to PSOs will differ depending on whether the risk-sharing entity involves a joint venture (e.g., IPA or PHO) or whether it is a more integrated organization (fully integrated medical group or IDS). Antitrust laws and Department of Justice (DOJ) enforcement policies were designed to promote competition in the relevant market. Recent efforts of the DOJ and the FTC included development of several policy statements intended to clarify instances where certain activities would not be subject to antitrust scrutiny. These "safety zones" were a good start, but not sufficient to address the rapidly changing health care market.

In August 1996, the DOJ and FTC released a new set of enforcement statements to further clarify antitrust enforcement policy. The most significant changes concern physician network joint ventures, where there were distinctions made between exclusive and nonexclusive ventures, and those that place the venturers at substantial financial risk. Joint ventures falling outside of the revised safety zones will not necessarily be challenged.

Q 13:75   What are other important considerations in establishing a PSO?

One of the most critical considerations in organizing a PSO is to structure it for success. Many organizations will become PSOs in name, but will not succeed because of the failure to integrate essential functions. If the purpose of organizing a PSO is to protect the existing systems from managed care penetration, rather than compete in the market with a new product, it will likely fail. If the system has not worked out the organizational and governance issues when historical competitors are brought together, it will encounter problems associated with disjointed vision and distrust.

HMOs will view PSOs with distrust. Even the community health plan model may encounter difficulties in finding an HMO partner because of a perceived competitive threat. If the PSO is too large, it may be perceived as a threat to other MCOs and insurers. This could impair its ability to obtain contracts for commercial lives.

There will always be resistance on the part of the physicians unless the PSO is one sponsored by the physicians. Even then, competition among physician groups and control issues will impede effective integration efforts. This correlates with the likely overcapacity of physicians in certain specialties and the unnecessary duplication of services available from participating facilities. Finally, if the PSO is unable to effectively manage the care, it is likely to encounter serious problems in managing costs. These issues should be addressed during the organizational and development stages of forming a PSO or PSN.

ALTERNATIVE DELIVERY SYSTEMS

Q 13:76   What is a community health care organization (CHCO)?

As described by John R. Griffith, a CHCO is an innovative systems approach to the community hospital model.[24] Building on the strength and history of the community hospital, the CHCO continues the commitment to the local community, while incorporating a more diverse representation on its governing board. Its success is based on its ability to integrate physicians, provide low-cost, high-quality care, and govern itself aggressively in a demanding market.

Griffith suggests that the CHCO should incorporate five areas into its strategic vision:

1. health
2. cost containment
3. progress
4. respect
5. collaborative approach

Using these as goals, the CHCO should be much more nimble than its competitors in accommodating change, integrating different perspectives, and responding to local community needs.

Q 13:77   What is an integrated health care network?

The SMG Marketing Group, Inc., in its May 1997 *Market Letter*, described an integrated health care network (IHN) as a system of health care providers that come together into an organizational structure that allows the IHN to cover a broad range of health care services, including wellness programs, preventive care, ambulatory clinics, outpatient diagnostic and laboratory services, emergency care, general hospital services, rehabilitation, long-term care, congregational living, psychiatric care, and home health and hospice care.[25] The *Market Letter* goes on to address the fact that not all the services have to be provided directly, but can be contracted out to nonmember entities. This allows the IHN to achieve the efficiencies of an integrated system, while also assuming financial risk in capitated contract arrangements. In all respects, the IHN is a form of IDS as described in this chapter.

Q 13:78   What does an IHN look like?

Most IHNs function as provider organizations with the participating health care entities and MCOs as formal members of the IHN. These are more likely to be further along in achieving integration than IHNs that have not formalized their network memberships. Hospitals, medical groups, and physician practices usually constitute the majority of members in an IHN, however, many IHN members also include nursing homes, MCOs, HMOs, home health agencies, diagnostic imaging centers, free-standing outpatient surgery centers, and other networks.

Q 13:79   What are the important areas of integration for an effective IHN?

Although there is no formula for the optimal functioning IHN, the important areas of integration should include:

- decision making
- board of directors
- centralized purchasing
- contracts with group purchasing organizations
- networkwide managed care contracts
- information systems

These and other areas of integration among IHNs include those items shown in Figure 13–7.

Q 13:80   Have the IHNs been successful in obtaining managed care contracts?

PacifiCare awarded a 10-year contract to the Memorial Health Services hospital system in Long Beach, California. This was an unprecedented

Centralized Decision Making
Board of Directors
Purchasing
Contracts with Group Purchasing Organizations
Networkwide Managed Care Contracts
Information Systems
Medical Services
Capitated Contracts with MCOs
Disease Management Programs
Case Management Programs
Capitated Contracts with Employers
Formulary
Centralized and Integrated Credentialing

Figure 13–7 Key Features of an IHN (By areas of integration and order of prevalence in operating IHNs)

event based, in substantial part, on PacifiCare's recognition of its ability to tap into a health system with established standardized and medically based treatment protocols that were outcome- and success-rate driven for acute and chronic conditions. This represents one of an increasing number of such arrangements involving HMOs (some of which are members of an IHN) and health care organizations.

As IHNs increase their levels of integration, the *Market Letter* predicts an increase in the establishment of formularies. This will most likely have an effect on health care product manufacturers and pharmaceutical companies who will be dealing with an IHN rather than an individual facility or organization. In addition, exclusivity is not a necessary or even desired arrangement for an IHN member organization. Successful IHNs will want the MCO to contract with other facilities beyond the IHN.

Q 13:81   How does an IDS differ from an IHN?

Although the distinction is subtle, it is significant. An integrated delivery system is a more tightly structured, controlled organizational structure. It is more likely that the IDS will be under common ownership or sponsorship of a health care organization. An integrated health care network is an organization of more independent entities that come together for the purpose of sharing contracts and services. The analogy is similar to the difference between a medical group practice that employs its physicians to service contracts and patients, and an IPA that contracts for medical services with independent practices as its network of participating providers.

INTEGRATED CREDENTIALING AND PEER REVIEW

Q 13:82   What is the relevance of the Health Care Quality Improvement Act (HCQIA) to selection and deselection of providers in an IDS?

In organizing an IDS or MCO, the organizers should determine whether the benefits of HCQIA protection, including antitrust immunity and access to the data bank, outweigh its drawbacks. The drawbacks include mandatory reporting to the National Practitioner Data Bank of adverse credentialing decisions based on clinical competence or conduct, and compliance with the requirements of the statutorily defined due process. Due process, at a minimum, means that the entity must offer the affected provider notice of the reasons for the adverse action and an opportunity to respond or rebut those reasons. There continues to exist a debate among attorneys and other interested parties as to whether an IDS should afford due process to providers who are either not selected or who are deselected from participation in the IDS; and whether HCQIA even applies to entities such as an IDS.

Q 13:83   Are the credentialing materials used by an IDS discoverable?

The issue of discoverability of confidential credentialing information has been the subject of many treatises and court decisions. The most common request is from plaintiff attorneys requesting information in malpractice suits and from physician plaintiffs in antitrust suits. In the absence of a statutory privilege protecting against the discovery of such information, a few courts have allowed discovery of peer review documents (see *Kenney v. Superior Court of Co.*, 255 Cal. App. 2d 106 [1967]). Most courts, however, have tended to restrict discovery by the malpractice plaintiff reasoning that the harm to the peer review process outweighs the advantages to the plaintiff who has other means for obtaining the information. Courts have been more liberal in granting discovery requests by physician plaintiffs, reasoning that there is a due process right to the information pertaining to their own case and a greater need for information pertaining to general practices of the committee.

Q 13:84   What are the advantages of centralizing and integrating the credentialing and peer review process systemwide?

With the development of integrated delivery systems (hospitals, clinics, and physician organizations), some of which include licensed health plans (insurance or HMO plans), there is an increasing level of redundancy inherent in the credentialing and peer review process. Accreditation organizations such as National Committee for Quality Assurance, Joint Commission on the Accreditation of Healthcare Organizations, and Utilization

Review Accreditation Commission place much emphasis on the credentialing and peer review program as part of the overall measurement of quality and outcomes of a network or health plan. Few systems have attempted to centralize the credentialing function, and fewer have attempted to integrate credentialing and peer review activities within the integrated delivery system, although several are evolving in that direction. By eliminating redundancy of effort, the process becomes easier to administer and understand. Centralizing and integrating the credentialing functions will reduce the potential for inconsistent credentialing decisions. This is an important risk management consideration.

By centralizing the credentialing process within the IDS, the risk that one system entity will take unfair action against a practitioner is minimized. Credentialing is costly to the IDS. By eliminating redundancy of effort, the process consumes less time and money, and takes advantage of existing resources and capacity.

The potential for sharing of information among the IDS entities will only improve the quality of information on which credentialing decisions are made and outcomes are measured. A well-organized, centralized, and professional credentialing office is likely to be delegated credentialing functions by other provider organizations and payers.

Q 13:85   What is centralized credentialing in an IDS?

Centralized credentialing involves the consolidation of the application and verification activities for multiple organizations into a central clearinghouse. The process respects the separate oversight and decision making of each organization, which retains its own standards for review, appraisal, and decision making, even though these organizations may be related entities. A credentialing program can be centralized, but not integrated, or may be centralized and integrated.

Q 13:86   What is integrated credentialing in an IDS?

Integrated credentialing involves both the consolidation and integration of the review and appraisal process beyond a clearinghouse function within a health care system. Such a consolidation has the capability of allowing a single credentialing process and standard to be used by related organizations within the same health care system. Parts of a credentialing program may be integrated even though other parts may not even be centralized.

Q 13:87   What are the goals of a centralized and integrated credentialing program?

The goals of centralized and integrated credentialing for an IDS should be to

- provide an accurate base of information for assessment of the qualifications of physicians and other clinical personnel
- ensure a fair and understandable process to those administering the credentialing program as well as to the applicants who would be subject to the process
- serve as a clearinghouse for information received from the many sources within and outside of the IDS
- protect the confidentiality of the peer review process to the fullest extent possible under applicable state and federal law
- provide immunity from suit for those administering the process to the fullest extent allowed by law
- respect the differences among the IDS entities and ensure that each entity meets its unique fiduciary, licensing, certification, and accreditation requirements
- improve the IDS's systemwide risk management and loss control through an effective credentialing and peer review program
- be efficient, cost-effective, and integrated, both functionally and organizationally, with each IDS entity

Q 13:88   What is the functional design of a centralized and integrated credentialing program?

The proposed design represents an incremental approach using a modular design that can be expanded and optimized over time. Figure 13–8 depicts the model for integrated credentialing. Figure 13–9 represents the current credentialing process for most IDS entities: a decentralized process

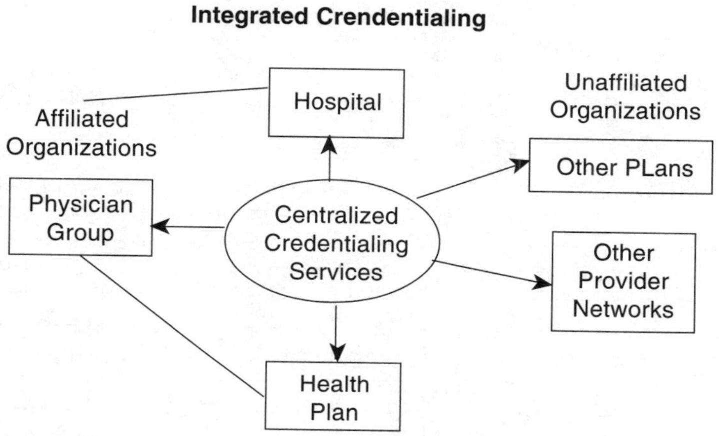

Integrated Crendentialing

Figure 13–8 Model for Integrated Credentialing

with no integration of functions. Each IDS entity has a separate verification and review process. The objective of this project is to move the IDS to a more centralized and integrated credentialing process. There are, however, differences between centralizing the credentialing process and integrating the credentialing function within a health care system. These vary from having centralized verification of primary source information to achieving coordinated qualitative appraisal, reappraisal, and peer review.

Q 13:89 How can information technology facilitate health care integration?

One of the critical elements of a successful integrated health care system as described by Dr. Stephen Shortell in *Remaking Health Care in America: Building Organized Delivery Systems,* is the availability of information technology that can link the various functions of the IDS.[26] It is this blending of clinical with financial information that will allow improved quality of care and outcome measurement. The future health care organizations will be able to use information systems to

- provide utilization management and case management information
- establish and monitor physician profile information

Unintegrated Credentialing

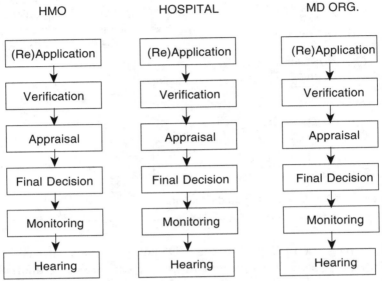

Figure 13–9 Credentialing Process of Most IDS Entities: No Integration of Function

- perform provider credentialing
- produce outcome measurements
- generate Health Plan Employer Data and Information Set information and create reports and report cards
- establish and monitor clinical protocols
- allow linkages among providers and between networks
- monitor disease state and wellness programs

NOTES

1. The Advisory Board Company, *The Grand Alliance Vertical Integration Strategies for Physicians and Health Systems* (1993).
2. J.D. Cochrane, Second Annual Symposium on Integrated Healthcare, Aspen, Colorado, March 28–29, 1994.
3. G.R. Peters, "Healthcare integration: A legal manual for constructing integrated organizations," *The Focus Series* (National Health Lawyers Association, 1995), 4–5.

4. Peters, "Healthcare integration: A legal manual for constructing integrated organizations," 6.

5. P.N. Grant and K.M. Morenchuk, *Medicare+Choice Provider Sponsored Organizations, a Workbook,* September 1997.

6. S.M. Shortell et al., *Remaking Health Care in America, Building Organized Delivery Systems* (San Francisco: Jossey-Bass Publishers, 1996).

7. B.J. Weiner and J.A. Alexander, "The challenges of governing public-private community health partnerships," *Health Care Management Review* 23, no.2 (1998): 39–55.

8. Combe and Talbot, *The Employee Benefits Answer Book* (New York: Panel Publishers, 1996). (The nondiscrimination rules associated with such benefit plans exceed the scope of this book; see alternate source of reference.)

9. IRS Exemption Ruling, Friendly Hills Healthcare Network, 29 January, 1993; 93 TNT 40-113. One of the earliest determinations for an integrated health organization was this ruling, wherein the Internal Revenue Service set out certain safe harbors for avoiding the possibility of physicians having too much control over or receiving too much benefit from the organization. The specific safe harbors address board composition, committee structure, compensation, medical staff, nondiscrimination among patients, emergency services, and other community benefit requirements. The Internal Revenue Service will allow covenants not to compete and, in one case, actually required this covenant as part of a transaction.

10. 42 U.S.C. § 1395nn, Medicare 1877.

11. The enabling statute for the foundation model in California is in the Health and Safety Code 1206(1). This statute establishes five criteria for the foundation model that include (1) a clinic; (2) operated by a tax-exempt 501(c)(3) nonprofit corporation; (3) that conducts medical research and health education; and (4) that provides health care through (a) a group of 40 or more physicians and surgeons; (b) who are independent contractors; (c) representing not less than 10 board-certified specialists; and (d) not less than two thirds of whom practice on a full-time basis at the clinic.

12. The Texas 5.01(a) nonprofit medical corporation is organized under the Texas Non-Profit Corporation Act, but it is not necessarily tax-exempt. It is authorized under Section 5.01(a) of the Medical Practice Act to function as a medical practice entity provided (1) the board of directors are physicians, (2) the board controls all clinical activities; however, (3) the member has an equal voice with the board on financial matters, and (4) the member can nominate new board members.

13. G.R. Peters, *Healthcare Joint Ventures, the Next Generation* (National Health Lawyers Association, 1991), 211.

14. R.C. Coile, "PHOs are training wheels for PSN direct contracting," *Health Care Trends* 8, no. 2 (1995): 2–3.

15. Florida, Idaho, Maine, New Hampshire, New York, Pennsylvania, South Carolina, Tennessee, Virginia, Washington, and Wisconsin.

16. Colorado, Illinois, Minnesota, Missouri, North Carolina, Ohio, North Dakota, Texas, and West Virginia.

17. Hawaii, Indiana, Kentucky, Louisiana, Mississippi, Nebraska, New Jersey, New Mexico, and Vermont.

18. California, Georgia, Massachusetts, Michigan, Nevada, North Dakota, Oklahoma, Rhode Island, and Wyoming.

19. Alabama, Alaska, Arizona, Arkansas, Connecticut, Delaware, Iowa, Kansas, Maryland, Montana, Oregon, and Utah.

20. PHOs and the assumption of insurance risk: A 50-state survey of regulators' attitudes toward PHO licensure. Group Health Association of America, Washington, DC, 10 July, 1995. (PPRC Report:212.)

21. Coile, "PHOs are training wheels for PSN direct contracting," 2–3.

22. Section 1855(d), Social Security Act enacted under the BBA. The BBA directs the Secretary of HHS to issue regulations to explain, further, the definition of the term PSO and provides the Secretary with guidelines for developing the definition of the key term "substantial proportion" that is used in the definition of the term PSO. The act also sets forth the definitions for the important terms "affiliated," "control" and "health care provider," which are used within the definition of the term PSO.

23. *Federal Register* 63: 34968–35116, adding 42 C.F.R. part 400 et al.

24. J.R. Griffith, *Health Care Management Review* 22, no. 3 (1997): 82–91.

25. SMG Marketing Group, Inc., "SMG market letter, May 1997," *Medical Benefits* 14, no. 14 (1997): 1–2.

26. SMG Marketing Group, Inc., "SMG market letter, May 1997," 1–2.

CHAPTER 14

Health Care Database and Information Management

Kathleen Loeb and Clifford C. Dacso

INTRODUCTION

Surveys have identified information technology as the most challenging aspect of managed care. It has long been axiomatic that the party that controls information flow in a health maintenance organization (HMO) or any managed care setting effectively controls the flow of funds. Thus, payers, providers, and third parties have invested an enormous amount of their treasure in ensuring, if not control, at least meaningful participation in the flow of financial and patient care information.

As organizations become legally, functionally, or virtually integrated in response to changes in health care delivery and reimbursement, the information system technology must be capable of supporting a more dynamic organization. Health care entities will succeed or fail based on their ability to

- capture, manage, and effectively transform data into accessible information
- leverage this information as a competitive advantage

An ideal environment will provide the information to enable the health care entity, be it provider or payer, to

- enhance quality of care
- reduce costs of care
- manage populations, not just individual patients
- self-monitor delivery and outcomes of care

Unfortunately, the government and private industry have not yet resolved such important issues as privacy of medical information or generation of reliable and comparative data. Private sector efforts to improve information technology have far surpassed the industry's ability to leverage such information in a meaningful way.

Q 14:1   What are the priorities for information system technology that are specific to managed care?

Improving managed care capability, supporting decision making, and monitoring quality for outcome measures are critical features of information technology for managed care. In the report by Deloitte & Touche/ VHA, *Redesigning Health Care for the Millennium*, the information system priorities for the next two years, in the order of priority, are to[1]

- improve managed care capabilities
- improve decision support for clinicians
- improve ambulatory and outpatient capabilities
- improve patient care capabilities
- improve productivity and cost reductions
- tie costs of care to outcomes
- use local area networks and connectivity
- integrate databases
- use emerging technologies
- justify benefits of technology
- improve cash flow and collections
- improve patient accounting capabilities
- change Joint Commission on Accreditation of Health Care Organizations and government requirements
- improve general accounting capabilities

Q 14:2   Why is the ability to access information critical for all health care entities?

Most health care organizations remain data rich and information poor even in a new world of managed care. Data exist throughout the enterprise in disparate, disjointed, and in many cases not systematized formats (i.e., paper). To manage health care as the business it has been forced to become, all health care entities will survive or fail based on their ability to harvest and leverage their data into information that drives nearly every decision that is made. Data warehousing, as other industries have discovered, is the way many health care organizations will address this need.

Many health care providers have already adopted interface engines as a means to enable their somewhat vertically oriented operational systems to communicate—this has been one step along the way to effective information management within the provider segment. Additionally, large health care application vendors have developed and are relatively successful in deploying clinical data repositories as a part of their overall clinical information system solutions. Enterprise resource planning vendors are deploying their package solutions for the human resources, financial, and materials management side of the equation. These new packages move the health care enterprise one step away from their mostly legacy world of information technology; however, this doesn't solve the entire puzzle for the health care entity. The next step is understanding what information they need to drive their business to success, upgrading the often down-level technology infrastructure to support this new layer of information applications, and building and executing the plan that will take them to the right information at the right time for the right users. This may include building an enterprisewide view of critical business information that is longitudinal in nature allowing analysis at the provider, patient, population, or diagnosis-related-group level: a data warehouse.

Without a way to seamlessly integrate the access and delivery of critical health care business information including subject area focus on financial data, provider profiling, outcomes, population management, and utilization, the health care entity will be significantly challenged in a managed care environment. Significant strides are being made by those who are investing now in information technology as a strategic business enabler, but health care as an industry historically has lagged behind.

Q 14:3   What effect has the Health Insurance Portability and Accountability Act of 1996 (HIPAA) had on health information technology?

With the passage of HIPAA—also known as the Kassebaum-Kennedy Bill—deadlines for adopting technical standards for health data communication related to privacy and security of personal medical information were set. The ownership and control of health data and accountability for such information also was standardized. As the larger, well-funded private sector moves toward the establishment of health information systems, public programs lag behind; however, despite the improved capability of electronic commerce via Internet technologies, privacy concerns are always being balanced against the need to access and share critical information.

Q 14:4   Why have health information networks lagged behind other industries such as financial services and air travel?

One of the major reasons the health care industry lags behind other industries in designing and applying information technology as a strategic business enabler is that it did not have the impetus to manage itself as a business focused on profit and loss. HMOs and managed care have created a new playing field and now the health care industry has been forced to apply technology as a strategic business enabler or accept the consequences of not having done so.

Additionally, the consumer has not, until recently, driven the health care industry to the same extent as other industries. Consumers are now demanding choice. Consumers are shopping for health care in much the same way they shop for airlines, banking services, and other services. They want the highest quality of care, with the greatest convenience at the lowest cost. One of the ways the health care provider or HMO can compete in a consumer-driven model is by exploiting and leveraging leading edge information technology. Internet accessibility allows the consumer to begin to understand, assess, and ultimately make choices for health care services. Those health care entities not able or willing to participate in this movement will not be chosen by the discerning consumers and are less likely to survive in the long term.

Q 14:5   What are the key issues for future information technology systems?

There are several areas that deserve special attention when developing effective health care information systems.

The first area is connectivity or linkage among health care providers—be it physicians within a common clinic or between the clinic setting and other health care facilities or health plans. This involves enabling infrastructure through traditional networking (local area networks or wide area networks) and Internet-working where extranets, intranets, and the Internet serve as the underlying network. Most health care entities (as evidenced by the Healthcare Information and Management Systems Society 1998 chief information officer survey) view investments in upgrading their technical infrastructure as one of their top priorities for the next two years.

The second area involves the use of Internet-based health care applications that are becoming the next generation of community health information networks (CHINs). Many health care entities have already begun to exploit their own Web sites as a means of providing linkages between consumers and providers and, in some cases, health plans.

The third area that deserves attention is the integration, as previously discussed, of the various forms and types of health care information systems. The clinical, financial, human resource, and materials management data have begun to form a new layer of application architecture on top of the legacy layer. When this application architecture layer is completed by the health care entity, much of this in preparing for Year 2000 compliance, the next major step will be the integration step. This represents the information application level facilitating effective enterprisewide decision management and support. Clearly, the successful health care entities will be moving in this direction in parallel to their efforts on enabling both infrastructure and health care applications. Investments in health care information technology will be front-end loaded and will need to climb to new levels. Those who recognize the value of this investment are more likely to prosper.

HEALTH PLANS AND MANAGED CARE INFORMATION

Q 14:6   What is the capability of health plans related to the collection and use of health care information?

Current capabilities to collect data vary widely from one plan to another. A few plans have up-to-date, comprehensive clinical information systems but others must gather data by hand for anything beyond enrollment information; however, health plans vary considerably in their ability to collect and report data.

Q 14:7   What data are usually collected by health plans?

Data are collected for internal purposes such as utilization management, payment of providers, premium setting, and quality improvement. Many plans collect Health Plan and Employer Data Information Set (HEDIS) data to meet emerging demands for information about performance and costs. The types of data being collected by health plans include enrollment, survey, encounter (claims), and clinical data. Each type has multiple uses, which may require different data elements and quality of data.

Enrollment Data. Most health plans have basic information on enrollment and disenrollment, benefits, and purchase of care. Some plans collect information on the subscriber only, rather than on the other family members. Demographic data are routinely collected, but usually at the time of enrollment or annual renewal. These items may include employment status, ethnicity, and family status.

Survey Data. Surveys are used to query patients on their health perceptions, the quality of care they received, their access to care, functional status, symptoms, health knowledge, satisfaction with care, and health-related behavior such as diet. Survey data allow plans to satisfy the HEDIS requirements for surveys. HEDIS requires plans to survey a sample of their enrollees to determine health status and patient satisfaction with care.

Encounter and Claims Data. Encounter and claims data document processes of care, such as the number of visits, the purpose of the visit, the procedures or care given, and such other information as the name of the patient and the provider; date and site of service; and the diagnosis necessitating the service. Providers must generate all encounter data before they are transmitted to health plans. There are differences between encounter data for fee-for-service providers and those for the various types of capitated providers. There are also differences between encounter data for physicians and those for hospitals, which make the capture of such data more challenging.

Clinical Data. Clinical data include signs and symptoms, diagnoses, functional status, and results of tests and procedures, as well as ultimate outcomes such as mortality, morbidity, complications, and completeness of recovery. Some of these data are available in automated form such as the results of blood tests, radiology exams, and pathology reports; however, most of the clinical data must be obtained from the patient medical record. Few providers and health plans have computerized clinical information systems.

Q 14:8   What are the considerations for external reporting of health plan data?

When deciding to collect and use health plan data, it is important to define the uses of the data in advance. Data need to be accurate, complete, standardized, and comparable across plans. Cost and confidentiality need to be considered. Uses of data often relate to access to care and quality of care, risk adjustment related to payment, or use and outcomes measures as well as for plan comparison as a consumer selection tool. Data accuracy and completeness are also important to the ultimate purchasers of the product. Because the majority of information is in the hands of providers, many health plans have incorporated economic or noneconomic incentives for providers to report this information. Such economic incentives can be punitive, such as the use of penalties and withholding for not reporting, or positive, such as incorporating the reporting incentive into the plan's bonus methodology. Noneconomic incentives include giving the providers access to the analyzed data for their own internal use.

Another important consideration in external reporting is the standardization of data. This is essential if the data are to be useful and credible. Data need to be standardized as to their format and definitions. An important development in the area of standardization occurred with the passage of HIPAA. With respect to various health care transactions, HIPAA requires the Secretary of Health and Human Services (HHS) to adopt transactions including claims and encounters, uniform standards and definitions for data elements, and technical standards for transmission of the data. The intent of the law is to promote administrative efficiency by enabling health care entities to communicate in a common language. Health plans and providers will be required to report data in the standardized format if requested by the data's recipient. This is not a mandatory reporting requirement, but rather a right of access and transmission. There are always issues of privacy and confidentiality that arise when patient-specific and identifying information is being collected for external use. Particularly sensitive items include mental health conditions, acquired immune deficiency syndrome testing and treatment, and genetic testing. Recent legislation has attempted to address not only the confidentiality of this information, but also its use in a nondiscriminating manner.[2]

Q 14:9   What is the reason for disparity among health plans in collecting and using information?

There are many reasons for disparity when collecting and using health care services information. Some providers are unwilling or unable to furnish information to health plans. Data from different sources may be incompatible. Valid data are costly to obtain, and incorrect or misinterpreted data can do more harm than good. Finally, external reporting of data by health plans requires considerations such as standardization, comparability of data across plans, and confidentiality of medical information.

COMMUNITY HEALTH INFORMATION NETWORKS

Q 14:10   What is a CHIN?

CHINs were the vanguard of integration in information technology. Although few have survived in their original incarnations, the concept of information systems as the backbone of the integrated system is useful to revisit.

A CHIN is a concept for a data highway that connects networks of health care entities into data networks to permit the exchange of clinical and financial information among participating hospitals, physicians, insurers, and other providers such as pharmacies and durable medical equipment providers. Unlike the healthcare data organization, which functions at a regional or national level for a clearly public purpose, the CHIN was to function at the community level as either a private or public enterprise or some combination thereof. The CHIN facilitates patient care by allowing a master patient index to serve all of its components.

CHIN vendors have included Ameritech Health Connections, Chicago; Health Communications Services, Inc., Richmond, Virginia (a joint venture with Hughes Aircraft Company of Fullerton, California); Integrated Medical Systems, Inc., Golden, Colorado; and Health Data Exchange, Malvern, Pennsylvania. The Wisconsin Health Information Network,

Brookfield, Wisconsin, was a CHIN-like structure. Others were located in Texas, Indiana, Illinois, and California.

Aurora Health System and Ameritech started the first functioning CHIN in 1993. Called the Wisconsin Health Information Network, it linked 16 hospitals, 8 clinics, 3 nursing homes, 7 insurers, 4 billing services, and more than 1,300 physicians.[3] In addition to transmitting claims and other administrative data, the system had the ability to allow physicians to check on the inpatient status of their patients, including their laboratory results.[4] Another successful CHIN operated on a voluntary basis in Utah. The Utah Health Information Network was a public and private partnership that included the department of health, all hospitals in the state, more than 85 percent of physicians, 80 percent of all other practitioners, and all but one of the major payers.[5] The largest CHIN, located in California, was run by the Health Data Information Corporation, a nonprofit group made up of more than 40 members covering more than one half of the insured population of California.

Q 14:11   What is a community health management information system (CHMIS)?

A CHMIS is a form of a CHIN that functions as a data network and also as a data repository that can be used to allow comparison of cost and quality of care provided by competing providers in a community.

Q 14:12   What is the difference between a CHIN and a CHMIS?

A CHIN is made up of sponsors or shareholders and operates for private, rather than public, purposes. A CHIN does not have a commitment to make public community-level health data; however, the CHIN projects have encountered the same challenges to survival as have the CHMIS projects.

Q 14:13   How did the concept of the CHMIS evolve, and how is it organized?

The concept of moving clinical and administrative information electronically throughout the health care system evolved through the efforts of the John A. Hartford Foundation of New York. The Foundation provided grants to interested communities to support the development of a CHMIS. The model requires that the organization represent all local public and private stakeholders, purchasers, and providers. Data extracted from the digital flow would be publicly available and the organization would look for guidance on how to protect the confidentiality and security of individually identifiable records.

Hartford financed seven CHMIS initiatives in Minnesota, Iowa, Ohio, Vermont, and Washington State, each with a nonprofit grantee that had both purchaser and provider representation. A sixth CHMIS initiative in New York was based in the state's department of health and a seventh in Tennessee was regional in scope and run by a business coalition.

In Iowa, the CHMIS developed through the efforts of local businesses and labor, as well as through the legislative efforts of the Iowa senate.[6] The grant was awarded to the Health Policy Corporation of Iowa, which developed a plan for a community health care network that was implemented through the creation of a state information management system that captures all electronic claim data into a central information depository. The legislation will mandate electronic claims submission, and it is anticipated that clinical information will be available to all providers by 1999. The unique aspect of the Iowa experience is that it represents a networking among the providers, the employers, and the government, all of whom have committed to the concept.

Q 14:14   How successful are CHMISs?

The most successful CHMISs and CHINs seem to be those linked with state health care reform efforts. The Iowa project benefited from mandated compliance with statewide CHMIS; Minnesota and Washington State followed suit.

Of those initiatives undertaken in many other states, the lack of cooperation resulted in the demise of Vermont's and Tennessee's CHMIS projects. For the most part, the problems were related to competitive issues that undermined cooperative efforts. For example, in Vermont, although the Vermont Health Care Information Consortium was able to bring together the essential stakeholders, one of the hospitals decided to start its own information network. The Memphis project collapsed when one of the hospital system members decided to contract for network services with a private company.

Other barriers to effective implementation have included access to capital and the rise of managed care. With many of the network participants in CHMIS developing independent networks, there was a need to reconsider the structure as a more decentralized network of networks. Unfortunately, this decentralization affected the CHMIS' ability to charge and be financially self-supporting. Finally, Internet technology with encryption has allowed many of these systems to use less expensive and simpler technology to access data and information within a defined system. Many of the Hartford grantees have shifted their focus in response to this technology.

Q 14:15   How have state government entities addressed health information systems?

Information technology has allowed many state governments to access important tools that positively affect their role in monitoring, purchasing, and providing services in the interest of public health and welfare. Federal legislation, such as HIPAA, has increased state and private-sector attention on electronic communication capabilities. Efforts commonly undertaken by most states have included providing meaningful data to state decision makers, disseminating information collected by state governments, coordinating services delivered by government providers, creating transaction systems for public and private sectors, and supporting telemedicine services.

Providing Data. Collection of data has been a long-standing role for state government. Unfortunately, dissemination of collected data was often fragmented and poor. Many states have developed improved information systems and communication tools to streamline dissemination of health information.

Disseminating Public Information. States have always functioned as a repository of public information from such sources as hospital discharges, vital statistics, and communicable disease records. Some state government agencies have taken on a more expanded customer base and seek to share this internal public health information with external audiences. Prospective users of this information include purchasers and consumers and providers and researchers.

Better Coordination of Government Services. One of the advantages of improved information technology is the state's ability to manage information across different agencies through an integrated information system. Texas recently bid its information management support to centralize and integrate information within the agencies under the commissioner of health. This will allow the state to better monitor and integrate welfare recipients within its Medicaid program to reduce fraud by both those individuals who misrepresent their eligibility status, and those providers who abuse the Medicaid system.

Supporting Health Transactions. HIPAA calls for the development of data standards at the national level and will require coordination and standardization at the state level. Despite the use of capitation, health care claims and encounter submission will remain a dominant means for reimbursement for services and is a major area of inefficiency. This is one of the potential applications of the CHMIS or CHIN programs. Some states have encouraged efficiency by requiring insurers and health plans to rely on electronic communications. For example, Texas has established an electronic data interchange among providers, payers, and the Texas Department of Health using a Medicaid management information system called TexMedNet.[7] This program includes electronic eligibility verification and claims processing, electronic appeals, electronic claims submission and editing, electronic remittance and status reports, electronic files transfer, an electronic bulletin board system, and e-mail and software to allow access. Users include businesses (e.g., billing companies, vendors, and clearinghouses) and providers (who pay no fee).

Telemedicine/Telehealth Services. The ability to use telecommunications in the education and delivery of health care services takes health care delivery where it has not gone before. The ability to extend health care services to rural and underserved areas offers significant benefits to historically underserved areas. Several states have passed legislation enabling such technology to be used and reimbursed. (This is discussed in more detail in Q 14:18.)

Q 14:16   What are the major challenges faced by states in facilitating information technology initiatives?

There are many challenges to pursuing information-based solutions to enhance health care capabilities. How should states regulate these activities? How should they be governed? What type of management is necessary to ensure the success of these activities? Where will they get funding? How will personal records remain confidential and secure? The solutions to these issues are evolving as the technology becomes more sophisticated.

Q 14:17   What are the lessons learned from states' involvement in information technology?

In a study of state initiatives related to health information systems, Daniel Mendelson and Eileen Salinsky developed the following guiding principles for system and organizational design:[8]

- Broad public and private participation is essential.
- Demand must exist for administrative savings.
- State government needs to be organized and actively involved.
- Systems should maximize use of existing data, technology, and expertise.
- States should support efforts to obtain outside funding.
- Shared governance between public and private interests is important.
- Efforts should be made to collaborate rather than compete with existing private networks.
- Access should be available to the greatest possible number of users, using low-cost platforms.
- Training should be made available in the use of the system.
- Communications capabilities should be sufficiently flexible to evolve as technology advances.
- All data should be encrypted for security and confidentiality.
- Goals and objectives should be focused and realistic.
- Communication solutions should follow widely accepted technical standards.
- Telehealth and telemedicine should be goals.

Q 14:18   What is telehealth and telemedicine?

According to a report to Congress on telemedicine in January 1997,[9] telemedicine is the use of medical information exchanged from one site to another via electronic communications for the health and education of the patient or health care provider, and for the purpose of improving patient care.

According to a recent report to Congress by the U.S. Departments of Commerce and Health and Human Services,

> Telemedicine has the potential to make a difference in the lives of many Americans. In remote rural areas, where a patient and the closest health professional can be hundreds of miles apart, telemedicine can mean access to health care where little had been available before. In emergency cases, this access can mean the difference between life and death. In particular, in those cases where fast medical response time and specialty care is needed, telemedicine availability can be critical. For example, a specialist at a North Carolina University Hospital was able to diagnose a rural patient's hairline spinal fracture at a distance, using telemedicine video imaging. The patient's life was saved because treatment was done on-site without physically transporting the patient to the specialist who was located a great distance away.
>
> Telemedicine also has the potential to improve the delivery of health care in America by bringing a wider range of services such as radiology, mental health services and dermatology to underserved communities and individuals in both urban and rural areas. In addition, telemedicine can help attract and retain health professionals in rural areas by providing ongoing training and collaboration with other health professionals.

Q 14:19   What are the major forms of telemedicine?

A 1997 survey in *Telemedicine Magazine* showed that teleradiology is the most popular application of this technology. Close behind, though, is telecardiology, teledermatology, psychiatry, and emergency medicine. Of the surveyed sites, 57 percent performed teleradiology services. Telemedicine-mediated cardiology is provided at 46 percent of sites, followed by dermatology (44 percent), psychiatry (43.5 percent), emergency medicine (39.8 percent), home health care (23.1 percent), pathology (21.3 percent), and oncology (20.4 percent). Seventy-two percent of the sites responding had interactive video capability.

Not surprisingly, the Internet is becoming a major telemedicine tool, particularly with the so-called store-and-forward technology. This technology allows asynchronous transfer of data and images over the Internet and is most amenable to desktop applications. In the magazine survey on telemedicine, about 10 percent of the 296 program managers surveyed indicated that they used the Internet for a number of purposes, including medical image transfer (74.2 percent), patient-care consulting (51.6 percent), patient records (41.9 percent), and video transfer (38.7 percent). Video transfer exploits the high-speed data transmission capabilities emerging on the Internet.

Despite the growth of the technology and the diversity of the applications available, managers at 68 percent of sites reported that their services were underutilized and nearly one half cite lack of physician and staff acceptance of telemedicine as the cause.

Q 14:20   Where is telemedicine being used?

Telemedicine is being supported through pilot studies and with state funding in Georgia, California, and Texas, among other locations. In 1997, *Telemedicine and Telehealth Networks* outlined criteria for excellence in telemedicine. These criteria are:[10]

- *Fulfills a defined need.* Programs implemented solely because federal funding is available, or because of an attraction to the technology, are doomed to fail. Only those that apply technology in an appropriate way to a defined need have a chance at long-term success.
- *Is sustainable or self-funded.* Those willing to invest their own funds in telemedicine start-up and operations are more likely to ensure that there is a sound business reason for doing so. As a result, chances for success are higher.
- *Has demonstrated organizational support.* Creating an environment in which top management as well as end users are engaged requires both financial and resource investment. Demonstrated support also means developing a strategic vision. Evidence of such can be found in policies related to confidentiality, satisfaction, operations, liability, and future expansion.

- *Is accepted by physicians, allied health providers, and patients.* It has been demonstrated repeatedly that without the involvement and support of those who are expected to use the technology, the service will fail.
- *Tracks data on costs, quality, and outcomes.* Programs demonstrate a commitment to the service they are providing when they monitor its success.

Q 14:21   What are the barriers to the widespread use of telemedicine/telehealth?

States face obstacles in the form of payment policies, resources, state licensure requirements, Medicaid practice issues, and training required to establish the systems. Physicians may be reluctant to use the technology because of unfamiliarity, fear of liability, or lack of access. Questions of "turf" arise when unacquainted specialists provide patient consultation. Patient and record confidentiality issues have to be addressed. Finally, quality standards are not yet in place.

The Health Care Financing Administration has chosen to define teleconsultation for reimbursement as real-time communication—thus effectively blocking reimbursement for the store-and-forward technology that is becoming more widespread. Additionally, the proposed rates are not favorable to substituting telecommunication for on-site consultation. Although the rules, definitions, and schedules are not settled at the time of this writing, telemedicine and payment for it is clearly a work in progress.

Physician acceptance of telemedicine is spotty (see Q 14:19). Several institutions have embraced telemedicine, including Baylor College of Medicine and Texas Children's Hospital, Houston, which have a long-standing distance consultation link; The University of Texas Medical Branch, which has led in a contract with the Texas Department of Corrections; Partners in Boston; and Texas Tech University.

Q 14:22   What are the potential legal issues associated with telemedicine?

Legal issues associated with telemedicine include:

- licensing and credentialing
- financial reimbursement
- malpractice liability
- privacy and confidentiality
- intellectual property
- food and drug regulation
- fraud and abuse

Questions that arise in the context of licensure relate to the interprofessional consultations and use of the technology. Each state regulates health care as part of its public health and consumer protection policies. When a physician in Texas is providing services to a patient in New Mexico, the regulators become concerned. Many states have initiated efforts to address these concerns through statutes; however, others retain restrictive practice and license statutes that make the use of telemedicine challenging.

Saltzman[11] observed, "The cause of much of the uncertainty with regard to liability related to telemedicine is a lack of relevant legal precedents. Much telemedicine technology is so new that telemedicine malpractice cases have not made their way through the legal system yet." It is likely that the courts will continue to apply existing malpractice tests in telemedicine cases, which currently hinge on two legal questions:[11]

1. whether a doctor-patient relationship existed
2. whether the physician breached his or her duty of care

Both of these questions present difficult issues in the realm of telemedicine. For example, a physician's review of a patient's medical records could be interpreted as either an informal consultation between two doctors or the establishment of a doctor-patient relationship; moreover, the legal system currently relies on professional standards to determine appropriate levels of care in malpractice cases. Because there are few existing telemedicine standards, the courts will face a challenge in determining whether the physician breached his or her duty of care.[12]

Q 14:23   What is the role of the Internet?

The Internet has been a vehicle for research and dissemination of medical knowledge along with the all-but-indispensable electronic mail.

Recent efforts have expanded to include use of the World Wide Web (Web) to exchange medical records. The National Library of Medicine has funded projects using Internet technology. The projects are administered through the agency's High Performance Computing and Communications project. These projects include:

Columbia University, New York City. The facility is using personal computers and Web-based technologies to manage chronic illnesses in the home setting and to demonstrate the ability to safeguard electronic medical records on the Internet. Patients will enter medical data, such as blood pressure and glucose levels, into an electronic medical record through home-based personal computers connected to the medical center via the Internet. They will also be able to communicate with health care providers, review their medical records, and access related information that addresses their specific health care concerns.

University of Washington Academic Medical Center, Seattle. The site is linking clinical and public health partners at selected facilities in a five-state area through a regional telemedicine network. The network includes a Web interface to electronic medical records, secure clinical e-mail for clinician-to-clinician and clinician-to-patient interactions, electronic delivery and management of X-rays and other clinical images, and access to medical library resources.

University of California at San Diego and Science Applications International Corporation. The two are jointly developing a system that improves the security of medical records on the Internet. The project is designed to enable patients, health care providers, and medical researchers to access clinical information over the Internet in a secure environment. It uses standard Web technology to support information search and retrieval. Additional security measures ensure patient privacy and information integrity, including implementation of role-based access controls that will authorize patients, researchers, and physicians to access different parts of the system for specific purposes.[13]

Q 14:24   What is the status of the Web-based computerized patient record (CPR)?

As managed care is becoming more population-based, the CPR takes on uses other than simply the transmission of medical information about an individual patient to an individual physician. Other applications include a population-based record for care management and public health purposes.

TeleMed is a distributed diagnosis and analysis system that permits physicians in various locations to simultaneously view, edit, and annotate a patient record via the Internet. Under development for the past three years by researchers at Los Alamos National Laboratory in New Mexico and physicians at the National Jewish Center for Immunology and Respiratory Medicine in Denver, TeleMed is one of the first implementations of a Web-based CPR system. The Department of Energy and the U.S. Army fund the project.

TeleMed uses distributed object technology to call up health care data on demand. The system provides access to patient-record components over a wide area network, building the complete patient record from various partial records and displaying the information in an integrated manner. A patient's record is constructed from data that may reside at several sites but that can be quickly assembled for viewing by pointing to the patient's name on the computer screen.

The data are displayed in a graphical patient record (GPR). This virtual document is empty until requests for distributed objects are made. Icons representing laboratory tests, radiographic studies, and drug treatments are drawn on the GPR template. Each of the icons is mouse-sensitive and, when clicked, summons up additional user interfaces and related data.[14]

NOTES

1. Deloitte & Touche LLP and VHA, *1997 Environmental Assessment: Redesigning Health Care for the Millennium* (1997).

2. The Health Insurance Portability and Accountability Act of 1996 looks to Congress or the Secretary of HHS to develop measures to protect the security of medical information. In July 1997, legislation was signed into law prohibiting insurers from using genetic information to discriminate in insuring individuals with a genetic predisposition to a particular condition.

3. P. Starr, "Smart technology, stunted policy: Developing health information networks," *Health Affairs* 16, no. 3 (May–June 1997): 91–105.

4. J. Ziegler, "Health care's search for an information injection," *Business and Health* (April 1996): 33.

5. Starr, "Smart technology, stunted policy: Developing health information networks," 91–105. (Report on an interview with Bart Killian, Executive Director, UHIN on 26 August, 1996; report on article by D. Wise, "Big savings from tackling the basics: Coalition report," *Business and Health* [August 1995]: 53.)

6. J.J. Moynihan, "CHINS: The Iowa experience," *Healthcare Financial Management* (April 1995): 70.

7. The Texas Medicaid Network (TexMedNet) can be found on the Internet at http://www.tdh.state.tx.us/hcf/tmnstart.htm.

8. D.N. Mendelson and E.M. Salinsky, "Health information systems and the role of state government," *Health Affairs* 16, no. 3 (May–June 1997): 106–119.

9. Telemedicine Report to Congress, Office of Rural Health Policy, Health Resources and Service Administration, Department of Health and Human Services (1998).

10. D.R. Dakins and K. Kincade, "The best in the U.S.: Programs of excellence 1997," *Telemedicine and Telehealth* (December 1997).

11. K.M. Saltzman, "Health care technology and the law," *Medical Group Management Journal* (July/August 1998): 68–74. (Citing R.F. Pendrak and P. Ericson, "Telemedicine and the law," *Healthcare Financial Management Journal* 50, no.12 [1996]: 46.)

12. Saltzman, "Health care technology and the law," 68–74.

13. K. Kincade, "Web-based records spin closer to reality," *Telemedicine and Telehealth* (February 1997).

14. Kincade, "Web-based records spin closer to reality."

AFTERWORD

The story of the health maintenance organization (HMO) has not yet been written. There has been a rapid evolution over the past several years; therefore, this work is a snapshot. Predicting the future is an exercise fraught with peril. Either the prediction is so general as to be fortune cookie–like and *prima facie* true or it is merely a possible one of alternative scenarios. Several important trends have emerged recently that have been elucidated in some ways in the context of the previous chapters but could also bear identifying explicitly.

Health care inflation can no longer be tamed merely by cost cutting. At the dawn of the era of rapid HMO growth, many economists predicted (correctly, it turns out) that the savings accruing from a massive shift of the risk of health care from the payer to the provider would turn in a one-time savings only. Trends in health care insurance premiums clearly show a growth trend and unless unforeseen price controls temporarily halt the growth, the trend is likely to continue.

Quality metrics are now in place, and the sophistication they bring to medical practice management is not likely to be undone. In fact, it is reasonable to assume that as HMOs become more sophisticated in their offerings, quality metrics will become product differentiates. We can expect that along with this growth of quality indicators will come the inevitable marketing hyperbole, such as "four out of five doctors recommend. . . ."

The market will demand ever-increasing choice in health care product offerings. The variety of options offered by even the most traditional HMOs can be expected to increase—but with choice comes cost. If the economy declines or the growth rate slows, we can reasonably expect that the trend to increased choice will reverse promptly. In a state of economic contraction, the uninsured and underinsured population is likely to increase as well.

Consolidation in the payer market can be expected to continue, but the influence of the Balanced Budget Act and the creation of provider sponsored vehicles will increasingly squeeze margins as "insurance companies" do not insure, but merely pay claims.

Vertical integration is likely to give way to so-called *horizontal integration* where a range of health care services are tied together rather than owned by one entity. A companion to this theory is the *disaggregation of physician services* accompanied by the failure of many practice management arrangements.

The rise of disease state management will supersede quality assurance and utilization management. The notion of the managed care organization as policeman can be expected to yield to the concept that the cheapest medicine is that medicine that is best for the patient. This is accompanied by the implementation of long-term case management for such chronic illnesses as asthma, renal failure, diabetes, cystic fibrosis, and others where it can be shown that preventive medicine and education can have a favorable impact on the health of the patient, as well as the cost of the patient's care.

Price competition can be expected to yield to value competition as cost of care is squeezed as much as it possibly can be. Value items will include added benefits, increased accessibility, increase in choice, and more emphasis on quality.

As usual, there are alternatives to the optimistic scenario. In this scenario, consolidation in the payer community is mirrored by defensive organizations of providers, both hospitals and physicians. Animosity between these groups affects the most vulnerable participant in health care: the patient. Value-added services are eliminated, as price competition becomes increasingly fierce. Major victims of this scenario are research and education that succumb to financial starvation. Then, of course, there is government regulation that capitalizes on the popular sentiment against HMOs to impose more onerous regulations and avenues for legal relief, as the trial lawyers sigh contentedly.

As usual, the truth may lie somewhere between these divergent paths, or on another path entirely; however, it is clear that neither the quality and prevention aspect nor the price benefits of managed care have been realized, and a reordering of priorities is on the way. The HMO will play a role in the future, although its guise is likely to evolve dramatically over time.

ACRONYMS AND TERMS

For the reader's convenience, commonly used acronyms are defined in the first section and then further defined in the terms section.

ACRONYMS

AAHC	Association of Academic Health Centers
AAHP	American Association of Health Plans
AAMC	Association of American Medical Colleges
AAPCC	Average Area per Capita Cost (Medicare)
AARP	American Association of Retired Persons
ABMS	American Board of Medical Specialties
ACG	Ambulatory Care Group
ADA	Americans with Disabilities Act
AFDS	Alternative Financing and Delivery System
AHCPR	Agency for Health Care Policy Research
ALOS	Average Length of Stay
AMA	American Medical Association
AMC	Academic Medical Center
ASC	Ambulatory Surgery Center
BBA	Balanced Budget Act
Ca	Cancer
CABG	Coronary Artery Bypass Graft
CAGR	Cumulative Annual Growth Rate
CalPERS	California Public Employees' Retirement System
CAT	Computerized Axial Tomography
CBO	Congressional Budget Office

CCM	Certified Case Manager
CCMC	Commission for Case Management Certification
CHIN	Community Health Information Network
CHMIS	Community Health Management Information System
CISN	Community Integrated Service Network
CLEAR	Consolidated Licensure for Entities Assuming Risk
CLIA	Clinical Laboratory Improvement Act
CMI	Case-Mix Index
CMP	Competitive Medical Plan
CMSA	Case Management Society of America
CMSA	Consolidated Metropolitan Statistical Area
COBRA	Consolidated Omnibus Budget Reconciliation Act
CON	Certificate of Need
CPEP	Clinical Practice Expert Panel
CPI	Consumer Price Index
CPI-U	Consumer Price Index for Urban Consumers
CPR	Computerized Patient Record
CPS	Current Population Survey
CPT-4	Current Procedural Terminology, 4th edition
CRS	Congressional Research Service
CT	Computerized Tomography
DCG	Diagnostic Cost Group
DHHS	Department of Health and Human Services
DOD	Department of Defense
DOJ	Department of Justice
DRG	Diagnosis-Related Group
DSH	Disproportionate Share
DUR	Drug Utilization Review
E/M	Evaluation and Management
EBRI	Employee Benefit Research Institute
EC	Emergency Center
ECI	Employment Cost Index
ED	Emergency Department
EMR	Electronic Medical Record
EMT	Emergency Medicine Technician
ENT	Ear, Nose, Throat (Otorhinolaryngology)
EOB	Explanation of Benefits Statement
EPO	Exclusive Provider Organization
ERISA	Employee Retirement Income Security Act

F&A	Fraud and Abuse
FAS	Financial Accounting Standard
FCA	Fraudulent Claims Act
FDA	Food and Drug Administration
FFS	Fee-for-Service
FNP	Family Nurse Practitioner
FP	Family Practitioner
FR	Federal Register
FY	Fiscal Year
GAF	Geographic Adjustment Factor
GAO	General Accounting Office
GDP	Gross Domestic Product
GI	Gastroenterology
GPCI	Geographic Practice Cost Index
GPR	Graphical Patient Record
GPWW	Group Practice without Walls
H&P	History and Physical Examination
HCC	Hierarchical Coexisting Conditions
HCFA	Health Care Financing Administration
HCQIA	Health Care Quality Improvement Act
HER	Health Economics Research, Inc.
HI	Hospital Insurance
HIAA	Health Insurance Association of America
HIV	Human Immunodeficiency Virus
HMO	Health Maintenance Organization
HPCC	High Performance Computing and Communications
HPSA	Health Professional Shortage Area
IBNR	Incurred But Not Reported
ICD-9-CM	International Classification of Diseases, 9th Revision, Clinical Modification
ICF	Intermediate Care Facility
ICU	Intensive Care Unit
IDS	Integrated Delivery System
IMG	International Medical Graduate
IPA	Independent Practice Association
IRS	Internal Revenue Service
ISN	Integrated Service Network
LOS	Length of Stay
MCBS	Medicare Current Beneficiary Survey

MCO	Managed Care Organization
MedPAR	Medicare Provider Analysis and Review file
MEI	Medicare Economic Index
MGCRB	Medicare Geographic Classification Review Board
MIG	Medicare Insured Group Demonstration
MMIS	Medicaid Management Information System
MOB	Medical Office Building or Maintenance of Benefits
MPCC	Medicare per Capita Cost
MPR	Mathematica Policy Research, Inc.
MRI	Magnetic Resonance Imaging
MSA	Medical Savings Account
MSA	Metropolitan Statistical Area
MSO	Medical Services Organization
MTS	Medicare Transaction System
NASHP	National Academy for State Health Policy
NCHS	National Center for Health Statistics
NCI	National Cancer Institute
NCQA	National Committee for Quality Assurance
NHIS	National Health Interview Survey
NIH	National Institutes of Health, HHS
NMES	National Medical Expenditure Survey
NP	Nurse Practitioner
NPDB	National Practitioner Data Bank
OBG	Obstetrics-Gynecology
ODS	Organized Delivery System
OIG	Office of the Inspector General
OMB	Office of Management and Budget
OR	Operating Room
OSHA	Occupational Safety and Health Act
PA	Physician Assistant
PACE	Program of All-Inclusive Care for the Elderly
PAR	Preadmission Review
PATH	Physicians at Teaching Hospitals
PCCM	Primary Care Case Management
PCP	Primary Care Provider
PHO	Physician-Hospital Organization
PHP	Prepaid Health Plan
PMPM	Per Member per Month

PMPY	Per Member per Year
PMSA	Primary Metropolitan Statistical Area
POS	Point of Service
PPMC	Physician Practice Management Corporation
PPO	Preferred Provider Organization
PPRC	Physician Payment Review Commission
PPS	Prospective Payment System
ProPAC	Prospective Payment Assessment Commission
PSN	Provider Sponsored Network
PSO	Provider Sponsored Organization
PTCA	Percutaneous Transluminal Coronary Angioplasty
QDWI	Qualified Disabled and Working Individual
QI	Quality Improvement
QIO	Quality Improvement Organization
QM	Quality Management
QMB	Qualified Medicare Beneficiary
RBRVS	Resource-Based Relative Value Scale
RTI	Research Triangle Institute
RUC	RVS Update Committee
RVS	Relative Value Scale
RVU	Relative Value Unit
SAF	Standard Analytical Files (Medicare)
SCH	Sole Community Hospital
SLMB	Specified Low-Income Medicare Beneficiary
SMI	Supplementary Medical Insurance
SNF	Skilled Nursing Facility
SSA	Social Security Administration
TANF	Temporary Assistance for Needy Families
TEFRA	Tax Equity and Fiscal Responsibility Act
TPA	Third-Party Administrator
TQM	Total Quality Management
TURP	Transurethral Resection of the Prostate
UB-92	Uniform Billing Code of 1992
UCR	Usual, Customary, and Reasonable
UR	Utilization Review
URAC	Utilization Review Accreditation Commission
USPCC	U.S. per Capita Cost
VA	Department of Veterans Affairs
Y2K	Year 2000

TERMS

Academic Medical Center—A group of related institutions including a teaching hospital or hospitals, a medical school and its affiliated faculty practice plan, and other health professional schools.

Access—The ability to obtain needed health care services.

Accountable Health Plan (AHP)—An organization proposed under health care reform proposals that combines health insurance and caregiving functions; it would function much like an HMO but could also be a more loosely organized network.

Activities of Daily Living (ADLs)—Activities such as bathing, dressing, and toileting that are needed for self-care; ADLs are measured to evaluate the continued feasibility of self-care.

Adjusted Average per Capita Cost (AAPCC)—The HCFA's best estimate of the amount of money it costs to care for Medicare recipients under fee-for-service Medicare in a specific geographic region. See also Average Payment Rate.

Adjusted Community Rate (ACR)—A rate-setting methodology used by managed care plans to set rates based on expected use of health care services by a group; includes the normal profit of a for-profit HMO or CMP; may be equal to or lower than the APR, but can never exceed it.

Administrative Contract Services (ACS)—A contract between an insurance company and a self-funded plan where the insurance company performs administrative services only and does not assume any risk; services usually include claims processing—but may include other services such as actuarial analysis—and utilization review, also called administrative services only contract (ASO).

Adverse Selection—Adverse selection occurs when a larger proportion of people with poorer health status enroll in specific plans or insurance options, whereas a larger proportion of people with better health status enroll in other plans or insurance options. Plans with a subpopulation with higher than average costs are adversely selected. Plans with a subpopulation with lower than average costs are favorably selected.

Age Discrimination in Employment Act of 1967 (ADEA)—As amended in 1978, requires employers with 20 or more employees to offer active employees older than age 40 (and their spouses) the same health insurance coverage that is provided to younger employees.

Agency for Health Care Policy and Research (AHCPR)—An agency of the U.S. Public Health Service, Department of Health and Human Services, that conducts scientific research, assesses health care technologies, and supports clinical practice guideline development.

Aid to Families with Dependent Children (AFDC) Program—A program established by the Social Security Act of 1935 and eliminated by welfare reform legislation in 1996. AFDC provided cash payments to needy children (and their caretakers) who lacked support because at least one parent was unavailable. Families had to meet income and resource criteria specified by the state to be eligible. A new block grant program has replaced AFDC, but AFDC standards are retained for use in Medicaid.

Allowed Charge—The amount Medicare approves for payment to a physician. Typically, Medicare pays 80 percent of the allowed charge and the beneficiary pays the remaining 20 percent. The allowed charge for a nonparticipating physician is 95 percent that for a participating physician. Nonparticipating physicians may bill beneficiaries for an additional amount above the allowed charge.

Alternative Delivery Systems (ADS)—Nontraditional methods of providing health care services such as ambulatory surgery and transitional care.

Alternative Dispute Resolution (ADR)—Methods of resolving disputes, claims, and disagreements other than by the traditional method of a lawsuit.

Ambulatory Patient Group (APG)—A modification of an ambulatory visit group, developed as an outpatient classification scheme for HCFA. The reimbursement methodology for outpatient procedures provides for a fixed reimbursement to an institution for outpatient procedures or visits, incorporates data regarding the reason for the visit and patient data, and prevents unbundling of ancillary services.

Ambulatory Surgical Center (ASC)—Setting for surgery of an uncomplicated nature that has traditionally been done in the more expensive inpatient setting but that can be done with equal efficiency without hospital admission. Centers may be hospital-based or hospital sponsored or independently owned in competition with hospitals; also called same-day surgery center.

American Association of Health Plans (AAHP)—A trade association serving nearly 1,000 HMOs, PPOs, and other managed care organizations representing nearly 100 million enrollees, created with the merger of GHAA and AMCRA.

American Association of Physician-Hospital Organizations (AAPHO)— A resource for PHOs, established in 1993 (P.O. Box 4913, Glen Allen, VA 23058–4913).

American Association of Preferred Provider Organizations (AAPPO)—A trade association of preferred provider organizations (1101 Connecticut Avenue, Suite 700, Washington, DC 20036).

American Managed Care and Review Association (AMCRA)—A national trade association of managed care organizations such as HMOs, PPOs, IPAs, and UROs (1227 25th St., N.W., Suite 610, Washington, DC 20037).

American Medical Peer Review Association (AMPRA)—A national trade association representing federally designated PROs (810 First St., N.E., Suite 410, Washington, DC 20002).

Americans with Disabilities Act (ADA)—A federal law enacted in 1990 that prohibits discrimination against people with disabilities in such areas as public accommodations and terms and conditions of employment.

Ancillary Outpatient Services—Services to support the diagnostic workup of the patient, or supplemental services needed as part of providing other care; includes anesthesia, lab, radiology, or pharmacy, but not room, board, medical, and nursing services.

Any Willing Provider Laws (AWP)—State laws that challenge and establish policy governing managed care organizations; requires the granting of network enrollment to any provider who is willing to join, as long as it meets provisions outlined in the plan. The central issue is the fairness of physician deselection by a plan, and, conversely, the plan's ability to reduce medical costs by eliminating overusing physicians.

Assignment (Medicare)—A process under which Medicare pays its share of the allowed charge directly to the physician or supplier. Medicare will do this only if the physician accepts Medicare's allowed charge as payment in full (guarantees not to balance the bill). Medicare provides other incentives to physicians who accept assignment for all patients under the Participating Physician and Supplier Program.

Average Length of Stay (ALOS)—The average number of patient days of hospitalization for each admission, expressed as an average of the population within the plan for a given period of time.

Average Payment Rate (APR)—The amount of money that the HCFA could conceivably pay an HMO or CMP for services to Medicare recipients under a risk contract. The figure is derived from the AAPCC for the service area and is adjusted for the enrollment characteristics the plan would expect to have. The payment to the plan, the ACR, can never be higher than the APR, but may be less.

Balance Billing—In Medicare and private fee-for-service health insurance, the practice of billing patients in excess of the amount approved by the health plan. In Medicare, a balance bill cannot exceed 15 percent of the allowed charge for nonparticipating physicians.

Behavioral Offset—See Volume Offset.

Beneficiary—Someone who is eligible for or receiving benefits under an insurance policy or plan. The term is commonly applied to people receiving benefits under the Medicare or Medicaid programs.

Benefit Package—Services covered by a health insurance plan and the financial terms of such coverage, including cost sharing and limitations on amounts of services.

Block Grant—Federal funds provided to the state level as a nucleus of support for Medicaid provisions by the state to its beneficiaries.

Blue Cross/Blue Shield (BC/BS)—An umbrella term for independent Blue Cross/Blue Shield health plans across the country. Also called "The Blues."

Board-Certified—A term applied to a physician or other health professional who has passed an exam from a recognized medical specialty board and thereby is certified to provide care within that specialty.

Bonus Payment—An additional amount paid by Medicare for services provided by physicians in Health Professional Shortage Areas. Currently, the bonus payment is 10 percent of Medicare's share of allowed charges.

Budget Neutrality—For the Medicare program, payment rate adjustments when policies change so that total spending under the new rules is expected to be the same as it would have been under the previous payment rules.

Bundled Payment—A single comprehensive payment for a group of related services.

Buy-In—Refers to the arrangements states make for paying Medicare premiums on behalf of those they are required or choose to cover.

Capitation (CAP)—A payment arrangement on a per member basis for a given number of patients under a provider's care; a set amount of money received or paid out, based on a prepaid agreement rather than on actual cost of separate episodes of care and services delivered, usually expressed in units of PMPM; may be varied by such factors as age, gender, and benefit plan of the enrolled member.

Carrier—A private contractor that administers claims processing and payment for Medicare Part B services.

Carve-Out—A category of health care not covered as a benefit within the contract, usually an area of high cost or requiring special expertise—such as behavioral, subacute, podiatry, chiropractic, X-ray, transplants—that is not subject to discretionary utilization and not included within the capitation rate.

Case Management (CM)—The control of health care services including either medical or ancillary health care resources, for efficient and medically appropriate ends for enrolled members; designed to achieve the optimal patient outcome in the most cost-effective manner.

Case Manager—A nurse, doctor, or social worker who works with patients, providers, and insurers to coordinate all services that provide a patient with medically necessary and appropriate care.

Case Mix—The frequency and intensity of hospital admissions or services reflecting different needs and uses of hospital resources; can be measured based on patient diagnoses or the severity of their illnesses, the utilization of services, and the characteristics of a hospital. It influences ALOS, cost, and scope of services provided by a hospital.

Case Rate—A reimbursement model used by hospitals to establish a flat rate per admission based on an assumed average length of stay per admission. The HMO is charged this rate for each member admitted; unique rates may be set or grouped by diagnosis type by categories such as medical/surgical, obstetrical, critical care, or cardiac. Other elements may include sliding scale volume, ALOS by type, volume of ancillary per patient, and contribution margin.

Categorically Needy—Aged, blind, or disabled people or families and children under established financial thresholds of eligibility for AFDC, SSI, or an optional state supplement.

Center of Excellence—A credentialed health care institution that has demonstrated, through clinical expertise and capital equipment improvements, the ability to provide a major resource-intensive procedure such as organ or bone marrow transplant, open-heart surgery, high-risk OB, or neonatal intensive care in a more effective and efficient manner than possible anywhere else within a specific geographic region. Centers of excellence are listed in the *Federal Register.*

Certificate of Authority (COA)—The state-issued operating license for an HMO.

Certificate of Coverage (COC)—A document provided to covered employees by the insurance carrier or managed care plan that outlines the benefits, covered services, and principal provisions of the group health plan provided under contract by the insurer or managed care organization.

Certificate of Need (CON)—The requirement that a health care organization obtains permission from an oversight agency before making changes (federally qualified HMOs are exempt).

Chemical Dependency Services—Services in support of patients who are addicted to various chemicals, drugs, or alcohol, as classified by the U.S. Department of Health and Human Services.

Civilian Health and Medical Program of the United States (CHAMPUS)— A health benefit program that provides coverage for armed forces personnel receiving care outside a military treatment facility.

Claims Services Only (CSO)—A contract designed for fully self-insured employers that need little administrative assistance. Under a CSO arrangement, the insurer administers only the claims portion of the plan. See also Administrative Contract Services (ACS or ASO).

Clinic without Walls—A centralized business operation serving medical groups in a network while the delivery of care remains decentralized, usually involving professional management services, group purchasing and support systems, centralized billing and accounting, uniform fee schedule, and employment of all nonphysician staff.

Closed Panel—A managed care plan that contracts with physicians on an exclusive basis for services and does not allow those physicians to see patients for another managed care organization (e.g., staff and group model HMOs or a large private medical group that contracts with an

HMO); a physician must normally meet strict criteria to join the closed panel of a plan's providers.

Closed PHO—A closed physician-hospital organization limited to providers that have expertise in managing utilization and are continually approved as meeting certain standards. It provides similar governance to an open PHO but is more attractive to payers because of demonstrated cost reductions and increased feedback to providers of personal and peer practice utilization. This model does not contain the more advanced incentives of equity sharing from venture profits.

COBRA (Consolidated Omnibus Budget Reconciliation Act)—A federal law that, among other things, requires employers to offer continued health insurance coverage for a certain length of time to certain employees and their beneficiaries whose group health insurance coverage has been terminated.

Coinsurance—A type of cost sharing where the insured party and insurer share payment of the approved charge for covered services in a specified ratio after payment of the deductible by the insured. Under Medicare Part B, the insured pays coinsurance of 20 percent of allowed charges.

Community Health Information Network (CHIN)—A system that electronically links providers, payers, employers, and consumers in communities to improve health care quality and promote community wellness.

Community Health Purchasing Alliance (CHPA)—A purchaser of health care benefits on behalf of employer groups.

Community Rating—The method of establishing a premium level that does not take into account the actual claims experience of a group (as in experience rating), but predicts the utilization of the entire community. A community rating is required for any federally qualified HMO and for many state-qualified HMOs, as well as for some indemnity plans.

Community Rating by Class—A form of community rating in which separate groups of enrollees can have different actuarial premium rates depending on the age, gender, marital status, and industry component. It is not equivalent to experience rating because no actual cost experience data is analyzed for the specific group of patients under review.

Competitive Bidding—A pricing method that elicits information on costs through a bidding process to establish payment rates that reflect the costs of an efficient health plan or health care provider.

Competitive Medical Plan (CMP)—A federal designation that allows a health plan to obtain eligibility to receive a Medicare risk contract without having to obtain qualification as an HMO; requirements for eligibility are somewhat less restrictive than for an HMO.

Concurrent Review—A screening assessment of hospital admissions at the time they occur, performed by a professional managed care support staff during a patient's hospitalization, either by telephone or through a representative's visit to the hospital location; this review ensures that utilization is appropriate.

Continuing Care Retirement Community (CCRC)—A community, which in exchange for an entrance fee and a monthly charge, guarantees lifetime housing and nursing care as required.

Continuum of Care—A spectrum of health care options ranging from limited care needs through tertiary care to provide the appropriate expertise for the patient without providing a more expensive setting than necessary. An integrated delivery network can take full advantage of the continuum by ensuring good communication throughout the patient episode and by using step-down, long-term care, rehabilitation, subacute, or assisted living center features as soon as they become an option, rather than more costly hospitalization choices.

Contractual Allowance—A bookkeeping adjustment to reflect the difference between established charges for services rendered to insured people and rates payable for those services under contracts with third-party payers (similar to a trade discount).

Conversion Factor—The dollar amount of one unit of service rendered; used to convert various medical procedures into an established fee-schedule payment structure in which the conversion factor times the relative value unit equals the payment amount.

Conversion Factor Update—Annual percentage change to the conversion factor. For Medicare, the update is either established by the Congress or set by a formula to reflect whether actual expenditure growth from two years earlier fell below or above the target rate.

Coordination of Benefits (COB)—A cost-control mechanism used by most insurers and managed care plans to avoid duplication of benefits.

Copayment—A type of cost sharing under which the insured party is responsible for paying a fixed dollar amount per service. Sometimes used more generally as a synonym for cost sharing.

Cost Compression—A marketplace factor in which the amounts of revenue or premium are reduced (perhaps quite quickly) as managed care practices begin to occur. Cost compression occurs due to pricing, utilization, and premiums.

Cost HMO—One of the three distinct types of managed care contracts with the HCFA. The HMO is paid by Medicare and receives a predetermined monthly amount per beneficiary based on a total estimated budget, with adjustments at year-end for any variations from the budget. Medicare enrollees are not locked into the networks, and they are structured like point-of-service programs. Medicare will pay its share for non–plan providers (after the member's coinsurance and annual deductible, as in the traditional FFS system), but the cost HMO will not pay anything.

Cost Sharing—A health insurance policy provision requiring the insured party to pay a portion of the costs of covered services. Deductibles, coinsurance, copayment, and balance bills are types of cost sharing.

Cost Shifting—Practice whereby a health care provider charges certain patients or third-party payers more for services in order to subsidize service provided below cost or free to the poor or uninsured.

Covered Lives—The number of people enrolled within a particular health plan or enrolled for coverage by a provider network, including covered dependents.

Covered Services—Those services specified in a managed care contract; specific services and supplies for which Medicaid will provide reimbursement; a combination of mandatory and optional services within each state.

CPT-4 (Current Procedural Terminology, 4th edition)—A unique set of five-digit codes established by the AMA that apply to the medical service or procedure performed by providers and used as a standard in the industry; used for billing purposes.

Credentialing—The review process by a hospital or insurer to approve a provider; careful review of documents, medical license, evidence of malpractice insurance (in cases where the insurance is needed or not provided by the supporting hospital or HMO by agreement), history involving actual or alleged malpractice, and educational background of professional providers; may apply to seeking candidacy on care panels.

Customary, Prevailing, and Reasonable (CPR)—Medicare's method of determining approved charges for a Part B service from a specific physician or supplier.

Days per Thousand—The number of hospital days used in a year for each 1,000 covered lives, derived by first taking the number of bed days divided by member months and then multiplying by each 1,000 members, also multiplied by the number of months under consideration; also called bed days/1,000.

Deductible—The minimum threshold payment that must be made by an enrollee each year before the plan begins to make payments on a shared or total basis; the amount of loss the plan must sustain for each member in each contract year for each category of coverage before any benefits become payable under the agreement; for example, if an enrollee has a $100 annual deductible, no payment assistance comes from the plan until at least a total of $101 in eligible claims are processed within the calendar or contract year. Plans will typically reduce the deductible if they wish to create an added incentive for patients to enroll, or will use reduced deductibles to get reluctant patients to try some form of managed care.

Defined Benefits Coverage—An approach to providing health benefits whereby employers and other purchasers promise coverage for a specific package of health benefits.

Defined Contribution Coverage—A funding mechanism for health benefits whereby employers make a specific dollar contribution toward the cost of insurance coverage for employees.

Demand Management—Strategies designed to ensure patient care quality while reducing traditional demand on a primary care physician, such as workplace health promotion or wellness programs, lifestyle management (behavioral changes that avoid or reduce health risks), self-management of minor acute conditions, or self-help to manage chronic conditions; support systems for demand management include telephone-based hot lines, trained nurse counselors, and educational and psychosocial support for informed choice.

Dental Carve-Out—A carve-out segment of the PMPM or contract pricing that may require that oral surgeons be participating providers if oral surgery is included.

Dental Maintenance Organization (DMO)—Type of managed dental care plan that provides comprehensive dental services to enrollees for a fixed per capita fee, similar to an HMO, using a closed panel of dentists.

Dental Service Corporation (DSC)—A nonprofit organization that underwrites or administers contracts for managed dental care plans.

Deselection—A process by which an HMO removes a physician from its panel of providers.

Diagnosis-Related Groups (DRGs)—A system of classification used by Medicare for inpatient hospital services based on principal diagnosis, secondary diagnosis, surgical procedures, age, gender, and presence of complications. This system of classification is used as a financing mechanism to reimburse hospitals and other selected providers for services rendered.

Direct Contracting—The practice of providing care under a direct agreement between employers or business coalitions and providers, with no HMO or PPO intermediary; normally, hospitals offer price discounts and employers agree to limit the number of providers while creating incentives for employees to use in-network providers.

Disability—Physical or mental conditions that render an insured person incapable of performing one or more occupational duties temporarily, long-term, or absolutely.

Discounted Fee-for-Service (DFFS)—A payment method that is calculated as a certain percentage of discount from fee-for-service charges; among the least risky contracting approaches, second only to billed charges; may include a sliding scale tied to volume, with varying discounts by product line; similar to full FFS except that the HMO agrees to pay billed hospital charges or outpatient services, minus a fixed percentage that is based on the efficiencies of guaranteed payments.

Disenrollment—The termination of coverage. Normally, voluntary disenrollment is not allowed until the patient has remained within the plan for at least 6 to 12 months. A patient can be involuntarily disenrolled because of a change in employment.

Disproportionate Share Hospital (DSH)—A hospital where people covered by Medicaid or without any health insurance make up a large proportion of all patients served. Federal law authorizes special payments to these hospitals to help them meet the costs of serving those patients that are not covered by other revenue sources.

Downstream Risk—An arrangement where an entity (typically, a provider group) accepts risk from another entity (typically, a licensed organization like an HMO).

Drug Utilization Review (DUR)—Quantitative evaluation of prescription drug use, physician prescribing patterns, and patient drug utilization to determine the appropriateness of drug therapy.

Dual Choice—An employee option of joining an HMO or an indemnity insurance plan as a basic entitlement; the employer must give the HMO marketing opportunities at least equal to those given the current indemnity carrier (dual choice does not apply to CMPs); employers are not required to offer multiple HMOs of the same type unless the second HMO can prove that it has a unique service area. Title 13 of the Public Health Service Act requires employers of 25 or more people with employees residing in an

HMO's service area to pay minimum wage, to offer their employees health benefits to which they contribute, and to offer dual choice of plans.

Dual Eligible—A beneficiary who is eligible for Medicare and Medicaid.

Due Diligence—A review or investigation by a prospective party to a contract, such as a hospital evaluating a contract with a managed care organization or a physician practice to be acquired, in order to ascertain financial stability, proper legal structure, reputation, adequate supplier-provider relationships, and acceptable reimbursement or equity-sharing strategy for the resulting contract.

Durable Medical Equipment—Equipment that can endure repeated use without being subject to disposal after one use (e.g., insulin pumps, wheelchairs, home hospital beds, walkers, glucometers, motor-driven wheelchairs, and oxygen therapy equipment).

Electronic Data Interchange (EDI)—The computer-to-computer exchange of business or other information between organizations; data may be in either a standardized or proprietary format.

Electronic Medical Record (EMR)—An automated on-line medical record that is available to providers, ancillary service departments, pharmacies, and others involved in patient treatment or care. The electronic medical record system stores, processes, and retrieves patient clinical and demographic information; eliminates redundancy or illegibility; reduces human error; streamlines data entry; and centralizes management of the patient.

Emergency—Life-endangering bodily injury or sudden and unexpected illness that requires an enrollee to seek immediate medical attention under circumstances that effectively preclude seeking care through a plan physician or a plan medical center. An occurrence requiring immediate care needed to preserve life, limb, eyesight, bodily tissue, or to preclude unnecessary pain and suffering.

Employee Assistance Program (EAP)—Services designed to assist employees, their family members, and employers in finding solutions for workplace and personal problems; services may include assistance for family/marital concerns, legal or financial problems, elder care, child care, substance abuse, emotional/stress issues, violence in the workplace, sexual harassment, dealing with troubled employees, transition in the workplace, and other events that increase the rate of absenteeism or employee turnover, lower productivity, and affect an employer's financial success or employee relations management; can provide voluntary or mandatory access to behavioral health benefits through an integrated behavioral health program.

Employer Group Health Plan (EGHP)—A private, employment-originated health plan covering an individual who, due to being age 65 years or older, has Medicare as a secondary payer.

Encounter—A health care visit of any type that warrants payment of services by an enrollee to a provider of care or services.

Encounter Date—Description of the diagnosis made and services provided when a patient visits a health care provider under a managed care plan. Encounter data provide much of the same information available on the bills submitted by fee-for-service providers.

End-Stage Renal Disease (ESRD)—A variety of conditions ending in kidney failure requiring dialysis or transplantation. Those suffering from ESRD are eligible for Medicare benefits.

Enrollee—A covered member of a health care contract who is eligible to receive contract services.

Enrollment—The number of patients who have contracted with a carrier; the process or activity of recruiting and signing up individuals and groups for membership in a plan; a description of the covered lives in a plan.

ERISA (Employee Retirement Income Security Act)—A federal law enacted in 1974 that allows self-funded plans to avoid paying premium taxes or complying with state-mandated benefits even when insurance companies and managed care plans must do so; another provision requires that plans and insurance companies provide an EOB statement to a member or covered insured in the event of a denial of a claim explaining why a claim was denied and informing the individual of his or her rights of appeal.

Evaluation and Management (E/M) Service—A nonprocedural service, such as a visit or consultation, provided by physicians to diagnose and treat diseases and counsel patients.

Exclusive Provider Organization (EPO)—A form of managed care plan, similar to an HMO in that it uses primary care physicians as gatekeepers, often capitates providers, has a limited provider panel, and uses an authorization system, yet is generally regulated under insurance statutes rather than HMO regulations (not allowed in many states that maintain that EPOs are really HMOs).

Expenditure Limits—A mechanism that adjusts payment levels downward if spending levels or growth rates exceed predetermined spending caps.

Expenditure Targets—A mechanism that adjusts payment levels upward or downward depending on whether spending levels or growth rates meet prospectively determined targets or standards. Designed to hold spending to a predetermined budget trajectory.

Experience Rating—A system used by insurers to set premium levels based on the insured's past claims experience. For example, experience rating may be based on service utilization for health insurance or on liability experience for professional liability insurance.

Explanation of Benefits Statement (EOB)—A statement mailed to a member or covered insured following the processing of a claim that explains how reimbursement was determined, why a claim was or was not paid, and the general appeal process.

Faculty Practice Plan—An organization created to bill, collect, and distribute income from professional fees of medical school faculty.

Fail-Safe Budget Mechanism—An overall limit on Medicare spending proposed in the Balanced Budget Act (H.R. 249) passed by Congress in November 1995.

Federal Employee Health Benefits Program (FEHBP)—The program that provides health benefits to federal employees. See Office of Personnel Management (OPM).

Federal Qualifications—Designation rendered by the HCFA following a methodical review to determine a plan's preparation of an HMO. It includes a review of documentation, contracts that are required for support by individual providers or hospital systems, infrastructure systems and facilities, marketing capabilities, and accountant's evidences of financial security.

Federal Trade Commission (FTC)—Reviews mergers and acquisitions of HMOs, hospitals, medical groups, and various levels of health networks and combinations thereof to ensure no infringements of antitrust laws.

Federally Qualified HMO—An HMO that has satisfied certain federal qualifications pertaining to organizational structure, provider contracts, health service delivery information, utilization review and quality assurance, grievance procedures, financial status, and marketing information, as specified in Title XIII of the Public Health Service Act.

Fee-for-Service (FFS)—The full rate of charge for a private patient without any type of insurance arrangement or discounted prospective health plan.

Fee Schedule—A list of predetermined payment rates for medical services.

Fee Schedule Payment Area—A geographic area within which payment for a given service under the Medicare Fee Schedule does not vary.

Five-Year Review—A review of the accuracy of Medicare's relative value scale that the Health Care Financing Administration is required to conduct every five years.

Flexible Benefit Plan—A variety of health plan coverage features offered to employees based on their needs or their ability to pay; decisions regarding which plan is needed may be made at the time health care services are needed.

Foundation Model—A nonprofit physician-hospital entity for markets that do not allow physicians to be directly employed by a hospital. It involves more advanced managed care integration than the GPWW, open PHO, or closed PHO; contains MSO centralized support and physician practice procurement features, but MSO costs are paid by the foundation, not physicians; may allow physicians to share in revenue.

Full-Time Equivalent (FTE)—The equivalent of one full-time employee. For example, two part-time employees are one-half FTE each, for a total of one FTE.

Generalists—Physicians who are distinguished by their training as not limiting their practice by health condition or organ system, who provide comprehensive and continuous services, and who make decisions about treatment for patients presenting with undifferentiated symptoms. Typically this includes family practitioners, general internists, and general pediatricians.

Generic Equivalents—Drug products not protected by a trademark that have the same active chemical ingredients as those sold under proprietary brand names; also generic drugs.

Geographic Adjustment Factor (GAF)—The GAF for each service in a particular payment area is the average of the area's three geographic practice cost indexes weighted by the share of the service's total RVUs accounted for by the work, practice expense, and malpractice expense components of the Medicare Fee Schedule.

Geographic Practice Cost Index (GPCI)—An index summarizing the prices of resources required to provide physicians' services in each payment area relative to national average prices. There is a GPCI for each component of the Medicare Fee Schedule: physician work, practice expense, and malpractice expense. The indices are used to adjust relative value units to determine the correct payment in each fee schedule payment.

Global Capitation—A reimbursement mechanism that pays for all the care needs for a population of patients, including physicians and hospitals; may involve payment from an HMO to each PCP at risk for a contractually determined PMPM amount that is to pay for the costs of all physician services; may involve payment to a provider network or IDS for all physician and hospital care, with other stated commitments or limitations for pharmacy, mental health, or other carve-outs; a portion of the global cap may be withheld in a reserve fund to pay for specialist care referred by the PCP (excess remaining each year is paid out, or shortages are carried forward against future global capitation payments to the PCP).

Global Fee—A reimbursement mechanism used by a provider for a given episode of care; the single fee for the entire charge of all aspects and services surrounding the episode (e.g., $1,600 for a normal vaginal delivery to include a stated amount of prenatal and postnatal care in addition to the delivery), best used with a large number of covered lives in order to spread risk.

Global per Diem—A reimbursement mechanism used by a provider to include all costs of care for a day, fixed regardless of case type.

Graduate Medical Education (GME)—The period of medical training that follows graduation from medical school; commonly referred to as internship, residency, and fellowship training.

Gross Domestic Product (GDP)—The total current market value of all goods and services produced domestically during a given period; differs from the gross national product by excluding net income that residents earn abroad.

Group Health Association of America, Inc.—A trade association for HMOs now part of AAHP.

Group Model HMO—An HMO model in which the physicians, employed by the HMO, are typically paid on a salary basis or fee schedule and may receive incentive payments based on their performance.

Group Practice—A combined practice of three or more physicians or dentists who may share office personnel, expenses, equipment, space, records, and income.

Group Practice without Walls (GPWW)—An early managed care market structure that allows physicians to retain their separate offices, combining centralized business operations with decentralized delivery of care to preserve traditional autonomy; comprising a group of physicians with varying interests and geographical locations, who may or may not have hospital affiliations as primary care or specialty orientations. GPWWs have failed to attract meaningful covered lives.

Guaranteed Issue—The requirement that each insurer and health plan accept everyone who applies for coverage and guarantee the renewal of that coverage as long as the applicant pays the premium.

Guaranteed Renewable—The requirement that each insurer and health plan continue to renew health policies purchased by individuals as long as the person continues to pay the premium for the policy.

HCFA 1500—A standardized claim form developed by HCFA that is used by providers to bill health carriers.

Health Benefit Organization (HBO)—HCFA-contracted entities that are required to provide a package of benefits that essentially matches Medicare's benefits package without exceeding current program cost-sharing levels. Under the Private Health Plan Option, these HBOs might be contracting with HCFA. Under the voucher proposals, beneficiaries could present vouchers worth 95 percent of the adjusted average beneficiary costs in an area to the HBO in return for services.

Health Care Financing Administration (HCFA)—The federal agency responsible for administering Medicare and overseeing states' administration of Medicaid; manages HMO qualification and other utilization and the quality review programs.

Health Care Prepayment Plan (HCPP)—A health plan with a Medicare cost contract to provide only Medicare Part B benefits. Some administrative requirements for these plans are less stringent than those of risk contracts or other cost contracts.

Health Care Quality Improvement Act of 1986 (HCQIA)—A federal regulation that affords antitrust immunity for good-faith peer review activities. The reporting requirement to the National Practitioner Data Bank (NPDB) is mandatory for settlements, acts involving licensure, and medical staff actions involving a physician's status.

Health Insurance Purchasing Cooperative or Coalition (HIPC)—One of many types of purchasing alliances, begun by California in 1992, without premium capitations or state price controls designed to spread the risk of small group and individual health care members among a broad representation of purchasers and guarantee insurance to small businesses of 3 to 50 employees. It acts as the purchasing agent for consumers under a system of managed competition in negotiating the best plan at the lowest cost from networks of doctors and hospitals or HMOs. It was proposed as part of the national health care reform in 1992. Many reform proposals surrounding President Clinton's Health Security Act also contained HIPC applications of restrictions for preexisting condition limits, portability, guaranteed renewals for groups, and universal access.

Health Insuring Organization (HIO)—Usually an organization that contracts with a state or federal agency to ensure the delivery of services to beneficiaries of a state or federal program such as Medicaid or Medicare. The HIO will contract with health services organizations—either on a discounted fee-for-service or a capitated basis—for the provision of hospital and physician services.

Health Maintenance Organization (HMO)—An organization that provides comprehensive medical care for a fixed annual fee. Physicians and other health professionals often are on salary or on contract with the HMO to provide services. Patients are assigned to a primary care doctor or nurse practitioner as a gatekeeper, who decides what health services are needed and when. There are four basic models of HMOs: group model, individual practice association, network model, and staff model.

Health Plan—An organization that acts as insurer for an enrolled population.

Health Plan Employer Data and Information Set (HEDIS)—A core set of performance measures to assist employers and other health purchasers in understanding the value of health care purchases and evaluating health plan performance; used by the National Committee for Quality Assurance to accredit HMOs.

Health Professional Shortage Area (HPSA)—An urban or rural geographic area, a population group, or a public or nonprofit private medical facility that the Secretary of Health and Human Services determines is being served by too few health professionals. Physicians who provide services in HPSAs qualify for the Medicare bonus payment.

Hierarchical Coexisting Conditions Model (HCC)—A risk-adjustment model that groups beneficiaries based on their diagnoses.

High Self-Insured Deductible (HSID)—A way for employers to improve cash flow by self-funding the first tier of any employee's health care expenses; also known as shared funding. Employers can thus retain funds that would normally be paid to the insurance company to cover current and future claims.

Highly Compensated Employees (HCEs)—As defined by Section 414(q), 5 percent owners, employees who earned more than $75,000 in (1991), the top paid 20 percent of employees who earned more than $50,000 (in 1991), and officers earning more than $45,000 (in 1991) who are not permitted to receive benefits disproportionately larger than other employees under the nondiscrimination rules applicable to employee benefits plans; also called highly compensated individual, highly compensated participant, and key employee.

HMO Act—A 1973 federal law outlining requirements for federal qualification of HMOs, including legal and organizational structures, financial strength requirements, marketing provisions, and health care delivery. The voluntary status of "federally qualified" is sought by HMOs to gain credibility with employers and to gain covered lives from dual choice mandates that require employee access to such plans.

Hold Harmless—A contractual provision that protects enrollees in the event of a health plan failure by prohibiting health care providers from collecting payment from enrollees for services rendered but not paid for by the plan.

Home Health Agency (HHA)—A facility or program licensed, certified, or otherwise authorized pursuant to state and federal laws to provide health care services in the home.

Hospital Insurance (HI)—The part of the Medicare program that covers the cost of hospital and related posthospital services. Eligibility is normally based on prior payment of payroll taxes. Beneficiaries are responsible for an initial deductible per spell of illness and copayments for some services. Also called Part A coverage or benefits.

ICD-9-CM (International Classification of Diseases, 9th Revision, Clinical Modification)—A statistical classification system of diagnoses and identifying codes for reporting by physicians to ensure accurate and consistent documentation for claims. The codes are revised periodically by the World Health Organization. Since the Medicare Catastrophic Coverage Act of 1988, the use of ICD-9 coding is mandatory for Medicare claims.

IME (Indirect Medical Education)—Part of the payment to academic medical centers for the indirect costs associated with educating residents.

Incurred but Not Reported (IBNR)—The amount of money that the plan should accrue for medical expenses that the authorization system has not captured and for which claims have not yet been submitted. Unexpected IBNRs have been the major cause of financial insolvency for many managed care plans and providers.

Indemnity—The insurance protection against injury or loss of health; although this type of traditional system is now being replaced with other forms of insurance that share risk with providers or employers; indemnity programs still exist to provide reimbursement to the enrolled members for benefits under the contract.

Independent Living Program (ILP)—A program of housing assistance, job retraining, and other types of assistance to help disabled individuals live as independently as possible.

Independent Practice Association (IPA)—A health care model that contracts with an entity, which in turn contracts with physicians, to provide health care services in return for a negotiated fee. Physicians continue in their existing individual or group practices and are compensated on a per capita, fee schedule, or fee-for-service basis.

Indigent—Having insufficient income or savings to pay for adequate medical care without depriving oneself or dependents of food, clothing, shelter, and other essentials of living.

Insured—Any person or organization under a contract or policy for benefits that are received in return for payment.

Integrated Delivery System (IDS)—A single organization or a group of affiliated organizations that provide the full range of health care services to a population of enrollees within a market area that consists of physicians, dispersed clinic settings, hospitals, a referral network, and full continuum of after-care offerings; may obtain an HMO license and retail health services, or may wholesale the provision of care services and seek to accept risk within components of the systems, such as a physician network or its hospitals, or may obtain global risk agreements with HMOs.

Integration—The construction or reorganization of a health care entity by connecting previously independent segments of the care continuum to emphasize economic interactions between segments for the most appropriate care, services, and use of resources (e.g., subacute versus traditional care).

Intermediate Care Facility (ICF)—A preferred, lower cost setting within the managed care environment for patients who require intermediate care; a center without hospital or skilled nursing facility capabilities but with facilities above that of an assisted living center.

IOM (Institute of Medicine)—An organization of the National Academy of Sciences often called upon by Congress to provide objective opinions on health care issues.

Joint Commission on the Accreditation of Healthcare Organizations (Joint Commission)—A private, not-for-profit organization that evaluates and accredits hospitals and other health care organizations providing home care, mental health care, ambulatory care, and long-term care services.

Joint Venture (JV)—An arrangement involving risk and benefit sharing between one or more entities, whose rights and obligations are specified in contractual terms, for a specific purpose; examples include a hospital JV with a provider group for 50 percent of the group profits or downside risk, a hospital JV with an HMO for 50 percent exposure to the mutual patient business, or a hospital buying a certain percent of common shares of an HMO to broaden sharing of business.

Length of Stay (LOS)—The number of days that a covered person stayed in an inpatient facility. See also Average Length of Stay.

Limited Liability Company or Corporation (LLC)—A legal entity that provides for partnership agreements and liability protection of the owners; an excellent way to share risk and equity between hospital systems and physician practices.

Limiting Charge—The maximum amount that a nonparticipating physician is permitted to charge a Medicare beneficiary for a service, in effect, a limit on balance billing. Starting in 1993, the limiting charge has been set at 115 percent of the Medicare-allowed charge.

Long-Term Care (LTC)—The segment of the health care continuum that consists of maintenance, custodial, and health services for the chronically ill or disabled; may be provided on an inpatient (rehabilitation facility, nursing home, mental hospital) or outpatient basis, or at home.

Loss—Paid claims and incurred claims plus expenses belonging to the contract year; does not include: claim administration expenses or salaries paid to employees of the plan, any amount paid by the plan for punitive, exemplary, extracontractual, or compensatory damages awarded or paid to any member arising out of the handling, investigation, litigation, or settlement of any claim or failure to pay, or delay in payment of, plan benefits, or any statutory penalty imposed on the plan due to any unfair trade practice or any unfair claim practice, or amounts paid by the plan after the three-month period following the contract year without the express written approval of the reinsurer.

Maintenance of Benefits (MOB)—A type of coordination of benefits that limits the total reimbursement from all health plans to a given individual for a program of treatment.

Maintenance of Effort (MOE)—A requirement that employers increase benefits or provide refunds to Medicare primary employees to compensate for the reduced wraparound plan costs that resulted from the increased Medicare coverage of the MCCA.

Malpractice Expense—The cost of professional liability insurance incurred by physicians. A component of the Medicare relative value scale.

Managed Behavioral Care—Mental health or chemical dependency treatment that is screened and monitored for meeting utilization criteria, treatment effectiveness, or quality.

Managed Care—Any method of health care delivery designed to reduce unnecessary utilization of services, contain costs, and measure performance while providing accessible, quality, effective health care. Managed care generally involves a third party in the health care payment decision.

Managed Care Organization (MCO)—A generic term for any organization that manages and controls medical service. It includes HMOs, PPOs, CMPs, managed indemnity insurance programs, and managed BC/BS programs.

Management Information System (MIS)—The common term for the computer hardware and software that provides the support for managing a plan.

Management Services Organization (MSO)—A legal entity that offers practice management and administrative support to physicians or that purchases physician practices and obtains payer contracts as a PHO. It can be wholly owned, a for-profit subsidiary of a hospital, a hospital-physician joint venture, or a private joint venture with physicians or hospital/physicians; offers a menu of services through shared practice management (group purchasing discounts, practice management, consulting, information newsletters and educational seminars, computer/information systems, marketing, employee leasing for office coverage, claims processing), and creates economies and allows physicians to delegate management and administration, but yields some profit for these functions. Corporate examples include Coastal, MedPartners, and PhyCor; also called physician practice management or physician management corporation.

Maximum Allowable Charge or Cost (MAC)—The maximum that a vendor may charge for something; often used in pharmacy contracting. A related term, used in conjunction with professional fees, is fee maximum.

Medicaid—A medical program of aid provided by the federal government and administered at the state level to provide benefits according to established criteria for the poor, aged, blind and disabled, and dependent children; current legislative proposals would provide block grants to the states, or establish other strategies to make them responsible for the program with less dependence on the federal level. The general enabling legislation is sometimes referred to as Title XIX.

MediCal—The California version of the Medicaid federally funded, state operated and administered program that provides medical benefits for certain low-income people in need.

Medical Care Evaluation (MCE)—A component of a quality assurance program that looks at the process of medical care.

Medical Group Management Association (MGMA)—An association of large medical groups that collects data from its members for the purpose of benchmarking.

Medical Loss Ratio—A ratio of costs to provide health benefits to revenue from premiums (or total medical expenses of paid claims plus the IBNR component, divided by premium revenue); a common way to describe efficiency of an HMO plan, medical loss ratios are being reduced during the 1990s from the low 90 percentile to the mid-70 percentile.

Medical Savings Account (MSA)—The Medicare Plus proposal that offers a medical savings account (MediSave) option to all seniors, now incorporated into the Balanced Budget Act. A senior choosing MediSave would get a high-deductible insurance policy along with a cash deposit in an MSA that would cover a significant portion of the deductible; the high-deductible policy would have no copays, so that seniors would be ensured a limit on their out-of-pocket costs. This plan is designed to give a patient incentive to save unnecessary care expenses, yet give him or her control to spend for whatever needs may exist, or to purchase long-term insurance.

Medicare—A national program of health insurance that provides benefits primarily to people over the age of 65 and others eligible for Social Security benefits; covers the cost of hospitalization, medical care, and some related services; Part A includes inpatient costs and Part B includes outpatient physician costs. Medicare has been operated by HCFA since its creation by title XVIII, Health Insurance for the Aged, in 1965 as an amendment to the Social Security Act.

Medicare Catastrophic Coverage Act of 1988 (MCCA)—A federal law that added significant coverage and substantially increased the cost of Medicare; repealed in 1989.

Medicare Choices Demonstration—A demonstration project designed to offer flexibility in contracting requirements and payment methods for Medicare's managed care program. Participating plans include PSOs and PPOs. Plans are required to submit encounter data to HCFA, and most will test new risk-adjustment methods.

Medicare Cost Contract—A contract between Medicare and a health plan under which the plan is paid on the basis of reasonable costs to provide some or all Medicare-covered services for enrollees.

Medicare Part A—An insurance program that provides basic protection against the costs of hospital and related posthospital services for individuals age 65 years or over who are eligible for retirement benefits under the Social Security or the Railroad Retirement System; individuals under age 65 entitled for not less than 24 months to benefits under the Social Security or Railroad Retirement System on the basis of disability; and certain other individuals with end-stage renal disease who are covered by the Social Security or Railroad Retirement System. After various cost-sharing requirements are met, Part A pays for inpatient hospital costs and home health care. It is financed from a separate trust fund maintained by a payroll tax levied on employers, employees, and the self-employed. It is also called hospital insurance program.

Medicare Part B—A voluntary portion of Medicare that covers physician costs within various outpatient or ambulatory settings; also called supplementary Medicare Insurance.

Medicare Risk Contract—A contract between Medicare and a health plan under which the plan receives monthly capitated payments to provide Medicare-covered services for enrollees, and thereby assumes insurance risk for those enrollees. A plan is eligible for a risk contract if it is a federally qualified HMO or a competitive medical plan.

Medicare SELECT—A demonstration project that allows Medigap insurers to experiment with the provision of supplemental benefits through a network of providers. Coverage of supplemental benefits is often limited to those services furnished by participating network providers and emergency, out-of-area care.

Medicare Transaction System (MTS)—MTS is a new electronic claims processing and information management system under development by HCFA. When implemented it will act as a single, standardized repository of information related to fee-for-service Medicare, Medicare managed care plans, and beneficiaries' secondary insurance.

Medigap Insurance—Privately purchased individual or group health insurance policies designed to supplement Medicare coverage. Benefits may include payment of Medicare deductibles, coinsurance, and balance bills, as well as payment for services not covered by Medicare. Medigap insurance must conform to 1 of 10 federally standardized benefit packages.

Mental Health Carve-Out—Specified services for mental health or substance abuse that can be provided more efficiently through either a focused effort or separate entity contract; for example, $1.75 to $2.50 PMPM for annual benefits of 30 inpatient days and 20 visits, with varying copay and deductible, they may include UM for preauthorization, concurrent review, retrospective review, discharge planning, and CM.

Messenger Model—Nickname for an early model of physician integration, normally fostered by a supporting hospital entity, to help local physicians move toward more sophisticated managed care; this formation signals nonaffiliated physicians and insurers that capabilities are being enhanced to manage care and accept risk. Typically, membership is both easy to obtain and inexpensive.

Midlevel Practitioner or Provider—Physician assistants, clinical nurse practitioners, nurse midwives, nutritionists, aides, medical technicians, physical therapists, and so forth who deliver medical care as nonphysicians generally under the supervision of a physician, but often at less cost. Practitioners sometimes consider this term pejorative.

Mixed Model—A managed care plan that mixes two or more types of delivery systems, such as an HMO and a closed and open panel system; also called a hybrid model.

Modified FFS—A reimbursement mechanism that pays providers on a fee-for-service basis but with certain fee maximums established by procedure; distinct from a discounted FFS in that it may not always be the same percentage discount from the prevailing FFS. This unit-of-service arrangement is a typical reimbursement mechanism for many arrangements that are considered to involve managed care but have not yet evolved to global risk, and may involve a PCR holding.

Most Favored Nations—A status granted to insurers in contracts between insurers or managed care organizations and providers by stating that any time the provider gives a better price to a second or subsequent insurer or patient, it will notify the first insurer and give the same price reductions.

Multiple Employer Trust (MET)—A mechanism that allows small employers in the same or a related industry to provide group insurance to their employees under a trust arrangement. See also Multiple Employer Welfare Arrangement.

Multiple Employer Welfare Arrangement (MEWA)—An employee welfare benefit plan or other arrangement designed to provide benefits to employees of two or more employers that form an association for the purpose of purchasing group health insurance. See also Multiple Employee Trust.

Multispecialty Group Practice—A group of providers in which at least one physician is a family practitioner, internist, or general medical officer and the others physicians practice other specialties.

National Association of Insurance Commissioners (NAIC)—A trade organization of state insurance regulators that has addressed the development of uniform standards in the regulation of insurance (120 W. 12th Street, Suite 1100, Kansas City, MO 64105).

National Claims History System—An HCFA data reporting system that combines both Part A and Part B claims in a common file. The National Claims History system became fully operational in 1991.

National Committee for Quality Assurance (NCQA)—An independent, nonprofit group that accredits HMOs (1350 New York Avenue, Suite 700, Washington, DC 20005).

National Practitioner Data Bank (NPDB)—A database on physician discipline or malpractice payment experience; queried by HMOs, private and federal hospitals, and health systems; used for credentialing a provider for clinical privileges or granting status as medical director or for medical staff positions. Query of NPDB is required at two-year intervals for reappointment.

Network Model HMO—An HMO that contracts with several different medical groups, often at a capitated rate. Groups may use different methods to pay their physicians.

Nominal Value—Measurement of an economic amount in terms of current prices.

Nonparticipating Physician—A physician who does not sign a participation agreement and, therefore, is not obligated to accept assignment on all Medicare claims.

Occupational Safety and Health Act (OSHA)—A federal law that provides national standards for health and safety in a workplace.

Office of Personnel Management (OPM)—The federal agency that administers the FEHBP; the agency that a managed care plan contracts with to provide coverage for federal employees.

Office of Prepaid Health Care (OPHC)—The federal agency that oversees federal qualification and compliance for HMOs and eligibility for CMPs; was once part of the Public Health Service, now part of HCFA; also known as the "central office" in HMO circles.

Open Access—Patient access to providers of specialty care without going through a gatekeeper or primary care provider, as long as the specialist participates in the network.

Open Enrollment Period—The time allowed for subscribers to choose a health plan, either by reenrolling in their existing plan or switching to a competitor's plan; open enrollments are at least 30 days and provide for a first-come, first-served basis to the limit of the plan's capacity, usually without evidence of insurability or waiting periods; most managed care plans have half their membership up for open enrollment in the fall for an effective date of January 1.

Open PHO—An early-stage managed care physician-hospital model with an open and almost nonrestrictive policy for allowing physicians to join in an attempt to build a network for payer contracts. It commonly features joint governance between hospital and physician leadership, varying degree of MSO support and centralization; has shown weak attraction for covered lives, a lack of physician practice behavior modification, and little long-term loyalty from providers.

Other Weird Arrangement (OWA)—Any new and bizarre managed care plan or provider arrangement.

Outcome—An indicator of the effectiveness of health care measures upon patients also called health outcome; or the result of a process of prevention, detection, or treatment.

Out-of-Area—Any area (where health care services or supplies may be received) outside the HMO's service area and where only emergency services are allowed.

Out-of-Pocket Expenditures—Health-related expenditures for which beneficiaries are financially liable. For Medicare beneficiaries, the total amount includes: cost sharing for Medicare-covered services (e.g., deductibles, copayments, and balance bills); cost of Medicare Part B and private health insurance premiums; and cost of noncovered services.

Outpatient—An enrollee who receives treatment or services without being admitted to a hospital.

Packaged Pricing—A reimbursement strategy used by hospitals that offers flat fees on a limited number of case types (which may include category-based pricing) in order to offer employers and insurers preferred pricing on DRGs that the hospital can manage well, without setting a fixed fee for all diagnoses.

Paid Amount—The portion of a submitted charge that is actually paid by both third-party payers and the insured, including copayments and balance bills. For Medicare, this amount may be less than the allowed charge if the submitted charge is less, or it may be more because of balance billing.

Par Provider—Abbreviation for participating provider.

Partial Capitation—An insurance arrangement where the payment made to a health plan is a combination of a capitated premium and payment based on actual use of services; the proportions specified for these components determine the insurance risk faced by the plan.

Partial Risk Contract—A contract between a purchaser and a health plan in which only part of the financial risk is transferred from the purchaser to the plan.

Participating Physician—A physician who signs a participation agreement, agreeing to accept assignment on all Medicare claims for one year.

Participating Physician and Supplier Program—A program that provides financial and administrative incentives for physicians and suppliers to agree in advance to accept assignment on all Medicare claims for a one-year period.

Participating Provider—An individual provider, hospital, integrated delivery network, pharmacist, dentist, optometrist, chiropractor, podiatrist, nurse, group practice, nursing home, behavioral or mental health entity, skilled nursing facility, long-term care facility, or other medical institution agreeing to provide care or services to enrolled members of a particular plan, according to stated rates and conditions. In most prepayment relationships, including CHAMPUS, the participating provider receives payment directly from the plan, but the patient must pay any cost share or deductible.

Patient Dumping—The practice of refusing services to uninsured indigent patients or of transferring them to a public hospital or a private, nonprofit hospital willing to treat indigents.

Patient Self-Determination Act (PSDA)—An act passed by the U.S. Congress in 1990, effective December 1991, that requires most hospitals, nursing homes, and other patient care institutions to ask all admitted patients whether they have made advance directives as to their wishes for the use of medical interventions for themselves in case of the loss of their own decision-making capacity. The institution is required to furnish each patient with written information about advance directives.

Payment Rate—The total amount paid for each unit of service rendered by a health care provider, including both the amount covered by the insurer and the insured person's cost sharing; sometimes referred to as payment level. Also used to refer to capitation payments to health plans.

Peer Review—An evaluation by a group of unbiased practicing physicians of the effectiveness and efficiency of care rendered under a plan's benefits.

Peer Review Organization (PRO)—An entity established by the Tax Equity and Fiscal Responsibility Act of 1982 (TEFRA) to review quality of care and appropriateness of admissions, readmissions, and discharges for Medicare and Medicaid. Such an organization is held responsible for maintaining and lowering admission rates and reducing lengths of stay while ensuring against inadequate treatment.

Per Diem Rate—A single set fee paid to a hospital for each day that a member of an HMO is hospitalized.

Per Member per Month (PMPM)—Revenue or cost for each enrolled member each month.

Per Member per Year (PMPY)—Revenue or cost for each enrolled member per year.

Performance Measure—A specific measure of how well a health plan does in providing health services to its enrolled population. It can be used as a measure of quality. Examples include percentage of diabetics receiving annual referrals for eye care, screening mammography rate, and percentage of enrollees indicating satisfaction with care.

Performance Standard—The target rate of expenditure growth set by the Volume Performance Standard System.

Physician Payment Review Commission (PPRC)—A group created by Congress in 1986 to recommend changes in reimbursement procedures for physicians under Medicare; prepares an annual report to Congress.

Physician Work—A measure of the physician's time, physical effort and skill, mental effort and judgment, and stress associated with providing a medical service. A component of the resource-based relative value scale.

Physician-Hospital Organization (PHO)—A legal entity formed and owned by one or more hospitals and physician groups in order to obtain payer contracts and to further mutual interests. Physicians maintain ownership of their practices while agreeing to accept managed care patients under the terms of the PHO agreement. The PHO serves as a negotiating, contracting, and marketing unit.

Plan Age—Plan age refers to the number of full years an HMO has been in operation as of January 1, 1996. The operational date is the date when the HMO first offered prepaid medical services to an enrolled population.

Point of Service (POS)—A provision that allows patients in managed-care plans that limit choice of doctors and hospitals to seek treatment outside of the plans; patients who use this option typically are required to pay more.

Portability—The requirement that insurers waive any preexisting condition exclusion for someone who was previously covered through other insurance as recently as 30 to 90 days earlier.

POS Plan—A plan that provides flexibility for an enrollee to choose to receive a service from a participating or nonparticipating provider, with corresponding benefit or penalty of copay depending on the level of benefit selected, with the goal of encouraging the use of network or participating provider care options. POS maintains the popularity of choice by offering the typical HMO provision, PPO, or combinations of both. In many POS plans, enrollees coordinate their care needs through the PCP. HMOs pay nonparticipating providers at an FFS rate; also called HMO swing-out plan or out-of-plan rider to an HMO.

Practice Expense Relative Value—A value that reflects the average amount of practice expenses incurred in performing a particular service. All values are expressed relative to the practice expenses for a reference service whose value equals one practice expense unit.

Practice Expense—The cost of nonphysician resources incurred by the physician to provide services. Examples are salaries and fringe benefits received by the physician's employees, and the expenses associated with the purchase and use of medical equipment and supplies in the physician's office. This is a component of the Medicare relative value scale.

Practice Guideline—An explicit statement about the benefits, risks, and costs of particular courses of medical action based on the medical literature and expert judgment. Practice guidelines are intended to help practitioners, patients, and others make decisions about appropriate health care for specific clinical conditions.

Preadmission Certification or Review—A certification that acute hospitalization or surgery performed before the patient's admission is necessary, based on the judgment of medically appropriate care by a qualified peer.

Preadmission Review (PAR)—A utilization review mechanism for plans that utilize telephone-based nurses to review cases, assign expected lengths of stay, and issue an authorization number. The PAR is also referred to as precertification.

Preauthorization—Sanction by the managed care company that treatment is needed, thereby providing authorization for payment for service provided to beneficiary of contract.

Preexisting Condition—Any single or multiple physical or mental impairment or disease of an enrollee that exists before insurance begins. Many plans stipulate a waiting time before an enrollee can begin to receive care for preexisting conditions to establish that his or her health condition is relatively stable (e.g., posttransplant enrollees).

Preferred Provider—Any entity defined as a provider that has agreed to contract for the provision of health services for all enrolled members of a plan.

Preferred Provider Arrangement (PPA)—Same as a PPO, but sometimes refers to a less restrictive type of plan in which the payer (i.e., the employer) makes the arrangements rather than the providers.

Preferred Provider Organization (PPO)—A plan or an affiliation of providers seeking contracts with a plan (by virtue of their ability to cover a broad geographical area or provide multispecialty skills). Incentives for providers to participate include quick turnaround of claims payment, a valuable pool of patients, and FFS payment. Payer incentive is negotiated discounts to FFS. Usually a PPO doesn't prepay physicians. A physician-sponsored PPO increasingly will bear risk when seeking arrangements with insurance companies or self-insured companies. There is great consensus that PPOs are early-stage managed care relationships that are formed in response to HMO pressure or competition, but do not bring the same savings in health care costs.

Premium—An amount paid periodically to purchase health insurance benefits.

Prevailing Charges—The fees most frequently charged by physicians in a specific geographic area for Medicare; 75 percent of the customary charges made for similar services in the same locality (the maximum Medicare rate is controlled by an economic index); other plans may pay a different percentage based on the prevailing charge.

Primary Care Case Management (PCCM)—A case management that requires a gatekeeper to coordinate and manage primary care services, referrals, preadmission certification, and other medical or rehabilitative services; the primary advantage of PCCM for Medicaid eligibles is increased access to a PCP while reducing use of hospital outpatient departments and emergency rooms. (Encourages choices within Medicaid to provide PCP coordination for patients being treated by a wide variety of specialists but who no longer have a PCP for oversight.)

Primary Care Physician (PCP)—A physician whose practice is largely devoted to general internal medicine, family/general practice, and pediatrics.

Privileges—Formal authority by an HMO or hospital-based system to treat patients at a hospital or within a system as granted by a governing authority.

Professional Liability Insurance (PLI)—The insurance physicians purchase to help protect themselves from the financial risks associated with medical liability claims.

Professional Review Organization (PRO)—A physician-sponsored organization charged with reviewing services provided to patients to determine if the services rendered are medically necessary; are provided in accordance with professional criteria, norms, and standards; and are provided in the appropriate setting.

Professional Standards Review Organization (PSRO)—One of 203 physician groups that reviewed the care rendered to Medicare and Medicaid patients pursuant to a 1972 law. The PSRO program was repealed in 1982 and replaced by the PRO program.

Profiling—Expressing a pattern of practice as a rate of some measure of utilization (costs of services) or outcome (functional status, morbidity, or mortality) aggregated over time for a defined population of patients to compare with other practice patterns. May be done for physician practices, health plans, or geographic areas.

Program for All-Inclusive Care for the Elderly (PACE)—HCFA demonstration using managed care programs to serve frail elderly people who are, for the most part, dually eligible for Medicare and Medicaid and have been assessed as eligible for nursing home placement. The program provides adult day health care and case management to help the program participant maintain independent living in the community.

Prospective Payment System (PPS)—Established by title VI of the Social Security Amendments of 1983 and developed and implemented by HCFA to pay health care facilities for Medicare patients; replaced the retrospective cost-based method that was begun in 1968. The primary prevention against premature discharge of patients is the presence of sound quality assurance programs.

Provider—A physician, pharmacist, dentist, optometrist, chiropractor, podiatrist, nurse, hospital, group practice, nursing home, behavioral or mental health entity, skilled nursing facility, long-term care facility, pharmacy, other medical institution, or any individual or group of individuals that provides health care services. A distinction between provider and supplier within Medicare policy will determine payment on a charge basis for suppliers and a prospective or retrospective cost-related basis for providers.

Provider Sponsored Network (PSN)—A formal affiliation of health care providers organized and operated to provide a full range of health care services. The Balanced Budget Act allows Medicare to contract directly with PSNs on a full-risk capitated basis in a way that would eliminate some HMOs as middlemen. The degree to which PSNs must be subject to licensing, financing, and insurance considerations, as regulated by state insurance commissioners, will determine the number of providers to qualify compared to the more rigid HMO standards under which provider networks must currently qualify.

Provider Sponsored Organization (PSO)—Any organization created through the formal affiliation of health care providers that seeks to act as insurer for an enrolled population. PSOs can be physician-based, hospital-based, or a combination of both; typically, they are local health delivery systems.

Qualified HMO—An HMO found by HCFA to be qualified within the meaning of Section 1310 of the PHS Act and subpart D as either an operational, preoperational, or transitional qualified HMO.

Qualified Medicare Beneficiary (QMB)—Medicare beneficiaries whose incomes are at or below 100 percent of the poverty level and whose resources do not exceed 200 percent of that allowed under the Supplemental Security Income program in each state. QMBs are entitled under federal law to have their Medicare premiums, coinsurance, and deductibles paid by the state in which they reside.

Quality Assurance—Program activities that are conducted from the perspective of individual hospitals or insurers, and reviewed by internal leadership or external entities such as NCQA to ensure that medical care and service meet clinical standards of quality; includes elements of peer review and audits of care, medical protocols, credentialing, and assessment of patient satisfaction.

Quality Improvement (QI)—A management-engineering theory applied to the medical industry to effect continuous and incremental improvements through the identification of problems in health care delivery, the testing of solutions to those problems, and the tracking of solutions. QI seeks to identify the optimal process to accomplish a task and then to eliminate process deviation that causes waste or delay; the "clean sheet of paper" approach, a more nonlinear theory of reengineering, that allows a team to design a preferred process as if no process were already in place, called linear improvement.

Quality Improvement Organization (QIO)—An organization contracting with HCFA to review the medical necessity and quality of care provided to Medicare beneficiaries. Previously, these were called Peer Review Organizations.

RAPs—Diagnosis-Related Groups (DRGs) for radiologists, anesthesiologists, and pathologists used by HCFA to reimburse these specialists for care to Medicare recipients.

Real Value—The measurement of an economic amount corrected for change in price over time (inflation), thus expressing a value in terms of constant prices.

Reasonable and Customary Charge (R&C)—The amount of money usually billed for individual health care services within a specific geographic region; sometimes all fees in the 80th or 90th percentile are averaged to determine R&C, other times R&C is synonymous with fee schedule rate ceilings, when the rates are relatively high.

Referral—The request for additional care, usually of a specialty nature, by a primary care physician or by a specialist needing additional medical information on behalf of the patient. Referrals within the context of managed care are more restricted in that a PCP who accepts financial risk for downstream medical care is more sensitive to the balance between medical necessity and cost. Good information systems are needed to track referral costs to aid physicians in learning more about this factor.

Refinement—The correction of relative values in Medicare's relative value scale that were initially set incorrectly or have become incorrect due to changes in medical practice.

Reinsurance—Insurance procured by an insurance company, provider, or employer to guard against the partial or complete loss of money from medical claims. Typical coverage is purchased for individual stop-loss, aggregate stop-loss, out-of-area care, or insolvency protection. A larger health plan typically reduces reinsurance coverage as it grows; also called risk-control insurance or stop-loss insurance.

Relative Value Scale (RVS)—An index that assigns weights to each medical service; the weights represent the relative amount to be paid for each service. The RVS used in the Medicare Fee Schedule consists of three components: physician work, practice expense, and malpractice expense.

Relative Value Unit (RVU)—The building block of RBRVS; for each service, there are three RVUs to cover work, practice expenses, and the cost of professional liability insurance.

Reserves—Fiscal method of providing a fund for incurred but not reported health services or other financial liabilities; also refers to deposits and/or other financial requirements that must be met by an entity as defined by various state or federal regulatory authorities.

Resource-Based Relative Value Scale (RBRVS)—A fee schedule introduced by HCFA to reimburse physicians' Medicare fees based on the amount of time, resources, and expertise expended in selected specific medical procedures. Adjustments are made for regional variations in rents, wages, and other geographical differences. Developed by Dr. William

Hsiao and a Harvard research team, it divides Medicare treatments into 7,000 procedures with specific scales.

Respondeat Superior—The legal doctrine of vicarious liability, which may be applied in the case of a suit against a health care provider by a patient, making the employer responsible for the employee's negligent acts because the employer has the right to control that behavior.

Retention—The administrative fee that normally serves as the profit for a plan; retention funds may be either reinvested in the organization that administers the plan, applied toward the cost of medical claims and miscellaneous expenses, or, in the case of for-profit entities, passed to shareholders.

Retrospective Review—A method of determining medical necessity and/ or appropriate billing practice for services that have already been rendered.

Revenue Share—The proportion of total revenue devoted to a particular type of expense. For example, the practice expense revenue share is that proportion of revenue used to pay for practice expense.

Risk—The loss foreseen by a provider, IDN, or insurer in providing health care services. It also refers to the generic arrangements within managed care that involve a departure from FFS medicine toward prepayment, which focuses on the care of a given population by a primary care provider or hospital system taking full economic responsibility for that population's care needs.

Risk Adjuster—A measure used to adjust payments in order to compensate for spending that is expected to be lower or higher than average, based on the health status of demographic characteristics of enrollees.

Risk Adjustment—The process used to adjust payments to plans to compensate for differences in health status of enrollees across plans.

Risk Analysis—The methodology for evaluating the expected medical care costs for a prospective group, assuming the best application of all available products (with the employer-customer in mind) and benefit levels and prices that best meet the needs of the group under evaluation.

Risk Contract—A contract involving medical claims risk on a prepayment basis between two entities, such as a provider and an HMO, the HCFA and a federally qualified HMO, or an integrated delivery network and an individual PCP or medical group. It will specify the medical services to be included, together with the associated reimbursement structure, and the amount to be withheld or physician contingency reserve to be set aside for potential claims above estimates, or incremental risk corridors. If claims run above projections, it is the responsibility of the party that bears risk under the contract to pay those excess costs; any savings are similarly allocated to the party bearing risk.

Risk Corridor—A mechanism to share risk within a stated range of performance, wherein providers are assessed penalties or given financial rewards if their actual claims per member per month fall outside a specific percentage above or below an established claims target (e.g., for a 10 percent corridor on a PCP set at $23 PMPM, a physician will be subject to rewards for amounts less than $21.70 and penalties for more than $25.30 in PMPM claims costs).

Risk Selection—Any situation in which health plans differ in the health risk associated with their enrollees because of enrollment choices made by the plans or enrollees. As a result, one health plan's expected costs differ from another's due to underlying differences in their enrolled populations.

Risk Sharing—Any mechanism that gives financial incentive to managed care providers for rendering cost-effective, high-quality care.

Rural Area—Any geographic region not listed as having a population of 2,500 or more in the "Number of Inhabitants" Document PC(1)A of Table VI "Population of Places" and not listed as an urbanized area in Table XI "Population of Urbanized Areas" of the most recent update of the Bureau of Census, U.S. Department of Commerce.

Scored Savings—The amount of savings expected to result from enacting new legislation. Estimated by the Congressional Budget Office by calculating the difference in spending projected under current law and under the proposed legislation.

Secondary Insurance—Any insurance that supplements Medicare coverage. The three main sources for secondary insurance are employers, privately purchased Medigap plans, and Medicaid.

Selective Contracting—State mechanism used as a cost-control measure for obtaining services for Medicaid patients from fewer than all available providers through a competitive bidding process.

Self-Insurance—A risk strategy that allows the potential profit that an HMO or carrier traditionally receives from funding insurance risk to be experienced instead by an employer or other legal entity, such as a hospital-based delivery network. It is different from reinsurance in that an external insurance protection is not used as a general format, but certain protection may be sought for a segment such as catastrophic coverage. Essentially, the health benefits are funded from internal resources without purchasing insurance. Self-insurance entities may obtain outside administrative assistance to manage requirements.

Self-Insured Health Plan—Employer-provided health insurance in which the employer, rather than an insurer, is at risk for its employees' medical expenses.

Shared Risk—An arrangement where any two entities, such as a health plan and a provider, agree to share in the risk to some contracted percentage of hospital costs that may come in over budget, as well as share profits for care provided under budget.

Site-of-Service Differential—The difference in the amount paid to the physician when the same service is performed in different practice settings, for example, a colonoscopy in a physician's office or a hospital clinic.

Sixth Omnibus Reconciliation Act of 1985 (OBRA/SOBRA)—A federal law, a portion of which created quality review organizations (QROs) and empowered QROs and peer review organizations (PROs) to monitor quality of care for Medicare recipients enrolled in HMOs or CMPs, provided for civil monetary penalties for plans that failed to provide proper care, and restricted the types of physician incentives that a managed care plan may use when providing care for Medicare recipients. It also made disenrollment from HMOs and CMPs far easier for Medicare recipients.

Skilled Nursing Facility (SNF)—A facility that provides health and social services to patients on a less than acute basis where ongoing skilled care is required; commonly referred to as nursing homes.

Social Health Maintenance Organization (SHMO)—Federally funded demonstration project for the elderly that provides comprehensive health and long-term care benefits to Medicare beneficiaries; unlike other Medicare-enrolling HMOs, care in a social HMO is reimbursed at 100 percent.

Specified Low-Income Medicare Beneficiary (SLMB)—Medicare beneficiaries who have income below 120 percent of the federal poverty level and whose resources do not exceed 200 percent of that allowed under the SSI program in each state. States are required, under federal law, to pay the Medicare Part B premiums for resident SLMBs.

Staff Model HMO—An HMO in which physicians practice solely as employees of the HMO and usually are paid a salary.

Standard Benefit Package—A defined set of health insurance benefits that all insurers are required to offer.

Stark I—A section of 1989 OBRA, effective January 1992, that precludes patient referrals by a physician to an entity in which a physician has financial interest, such as a clinical laboratory owned by a relative. Formally called the Ethics in Patient Referrals Act, it contains several exceptions to referral relationships or purposes.

Stark II—Legislation, effective August 1993, that strengthened restrictions imposed by Stark I; precludes patient referrals to an expanded list of health care services by a physician having a financial interest in the referral entity.

Stop-Loss Insurance—Insurance that is designed to stop the loss, or limit risk exposure beyond a stated amount, for either the catastrophic loss of individual patients or group claims. Stop-loss insurance is sought by nearly any entity that accepts risk. It is also called "stop-loss" because the more protection the higher the insurance cost. A point of attachment to stop-loss at $75,000 might cost $2.50 PMPM, whereas an attachment at $100,000 might cost $2.

Subcapitation—Any capitation arrangement at a level subordinate to global capitation, such as a subcap between an IDS and primary care physicians, specialists, or ancillary services.

Submitted Charge—The charge submitted by a provider to the patient or a payer.

Supplemental Security Income (SSI)—A program of income support for low-income, aged, blind, and disabled people established in Title 16 of the Social Security Act.

Supplementary Medical Insurance (SMI)—The part of the Medicare program that covers the costs of physicians' services, outpatient laboratory and X-ray tests, durable medical equipment, outpatient hospital care, and certain other services. This voluntary program requires payment of a monthly premium, which covers 25 percent of program costs with the rest covered by general revenues. Beneficiaries are responsible for a deductible and coinsurance payments for most covered services. Also called Part B coverage or benefits.

Supplier—A provider of health care services other than a practitioner that is permitted to bill under Medicare Part B. Suppliers include independent laboratories, durable medical equipment providers, ambulance services, orthotists, prosthetists, and portable X-ray providers.

Surplus—The funds remaining relative to a risk product or arrangement for payout as bonus or retention, either at the level of an HMO, a hospital withhold pool, an IPA, medical group, pod-level entity, or individual PCP under full personal capitation.

Sustainable Growth Rate System—A revision to the Volume Performance Standard system, proposed by Congress and the Administration. This system would provide an alternative mechanism for adjusting fee updates for the Medicare Fee Schedule. The mechanism would use a single conversion factor, base target rates of growth on growth of gross domestic product, and change the method for calculating the conversion factor up date to eliminate the two-year delay.

Sustainable Growth Rate—The target rate of expenditure growth set by the Sustainable Growth Rate system. Similar to the performance standard under the Volume Performance Standard system, except that the target depends on growth of gross domestic product instead of historical trends.

Tail Policy—A policy that covers incidents of medical risk that originated during the policy period but were not reported until after the policy period ended; coverage provided to a physician who leaves a program to retire or join another plan; also known as Tail Coverage.

Tax Equity and Fiscal Responsibility Act of 1982 (TEFRA)—A federal law that created the current risk and cost contract provisions under which health plans contract with HCFA and which defined the primary and secondary coverage responsibilities of the Medicare program.

Technical and Miscellaneous Revenue Act of 1988 (TAMRA)—A federal law that revised the Section 89 nondiscrimination rules and amended the penalties for noncompliance with COBRA.

Temporary Assistance for Needy Families (TANF)—A new block grant program created under federal welfare reform legislation (Pub. L. 104–193). It replaces Aid to Families with Dependent Children (AFDC). Medicaid eligibility is not linked to TANF as it has been to AFDC.

Third-Party Administrator (TPA)—Any third-party entity that administers health plan entitlements and is supported by the infrastructure to process claims. A TPA does not underwrite the risk of a contract, but performs largely administrative functions that are supported by computer systems; as markets mature, many TPAs are looking to evolve into other lines of business because HMOs and providers are becoming more able to perform the TPA's primary mission.

Tolerable Loss Ratio (TLR)—The loss ratio an insurer can fund without losing money on the group.

Total Quality Management (TQM)—An organizationwide process of improving the quality of products and services in any organization; also referred to as CQI (Continuous Quality Improvement) or TQM/CQI.

TRICARE—The acronym applied to the U.S. Department of Defense program of managed care, which uses a commercial HMO to supplement the health care services the collective military treatment facilities provide. It includes a triple option array of HMO (TRICARE Prime), PPO (TRICARE Extra), and indemnity-type coverage (TRICARE Standard or traditional CHAMPUS). The coverage for the 50 United States is divided into 12 regions, which offer competitive bidding for the service contracts.

U.S. per Capita Cost (USPCC)—The national average cost per Medicare beneficiary, calculated annually by HCFA's Office of the Actuary.

Undergraduate Medical Education—The medical training provided to students in medical school.

Underwriting Cycle—The cyclical pattern of insurer profitability and premium prices in group health insurance. The underwriting cycle consists of three phases: Phase I is characterized by rapid price increases and rising revenue for insurance companies; phase II is marked by relatively stable premium prices and an increase in insurers' capital reserves; and phase III consists of increasing premium price competition and the depletion of insurers' capital reserves.

Underwriting—The process by which an insurer determines whether and on what basis it will accept an application for insurance. Some insurers use medical underwriting to exclude individuals, groups, or coverage for certain health conditions that are expected to incur high costs.

Unified Insurance—Health insurance coverage that is provided through a single insurance policy.

Uniform Billing Code of 1992 (UB-92)—The federal directive requiring hospitals to follow specific billing procedures and use a standard billing form for Medicare services. The most current code was implemented October 1, 1993.

Usual, Customary, and Reasonable—A method used by private insurers for paying physicians based on charges commonly used by physicians in a local community. Sometimes called customary, prevailing, and reasonable charges.

Utilization Management (UM)—The process of evaluating the necessity, appropriateness, and efficiency of health care services. A review coordinator or medical director gathers information about the proposed hospitalization, service, or procedure from the patient or provider, then determines whether it meets established guidelines and criteria, which may be written or automated protocols approved by the organization. A provider or IDN that proves it is skilled in UM may negotiate more advantageous pricing if UM is normally performed by the HMO but could be more effectively passed downward at a savings to the HMO.

Utilization Review (UR)—A formal assessment of the medical necessity, efficiency, or appropriateness of health care services and treatment plans on a prospective, concurrent, or retrospective basis.

Utilization Review Accreditation Commission (URAC)—An independent accreditation organization for utilization review organizations with a goal of encouraging effective and efficient UR processes and providing a method of evaluation and the accreditation for UR programs (1130 Connecticut Avenue, N.W., Suite 450, Washington, DC 20036).

Utilization Review Organization (URO)—An organization that conducts UR activities for managed care organizations.

Vision Carve-Out—The specific reference to eye care that is a carve-out segment of the PMPM or contract pricing. It may require that ophthalmologists be participating providers in the case that ophthalmology services are included in the coverage.

Volume and Intensity of Services—The quantity of health care services per enrollee, taking into account both the number and the complexity, or mix of the services provided.

Volume Offset—The change in the number and mix of services that is projected to occur in response to a change in fees. A 50 percent behavioral offset means that half the savings from fee reductions will be offset by increased volume and intensity of services. It is used to estimate budget effects for Medicare payment changes, and is also referred to as behavioral offset.

Volume Performance Standard (VPS)—The desired growth rate for spending on Medicare Part B physician services, which is set each year by Congress.

Voluntary Employees' Beneficiary Association (VEBA)—A means of accumulating tax-free income-producing reserves for life, sick, accident, or other benefits. The association was initially formed and funded by employees, but changes in the law have allowed it to be used as an employee benefits vehicle by employers; also known as a Section 501(c)(9) trust.

Work Relative Value—A value that reflects the average amount of physician work incurred in performing a particular service, relative to that of other services.

Workers' Compensation—A program that provides liability insurance for an employer and benefits to the employees in the case of job-related injury, with added consideration for family members of employees who are killed in the line of duty. The employer pays the premium. Rehabilitation entities attempt to reduce health care costs and the costs of lost employment value by speeding recovery and return to work.

United States Department of Health and Human Services Negotiated Rulemaking Committee on PSO Solvency Standards

AGREEMENT

The Negotiated Rulemaking Committee on provider sponsored organization (PSO) Solvency Standards considered the technical and policy issues in establishing solvency standards for provider-sponsored organizations applying for a waiver of State licensure requirements. See sections 1855 and 1856 of the Social Security Act, as amended by the Balanced Budget of 1997.

The parties whose signatures appear on this document agree that

1. The individual signing this agreement is authorized to commit the party to the terms of this agreement.
2. The party concurs in the attached written statement dated March 5, 1998 (Committee Statement), when considered as a whole.
3. The Department of Health and Human Services, through the Health Care Financing Administration [HCFA], agrees to use the Committee Statement as the basis of an interim final rule to the maximum extent possible consistent with the Department's legal obligations.
4. Each party agrees not to file negative comments on the interim final rule or on its preamble to the extent the rule and preamble have the same substance and effect as the Committee Statement. This does not prohibit a party from submitting comments of any nature on any matter on which the Committee Statement provides that comments will be expressly solicited.

5.   The Health Care Financing Administration, consistent with its obligations under the Federal Administrative Procedure Act, will consider all relevant comments submitted on the interim final rule and will make such modifications in the regulations and preamble as are necessary when issuing final regulations. After the close of the comment period on the Notice of Interim Final Rulemaking, the facilitator will consult with the committee to determine whether the negotiating committee will reconvene to consider the comments before the final rule is circulated for review and approval within the appropriate Federal agencies.

6.   Each party agrees not to take any action to inhibit the adoption of the recommended interim final rule as final regulations to the extent the final regulations and their preamble have the same substance and effect as the Committee Statement.

7.   No party is bound under Article 4 or Article 6 with respect to any matter that is not addressed in the Committee Statement.

Signatories:
American Association of Health Plans
American Association of Homes and Services for the Aging/American Health Care Association/Home Health Services and Staffing Associations/National Association for Home Care
American Association of Retired Persons
American Hospital Association
American Medical Association
BlueCross/BlueShield Association
Catholic Health Association/Premier
Consortium for Citizens with Disabilities
Federation of American Health Systems
Health Care Financing Administration
Health Insurance Association of America
National Association of Insurance Commissioners
National IPA Coalition/The IPA Association of America
National Rural Health Association

NEGOTIATED RULEMAKING COMMITTEE ON PSO SOLVENCY STANDARDS

COMMITTEE STATEMENT—MARCH 5, 1998

The Negotiated Rulemaking Committee on PSO Solvency Standards has concurred in the following recommendations, considered as a whole, on the content of an interim final rule (and its preamble) pursuant to section 1856(a) of the Social Security Act, establishing solvency standards that entities must meet to qualify as provider-sponsored organizations (PSOs) under Part C of Title XVIII of the Social Security Act. In its negotiations, the Committee took into account the factors listed in the Act. Some of these factors are explicitly mentioned in the Committee Statement. Others are implicitly reflected in the recommended provisions. For example, the ability to deliver care directly (including the concept of "sweat equity") is reflected in the provision on "subordinated liabilities" and the treatment of intangible assets, and projected losses in the financial plan may be reduced through the use of reinsurance.

INITIAL STAGE (AT APPLICATION)

1.   NET WORTH
   1)   *Minimum Net Worth Amount:* $1.5 million, with HCFA discretion to lower to no less than $1 million based on business/financial plan demonstrating that the PSO has or has available to it an administrative infrastructure that will reduce the PSO's start-up costs.
   2)   *Calculation—Health Care Delivery Assets:* Admit 100% of book value (GAAP depreciated value) of Health Care Delivery Assets on the balance sheet of the legal entity that applies for a waiver.

   Health Care Delivery Assets = any tangible asset that is part of PSO operation, including:
   Hospitals, medical facilities, and their ancillary equipment, and such property as may reasonably be required for the PSO's principal office or for such purposes as may be necessary in the transaction of the business of the PSO.

Statement on asset concentration and quality standards for Health Care Delivery Assets:

The Committee agreed that HCFA will look at SAP codification after codification is completed and will consider whether any codification standard on asset concentration or quality applicable to Health Care Delivery Assets should be applied to waivered PSOs. HCFA will request comment on whether to use and/or modify any such standard. Comments will be sought in the notice on the NAIC RBC (see below). Meanwhile, HCFA may apply judgment in evaluating Health Care Delivery Assets for concentration and quality.

    3)   *Calculation—Intangible Assets:* If at least $1 million of the initial minimum net worth requirement is met by cash or cash equivalents, then HCFA will admit the GAAP value of intangible assets up to 20% of the minimum net worth amount required.

If at least $1 million of the initial minimum net worth requirement is met by cash or cash equivalents or HCFA has used its discretion to reduce the initial net worth requirement below $1.5 million, then HCFA will admit the GAAP value of intangible assets up to 10% of the minimum net worth amount required.

Deferred acquisition costs will not be admitted.

If, once the three-year waiver period ends, the PSO intends to continue to contract with Medicare, it must demonstrate, through the required financial plan (I.B.), how it will comply with State minimum net worth requirements under State standards for admitting intangible assets at the end of the three-year waiver period.

    4)   *Calculation—Other Assets:* SAP treatment to be given to other assets not used in the delivery of health care for purposes of meeting the minimum net worth requirement.

2.   FINANCIAL PLAN

    1)   *Plan Content and Coverage:* At the time of application, the PSO (which has been waived under subsection xxxx) [or the legal entity of which the PSO is a component,] must submit a financial plan, satisfactory to HCFA, covering the first twelve months of operation under the contract and meeting the requirements of (stated below). If the plan projects losses, the financial plan must cover the period through twelve months beyond projected break-even.

A financial plan must include

(A) A detailed marketing plan
(B) Statements of revenue and expense on an accrual basis
(C) A cash flow statement
(D) Balance sheets

  (E) The assumptions in support of the financial plan

  (F) If applicable, availability of financial resources to meet projected losses

 2) *Funding for Projected Losses:* In the financial plan, the PSO must demonstrate that it has the resources available to meet the projected losses for the entire period to break-even. Except for the use of guarantees as provided in section (a) below, letters of credit as provided in section (b) below, and other means as provided in section (c) below, the resources must be assets on the balance sheet of the PSO in a form that is either cash or will be convertible to cash in a timely manner, pursuant to the financial plan.

Guarantees will be acceptable as a resource to meet projected losses, under the following conditions:

- HCFA's requirements for guarantors/guarantees are met. These requirements will be modified for PSOs by HCFA.
- In the first year, the guarantor must provide the PSO with cash or cash equivalents to fund the projected losses, as follows: (1) prior to the beginning of the first quarter, in the amount of the projected losses for the first two quarters; (2) prior to the beginning of the second quarter, so that the PSO has cash or cash equivalents sufficient to meet projected losses through the end of the third quarter; and (3) prior to the beginning of the third quarter, so that the PSO has cash or cash equivalents sufficient to meet the projected losses through the end of the fourth quarter.
- If the guarantor provides the cash or cash equivalents to the PSO in a timely manner on the above schedule, this will be considered a sign of the guarantor's commitment to the PSO. In the third quarter, the PSO shall notify HCFA if the PSO intends to reduce the period of funding of projected losses. HCFA shall notify the PSO within 60 days of receiving the PSO's notice if the reduction is not acceptable.
- If the above guarantee requirements are not met, HCFA may take appropriate action, such as requiring funding of projected losses through means other than a guarantee. HCFA retains discretion, however, to require other methods or timing of funding, considering factors such as the financial condition of the guarantor and the accuracy of the financial plan.

An irrevocable, clean, unconditional letter of credit may be used in place of cash or cash equivalents if satisfactory to HCFA.

If approved by HCFA, based on appropriate standards promulgated by HCFA, PSOs may use the following to fund projected losses for periods after the first year: lines of credit from regulated financial institutions, legally binding agreements for capital contributions, or other legally binding contracts of a similar level of reliability.

The exceptions in (a), (b) and (c) may be used in an appropriate combination or sequence.

   3)   *Liquidity:* The PSO must have sufficient cash flow to meet its obligations as they become due.

In determining the ability of a PSO to meet this requirement, HCFA will consider the following:

   (a)   The timelines of payment.
   (b)   The extent to which the current ratio is maintained at 1:1, or whether there is a change in the current ratio over a period of time.
   (c)   The availability of outside financial resources.

The following corresponding remedies apply:

- If the PSO fails to pay obligations as they become due, HCFA will require the PSO to initiate corrective action to pay all overdue obligations.
- HCFA may require the PSO to initiate corrective action if any of the following are evident: 1) the current ratio declines significantly; or 2) a continued downward trend in the current ratio. The corrective action may include a change in the distribution of assets, a reduction of liabilities or alternative arrangements to secure additional funding requirements to restore the current ratio to 1:1.
- If there is a change in the availability of the outside resources, HCFA will require the PSO to obtain funding from alternative financial resources.
- Amount of minimum net worth requirement to be met by cash or cash equivalents: $750,000 cash or cash equivalents.

ONGOING (STARTS DAY ONE OF OPERATION, LIKE HMO MODEL ACT.)

1.   NET WORTH
   1)   *Amount of Minimum Net Worth:* Every PSO must maintain a minimum net worth equal to the greater of:
   (a)   One million dollars ($1,000,000); or

(b) Two percent of annual premium revenues as reported on the most recent annual financial statement filed with HCFA on the first $150,000,000 of premium and one percent of annual premium on the premium in excess of $150,000,000; or

(c) An amount equal to the sum of three months uncovered health care expenditures as reported on the most recent financial statement filed with HCFA; or

(d) An amount equal to the sum of:
1. Eight percent (8%) of annual health care expenditures paid on a non-capitated basis to non-affiliated providers as reported on the most recent financial statement filed with HCFA; and
2. Four percent (4%) of:
   Annual health care expenditures paid on a capitated basis to non-affiliated providers plus
   Annual health care expenditures paid on a non-capitated basis to affiliated providers; and
   Zero percent (0%) of annual health care expenditures paid on a capitated basis to affiliated providers (regardless of downstream arrangements from the affiliated provider).

2) *Preamble Statement on NAIC RBC:* The Committee discussed whether to include, among the factors considered in setting ongoing net worth requirements for PSOs, the authorized control level capital requirement derived from the NAIC Managed Care Organization Risk-Based Capital Formula. The Committee agreed that HCFA should consider adding that RBC factor to the ongoing net worth requirements after evaluating whether it is a valid indicator of PSO solvency and after considering the manner in which states have regulated managed care plans using that factor. In 1999, after PSOs have begun to operate under the waiver requirements and after they have begun reporting financial data, HCFA will issue a notice requesting comment on adding this factor to the net worth calculation for PSOs. As part of HCFA's normal data collection process for all Medicare + Choice plans, HCFA would expect to be collecting information necessary to complete the RBC calculations.

3) *Calculation—liabilities:* In calculating net worth, liabilities shall not include fully subordinated debt or subordinated liabilities. For purposes of this provision, subordinated liabilities are claims liabilities otherwise due to providers that are retained by the PSO to meet net worth requirements and are fully subordinated to all creditors.

4) *Calculation—assets:* Asset rules same as initial stage, except for intangible assets. If at least the greater of $1 million or 67% of the ongoing minimum net worth requirement is met by cash or cash equivalents, then HCFA will admit the GAAP value of intangible assets up to 20% of the minimum net worth amount required.

If less than the greater of $1 million or 67% of the ongoing minimum net worth requirement is met by cash or cash equivalents, then HCFA will admit the GAAP value of intangible assets up to 10% of the minimum net worth amount required.

Deferred acquisition costs will not be admitted.

2. FINANCIAL PLAN

During the start-up phase, the pre-break-even financial plan requirements would apply. After the point of break-even, the financial plan requirement would be focused on cash needs and the financing required for the next three years.

If, however, a PSO [or the legal entity of which the PSO is a component] did not earn a net operating surplus during the most recent fiscal year, the PSO must submit a financial plan, satisfactory to HCFA, meeting all of the requirements [established for the initial financial plan].

3. FINANCIAL INDICATORS

The PSO must file an Orange Blank form, modified to include supplemental information relating to Federal PSO solvency standards, according to the following schedule:

- On a quarterly basis until break-even; and
- On an annual basis after break-even, if the PSO has a net operating surplus; or
- On a quarterly or monthly basis (as specified by HCFA) after break-even, if the PSO does not have a net operating surplus.

4. LIQUIDITY

The PSO must have sufficient cash flow to meet its obligations as they become due. In determining the ability of a PSO to meet this requirement, HCFA will consider the following:

(a) The timeliness of payment
(b) The extent to which the current ratio is maintained at 1:1, or whether there is a change in the current ratio over a period of time
(c) The availability of outside financial resources.

The following corresponding remedies apply:

(a) If the PSO fails to pay obligations as they become due, HCFA will require the PSO to initiate corrective action to pay all overdue obligations.
(b) HCFA may require the PSO to initiate corrective action if any of the following are evident:
1) The current ratio declines significantly; or
2) A continued downward trend in the current ratio. The corrective action may include a change in the distribution of assets, a reduction of liabilities or alternative arrangements to secure additional funding requirements to restore the current ratio to 1:1.
(c) If there is a change in the availability of the outside resources, HCFA will require the PSO to obtain funding from alternative financial resources.

Minimum of net worth that must be in cash or cash equivalents:
The greater of
$750,000 cash or cash equivalents; or
40% of the minimum net worth required (determined under the greater of test for minimum net worth at the ongoing stage).

Cash or cash equivalents held to meet the net worth requirement are current assets.

5.   INSOLVENCY
1) *Federal Bankruptcy vs. State Receivership:* While the Committee discussed this issue (including the implications for beneficiaries, providers, and regulators), the Committee concluded that resolution of the issue is outside the scope of its negotiations. HCFA will share information on PSO's financial condition with relevant State regulators on an ongoing basis.
2) *Uncovered Expenditures:* If at any time uncovered expenditures exceed ten percent (10%) of total health care expenditures [a PSO] shall place an uncovered expenditures insolvency deposit with HCFA, or with any organization or trustee acceptable to HCFA through which a custodial or controlled account

is maintained, cash or securities that are acceptable to HCFA. Such deposit shall at all times have a fair market value in an amount of 120% of the PSO's outstanding liability for uncovered expenditures for enrollees, including incurred but not reported claims, and shall be calculated as of the first day of the month and maintained for the remainder of the month. If a PSO is not otherwise required to file a quarterly report, it shall file a report within forty-five days of the end of the calendar quarter with information sufficient to demonstrate compliance with this section.

The deposit required under this section is . . . an admitted asset of the PSO in the determination of net worth. All income from such deposits or trust accounts shall be assets of the PSO and may be withdrawn from such deposit or account quarterly with the approval of HCFA. . . .

A PSO that has made a deposit may withdraw that deposit or any part of the deposit if (1) a substitute deposit of cash or securities of equal amount and value is made, (2) the fair market value exceeds the amount of the required deposit, or (3) the required deposit is reduced or eliminated. Deposits, substitutions or withdrawals may be made only with the prior written approval of [HCFA].

The deposit required under this section is in trust and may be used only as provided under this section. HCFA may use the deposit of an insolvent PSO for administrative costs associated with administering the deposit and payment of claims of enrollees.

3)   *Hold Harmless and Continuation of Coverage Benefits:* While the Committee discussed these issues, the Committee was advised that PSOs will be subject to the same hold harmless and continuation of coverage/benefits rules as other Medicare Part C contractors, which were published in the June 1998 Medicare Part C regulations.

INDEX